Jewish Immigrants of the Nazi Period in the USA
Volume 1   Archival Resources

Jewish Immigrants of the Nazi Period in the USA

Sponsored by the Research Foundation
for Jewish Immigration, New York

Herbert A. Strauss, Editor

Volume 1
Archival Resources

Compiled by Steven W. Siegel

K. G. Saur
New York—München—London—Paris

K. G. Saur Publishing Inc.
175 Fifth Avenue
New York, New York 10010
USA
Tel. (212) 477-2500
Telex 238386 KGSP UR

K. G. Saur Éditeur
38, rue de Bassano
F-75008 Paris
FRANCE
Tel. 72355-18
Telex Iso Bur. 630 144

K. G. Saur Verlag
Pössenbacher Strasse 2
P.O.B. 71 10 09
D-8 München 71
FEDERAL REPUBLIC OF GERMANY
Tel. (089) 79 89 01
Telex 5212067 saur d

Clive Bingley Ltd. &
K. G. Saur Ltd.
16 Pembridge Road
London W11
GREAT BRITAIN
Tel. 01-229-1825

LIBRARY OF CONGRESS CATALOGING IN PUBLICATION DATA

Jewish immigrants of the Nazi period in the USA.

Sponsored by the Research Foundation for Jewish Immigration.
CONTENTS: v. 1. Siegel, S. W. Archival resources.
1. Jews in the United States—Social conditions. 2. Refugees, Jewish—United States. 3. Jews in Germany—History—1933-1945. 4. United States—Emigration and immigration. 5. Germany—Emigration and immigration. I. Strauss, Herbert Arthur. II. Siegel, Steven W., 1946- III. Research Foundation for Jewish Immigration.

E184.J5J558   301.45'19'24073   78-26930
ISBN 0-89664-026-4

CIP-KURZTITELAUFNAHME DER DEUTSCHEN BIBLIOTHEK

Jewish immigrants of the Nazi period in the U.S.A./ ed. by Herbert A. Strauss. Sponsored by the Research Foundation for Jewish Immigration.—New York, München, London, Paris: Saur.

NE: Strauss, Herbert A. [Hrsg.]

Vol. 1. Archival resources / comp. by Steven W. Siegel.—1979.
ISBN 0-89664-027-2 (New York)
ISBN 3-598-08006-9 (München)

Copyright © 1978 by the Research Foundation for Jewish Immigration, Inc.

ISBN 0-89664-027-2
ISBN 3-598-08006-9

Editing: Service to Publishers, Inc.

Printed and bound in the United States of America by Edwards Brothers, Inc.

The Research Foundation for Jewish Immigration, Inc. gratefully acknowledges the support of the following foundations and organizations for this volume:

American Federation of Jews from Central Europe, Inc.
Council of Jews from Germany
Jewish Philanthropic Fund of 1933, Inc.
The Gustav Wurzweiler Foundation, Inc.

CONTENTS

PREFACE

With this volume, *Archival Resources*, the Research Foundation for Jewish Immigration, Inc., New York, inaugurates its series entitled *Jewish Immigrants of the Nazi Period in the U.S.A.* The aim of the Foundation is to offer research tools for, and to write the history of, a group of immigrants to the U.S.A. which, in its opinion, has not found the scholarly attention it deserves. The series is being published under the general editorship of the Foundation's Secretary and Coordinator of Research, who designed it and guided its preparation and publication through all its phases.

The series consists of six major divisions. Volume I offers a guide to archival resources in the U.S.A. that deal with the immigration, resettlement, and acculturation in the U.S.A. of Jews from Germany and Austria who were uprooted by Nazi persecution. Volume II offers a comprehensive, annotated bibliography of books and articles on the emigration, resettlement, and acculturation in the U.S.A. of Jewish immigrants of the Nazi period. Volume III will be a guide to the Oral History Collection of the Research Foundation for Jewish Immigration. These volumes will span the entire process of migration, from emigration-related persecution and Jewish responses in countries of origin, to the international aspects of migration, countries of intermediate settlement, resettlement in the U.S.A., German postwar reparations (*Wiedergutmachung*), the effects of persecution trauma, and similar subjects. Volumes IV and V are collections of documents and primary source materials dealing with the emigration and emigration-related persecution of Jews in Germany and Austria, the international aspects of migration, and the entire range of materials bearing on the admission, resettlement, and integration in the U.S.A. of Jewish immigrants from Germany and Austria. Also included will be selections from the Oral History Collection of the Research Foundation for Jewish Immigration related to these subjects. With Volume VI, a social and communal history of the Jewish émigrés from Nazi Germany, the Foundation expects to realize the first stage of its plan for a comprehensive history of Jewish immigrants from Nazi Germany in the U.S.A.

The Foundation, which has sponsored this series and other research and publication programs, was incorporated in 1971 as a not-for-profit educational foundation under the laws of the State of New York to further the study of the history of Jewish émigrés of the Nazi period. Its founding members, leaders of the American community of Jews from Central Europe and directors of many of its organizations, were motivated by a belief that the history of an influential and worldwide migration movement of the twentieth century had not found the institutional center it so richly deserved. Aided by a seed grant from the Council of Jews from Germany (London–New York–Jerusalem), the American Federation of Jews from Central Europe sponsored the Research Foundation. The Board of Directors of the Research Foundation—Rudolf Callmann (deceased), Hans J. Frank, Max Gruenewald, Fred W. Lessing, Joseph Maier, Gerald Meyer, Curt C. Silberman, Hermann E. Simon, Albert U. Tietz, Franz Winkler, and Herbert A. Strauss—then commissioned the Coordinator of Research to develop its program.

This program was inspired by the belief that the complexity of this Jewish migration movement from Central Europe, as well as its significance for twentieth-century culture and society, required that both research and writing be based on a thorough foundation. To this end, the Foundation commissioned a series of studies that would offer the scholarly community the necessary research tools. It began, in addition, a nationwide program of taped interviews with community leaders and informants from all walks of life to supplement, through an Oral History Collection, the information available from archives and secondary sources. The Foundation further commissioned the writing of a communal and institutional history of Jewish immigrants from Nazi Germany in the U.S.A.

Although the Foundation originated with the community whose history it was exploring, its sponsors are united in the belief that only a critical history, unfettered by any commitments but the constraints of critical methods of historical research and writing, is worth the effort and offers results that endure. Nativism or "contributionism" would have detracted from this critical commitment.

The Foundation understands the history of this unique group of victims of persecution as an integral whole composed of intersecting historical contexts.

As the history of a Jewish group, the persecution, emigration, and acculturation of Jews from Nazi Germany form part of the history of the Holocaust, indeed of its first victims.

As the history of an ethnic minority from Germany, the migration of German Jews continues a pattern of German history. Since 1555, emigration had been the only continuous and universal civil right open to dissenters that was recognized in the German states, or the German *Reich*. Repeating earlier German history, another creative minority entered into new patterns of acculturation with foreign cultures and societies after being driven from its homeland. In this context, Jews from Nazi-controlled Europe formed part of the stream of antifascist and antitotalitarian émigrés (if Stalinists are disregarded in this context), joined the refugee and émigré communities, and shared their political and intellectual energies in many lands.

Finally, as part of the large population displacements of twentieth-century Europe, indeed world civilization, Jews from Nazi Germany took part in the East-West trek of European populations. Their migration anticipated the drain of brains from oppressive or deprived to free and prosperous societies that has endowed professional and business careers with the international hue characteristic of the last quarter of the twentieth century.

These multitiered historical contexts have found appropriate expression in the Foundation's International Biographical Archives of Central European Émigrés, 1933–45, with over 25,000 files, and in its three-volume *International Biographical Dictionary of Central European Émigrés, 1933–1945* (1979-80). For the first time in any country, this publication links the research directions of West German *Exilforschung* and of international migration history in a cooperative venture between a German research center (Institut für Zeitgeschichte, Munich) and the Foundation. Seven years in the making, the *Dictionary*, a basic reference work, documents the entire range of migrants independent of race, political creed, religion, national origin, or self-perception. The impact of the Archives and *Dictionary* on research and writing is expected to continue for a long time to come.

The Foundation is grateful to the organizations and foundations that have believed in and supported its program: the Council of Jews from Germany (London-New York-Jerusalem); the American Federation of Jews from Central Europe, Inc., New York; the Jewish Philanthropic Fund of 1933, Inc., New York; the Gustav Wurzweiler Foundation, Inc., New York; the Whittier Street Foundation, Scarsdale, NY; the Deutsche Forschungsgemeinschaft, Bad Godesberg, BRD; the National Endowment for the Humanities, Washington, DC; and the Research Foundation of the City University of New York. It thanks its dedicated assistants, associates, advisers, and fellows who have worked, often at financial sacrifice, so that the tragedies and triumphs of contemporary history may not vanish from the collective memory of our time.

Research Foundation for Jewish Immigration, Inc.

THE MIGRATION OF JEWS FROM NAZI GERMANY

1. EMIGRATION: NAZI ANTI-SEMITISM AND JEWISH PERCEPTIONS

On January 30, 1933, Adolf Hitler was installed as Germany's Reich Chancellor by the constitutional authority vested in Reich President Paul von Hindenburg. Hitler's appointment, and the subsequent penetration of Nazi power through the entire fabric of German society, culture, and economic life, signified the beginning of the end of 2000 years of Jewish history in Germany.

Selectively at first, in steps dictated by political opportunism, the Nazi government unleashed a wave of discrimination and defamation against its opponents—in particular, against the Jewish population in Germany. Waves of terror, organized or tolerated by the Reich government, swept the land in 1933. When the domestic economy and German foreign economic and diplomatic relations deteriorated under the impact of such violence, a policy of tactical deception was instituted to narrow, step by gradual step, the sphere in which Jews could work, follow their cultural interests, or worship in their temples and synagogues. In 1935, the Nuremberg Laws "legally" deprived Jews of the civic equality they had won in nearly 200 years of struggle. The well-staged Olympics of 1936, and Germany's continued vulnerability while she prepared aggressive plans for conquest, temporarily slowed down Nazi anti-Jewish measures. Jews believed themselves protected by reasons of Germany's economic need—as if Nazi policies followed economic reason.

By late 1937, however, the time had come to throw restraint to the wind. Germany's new economic policy in Eastern and Southeastern Europe had brought new independence from world markets and trade balances. Appeasement showed that deception worked and lamed the will to self-protection in the Western world. Rearmament in Germany proceeded vigorously, without dissenting voices being heard in public in Germany on any level of society.

Thus, it was no longer necessary to pay attention to the effect that radical and rowdy anti-Semitism might have on public opinion abroad or on foreign trade. Preparations to eliminate the Jews from Germany now entered the final

phase. In 1938, the Nazi government took a census of Jewish property to prepare its despoliation, and a series of measures were begun to hasten the "aryani-
zation" (forced sale at depressed prices) of business establishments. The
Anschluss of Austria of March 12, 1938, which had been greeted with enthusi-
asm by large segments of the Austrian population, led to crude violence and
atrocities committed by Austrians in the streets of Vienna. The reigning Catholic
primate, Kardinal Joseph Innitzer, sent a welcoming message to Hitler. Petty
Austrian Nazis enriched themselves with Jewish property, and Jews fled in panic
to escape Austrian brutality.

This lesson was not lost on Nazis in Germany. Radical proponents of
rowdyism and terror were now able to point to the Austrian way of eliminating
the Jews through violence as effective and rewarding. A pretext was found in
the murder of a German diplomat in Paris by a Jewish youth, unhinged by his
misfortunes and his family's mistreatment in Germany. On November 9-10,
1938, the greatest desecration of houses of worship known to German history
was staged "in retaliation." Nazi thugs murdered Jewish men and women,
burned the synagogues and temples, and destroyed and looted Jewish property.
They then interned tens of thousands of Jewish men in concentration camps, to
be released only upon proof that they would emigrate from Germany forthwith.
Neither the churches, the courts, the universities, women, lawyers, professors,
nor any other German group protested publicly against this great German
Kirchenschändung, the murders, the despoliations.

This attack inaugurated the largest mass exodus of Jews from Germany,
covering the years 1938 through 1940. Those unable (or unwilling) to leave
carried on Jewish life as well as possible under the threat of the oncoming holocaust. In some large cities, such as Berlin, a semblance of the old life and culture
was maintained against ever-increasing threats. In general, however, Jews were
coerced into forced labor, and harassment, illegality, and numerous petty
annoyances finally yielded up their victims to the great death that followed their
deportations to the Eastern European camps. By October 1941, a Himmler
decree made all emigration from Germany illegal. Only a few of those still left
escaped the destruction of German Jewry, either by hiding or by crossing a
frontier to freedom.

The 525,000 Jews of Germany—over 100,000 of whom were foreign, mostly
of Eastern European nationality—were ill-placed in 1933 to resist persecution
with barrels of guns they did not have. Small in number and scattered over the
land, too apolitical to fathom the nihilism and violence of their enemies, too
long partners in the bourgeois decencies of a past era, the Jews in Germany,
Austria, and Czechoslovakia resorted to the resistance open to the weak. They
rebuilt their spiritual and cultural lives. They flocked to the synagogues where
the rabbis spoke of spiritual victories over brutal aggression. For too long, many,
especially the well-to-do, believed themselves indispensable to German economic
recovery, and hoped, against the accumulating evidence of despoliation and
confiscation, that responsibility would tame, had tamed, Nazi radicalism.

Nazi anti-Semitic policies aided in this self-deception, although its goals had
never been concealed. Among Nazi radicals, including Hitler in one of his
psychotic guises, the mass murder of the Jews had always been an esoteric last

resort, a potential means to the end of eliminating the pathologically hated "World Jewry" from Germany and Europe. Like other Nazi policies, the tactics used to realize these goals were designed to tranquilize the victims. Each step was declared a "final step." The elimination of the Jews from public and intellectual life in 1933 was followed by assurances that the economic position of Jews in Germany would remain protected. Conservative officials serving the Nazi government in the responsible ministries opposed street terror as counterproductive for economic recovery. For a while, rowdy street brutalities appeared to be curbed by those who favored a "legal" way of establishing Jewish life in Germany on a separate and unequal basis. The Nuremberg Laws of September 1935 were characterized by Jewish representatives in public pronouncements "as a new basis for legal Jewish existence in Germany."

In the villages and hamlets where Jews had coexisted literally for centuries with their Christian neighbors, physical attacks and economic boycotts were driving Jews to the safety and anonymity of the larger cities, such as Hamburg, Frankfurt, or Berlin. Jewish policies as formulated by their central representations, the Reichsvertretung der Juden in Deutschland, and by the Prussian Landesverband jüdischer Gemeinden, supported this movement away from the unprotected small communities and thus unwittingly paved the way for later Nazi plans for despoliation and, finally, deportation and extermination.

Still, for the time being, internal migration and urbanization offered temporary respite and the opportunity to prepare one's emigration, as internal obstacles paced the callousness of a depression-ridden world closing its doors to the Jews.

Behind the tight news curtain of the totalitarian regime, no Jewish journalist, no community leader could speak his mind—even if German Jewish leaders had been more astute in anticipating such a radical "solution" as the Holocaust. At the time, only sick minds were capable of anticipating the murder of 6 million innocent people. That old Jewish quality, a misplaced belief in the ultimate rationality of man, an analytic penetration of reality schooled by centuries of intellectual training and habit, saw only too clearly the internal disunity of the regime, the struggle for power between old conservatives and new radicals, the economic impossibility of war, the irresponsibility of Nazi policies. Could rational minds have foreseen the appeasement of Hitler's aggression by those powers most immediately threatened? Nobody among the Jewish leaders, not even the Zionists, were aware of the techniques by which the Nazi government deceived the world; nobody called early enough for the only form of resistance available to this small minority—total emigration to escape total annihilation.

Thus, for the average German Jew, hope fed illusion and slowed his determination to escape a deteriorating situation. Despite their misplaced optimism, however, Jewish leaders from the very beginning had set out to prepare Jewish youth and those deprived of their livelihood for emigration, even if older generations of German Jewry would be forced to remain in Germany because of age, poverty, or inability to find a country that would admit elderly persons.

Three major Jewish organizations directed the emigration process in Germany. The Palästina-Amt organized the occupational retraining of younger groups, primarily students or commercial employees, for useful roles in Palestine's agricultural or craft sectors. Jews with some means—*Mittelstand*—under a special agreement with German authorities, were allowed to transfer part of their capital to Palestine. An organization was set up—Haavara—through which such transfers could be effected with a minimum of gain for the Nazi economy. The Hauptstelle für jüdische Wanderfürsorge, founded in 1917 to assist Eastern-Jewish migrants, aided Jews of foreign nationality in their emigration or remigration efforts. The Hilfsverein der Juden in Deutschland, established in 1904 to assist Jews in Eastern Europe, was charged with the task of aiding German Jewish émigrés to countries other than Palestine. Thus were the tables turned, and old philanthropies turned into life-saving agencies. Aided from the very beginning by their fellow Jewries in Palestine, England, America, and Western Europe, these organizations played a vital role in helping all those who needed assistance, from advice and information about prospective immigration countries to financial aid, help in obtaining visas, funds for travel, or the money immigrants had to have in their possession in some countries as a condition for their admittance. As Nazi measures impoverished German Jews—by 1938 every fourth Jew in Germany received social assistance in one form or another—the international Jewish effort to save the lives of German Jewry intensified. In addition, Jews in Germany contributed financial aid to their brethren to a degree never equaled in their history.

In spite of social assistance and organized aid to emigration, the decision to emigrate from Germany, and the emigration movement itself, remained matters of personal decision. German and international Jewish organizations—with the possible exception of the Jewish Agency for Palestine, which enjoyed semi-governmental status in its dealings with the British Mandatory Government in Palestine—never succeeded in directing or planning the flow of emigration. Like most Jewish migration, the emigration of German Jews was substantially an individual or family migration, and the decision to leave the result of all the complex factors and perceptions that have been effective in similar situations of evolving religious (now "racial") persecution. Emigration figures show that as many as 270,000 to 300,000 Jews (of a total of about 525,000 in January 1933) may have succeeded in leaving Germany, while between 180,000 and 196,000 German Jews perished in the Holocaust (about 30,000 of whom had already emigrated to Western European countries later overrun by the German armies and were deported from there to the death camps of Eastern Europe during World War II). To this figure of persons professing the Jewish religion is to be added the unknown number of persons of Jewish descent and not of the Jewish religion who were affected in various ways by Nazi "racial" measures and forced to leave Germany as émigrés or exiles. There may have been as many as 200,000 such persons in Germany in 1933.

In 1933, an estimated 47,000 Jews fled the country in panic. About 10,000 of these had returned by 1935, deceived by the apparent "legality" and "moderation" the Hitler regime was forced to follow if rearmament and foreign policy plans were to proceed without foreign intervention. For the next four years, the number of Jewish émigrés remained stable: 23,000 for 1934, 21,000 for 1935, 25,000 for 1936, and 23,000 for 1937.

Only in 1938-39, when the full brunt of Nazi economic destruction and the

Kristallnacht of November 9-10, 1938, signaled the end of illusions, did about 118,000 Jews escape in mass flight from Nazi Germany. In 1940-41, another 23,000 succeeded in leaving before all legal emigration from Germany ceased in October 1941. In 1945, about 5000 Jews emerged from the rubble of war-torn Germany. They had survived the war hidden from the Secret Police by Christian or leftist friends. Another 14,000 persons had been protected by marriages with Christian partners from being deported and murdered in Eastern Europe. Only about 5000 Jews returned from concentration camps, mainly Theresienstadt. The rest—95% of German Jewry—had either died of natural causes or suicide, had been murdered, or had emigrated. German Jewry and its history had indeed come to an end.

2. IMMIGRATION: THE CLOSED WORLD

If the emigration of Jews from Germany was thus conditioned by the ebb and flow of persecution and by the tactics of deception practiced by the Nazi government upon the Jewish population, not a single government of the world (with the exception of the British Crown Colony of Shanghai) admitted Jews freely to its territory. Sympathy with the victims of persecution did not change the population policies of governments in the face of the high unemployment rates and economic slowdowns or depressions of the 1930s. Foreigners, rarely welcome to natives, now appeared as penniless refugees and were perceived as competitors, economic burdens, subversive elements, or, at the worst, spies or a "fifth column" in the service of a foreign country in wartime. In many countries, the anti-Semitism of the 1920s, symbolized by Henry Ford's support for the (forged) *Protocols of the Elders of Zion*, influenced immigration legislation. "Ethnic homogeneity" for prospective immigrants became a code word for the exclusion of Jews.

A few examples will suffice to document the difficulties faced by German Jews in the 1930s in their quest for a haven from persecution. South Africa, which had experienced a considerable economic upturn in 1935, and, for 10 months, permitted thousands of Jews from Germany to enter, stopped the flow of immigrants on November 1, 1936, by stipulating that immigrants would not be allowed to work in occupations which the government considered already filled adequately by South Africans. Canada and Australia practically closed their doors to Jewish immigrants by demanding that immigrants be farmers. Less than 1% of German Jews had been farmers, or part-time farmers and cattle dealers. In 1937, Brazil, until then relatively open to Jewish immigration, closed its doors to Jewish immigration. Chile, Peru, and Bolivia did not admit Jewish immigrants before 1938-39 in any appreciable numbers. Beginning in 1935, Argentina offered limited opportunities for small groups of farmers ready to join an agricultural settlement.

In Europe, too, economic fears, xenophobia, and anti-Semitism combined to produce public hostility or government restrictions on immigration from Nazi Germany. The countries of Western Europe, especially France, Holland, and Belgium, had been the émigrés' most immediate and proximate goals during the first two years of Nazi rule. Language and cultural ties (French, a symbol of

European civilization, had been widely taught in secondary schools in Germany and Austria), political connections, especially on the Left, geographic proximity, family relations, and commercial ties or travel experience made these countries the preferred choice during the first two years of flight from Germany. Political refugees also wanted to be close to Germany when Hitler's regime would collapse, as expected and predicted by many who worked in word, and to some extent, deed, for its downfall. France especially, with its loose interstices between bureaucratic regulations, and Czechoslovakia, offering asylum more freely than classical countries of refuge, became centers of the political refugee community.

Great Britain, in the throes of mass unemployment and the severe economic crisis of the 1930s, refused to admit refugees unable to support themselves (except for intellectuals, for whom Britain was willing to serve as a "waiting room" until suitable employment could be found elsewhere, primarily overseas). In Great Britain, too, the prohibition against allowing refugees to work was strictly enforced, until, under the impact of the *Kristallnacht* and its senseless violence, public policy changed and Great Britain admitted a considerable number of refugees from Nazi Germany between November 1938 and September 1939. It also took in considerably more unaccompanied Jewish children and placed them in foster homes in 1938-39 than did the United States of America during the entire Nazi period.

Even Switzerland, reacting to the mass entry of penniless Jews from Austria streaming across the frontier in 1938, agreed with the Berlin Gestapo Office that Jews should have imprinted the red letter "J" (for *Jude*, Jew) in their passports so that Switzerland would keep German Jews so identified out of the country and be protected against being inundated by them once they became destitute. They were, of course, not permitted to earn their living in Switzerland.

Palestine began to absorb immigrants from Germany in larger numbers beginning in 1934. The first year of Nazi rule, 1933, served to prepare the two major forms of assistance to future *olim* (immigrants to the land of Israel—verbatim, "people ascending" to the temple in Jerusalem). One form of assistance was offered by the occupational retraining of primarily intellectually and commercially trained youth for manual labor in collective settlements, agricultural cooperatives, or as craftsmen. This *Hachscharah* (preparation) was organized under the auspices of the Zionist Organization, the various labor parties of Israel and their youth groups, or by Hechaluz, the worldwide coordinating agency for such retraining. Centers for *Hachscharah* were located in most European countries. Another form of assistance was offered to émigrés able to transfer a minimum of £1000 to Palestine. Early in 1933, Jewish citrus fruit growers from Palestine had approached Nazi German officials and worked out a scheme to transfer Jewish assets out of Germany which would offer German industry the opportunity to export its manufactured goods to the Near East, without earning Germany the foreign currency it might have used for its rearmament. German Jews would pay *Reichsmark* to the German Treasury; German manufacturers would export equivalent values in manufactured goods to Palestine; they would be paid with the money of the Jewish émigré to Palestine on a permit ("certificate") reserved for "capitalists" (A-I certificate). In Palestine, A-I certificate immigrants from Germany would receive the equivalent in pounds of what they had paid to the German Treasury. The German goods would be used for the industrial and agricultural reconstruction of the Jewish homeland, or sold on the free market. This scheme, *Haavara* (transfer of foreign currency), and the opportunities offered to the idealistic, the young, the poor, or the unemployed among German Jews by *Hachscharah* and agricultural resettlement made Palestine the single major overseas immigration country for Jews from Germany between 1934 and 1936. Then, the Arab riots of 1936 and the policies of the British Mandate Government culminating in the so-called Peel Report of 1938 severely curtailed immigration to Palestine. Still, as many as 56,000 Jews from Germany reached a safe haven in Palestine through legal or illegal (*Aliyah Bet*) immigration before the end of World War II.

Among the major overseas countries priding themselves on their sympathies for the "huddled masses" of the strife-torn world, the United States of America had traditionally been a haven for victims of political or religious persecution. The U.S.A. had achieved this eminent position despite the recurrent periods of nativism known to American history in the nineteenth century. In the late nineteenth and early twentieth centuries, the latest of these nativist trends had combined with the racial ideas of the time and had culminated in the immigration legislation of the 1920s. Under this legislation, natives of "Nordic" countries were admitted in larger numbers ("immigration quotas") than Southern or Eastern Europeans. The law effectively minimized or stopped the immigration of Orientals, Catholics, Southern and Eastern Europeans, the Greek Orthodox, and Eastern European Jews. The immigration quota for natives from Germany was fixed at about 25,000 persons per year, as compared to about 6000 persons for Italy, or 6500 persons for Poland.

Ironically, their birth in Germany would have made German Jews beneficiaries of the "Nordic" orientation of the law, since birth in Germany qualified a person for admission under the German quota. German Jews also had greater opportunities than other ethnic groups to obtain the "affidavits of support" required of all prospective immigrants, since Jews from Germany, especially from southern Germany, had come to the U.S.A. in some numbers in the early and mid-nineteenth century and thus qualified as relatives of prospective immigrants to submit the required proof that the immigrant would not be "liable to become a public charge."

In spite of this favorable position, however, Jews from Nazi Germany met considerable difficulties in entering the U.S.A. during the first four years of their plight. In 1930, President Herbert Hoover had enjoined consuls to demand stringent proofs from visa applicants that they would be self-supporting following their immigration. This measure, taken under the influence of growing economic difficulties and unemployment, called for assurances of support few applicants were able to provide. Consuls abroad followed the directives of their administrations in Washington.

In addition, the economic condition of the U.S.A., the lack of first-hand knowledge on the part of prospective immigrants of American life or the English language, the lack of cultural bonds of most German Jews with the English-speaking world, and the geographic distance of the country from continental Europe acted as retardants. The search for relatives financially capable of providing the required assurances took time, and public indifference toward the seriousness of the plight of Jews in Germany, once considered the most secure of Jewish groups, took its toll.

As a result of factors such as these, the number of Jewish immigrants from Nazi Germany to the U.S.A. remained minuscule during the first three years of Nazi rule. Efforts to place intellectuals met with greater success since they were able to enter the country as "non-quota" immigrants, once they found a university or college willing to offer them a position.

By fiscal year 1935-36, the number of Jewish immigrants from Germany began to increase, presumably because the preparations of prospective immigrants begun years earlier were now bearing fruit, and conditions in Germany were perceived as worsening enough to overcome the obstacles of distance and ignorance of cultural conditions.

Table I documents the (estimated) number of émigrés of the Jewish faith leaving Nazi Germany for the U.S.A. Table II suggests the general influx of "refugees" of all kinds during the Nazi period (last column).

TABLE I. Jewish Immigration from Germany to the United States of America, January 1933 to June 1938

January 1933 to December 1933	535
January 1934 to December 1934	2,310
January 1935 to June 1935	658
July 1935 to June 1936	6,750 (estimated)
July 1936 to June 1937	6,750
July 1937 to June 1938	10,000
Total (approx.)	27,000

Source: Werner Rosenstock, "Exodus 1933-1939, A Survey of Jewish Emigration from Germany" in *Leo Baeck Institute Year Book I.* London, 1956, p. 376 (reproduced with the permission of the publisher).

TABLE II. Total Number of Immigrants from All Countries Arriving in the United States of America, 1933-44

Year	From All Countries	From Europe	Number of Refugees, Gross Estimate	Number of Refugees, Refined Estimate
1933	23,068	14,400	11,869	1,919
1934	29,470	19,559	16,323	4,241
1935	34,956	25,346	21,915	5,436
1936	36,329	26,295	22,875	6,538
1937	50,244	35,812	31,537	12,012
1938	67,895	50,574	44,848	44,848
1939	82,998	68,198	61,882	61,882
1940	70,756	56,254	50,581	50,581
1941	51,776	36,989	30,808	30,808
1942	28,781	14,881	12,620	12,620
1943	23,725	8,953	6,629	6,629
1944	28,551	8,694	6,348	6,348
Totals	528,549	365,955	318,235	243,862

Source: Maurice R. Davie, *Refugees in America.* Harper & Brothers, New York, 1947, p. 24 (reproduced with the permission of the author's estate).

Finally, Table III indicates that during the first three years of Nazi rule in Germany, the outflow of émigrés from the U.S.A. exceeded immigration by considerable (if decreasing) amounts.

TABLE III. Admissions and Departures of Immigrants to and from the United States of America, 1931–44

Year	Immigrant Aliens Admitted	Emigrant Aliens Departed	Net Entries
1931	97,139	61,882	35,257
1932	35,576	103,295	-67,719
1933	23,068	80,081	-57,013
1934	29,470	39,771	-10,301
1935	34,956	38,834	- 3,878
1936	36,329	35,817	512
1937	50,244	26,736	23,508
1938	67,895	25,210	42,685
1939	82,998	26,651	56,347
1940	70,756	21,461	49,295
1941	51,776	17,115	34,661
1942	28,781	7,363	21,418
1943	23,725	5,107	18,618
1944	28,551	5,669	22,882
Totals	661,264	494,992	166,272

Source: Maurice R. Davie, *Refugees in America* (from *Annual Reports of the Immigration and Naturalization Service*, for the appropriate years). Harper & Brothers, New York, 1947, p. 21 (reproduced with the permission of the author's estate).

In 1937, President Franklin D. Roosevelt eased the restrictions imposed by the "Hoover Directive" of 1930, and the number of immigrants began to increase rapidly. In Germany, the waiting lists for prospective immigrants to the U.S.A. lengthened quickly as Nazi persecution began to eliminate Jews from the economic sector in which they had hitherto been assured a relatively undisturbed place. Now German Jews expected to wait months, soon years, before being considered by a U.S. consulate for an immigration visa.

The last chapter of this tragic policy began with the impact of the anti-Jewish atrocities committed by Austrian Nazis after the *Anschluss* of March 12, 1938. They motivated President Roosevelt to call an international conference to discuss the plight of "political" refugees from Germany. It met at Évian-les-Bains (at Lake Geneva, on French soil) but had no practical effect on the admission of Jewish immigrants to the participating countries. The one concession offered by the U.S.A. consisted in the combination of the German and Austrian quotas, which eased, in effect, the admission of Austrian-Jewish refugees to the U.S.A. (the annual Austrian quota had been about 1400 persons since 1929). This combined German–Austrian quota was filled only following the senseless violence of the *Kristallnacht*, but the allocation of visas to U.S. consulates in Germany was curtailed by an understanding that part of the

German quota would be set aside for the admission of Jewish refugees from Germany who had found temporary havens in such countries as Great Britain. There, they had been admitted as refugees for a temporary stay until they could remigrate to their final destinations.

All attempts to liberalize the U.S. quota system of immigration failed, even during the emergencies of the war and the Holocaust periods. However, in spite of this failure, about 130,000 Jews from Germany were admitted to the U.S.A. during the Nazi period, making the U.S.A. the country that took in more refugees from Nazi Germany than any other country. Many more could have been saved if the U.S. government and public had understood the seriousness of the Jewish plight of the Holocaust period, and had acted on that understanding.

3. GOVERNMENTS, INTERNATIONAL ORGANIZATIONS, AND VOLUNTARY AGENCIES

The expulsion of the Jews from Germany, Austria, and Nazi-occupied Czechoslovakia was caused by the Nazi government or occupation authorities. The executive agencies of this government, many of whose ranking officials had served under the Weimar Republic, participated in numerous ways in carrying out the policies of their government. Whatever resistance against anti-Semitic measures was dared during the first years of the Nazi regime did not affect long-range policy. Once the Nazi government, with the connivance of its general staff, had murdered, without trials, its own lunatic fringe, and had its murders certified as "legal" by Germany's foremost political philosopher Carl Schmitt and by its own parliament, all resistance *within* the government was cowed into ineffectiveness, and deflected to matters of administration, not policy. No resistance movement—even within the churches—ever developed over the issue of Nazi anti-Semitism against the Jews (i.e., members of the Jewish religious community). Individual civil servants, following their conscience, might mitigate harshness in executing Nazi measures, or might fight for departmental or ministerial influence in carrying them out. Some government agencies, including the Finance Ministry, parts of the Foreign Office, and the Economics Ministry, suggested more civilized ways of "solving the Jewish question" in Germany, often for mixed and tactical motives. Government departments were involved also in assisting Jews to emigrate from Germany. Nazi policy, in fact, favored Zionist tendencies because until 1941, it saw emigration as the solution of the "Jewish problem," and Zionists as the most energetic promoters of emigration.

Jews had to pass through a maze of offices before the Nazi government would certify their exit, from tax authorities to police to foreign currency office to passport agency to customs police, *und so weiter.* At least in one area—the transfer of Jewish funds abroad—a Nazi government agency was concerned directly with issues of immigration.

But Nazi policy aimed basically at dumping German Jews as impoverished refugees in whatever country was willing to open its doors to them. Nazi propaganda stressed repeatedly that Germany expected public opinion abroad to better understand and sympathize with Nazi anti-Semitism because of the "firsthand experience with the Jewish question" foreign countries acquired by unregulated Jewish immigration. The few attempts made by foreign governments or Nazi groups to plan Jewish settlement abroad (negotiations with the Inter-governmental Committee on Refugees in London in 1938; plans to settle Jews on the island of Madagascar discussed with French politicians in 1939) remained talk or fantasies. Despite Nazi radical sympathies with a Jewish national settle-ment in Palestine, the Nazi government never took any diplomatic steps to help ease immigration to Palestine.

To some extent, this policy succeeded in turning Jewish emigration from Germany into an international problem, and a national problem for the govern-ments of immigration countries. As early as 1933, the League of Nations As-sembly created a separate High Commissioner for Refugees (Jewish and Other) Coming from Germany and expected member states to help in solving "the economic, financial, and social problems created by the large number of persons from Germany, Jewish and other, seeking refuge" (Resolution of October 26, 1933). Like other efforts of the then-moribund League of Nations, the Commis-sion remained a pious hope and failed to impose order on chaos. Other inter-national efforts on government levels (like the Évian Conference of 1938) remained equally ineffective.

Member states continued to pursue their national interests and heed their public opinions. In many countries, including the U.S.A., however, restrictive immigration policies were challenged by groups sympathetic to liberalized immigration regulations. Such groups usually included parties and organizations on the Left, the liberal center, progressive church groups, committed individuals, and the Jewish communities. Their activities, as yet undescribed on a global scale, can be assumed to have been one of the factors under whose pressure admission policies were, in some cases, changed. In the U.S.A., their efforts fell short of the basic goal, a change in the quota system or in admission proce-dures, although the pressures generated by American liberal–progressive lobbies did bring about some concessions during the Roosevelt years—for example, the creation of the President's Advisory Committee on Political Refugees in 1939-40, and the subsequent admission of intellectual and political leaders stranded in Nazi-occupied Europe following the fall of Holland, Belgium, and France in 1940.

The task of caring for the refugees thus fell to voluntary organizations set up by many groups in many lands, and to organizations created by immigrants to help themselves. These organizations, driven by volunteer energy and motiva-tion, served the double function of acting on behalf of émigrés as their organized spokesmen and negotiating with government agencies on behalf of their clients, and of assisting the isolated émigré and immigrant forced into uprooting, migra-tion, or flight by historical causes he often dimly understood.

The self-selected clienteles served by these agencies were, to a large part, determined by the religious, political, or occupational group to which the mi-grants belonged. Political refugees, overwhelmingly members of left-wing political parties or of leftist sympathies, sought contact with the political national or international organizations corresponding to their political allegiance, and formed "parties-in-exile," or front organizations, to further their political goals. Often, they sought to relate their activities, through underground channels, with remnants of their parties in Nazi Germany or Austria, or with newly established resistance cells. In some countries, refugees allegedly worked for the Communist International in Moscow. Numerous émigrés fought in the International Brigade in the Spanish Civil War, or joined German communist exile groups in Stalin's Russia, Mexico, and other countries.

The Social Democratic Party and the middle class, or religion-oriented (Catholic Center) parties, as well as trade union leaders, also formed political organizations abroad (e.g., in Czechoslovakia and Great Britain), published newspapers in the German language, and established associated cultural and social organizations. Their activities form the subject of the history of the "political exile" of the Nazi period.

For professional groups, organizations in aid of refugees were founded in many countries, since academic teachers, writers, scholars, and artists had been among the first to be dismissed or ostracized, and had made up a significant percentage of the first wave of émigrés to flee Germany in 1933–34. Some of their organizations were linked with political groups. Others served refugees independent of political or religious allegiance, especially displaced scholars. In many countries, professionals, women, students, musicians, librarians, scientists, teachers, psychoanalysts, physicians, and many other groups joined forces in professional organizations, among university faculties, on campuses, or on national and local levels to help refugees to find jobs in their fields of competence. However, not all such organizations, in all countries, welcomed refugees because they feared competition on the part of refugee professionals in a closed or tight job market, or wished to defend economic monopolies or private ethnic preserves.

Christian refugees were helped by organizations often established by church groups to aid coreligionists among Nazi victims. Since Nazi persecution was based on "Jewish descent" rather than religious affiliation, such "non-Aryan Christians" were often persecuted no less than their Jewish relatives. In Nazi Germany, they were assisted by such organizations as the Paulus Bund, the Association of Non-Aryan Christians, Caritas, or the German office of the Society of Friends (Friends Service Committee). Upon arrival abroad, corresponding church organizations received them and worked to ease their integration in their new homelands.

Besides the communist or socialist network of agencies, the most intensive effort was made by the Jewish communities wherever Jewish refugees from Germany arrived in some numbers and could not be absorbed quickly by the traditional primary group, the family. In Germany, the work of rescue would not have been possible without political, financial, and organizational support by such major supranational organizations as the Jewish Agency for Palestine, the American Jewish Joint Distribution Committee (JOINT), the (U.S.) Hebrew Sheltering and Immigrant Aid Society (HIAS), and numerous smaller groups founded years before the Nazi take-over to assist Jews persecuted in Czarist Russia or the Middle East. In several countries, nationwide agencies were established by philanthropists, political leaders, and Jewish organizations to raise funds, plan for the resettlement or retraining of refugees, or channel the flow of immigrants beyond the ports of entry. Wherever possible, Jewish representatives, acting as political lobbies on national and international levels, promoted the cause of refugee immigration and resettlement. A Jewish representation was located at Geneva, Switzerland, as a nongovernmental organization with the League of Nations. In several countries and on several political levels, Zionists made political efforts to increase admissions to Palestine. The World Jewish Congress, established in 1936, kept drawing attention to the plight of refugees and the pattern of Nazi persecution.

In the U.S.A., too, fund raising and assistance to the immigrant from Germany were placed at the head of the Jewish agenda of the 1930s, once it was understood that Jews in Central Europe would not be able to retain their foothold in their homelands. Such assistance took many forms, and involved the entire pluralistic and divided American-Jewish community. Fund drives and national fund-raising organizations based part of their appeals on the need to aid refugees and assist in the building-up of Palestine, where about 56,000 Jews from Germany had to be absorbed. Persistent political pressure was kept up to obtain liberalized U.S. immigration practices or legislation. Such pressure ranged from the traditional high-level approaches characteristic of the American Jewish Committee, to the democratic styles of Jewish Labor groups, the American Jewish Congress, committees to boycott German imports, and numerous allies in the non-Jewish community. Shelter and social assistance were offered by HIAS, the National Refugee Service, or the National Council of Jewish Women in major cities such as New York, and by local affiliates across the country. The major religious branches of American Judaism, their national organizations, regional sections, and local synagogues and temples (especially among the Orthodox and Reform groups) offered religious hospitality in their houses of worship, sociability, and personal assistance to the new arrivals.

In every major city receiving refugees from Germany, the already established Jewish social service agencies received additional funds from local community drives to provide a variety of social and counseling services to refugees. In smaller communities, where no social service agencies had been in existence before 1933, local "refugee committees" were established to help the newcomers. Rabbis were assisted in finding new pulpits. In some instances, they achieved national prominence in serving the religious or political community, or in transplanting their scholarship to the U.S.A. Child care agencies found Jewish homes that would accept the small number of unaccompanied children admitted to the country. Zionist leaders who migrated to countries other than Palestine, or who had left the Jewish homeland again, were placed in diaspora Zionist groups or organizations that might benefit from their experiences. In spite of inevitable hesitations, frictions, pettiness, resentment, dissension, and doubts, the organized American-Jewish community proved equal to the task, undertaken under difficult economic and political circumstances, of giving assistance to newcomers.

The entire organized effort of the community, both Jewish and Christian or nondenominational, was rooted in the efforts of individuals from many walks of life, obeying varied impulses, driven by different motives, to help the victims of totalitarianism. Each new wave of persecution, the violence attending the Nazi take-over in Germany in 1933, the invasion and *Anschluss* of Austria on March 12, 1938, and the *Kristallnacht* of November 9-10, 1938 produced new volunteer responses. Professors and students, physicians and librarians, musicians and rabbis gave money, wrote affidavits of support, helped immigrants to find positions, and engaged in the numerous acts of personal warmth and sociability that make the alien less of a stranger, and encourage him to begin that process of personal readjustment at whose end new productive lives would be lived in a new land.

In most countries where they reached a "critical mass," Jews from Germany also organized to help themselves. In some instances, such as the New York New World Club, they joined organizations established before 1933 by Jews from Germany and, by their numbers and cultural energies, gave them new vitality and purpose. Mostly, they created new networks of organized life, often in the image of what they had known overseas in their cities, regions, or homelands. To defend their legal and political status, and represent their political, economic, or communal interest, they founded such national organizations as the New York-based American Federation of Jews from Central Europe and the supranational Council of Jews from Germany. Activities on the national level included co-operation with Jewish community agencies, lobbying, and a wide-ranging concern with the legislative and administrative aspects of postwar West German *Wiedergutmachung* (material reparations), initiated by the Allied occupation powers in West Germany and developed into a major worldwide program by postwar West German governments. A major supranational social agency, United Restitution Organization, was established after the war to provide social assistance to claimants under the *Wiedergutmachung* laws of the Federal Republic of Germany. These central refugee coordinating agencies, in coopera-tion with other social and cultural groups in many countries, also served as conduits for the new links sought by successive governments of the Federal Republic of Germany with their former nationals, so that the evil legacy of the past might be overcome by new bonds of confidence and mutual understanding, a task fraught with psychological and intellectual difficulties and misunder-standings on the part of Germans and refugees alike. The organizations created by refugees played major roles in these undertakings.

In addition, refugees from Germany organized social agencies to serve the needs of the old, the sick, and the poor. One major agency, the New York Selfhelp of Émigrés from Central Europe, established in 1936 by faculty members of the New School for Social Research, offered counseling services and job placement to newcomers in its first 10 years of existence. It developed later into a major social service agency for the aged. Other organizations established day-care centers for the children of working mothers, organized summer camps for children and adults, or, like Blue Card, gave aid to the poorest and neediest among refugees. Aided by German *Wiedergutmachung* funds, another agency established by refugees (United Help) built two large apartment complexes in New York City to house elderly refugees. Still another agency erected a model nursing home in New York on a nonprofit basis. An old age home was also built in Chicago, and in other cities arrangements were made to provide space for elderly refugees in communal homes. In addition, a scholarship program for Nazi victims and their children provided modest assistance to students in need.

Most universal, however, among refugee-created organizations were the religious congregations they established in nearly all countries of resettlement. Wherever they reached sufficient numbers, they separated from the hospitable but alien settled Jewish congregations which had received them with interest and kindness. They bought burial grounds, rented halls in which to meet on Friday evenings, Saturdays, and holidays, listened to old melodies and the accustomed Hebrew pronunciations, heard a rabbi's sermon in German and recreated the (sometimes local and provincial) religious ritual (*minhag*) that had meant home to them since childhood. Beyond the emotional core of such traditionalism, they were motivated by weight of habit, the need to relate to friends, obtain advice, continue the sociability and amenity of a lifetime, the shared memories of childhoods lost, persecutions endured, the new world faced and overcome in shared limitations of integration or acculturation. In these congregations, mutual aid and economic support were given as a matter not only of age-old Jewish religious duty but also as a face-to-face act of mutuality and old neighborliness.

Beyond this, some congregations succeeded in continuing, for decades, the patterns of Jewish religious thought and practice that had made them pioneers or paradigms of German-Jewish religious life. In Israel, Reform Judaism, viewed with hostility by the Orthodox establishment, pioneered progressive Judaism and new religious ideas current in the Germany of the 1920s. In South America, too, Reform Judaism broke entirely new ground because refugee rabbis founded the first major Reform Jewish congregations on the subcontinent, and succeeded in developing them beyond their original clientele of refugees.

In the U.S.A., with its developed divisions into religious subdenominations, few congregations grew beyond the nostalgia of the *Landsmannschaft*, and many suffered from the low intellectual levels and interests of their members. Others, especially the Orthodox community transplanted from Frankfurt am Main to New York, and the Conservative–Reform congregations established by some outstanding rabbis, brought new themes and vitality to their American coreligionists, not always with lasting results. Whatever their levels of contributions, here were spiritual homes away from home, centers of mutuality and social aid, sources of intellectual or leisure-time activity for the migrants, organizational connections with other like-minded congregations and national or supranational agencies—all bridges on the way to integration. Numerous new arrivals received the first impressions of their new homelands, the first sound advice and shrewd economic counsel, through membership in religious congregations.

Of similar significance were the social and leisure-time organizations of refugees, from singing societies, sports clubs, and light entertainment groups to social service agencies, fund-raising operations, and private care groups. Like the congregations, their impact on refugee perceptions and acculturation was not measured by the purposes for which they were organized. Whether they continued patterns of homeland organization, or catered in new forms to old needs, they structured a community whose social health triumphed over defamation and persecution precisely to the degree to which their social interaction and mutual aid transcended self-pity and dependence. Their establishment gave the lie to the invidious view that Jews from Germany had cut themselves off from their roots in Jewish community, tradition, and service. When, after the Holocaust, institutes and foundations (Leo Baeck Institute, Research Foundation for Jewish Immigration) were established by the former refugees to account for the history of Central European Jews, and for the vicissitudes of their migration and resettlement, their activities were recognized as part of that characteristic Jewish voluntarism which saw its finest hours during the Nazi persecution and the migration of Nazi victims.

Thus, the history of the Jewish émigré from Germany and of his uprooting and resettlement is formed by the complex interplay of influences, actions, reactions, and perceptions summarily told in this essay. It is a significant part of twentieth-century history, whether this history is focused on the Holocaust, the history of the homelessness of German liberal and democratic forces, the transfer of intellectual and social forms through migration, or the immigration and acculturation of a community made up of a few intellectual giants, an unusually large number of intellectuals, professionals, artists and community leaders, and numerous anonymous, essentially bourgeois men and women who had never dreamed of the extraordinary fate the century had in store for them. Their resettlement in numerous countries around the globe, and the socialization of their second and younger generations, were aided by men and women of all faiths, by agencies and organizations of many kinds and in many lands. That the refugees as a group avoided social and personal disintegration and found new forms of self-expression in often hostile and always alien environments links them with their fellowmen of all faiths who fell victim to the Holocaust. The moral and spiritual forces that guided them also guided the community of deportees and camp inmates whose sufferings, like theirs, remain paradigms of man's ability to endure and face oppression by asserting his humanity.

Herbert A. Strauss

INTRODUCTION

The emigration and resettlement of Jews from Nazi Germany—as emerges clearly from the foregoing pages—was a historical process of considerable complexity. It involved the activities and interactions of numerous individuals, organizations, and government and international agencies. Its history has yet to be told in a comprehensive manner. The present publication is designed to contribute to the exploration of one segment of this general history.

It aims at documenting primarily three social, political, and communal processes: the *immigration* process, involving legislative and executive government activities, politics, public opinion, lobbying, and individual or organized assistance to immigrants prior to arrival; the *resettlement* process, including individual or organized activities concerned with the reception, geographic location or relocation of immigrants, and all forms of social or other assistance; the *acculturation* process, involving the activities of individuals or organizations, including the immigrant's own organizations, relating to his linguistic, economic, social, religious, intellectual, professional, or subjective integration.

The scope of this volume, *Archival Resources*, was influenced by the state of research on the history of the Jewish immigrant from Germany in the U.S.A., which had concentrated on intellectual or political "élites" while disregarding, to a large extent, the social, political, and communal aspects of the immigrant's history. This volume was designed to document materials relevant for social and communal history, whose neglect may have been due, to some extent, to the emotional imprint the Holocaust has left upon the direction of Jewish research, or to the greater accessibility and more clear-cut methodology of political and intellectual history for traditional scholarship.

This volume restricts its documentation, on the whole, to archival resources located in the U.S.A. It excludes documentation on the persecution or extermination of Jews in Germany from 1933 to 1945. (Volumes IV and V in this series will offer documentation on the persecution and emigration/expulsion of Jews from Germany and their immigration to the U.S.A.) It further excludes docu-

1

mentation on the considerable body of archival materials ("papers") of individual immigrants. Immigrants from Germany included a higher percentage than did other immigrant groups of intellectuals, writers, professionals, businessmen, political and communal leaders, and other persons active in significant segments of culture and society, many of whom have left historically important papers and manuscripts. Specialized collections of materials left by immigrants are located at several repositories, primarily in the two Germanies. (The *International Biographical Dictionary of Central European Émigrés, 1933-1945*, and the literature on German exile writers and the "intellectual migration," document the location of relevant papers.)

The limitation of this publication to materials available in U.S. archives excludes references to some major collections of materials held by agencies and repositories abroad bearing not only on the migration, resettlement, and acculturation of Jews from Germany in countries from which they later remigrated to the U.S.A., but also primary information on the emigration process, the Holocaust period, the rescue efforts made during that period, and postwar rehabilitation and restitution on the part of the Federal Republic of Germany, all of which, in various ways, affected the immigration, resettlement, and acculturation of Jews from Germany in the U.S.A. Several publications listing the holdings of major archives pertaining to these areas are now in print.

The present volume, *Archival Resources*, was compiled by Steven W. Siegel, who has been involved with the development of the Research Foundation for Jewish Immigration's program almost since its inception. This publication, prepared over years of wide-ranging and painstaking research, owes its existence to his expertise in the field of Jewish archives and his perseverance in the face of considerable difficulties encountered in securing the material compiled in this volume.

Based on some materials submitted to the Research Foundation by the late Zosa Szajkowski of the YIVO Institute for Jewish Research, the compiler of this volume used the primary and secondary sources available in libraries and archives, including published guides to archival resources such as the *National Union Catalog of Manuscript Collections* and the unpublished finding aids of archival repositories. In addition, a nationwide mail inquiry was conducted with archival repositories and with organizations and individuals believed to hold relevant materials, and their responses were followed up by further correspondence. Numerous interviews and telephone conversations were held, especially to obtain information on individuals or organizations that had been active in connection with the immigration, resettlement, or acculturation of Jewish immigrants from Germany, but that had ceased to exist by the time our survey had begun.

In principle, efforts were made to document the entire range of relevant archival resources. Some of the archival materials originated with overseas agencies (including German-Jewish organizations) active in assisting prospective immigrants to the U.S.A. Other listings concern non-Jewish (Christian) and nondenominational agencies in the U.S.A. Since the archives of these organizations are relevant for the activities of Jewish agencies aiding immigrants, they were included. (Nazi persecution was based on "racial," not religious grounds, and a number of immigrants from Nazi Germany did not belong to the Jewish religion, although some members of families of immigrants might be formally affiliated with the Jewish faith. For this and similar reasons, the activities of such agencies overlapped those of Jewish agencies.) In addition, organizations that assisted professionals, students, women, children, and other special groups served both Jews and non-Jews and are included in this publication.

For Jewish organizations, however, some selectivity was applied in view of the practically universal involvement of the Jewish community in the U.S.A. in aid to refugees. Organizations located in American communities numbering fewer than 7500 Jewish persons in 1940, and organizations whose programs included aid to refugees in a minor way, or whose activities were of a purely local character, were generally not included. Listing such agencies or committees, even if traces of their archives could be found, would have exceeded the space, time, and funds available for this compilation.

In principle, this volume does not include reports on archival materials that have been destroyed by an agency, or that could not be located any longer without prolonged on-site inquiries. However, it became clear to the Research Foundation, in the course of the research undertaken for this publication, how much irreplaceable documentation had already been destroyed, either following World War II, when agencies restricted or phased out their activities and moved to smaller quarters, or because of a policy of routinely destroying "closed case files" or "old materials." In these ways, the files of some major agencies had been destroyed, or only unsystematically "selected" for archival preservation by social workers or other persons untrained in historical or archival research. The Research Foundation considered it incumbent upon itself to record this loss where major agencies were involved, in order to draw the attention of responsible Jewish organizations to the serious damage done to scholarship in this manner. Efforts to organize a national program to safeguard the materials on the history of this immigration proved fruitless in view of the financial and space problems pleaded by those whose professional responsibility should have included an aggressive policy of archival preservation.

Also excluded were such archival materials of an audiovisual nature as pictures, photographs, newsreels, and films bearing on the subject of the project.

The material included in this volume is arranged in four sections. Part One lists national organizations and projects and topics of national significance, arranged alphabetically by name of organization, project, or topic. Part Two documents the archives of regional and local organizations and is arranged alphabetically by state and by locality within each state. This section includes organizations and agencies founded by refugees as well as American-founded groups. Part Three lists, in alphabetical order, individuals whose papers reflect activities in connection with the immigration, resettlement, or acculturation of immigrants, including some immigrants who themselves were active in these fields for fellow immigrants. Part Four offers a listing of oral history and taped interview collections, many of which are still in progress.

The four sections are followed by an alphabetically arranged list of repositories and their archival holdings as cited in this volume, and by a general index for the volume's four sections.

The information compiled for each entry includes the following: name of individual, organization, project, or topic; general history or information; description of activities related to the immigration, resettlement, or acculturation of immigrants from Nazi Germany; references to significant literature discussing its history or background; description of records or papers with identification of finding aids (including published description, where applicable, in the *National Union Catalog of Manuscript Collections–NUCMC*) and information concerning restrictions of access, where known.

The names of organizations are given in their last known or current form; since considerable changing of names and fusions of organizations were characteristic during and immediately following the period covered by this volume, information on these aspects of organizational history is included. For individuals, years of birth and death are provided. References to the literature are selected for their potential usefulness for further research, and are neither inclusive nor exhaustive. Frequently cited references to literature are abbreviated; the abbreviations used are listed following this Introduction. Organizations or individuals included in the descriptions but listed separately as a main entry or discussed elsewhere within the body of the text are preceded by an asterisk (*), and can be located by means of the Index.

The information concerning archival resources rests on the data obtained by the approach described above. The compiler has not verified this information by examining the holdings so described. Thus, responsibility for the accuracy of the information included rests with the archival repositories, organizations, and individuals cooperating with the Research Foundation. In addition, the information compiled herein is not to be considered exhaustive, as new information continues to become available on archival resources pertaining to the immigration, resettlement, and acculturation of Jews from Germany. This publication reflects the results of a systematic effort stretching over a five-year period (1973–1978) and thus the information obtainable during this period.

Finally, the Research Foundation and the compiler of this volume acknowledge with gratitude the cooperation of numerous individuals who assisted in its preparation. We are especially indebted to Dr. Sybil Milton, the archivist of the Leo Baeck Institute, New York. Professor Herbert A. Strauss, the Coordinator of Research of the Research Foundation for Jewish Immigration, conceived the plan for this publication, designed its form, wrote some of the entries, and gave of his time, knowledge, and editorial expertise to make this volume, *Archival Resources*, possible.

Terminology. Immigrants from Nazi Germany were designated "refugees" during the period of their immigration in public discussions and in the literature of the period. The administration of President Franklin D. Roosevelt generally preferred to use the designation "political refugees" for immigrants from Nazi Germany, the large majority of whom were Jewish. The designation "refugees" was also used by the League of Nations High Commissioner for Refugees (Jewish and Other) Coming from Germany. In accordance with this usage, the term "refugee" is used in this publication to designate the Jewish immigrant from Germany of the Nazi period.

Frequently Cited Literature References

Abbreviation Used	*Reference in Full*
American Jewish Year Book	*American Jewish Year Book.* New York: American Jewish Committee, 1899/1900-.
Contemporary Authors	*Contemporary Authors.* Detroit: Gale Research Co., 1962-.
Current Biography	*Current Biography Yearbook.* New York: H. W. Wilson, 1940-.
D.A.B.	*Dictionary of American Biography.* New York: Scribner, 1928-.
Dictionary of Scientific Biography	*Dictionary of Scientific Biography.* New York: Scribner, 1970-78.
Encyclopaedia Judaica	*Encyclopaedia Judaica.* Jerusalem, 1971-72.
Feingold, *Politics of Rescue*	Henry L. Feingold, *The Politics of Rescue, The Roosevelt Administration and the Holocaust, 1938-1945.* New Brunswick, NJ: Rutgers Univ. Press, 1970.
Genizi, "American Non-Sectarian"	Haim Genizi, "American Non-Sectarian Refugee Relief Organizations (1933-1945)." *Yad Vashem Studies on the European Jewish Catastrophe and Resistance* (Jerusalem) XI (1976): 164-220.
Hertz, "Joint and Concurrent"	Richard C. Hertz, "Joint and Concurrent Efforts of Catholics, Protestants and Jews on Behalf of Present Day Refugees." Unpublished thesis, Hebrew Union College, Cincinnati, 1940.
International Biographical Dictionary	*International Biographical Dictionary of Central European Émigrés 1933-1945.* 3 volumes. Munich: K. G. Saur, 1979-81.
Jewish Book Annual	*Jewish Book Annual.* New York: Jewish Book Council of America, 1942-.
Leo Baeck Institute Year Book	*Leo Baeck Institute Year Book.* London: 1956-.
Lessing, *Oral History*	*Jewish Immigrants of the Nazi Period in the U.S.A.* Volume III: *Guide to the Oral History Collection of the Research Foundation for Jewish Immigration,* Joan C. Lessing, comp. New York: K. G. Saur, 1979.
National Archives, *Guide*	U.S. National Archives and Records Service, *Guide to the National Archives of the United States.* Washington, DC, 1974.
National Cyclopaedia of American Biography	*National Cyclopaedia of American Biography.* New York: J. T. White, 1893-.

Abbreviation Used	*Reference in Full*
NUCMC	U.S. Library of Congress, *National Union Catalog of Manuscript Collections*. Washington, DC, 1958-.
Romanofsky, *Social Service Organizations*	*The Greenwood Encyclopedia of American Institutions: Social Service Organizations*. Peter Romanofsky, ed. Westport, CT: Greenwood Press, 1978.
Universal Jewish Encyclopedia	*Universal Jewish Encyclopedia*. New York: 1939-43.
Wetzel, "American Rescue"	Charles J. Wetzel, "The American Rescue of Refugee Scholars and Scientists from Europe 1933-1945." Unpublished Ph.D. dissertation, Univ. of Wisconsin, 1964.
Who's Who in American Jewry	*Who's Who in American Jewry*, vol. 3. New York: National News Association, 1938-39.
Who's Who in World Jewry	*Who's Who in World Jewry*. New York, 1955-.
Wyman, *Paper Walls*	David S. Wyman, *Paper Walls, America and the Refugee Crisis, 1938-41*. Amherst, MA: Univ. of Massachusetts Press, 1968.

One

NATIONAL ORGANIZATIONS

1. AGUDATH ISRAEL OF AMERICA, INC.
5 Beekman St., New York, NY 10038

The Agudath Israel movement was founded by German and Russian rabbis in Kattowitz in 1912 in response to the refusal of the majority at the Tenth Zionist Congress in Basel to vote for a decentralization of cultural activities. Unites the separatist Orthodox communities of many countries for the pursuit of Orthodox goals and the representation of their interests. Developed far-flung activities in religious, economic, and political affairs, and in social welfare. Jacob Rosenheim, a cofounder and president of Agudath Israel World Organization 1929-65, immigrated to the U.S.A. in 1941 as a refugee from Nazi Germany.

Agudath Israel Youth Council of America (founded in 1922) established an Immigration and Refugee Division in 1940 to assist in the rescue of Orthodox Jews overseas. Agudath Israel of America (founded in 1939 and now the parent body of the Youth Council) took part in efforts to rescue European Jews during and after World War II. *Agudath Israel of Upper Manhattan, New York, was founded by German-Jewish refugees in 1939 as a branch of the original Youth Council.

Literature. *International Biographical Dictionary*, vol. I (J. Rosenheim).
Orthodox Youth, 1940-43, and its successor, *Orthodox Tribune*, 1943-45(?) (reprinted in Jerusalem, 1975), were published by Agudath Israel Youth Council and contain a considerable amount of information on the Agudath Israel movement's efforts to assist Orthodox Jews in Europe.

Records. Agudath Israel of America: records (which were being processed in 1978) include materials on the rescue activities of the organization.

2. AMERICAN ASSOCIATION OF FORMER AUSTRIAN JURISTS
c/o Joseph Haim (president), 60 E. 42 St., New York, NY 10017

Founded in 1941 in New York by Austrian immigrants. Inactive in 1976. Was primarily concerned with influencing *Wiedergutmachung* legislation in favor of immigrants from Austria.

Records. Fragmentary financial records are with the last treasurer, Paul E. Deutsch, 755 West End Ave., New York, NY 10025. Minutes have not been located and are presumed lost.

3. AMERICAN ASSOCIATION OF FORMER EUROPEAN JURISTS *Defunct*

Cofounded in 1939 in New York by *Bruno Weil under the name American Association of Former German Jurists as a professional service of the *New World Club, New York. Adopted above name by 1945. Inactive since 1970. Was primarily concerned with legal problems of *Wiedergutmachung* and with legislation concerning alien property in the U.S.A. Acted as information, discussion, and pressure group concerning legal and political issues related to the above and to postwar West Germany. Membership included leading former German jurists and organization heads.

Records. Records, consisting of minutes of meetings, are with the last secretary, Fritz Weinschenk, 630 Fifth Ave., New York, NY 10020.

4. AMERICAN ASSOCIATION OF UNIVERSITY WOMEN, INC. (AAUW)
2401 Virginia Ave., N.W., Washington, DC 20037

Founded in 1882 as an educational organization of women college graduates. Formed a Committee on Refugee Aid early in 1940 under its Committee on International Relations. Issued recommendations to local branches for programs in aid of refugees, provided assistance in placing refugee women scholars, participated in the Princeton Conference on Refugee Problems and Needs, February–March 1941, cooperated with the French Association of University Women in aiding displaced and refugee university women overseas, and raised funds for that purpose. Issued a pamphlet, by Helen M. Parkin, *Refugees*, December 1938; revised and enlarged edition, *Refugees–A World Problem*, January 1939.

Literature. AAUW, *Journal*, includes reports on aid to refugees.

Records. AAUW Library/Archives: records include case files of refugee women scholars, committee reports, minutes, and letters of recommendation.

5. AMERICAN CHRISTIAN COMMITTEE FOR REFUGEES, INC. (ACCR)
Defunct

Founded in 1934 in New York as the American Committee for Christian German Refugees. The name was changed in 1939 to American Committee for Christian Refugees, and in 1944 to American Christian Committee for Refugees. Principal fund-raising and coordinating agency of Protestant groups and organizations aiding refugees. Cooperated closely with the Federal Council of the Churches of Christ in America (*National Council of the Churches of Christ in the U.S.A.) and with Jewish and nonsectarian organizations aiding refugees. Cosponsored *Friendship House for Refugees, New York, in 1940.

Established a Personal Service Division to assist and find jobs for refugees. Maintained branch offices in Chicago and Boston. In 1947, the Committee was dissolved and its program and resources were transferred to the Committee on Displaced Persons of Church World Service (475 Riverside Dr., New York, NY 10027), which had been founded in 1946 to consolidate relief activities of various church groups.

Literature. ACCR, *Toward a New Life: 10 Years of Stewardship: The American Christian Committee for Refugees.* New York, 1945.
Romanofsky, *Social Service Organizations*, pp. 43-46, 238-241.
Wetzel, "American Rescue," pp. 302-308.

Records. Presbyterian Historical Society: records of the Committee have not been identified in the files of Church World Service and have presumably been destroyed. Some materials regarding the Committee's activities are included among the records of the Federal Council of Churches.

6. AMERICAN CIVIL LIBERTIES UNION, INC. (ACLU)
22 E. 40 St., New York, NY 10016

Civil rights organization, founded in 1920, which pressed for changes in immigration laws and for easing government restrictions on enemy aliens during World War II. Corresponded with governmental agencies on matters relating to immigration, naturalization, citizenship, alien legislation and registration, deportations, and related topics.

Records. Princeton Univ., Manuscript Library: records since 1912 consist of correspondence files, clippings, and case files, arranged by years.

New York Public Library, General Research and Humanities Div.; Brandeis Univ. Library; and State Historical Society of Wisconsin: records, 1912-50, are on microfilm (279 reels); original materials are at Princeton Univ.

Records, 1912-46, are generally assembled in scrapbooks. Some of the records for those years were segregated and were not placed in the scrapbooks nor subsequently microfilmed. Therefore, some materials dealing with refugees and enemy aliens are not filed in chronological sequence, but are included among the files of 1946 to ca. 1952. Finding aid: Alex Baskin, *The American Civil Liberties Union Papers: A Guide to the Records, ACLU Cases 1912-1946.* Stony Brook, NY: Archives of Social History, 1971.

Recent records are at ACLU's office.

The American Civil Liberties Union Records and Publications, 1917-1975 was issued in microform (96 reels) by Microfilming Corp. of America, Glen Rock, NJ. It includes minutes since 1926, mailings to the board of directors since 1942, ACLU Policy Guides since 1938, legal briefs, and ACLU publications since 1917. Finding aid: *The American Civil Liberties Union Records and Publications, 1917-1975: A Guide to the Microform Collection.* Glen Rock, NJ, 1976.

7. AMERICAN COMMITTEE FOR THE GUIDANCE OF PROFESSIONAL PERSONNEL *Defunct*

Founded in 1938 to assist refugee journalists and lawyers. Also known as the Committee for the Re-education of Refugee Lawyers, Inc./John W. Davis Fund. [Davis, a prominent lawyer, was a founder of the Committee and served on the management council of the Coordinating Foundation (*Intergovernmental Committee on Refugees).] The Committee granted fellowships to refugee lawyers for studies at U.S. law schools, and sought their admission to such schools. Nine fellowships were granted in 1939-40, nineteen in 1940-41. The Committee ceased operation after 1944.

Records. New York Public Library, Manuscripts and Archives Div.: records, 1938-44, 3.5 ft, form part of the records of the *Emergency Committee in Aid of Displaced Foreign Scholars (boxes 187-194). Include biographical material on refugee lawyers and correspondence dealing with the Committee's efforts to retrain and place them. *NUCMC* MS 76-1507.

8. AMERICAN COMMITTEE FOR THE PROTECTION OF FOREIGN BORN
799 Broadway, New York, NY 10003

Founded in 1931 to protect the legal rights of the foreign born, and to assist in their naturalization.

The Committee assisted some refugees of the Nazi era. One of its publications relevant to refugees was James B. Carey, *Refugees and Unemployment*, New York, 1940.

Literature. The Committee's periodicals of the era included *The Foreign Born*, 1937-39, *These United States*, 1940-41, *This Month*, 1941, *Action Memo*, 1941-42, *For Your Information*, 1943-?, and *The Lamp*, 1944-59.

Records. Univ. of Michigan, Labadie Collection: records, 34 file drawers, consist of several hundred case files, minutes, legal briefs, and publications.

Recent records are at the agency's office.

9. AMERICAN COMMITTEE OF OSE, INC. *Defunct*

The American Committee for the Protection of the Health of the Jews—OSE was founded in New York in 1929, financed by the *American Jewish Joint Distribution Committee. Later renamed the American Committee of OSE, it was dissolved in 1971 upon the death of Leon Wulman, M.D., its executive director, who had been active in OSE in Europe prior to his arrival in the U.S.A. in 1939.

OSE (Obtchestvo Sdravuchranenya Evreyev) was founded in 1912 at St. Petersburg, Russia, to combat the high mortality rate and improve the physical and mental health of Jews through preventive measures and the spread of information on hygiene. It was active in Russia and Eastern Europe following World War I in baby, child, and adult health care for Jews. The Central (international)

Committee of OSE was located in Berlin, later in Paris, from 1923 to 1952. In 1952, it was renamed World Union OSE. OSE was known in Western Europe as Oeuvre de Secours aux Enfants Israélites or as Organisation pour la Santé et l'Éducation.

OSE aided Jewish children in Western Europe, especially through its French section during the Nazi occupation, and cared for survivors of the Holocaust following World War II. *Ernst Papanek directed an OSE Children's Home and School for Refugee Children in France 1938-40. The American Committee of OSE provided financial support for the overseas activities of the organization.

Literature. World Union OSE and American Committee of OSE, *In Fight for the Health of the Jewish People (50 Years of OSE).* Dr. L. Wulman, ed. New York, 1968.

Records. YIVO Institute for Jewish Research: records, 1941-60s, 35 ft, contain materials on the rescue of Jewish children during World War II and correspondence between OSE in New York and OSE in France and other countries. They include records of World Union OSE, 1940-45, 3 ft, formerly a part of the central archives of OSE. *NUCMC* MS 64-1318. Finding aid: unpublished inventory (115 pp.).

Central Archives for the History of the Jewish People, Israel: records of World Union OSE (now defunct), 1945-67, 25 ft, reflect the administrative, financial, and legal activities of the agency.

10. AMERICAN COUNCIL FOR ÉMIGRÉS IN THE PROFESSIONS, INC. (ACEP)
345 E. 46 St., New York, NY 10017

Founded in 1945 by the *American Christian Committee for Refugees, with the support of the *National Refugee Service, to continue the work done by Else Staudinger and *Alvin Johnson in connection with the University in Exile (*New School for Social Research, Graduate Faculty of Political and Social Science) from 1933 to 1945. Carried on the activities of the *Emergency Committee in Aid of Displaced Foreign Scholars, which was disbanded in 1945. Originally known as American Committee for Refugee Scholars, Writers and Artists. The name changed in 1946 to American Committee for Émigré Scholars, Writers and Artists; the present name was adopted in 1955. In 1964 a Medical Division was formed to carry on the work of the *National Committee for the Resettlement of Foreign Physicians. In 1978, concerned primarily with the placement and retraining of professional émigrés in the U.S.A.

Literature. Lessing, *Oral History.*

Records. Univ. of Minnesota, Immigration History Research Center: records, 1945-60, ca. 33 ft, consist of case files and administrative materials.

Records since 1960 are at ACEP's office.

11. AMERICAN COUNCIL FOR EQUAL COMPENSATION OF NAZI VICTIMS FROM AUSTRIA, INC.

c/o Felix Harding (president), 88-35 Elmhurst Ave., Elmhurst, NY 11373

Austrian-Jewish immigrant organization founded in 1966 in New York to obtain improved compensation for Nazi victims from Austria.

Records. Records are with the president.

12. AMERICAN COUNCIL FOR NATIONALITIES SERVICE, INC. (ACNS)

20 W. 40 St., New York, NY 10018

Formed in 1959 by a merger of the Common Council for American Unity and the American Federation of International Institutes. The member organizations, many of which are known as *International Institutes, are autonomous non-sectarian agencies providing service and fellowship for all immigrant nationalities. ACNS cooperates with the foreign-language press and radio, nationality groups, the U.S. government, and other organizations serving the foreign born.

The Foreign Language Information Service, predecessor of the Common Council for American Unity, was founded in 1918. Its declared purpose was "to interpret America to the immigrant and the immigrant to America." Its legislative programs during the 1930s were aimed at making "immigration legislation humane and eliminating discrimination against the alien."

The Common Council for American Unity, organized in 1940 upon the dissolution of the Foreign Language Information Service, served European immigrants, ethnic and racial groups in the U.S.A., and second-generation immigrants. During World War II, the Council publicized information relevant to immigrants in foreign languages for the *U.S. Dept. of Justice and advised aliens on the alien registration provisions. Following the war, it helped to organize the *Citizens' Committee on Displaced Persons.

For the history of the American Federation of International Institutes, see *International Institutes.

Literature. Romanofsky, *Social Service Organizations*, pp. 52-55, 244-247, 311-315.

Records. Univ. of Minnesota, Immigration History Research Center: records since 1918, 175 ft, consist of materials originating primarily with the Foreign Language Information Service and the Common Council. Some records relate to the American Federation and the International Institutes.

Recent records are at the organization's office.

13. AMERICAN COUNCIL OF VOLUNTARY AGENCIES FOR FOREIGN SERVICE, INC.

200 Park Ave. S., New York, NY 10003

Social service agency founded in late 1943 through the initiative of *Joseph P. Chamberlain and Clarence Pickett (*American Friends Service Committee) to develop and coordinate American relief efforts in the liberated areas of Europe. Committees composed of representatives of member agencies focused on particular concerns. A Committee on Displaced Persons was active in the postwar period, and efforts were made to clarify the roles of the voluntary agencies active on behalf of displaced persons.

The agency has expanded its activities and offers technical assistance and disaster preparedness (1978).

Literature. Romanofsky, *Social Service Organizations*, pp. 55–59.

Records. Council office: records, 1943–date, consist of files arranged by committee and project and by name of individual associated with a Council activity, including Chamberlain and documentation regarding organizations and activities in aid of refugees.

14. AMERICAN DANZIG ASSOCIATION *Defunct*

Founded in New York in December 1941 by refugees from Danzig, as the Free City of Danzig Citizens Committee in the United States. Its chairman was Dr. Bernhard Kamnitzer, formerly a Senator of the Free City of Danzig. The Committee was organized to represent refugees from Danzig in matters relating to their alien status in the U.S.A. By 1945, the Committee was known as the American Danzig Association, with Kamnitzer as president. The Association continued to exist until the 1950s.

Records. Leo Baeck Institute Archives: the Sam Echt Collection includes records, 1941–52, ca. 1 in., formerly held by Kamnitzer, consisting of Committee minutes, 1941–43, Kamnitzer's correspondence as chairman and president, 1942–46, and a copy of an Association newsletter, 1950.

15. AMERICAN FEDERATION OF JEWISH FIGHTERS, CAMP INMATES AND NAZI VICTIMS, INC.
315 Lexington Ave., New York, NY 10016

Founded in 1971 by survivors of the Holocaust to perpetuate the memory of Holocaust victims and make Jews and non-Jews aware of the Holocaust and of Jewish resistance. Organizes countrywide memorial meetings and services on "Holocaust Day" (Yom ha-Shoa), supports research and publications on the history of the Holocaust, and holds an annual dinner in New York.

Records. Records are at the agency's office.

16. AMERICAN FEDERATION OF JEWS FROM AUSTRIA, INC.
c/o Gustav Jellinek, M.D. (president), 49 E. 86 St., New York, NY 10028

Austrian-Jewish immigrant organization founded ca. 1940 in New York and incorporated in 1945. Inactive in 1976. Coordinating agency for six Austrian immigrant agencies, all in New York: American Council of Jews from Austria,

*American Congregation of Jews from Austria, Hakoah Athletic Club, *Igul Alumni Association of Zionist Fraternities, *Jacob Ehrlich Society, and Jewish Foreign War Veterans. Represented the interests of Austrian-Jewish immigrants, was active in civil rights, cultural and welfare work for the needy and elderly, and claims for *Wiedergutmachung* from Austria.

Records. Records are with the president.

17. AMERICAN FEDERATION OF JEWS FROM CENTRAL EUROPE, INC.
570 Seventh Ave., New York, NY 10018

Founded in 1939 in New York in the wake of the increase of Jewish immigrants from Germany as the American Federation of Jews from Germany, and renamed in 1940 the American Federation of German and Austrian Jews, the Federation was incorporated in 1941 under the above name. Its founders included Max M. Warburg, Nathan Stein, *Max Gruenewald, Frederick W. Borchardt, and numerous political, religious, and organizational leaders of the former Jewish community in Germany. A membership organization, the Federation represented over 30 organizations and congregations founded by immigrants from Germany and Austria in the U.S.A. Its first activities (1941–45) concerned the protection of the civil rights of immigrants from Germany threatened by their status as "enemy aliens" following the outbreak of World War II, the promotion of liberalized immigration laws, aid to Jewish communities and individuals in Axis-occupied Europe, and participation in the relief, rescue, and rehabilitation efforts of U.S. and international organizations.

From 1946 on, the Federation, as the American representative of the *Council of Jews from Germany, participated in efforts in the U.S.A. and abroad to obtain *Wiedergutmachung* from Germany for material losses suffered by Nazi victims due to the impact of Nazism. It established the *United Restitution Organization in New York under joint directorship, with Herman Muller as executive officer, and represented the interests of the Nazi victim community (including Eastern European and Austrian victims) on political and diplomatic levels. As the U.S. representative of the Council of Jews from Germany, it established *United Help and assisted in the establishment of the *Leo Baeck Institute, distributed *Wiedergutmachungs*-funds to the social and cultural organizations of refugees through United Help, and participated in fund-raising campaigns for the social agencies of refugees. It also established its own fund-raising organization, the *Jewish Philanthropic Fund of 1933.

Beginning in 1964, with Herbert A. Strauss as executive officer, the Federation, while continuing existing programs and affiliations, accepted individuals as members, developed a cultural program of all-day study conferences (*Lerntage*) and publications, and founded the *Research Foundation for Jewish Immigration as part of the effort of the Council of Jews from Germany to do research and write the history of Jewish immigrants from Central Europe of the Nazi period.

Literature. American Federation of Jews from Central Europe, *Ten Years*

1941-1951, 1952. *Annual Meeting 1956*, 1956. *Twenty Years 1940-1960*, 1961. *The Twenty-Second Year 1961-1962*, 1962. *Annual Meeting 1964*, 1964.

Lessing, *Oral History.*

Herbert A. Strauss and Hanns G. Reissner, eds., *Jubilee Volume for Dr. Curt C. Silberman.* New York: American Federation of Jews from Central Europe, 1969.

Records. Federation's office: records since 1939, 50 ft, consist of minutes (annual meetings, meetings of board of directors, and committees), correspondence, financial files, internal publications, and files concerning the early years of United Restitution Organization. Subjects include civil rights, political and diplomatic activities, restitution and indemnification, and relationships between the Federation and other organizations. Restricted.

Leo Baeck Institute Archives: records, 1 ft, concerning the Federation's 1944 questionnaire survey of former Jewish communal property in Germany.

18. AMERICAN FRIENDS SERVICE COMMITTEE, INC. (AFSC)
1501 Cherry St., Philadelphia, PA 19102

Established in 1917 by the (American) Society of Friends to put into practice traditional Quaker concerns with philanthropy and reform. Established Friends Centers in Berlin, Vienna, Paris, and Geneva in the 1930s to assist non-Jewish persons persecuted by Nazism. Cooperated with Jewish organizations in the U.S.A. and abroad on a wide range of social work, political activities, publicity, fund raising, immigration, resettlement, and placement on behalf of refugees. Clarence Pickett was AFSC executive secretary from 1929 to 1950.

Services for refugees were coordinated by its Refugee Service Committee, established in 1938, and subsequently renamed Refugee Section (Foreign Service Section). In 1939, AFSC published *Refugee Facts* (in 250,000 copies) at the urging of the *American Jewish Committee, to counteract anti-immigration propaganda. Supported old age and residence homes for refugees, established summer camps for refugee children, and operated hostels for refugees traveling West in the U.S.A., and in Cuba.

In 1940, on the suggestion of the *American Jewish Joint Distribution Committee, AFSC sent a representative to Lisbon and established an office there in 1941 to create a liaison with U.S. consular officials (*U.S. Dept. of State), and to facilitate the granting of U.S. visas to war victims and refugees.

Literature. AFSC, *Annual Report.* 1933-45.

——, *Bulletin*, nos. 132, 135, 157, 171, 209, 209A. 1939-42.

Kathleen Hambly Hanstein, *Refugee Services of the American Friends Service Committee: An Historical Summary.* Philadelphia, 1967. Mimeo.

Romanofsky, *Social Service Organizations*, pp. 75-79.

Wetzel, "American Rescue," pp. 237-287.

Wyman, *Paper Walls.*

Records. AFSC Archives: records since 1917 include minutes, correspondence, and subject files, and a wide variety of other materials on refugees and immigration; case files are not included.

Balch Institute: over 20,000 case files of refugees and refugee families who had requested help from the Philadelphia office of AFSC between 1939 and 1950.

19. AMERICAN GUILD FOR GERMAN CULTURAL FREEDOM   *Defunct*

Founded in New York in 1936 by Hubertus Prinz zu Loewenstein, a political refugee, who served as its general secretary until 1940, when the Guild was dissolved. Gave financial assistance to exiled Jewish and non-Jewish intellectuals in Europe, and assisted in their resettlement in the U.S.A. *Alvin Johnson and *Oswald G. Villard were officers of the Guild.

Records. Records are at the Deutsche Bibliothek, Frankfurt am Main, Federal Republic of Germany.

The papers of *Nicholas M. Butler include correspondence with Loewenstein, 1936–46, and materials regarding the Guild. The papers of Villard include correspondence with Loewenstein.

20. AMERICAN IMMIGRATION AND CITIZENSHIP CONFERENCE, INC. (AICC)
20 W. 40 St., New York, NY 10018

Formed in 1960 by a merger of the National Council on Naturalization and Citizenship (NCNC), founded in 1930, and the American Immigration Conference (AIC), founded in 1954, the AICC represents the major U.S. social and political agencies interested in immigration. The AICC is concerned with immigration, resettlement, integration, and ethnicity in the U.S.A., and provides information on, recommends, and lobbies for changes in immigration law. Its efforts contributed to the passage of the U.S. Immigration Act of 1965. Its Committee on Integration conducts annual seminars concerning immigration laws, ethnicity, the theory and practice of integration, and social service to immigrants.

The NCNC was formed to share information and to coordinate the activities of organizations and individuals concerned with improving naturalization laws and procedures. Its accomplishments by 1945 included reduced naturalization fees, increased appropriations for naturalization administration, and the codification of nationality laws in the Nationality Act of 1940. Its activities following the war increased owing to changes in immigration patterns and the arrival of displaced persons. The *American Federation of Jews from Central Europe is affiliated with the AICC.

Literature. Romanofsky, *Social Service Organizations*, pp. 87-92, 519-523.

Records. Univ. of Minnesota Libraries, Social Welfare History Archives Center: records of NCNC, AIC, and AICC, 1890-1967, 27 ft, include material on immigration and naturalization for the 1930s and 1940s. Finding aid: unpublished inventory.

Recent records are at AICC's office.

21. AMERICAN IMMIGRATION CONFERENCE BOARD, INC.   *Defunct*

Founded in New York in the 1920s (incorporated in 1938) as an anticommunist organization devoted primarily to limiting both legal and illegal immigration into the U.S.A.

Records. Yale Univ. Library, Dept. of Manuscripts and Archives: records, 1929, 1933-39, ca. 8 ft, consist of correspondence, minutes, statements of aims and objectives, petitions, resolutions, financial material, writings, newspaper clippings, printed matter, and other items. Include documentation on activities opposing the immigration of refugees from Nazi Germany. *NUCMC* MS 71-2005. Finding aid: unpublished register.

22. AMERICAN JEWISH COMMITTEE, INC.
165 E. 56 St., New York, NY 10022

Founded in 1906 by American Jews in response to the persecution of Jews in Czarist Russia. By 1933 the Committee had developed into one of the major Jewish civil rights and public education agencies in the U.S.A.

Engaged in diplomatic activities and undertook numerous intercessions in the U.S.A. and abroad on issues connected with anti-Semitism, the persecution of Jews in Germany, and their immigration and resettlement in the U.S.A., Palestine, South America, and elsewhere. In its educational efforts it used direct and indirect channels to fight anti-Semitic developments. Opposed strong anti-Nazi boycott measures in 1933. Fought immigration restrictions in the U.S.A. Cooperated with other agencies in founding and maintaining information offices in Amsterdam and Paris in 1933. At one time in the 1930s, links with Vatican officials were mediated through Joseph K. Wirth, an ex-chancellor of the Weimar Republic, who fled to Switzerland in 1933. Cooperated with the non-Zionist wing of the Jewish Agency for Palestine (*World Zionist Organization—American Section) to open Palestine for the immigration of refugees. The members of the Committee's Executive Committee, including *Felix M. Warburg, *James N. Rosenberg, *Lewis L. Strauss, and *Samuel I. Rosenman, were active on their own to fight the persecution, and to promote the immigration and resettlement, of Jews from Central Europe in the U.S.A.

Literature. Annual reports of the Committee in the *American Jewish Year Book.*

Naomi W. Cohen, *Not Free to Desist: The American Jewish Committee, 1906-1966.* Philadelphia: Jewish Publication Society, 1972. Especially chaps. 8-10.

Records. American Jewish Committee, Blaustein Library/Archives and Records

Center: records include minutes of the Executive, Administrative, Steering, and other committees; subject, chronological, and administrative files; printed and unpublished materials concerning refugees, immigration, anti-Semitism, and numerous other topics; and the papers of *Morris D. Waldman and of Cyrus Adler, president 1929–40.

23. AMERICAN JEWISH CONFERENCE *Defunct*

Established in 1943 at the initiative of *B'nai B'rith International as a central coordinating agency of all major Jewish organizations and local communities to deal with the problems created by the Holocaust, and to support the Jewish settlement in Palestine. In 1943, the *American Jewish Committee seceded from the Conference when it adopted a Zionist position contrary to the policies then pursued by the American Jewish Committee.

The Rescue and Post-War Commissions of the Conference were active in political and public relations campaigns concerned with the opening of Palestine for Jewish immigration and other areas related to Jewish refugees and survivors. The Conference was dissolved in 1948.

Records. Zionist Archives and Library: records, 1943–48, ca. 40 ft, comprise the organization's original files.

American Jewish Historical Society: records, 1943–48, 2.5 ft, consist of verbatim transcripts of the meetings and published materials issued by the Conference. *NUCMC* MS 72-2.

24. AMERICAN JEWISH CONGRESS, INC.
15 E. 84 St., New York, NY 10028

Major U.S. Jewish organization established in 1920 for the defense of the civil rights of Jews and other groups. Rabbi *Stephen S. Wise was its president 1936–49, *Joseph L. Tenenbaum chairman of its executive committee 1929–36, and vice-president 1943–45.

Played a major role in the struggle to liberalize immigration laws and admit refugees to the U.S.A. in the 1930s and 1940s. In 1933, the Congress established a Boycott Committee, chaired by Tenenbaum, which, in 1935, became the *Joint Boycott Council of the American Jewish Congress and *Jewish Labor Committee. The Women's Division of the Congress operated a refugee shelter in New York City at Congress Houses on W. 68 St. 1934–41. By mid-1934, the Congress had formed a Physicians' Committee to assist in resettling refugee physicians; this committee functioned for a short time only.

Literature. American Jewish Congress, *Reports . . . to the National Convention,* 1945–51.
American Jewish Congress, What It Is and What It Does, 1936.

Records. American Jewish Historical Society: records, 1916–71, 125 ft, include minutes, correspondence, publications, and other materials of the Congress on national and regional levels, and materials relating to the Women's Div. on the national and local levels. *NUCMC* MS 72-1363.

Recent records are at the agency's office.

Wise's papers include extensive documentation about the Congress.

25. AMERICAN JEWISH JOINT AGRICULTURAL CORPORATION
(AGRO-JOINT) *Defunct*

Founded in 1924 by the *American Jewish Joint Distribution Committee (JDC) to promote the agricultural settlement of Jews, primarily in Russia. *James N. Rosenberg was founder and chairman. Trustees included *Herbert H. Lehman, *Lewis L. Strauss, and *Felix M. Warburg. Agro-Joint was dissolved in 1952.

Agro-Joint provided financial support to the *Dominican Republic Settlement Association (DORSA) and the settlement of German- and Austrian-Jewish refugees at Sosúa, Dominican Republic.

Records. Records of Agro-Joint are with the JDC at its office.

26. AMERICAN JEWISH JOINT DISTRIBUTION COMMITTEE, INC. (JDC)
60 E. 42 St., New York, NY 10017

Founded in 1914 by relief committees set up by German (American Jewish Relief Committee), Orthodox (Central Relief Committee), and Eastern European (People's Relief Committee) Jews to coordinate relief efforts for Jews in Palestine and Eastern Europe. JDC established five major committees (Medical, Child Care, Refugees, Reconstruction, and Cultural) and other subdivisions, and cooperated with other charitable agencies during World War I and after to finance relief programs in Europe and the Middle East.

With the advent of Nazism, JDC became the principal agency disbursing American Jewish funds to Jews in Germany and to émigrés. *Bernhard Kahn, JDC's European director, transferred the JDC European office from Berlin to Paris in 1933. The office subsequently moved to Bordeaux, France, and in 1940 to Lisbon, Portugal. Aid to refugees in Europe was funneled through local agencies aiding newcomers in France, Belgium, Holland, Czechoslovakia, Austria, Poland, Switzerland, and other countries. Substantial aid was granted also to agencies serving German-Jewish refugees in North Africa, Shanghai, Latin America, and other locations. By 1939, JDC's operations in aid of German-Jewish and other Nazi victims extended to over 50 countries.

Following the outbreak of World War II, JDC arranged for the payment of transportation and chartered ships to rescue refugees. It assisted refugees, sometimes through underground channels, in reaching neutral territory where passage to overseas havens could be arranged. Activities in aid of Jewish refugees in Nazi-occupied Europe were directed from a Swiss center (Saly Mayer, Zürich). The total number of refugees receiving help from JDC in flight and emigration is estimated at 200,000, including large-scale aid to Holocaust survivors.

The JDC Transmigration Bureau, founded in June 1940, acted as a clearing house for Americans who financed the resettlement of refugee families. In 1954, the Migration Dept. (Transmigration Bureau) merged with the *United Service for New Americans to form the *United HIAS Service.

Agencies related to JDC were the *American Jewish Joint Agricultural Corporation (Agro-Joint), *American Joint Reconstruction Foundation, *Dominican Republic Settlement Association (DORSA), and *Refugee Economic Corporation.

Literature. Yehuda Bauer, *My Brother's Keeper. A History of the American Jewish Joint Distribution Committee 1929-1939.* Philadelphia: Jewish Publication Society, 1974.

Oscar Handlin, *A Continuing Task: The American Jewish Joint Distribution Committee, 1914-1964.* New York: Random House, 1964.

Romanofsky, *Social Service Organizations*, pp. 92-98.

Records. JDC records constitute one of the principal archival sources regarding American-Jewish immigration, relief, and rescue activities since 1914. JDC files are kept partly in the Archives and Library at the JDC office, and partly in a warehouse inaccessible to researchers. Records for the 1933-45 period were being arranged in 1978 for research use. Files include minutes, correspondence, reports, and a wide variety of documentation reflecting JDC's role.

YIVO Institute for Jewish Research:

- General records on JDC, ca. 1930-69, consist of printed materials, photographs, and newspaper clippings.
- Records of the JDC Lisbon office, 1939-51, 279 files on microfilm (originals destroyed), form a part of the JDC-HICEM Lisbon collection. Consist of correspondence with other organizations, including significant materials on refugees of the Nazi period. Finding aid: unpublished inventory.
- Records of the JDC Warsaw central office, 1939-41, ca. 1 ft (photocopies; originals are in the Jewish Historical Institute, Warsaw, Poland; the JDC Archives and Yad Vashem, Jerusalem, Israel, have microfilm copies of these materials).
- Records of the JDC Personal Service (Migration) Dept. (Transmigration records), 1946-54, 1899 files on microfilm (97 reels, originals destroyed), include materials on financial aspects of migration and transportation, the location of relatives and sponsors, referrals to other agencies, financial support given to immigrants, medical matters, and correspondence with individuals and organizations. Finding aid: unpublished inventory.

27. AMERICAN JEWISH K C FRATERNITY, INC./MAX MAINZER MEMORIAL FOUNDATION, INC.
70-45 173 St., Flushing, NY 11365

Organized in 1939 as the Jewish Fraternal Organization of the New Yorker K C. The American Jewish K C Fraternity was incorporated in 1943 as the American successor to the Kartell-Convent der Verbindungen deutscher Studenten jüdischen Glaubens. K C, an organization of Jewish students' dueling societies at German universities, was founded in 1896 to unite German-Jewish university students and to represent their political and civic interests as Jews. K C shared the orientation of the Central-Verein deutscher Staatsbürger jüdischen Glaubens, the main Jewish defense and civil rights organization in Germany, founded in 1893.

The American Jewish K C Fraternity provides social and cultural activities and mutual aid for former members of K C. It established the Max Mainzer Memorial Foundation in 1956 to provide financial assistance to members of the organization and their children. K C holds national and international conventions in conjunction with K C groups in the U.S.A. and other countries. Affiliated with the *American Federation of Jews from Central Europe.

Publications include: *Bulletin*, 1939-date, irreg.; *K C Address Book*, 1940, 194?, 1953, 1958, 196?, and 1971, containing data on K C members worldwide; and *K. C. Treffen 1959, New York* [Souvenir Journal].

Literature. Adolph Asch, *Geschichte des K C.* London, 1964.
Lessing, *Oral History.*

Records. Records, including minutes, correspondence, financial statements, and publications, are at the above address and with various officers.

28. AMERICAN JOINT RECONSTRUCTION FOUNDATION, INC. (AJRF)
Defunct

Founded in 1924 by the *American Jewish Joint Distribution Committee (JDC) and the Jewish Colonization Association (ICA) to continue the reconstruction of Jewish economic life in Eastern Europe (with the exception of Russia) begun by JDC during World War I. *Bernhard Kahn was managing director of the European office 1924-39. The AJRF was dissolved in 1952.

Records. YIVO Institute for Jewish Research: records of the European office (Berlin, later Paris), 1924-39, 11.7 ft, include 2 files on emigration from Germany (correspondence between the AJRF offices in Paris and Germany, 1933-38, and correspondence with its Berlin office) and 2 files on *HICEM (minutes and reports dealing with the activities of HICEM for refugees in Germany, 1932-37). *NUCMC* MS 60-721. Finding aid: unpublished inventory (86 pp., Yiddish).

Other records concerning AJRF are with the JDC at its office.

29. AMERICAN LEGION (National Headquarters)
700 N. Pennsylvania St., Indianapolis, IN 46206

An organization of honorably discharged wartime veterans, founded in 1919.

A resolution was passed by the National Convention in September 1938 favoring the total restriction of all immigration to the U.S.A. for 10 years. Opposed several legislative attempts to help refugees, including the *Wagner-*Rogers bill in 1939 for aid to refugee children. The Legion's representatives testified repeatedly before Congressional committees against immigration.

Literature. Raymond Moley, *The American Legion Story.* New York: Duell, Sloan and Pearce, 1966.

Records. American Legion, National Headquarters Library: records concerning refugees and immigration consist of 2 folders of correspondence of Legion officials with members and public figures on the refugee issue, 1930s-40s.

30. AMERICAN LIBRARY ASSOCIATION, INC. (ALA)
50 E. Huron St., Chicago, IL 60611

Founded in 1876 to promote libraries and librarianship, the ALA encourages the recruiting of competent personnel for professional careers as librarians.

In 1940, the Committee to Aid Refugee Librarians was established to place refugee librarians through the ALA Personnel Division. Jennie M. Flexner, Readers' Adviser at New York Public Library, chaired this Committee and the ALA Committee on Work with Foreign Born until her death in 1944. The Committee to Aid Refugee Librarians was dissolved after 1945.

Literature. ALA, *Bulletin*, 1940-45, includes reports on the work of these committees.
"Jennie Maas Flexner," *D.A.B.*, suppl. 3, pp. 280-281.

Records. Univ. of Illinois at Urbana–Champaign, Univ. Archives: records, 1885-date, 616.9 cu ft, include 2 folders, Feb.-Dec. 1940 and June-Dec. 1941, dealing with the work of the Committee to Aid Refugee Librarians. This material is part of the records of the ALA Executive Director. Finding aid: American Library Association, *A Preliminary Guide to the American Library Association Archives.* Urbana, 1975.

Flexner's papers, originally with the New York Public Library Readers' Adviser's Office, have not been located and are presumed destroyed.

31. AMERICAN NATIONAL RED CROSS (ANRC)
17th and D Sts., N.W., Washington, DC 20006

Founded in 1881, the ANRC was chartered by an act of Congress in 1905 to carry out the obligations assumed by the U.S.A. under international treaties known as the Geneva or Red Cross Conventions. ANRC acts as the medium of voluntary relief and communication between the American people and their armed forces, and carries on a system of national and international relief to prevent and mitigate suffering caused by disasters. Norman H. Davis was chairman 1938-44. During the early years of World War II, enemy aliens in the U.S.A. (including German-Jewish refugees) were barred from participation in certain local Red Cross activities.

The International Committee of the Red Cross (ICRC), located at Geneva, Switzerland and composed of 25 Swiss citizens, serves as a neutral intermediary in times of war, with special concern for prisoners of war and internees. It considered itself lacking in legal authority to deal with the Jewish situation in Nazi-occupied Europe. On several occasions during the later years of World War II, ICRC representatives were permitted to visit Theresienstadt concentration camp —under Nazi supervision. The ICRC shipped food and medicine to Theresienstadt and to camps in Croatia, France, The Netherlands, Italy, Latvia, Poland, Slovakia, and Slovenia. At the end of the war, the ICRC rendered some help to Nazi victims in Germany.

Since 1955, the ICRC has directed the International Tracing Service in Arolsen, West Germany, which absorbed the activities of the U.S.-based *Central Location Index.

Literature. Foster Rhea Dulles, *The American Red Cross: A History.* New York: Harper, 1950.

Report of the International Red Cross on Its Activities During the Second World War, September 1, 1939–June 30, 1947. Geneva, 1948.

Romanofsky, *Social Service Organizations*, pp. 110–117.

Records. National Archives and Records Service, Washington National Records Center: ANRC records, 1881–1945, ca. 900 ft, in Record Group 200 (National Archives Gift Collection), include documentation about the ANRC's activities overseas and its cooperation with the ICRC.

Records since 1945 are at the agency's office.

Archives of the ICRC, at its headquarters in Geneva, Switzerland, are assumed to include materials relating to refugees and relief in Europe during and after World War II.

32. AMERICAN ORT FEDERATION, INC.–Organization for Rehabilitation Through Training
817 Broadway, New York, NY 10003

ORT (Obtchestvo Rasprostraneniya Truda sredi Yevreyev) was founded in 1880 by Jews in Russia to support and develop vocational schools for Jews, and to help Jewish agricultural colonies, model farms, and agricultural schools. The World ORT Union was established in Berlin in 1921 as an international organization to serve in areas formerly within the Russian Empire and in other European countries. The American ORT Federation, founded in 1922 to represent the World ORT Union in the U.S.A., developed into a broad community organization, serving as a clearing house for contacts with European and other ORT offices around the world, and as a center for vocational training for Jews in the U.S.A.

In 1933, the ORT Committee in Germany, hitherto an educational and fund-raising agency, launched a program of constructive relief to aid Jews who had lost their livelihood because of Nazi persecution. *William Graetz, president of ORT in Germany, traveled abroad to enlist foreign aid. As a result, the World ORT Union began to organize industrial and agricultural training schools in Germany and other countries, including England, France, Switzerland, China, Canada, and Argentina. (The central offices of World ORT Union moved from Berlin to Paris in 1933. After relocating several times within France 1939-40, the offices moved permanently from Marseilles to Geneva, Switzerland, in 1943.)

The American ORT Federation established two vocational training schools in New York City in response to the arrival of large numbers of refugees: New

York ORT Trade School (later known as Litton Trade School), 1940-57, and Bramson ORT Trade School, 1942-date. *B. Charney Vladeck was national chairman of the Federation 1932-38.

Literature. *International Biographical Dictionary*, vol. I (W. Graetz).
Jack Rader, *By the Skill of Their Hands, the Story of ORT.* New York, 1970.
Romanofsky, *Social Service Organizations*, pp. 117-121.
World ORT Union, *80 Years of ORT: Historical Materials, Documents, and Reports.* Geneva, 1960.

Records. YIVO Institute for Jewish Research: Federation records, 1922-58, ca. 8 ft, include correspondence, reports, and financial records, and consist mainly of correspondence between the Federation in New York and ORT offices abroad. Finding aid: unpublished inventory (42 pp.).

American ORT Federation: recent records and records relating to the operation of the two trade schools. The latter, ca. 8 file drawers, consist of case histories, correspondence, and registration forms of former students of the schools.

YIVO Institute for Jewish Research: partial records of World ORT Union, 1923-55, 1.25 ft, include documents from the Central Board Office in Paris and records concerning ORT offices in various countries. Finding aid: unpublished inventory (18 pp.).

Other records are at the office of World ORT Union, 1-3 Rue de Varembé, 1211 Geneva 20, Switzerland.

Leo Baeck Institute Archives: Graetz' papers include materials about ORT, 1926-70.

33. AMERICAN PHILOSOPHICAL ASSOCIATION, INC.
Eastern Div.: c/o Ernest Sosa (secretary-treasurer), Box 1158,
Brown Univ., Providence, RI 02912
Western Div.: c/o Kenneth R. Pahel (secretary-treasurer), Dept. of
Philosophy, Knox College, Galesburg, IL 61401

An organization of professional philosophers and teachers of philosophy, founded in 1900.

Each Division formed a Committee on Exiled Scholars in 1938-39 to assist in resettling refugee philosophers. The Eastern Div.'s Committee was still active in April 1942.

Records. Minutes of the Eastern Div.'s Executive Committee, with the secretary-treasurer, contain some references, 1938-40, to its Committee on Exiled Scholars.

Minutes of the Western Div.'s Executive Committee have not been located.

34. AMERICAN PSYCHOANALYTIC ASSOCIATION, INC.
1 E. 57 St., New York, NY 10022

Professional organization of psychoanalysts and a federation of American psychoanalytic societies, founded in 1911.

In 1938, the Association formed an Emergency Committee on Relief and Immigration which was co-chaired by Drs. *Lawrence S. Kubie and Bettina Warburg. Assisted with the immigration and resettlement of European refugee psychoanalysts, psychiatrists, and related professionals. Cooperated with other agencies aiding refugees, including the *National Committee for the Resettlement of Foreign Physicians, of which Kubie was a founder and officer. A Psychoanalytic Fund was created to help individuals unable to leave Europe, or otherwise in emergency situations. Although the active phase of the Committee's work ended in 1943, the books were not closed until 1948. After the war, two subcommittees were formed to aid psychoanalysts in Holland and Hungary.

Literature. American Psychoanalytic Association, *Bulletin* 1 (June 1937/June 1938): 65-68, 2 (June 1938/June 1939): 41-49, 3 (June 1939/June 1940): 55-65.

Laura Fermi, *Illustrious Immigrants: The Intellectual Migration from Europe, 1930–41.* Chicago: Univ. of Chicago Press, 1968, pp. 148-150.

Records. American Psychoanalytic Association: extant Committee records, 1938-48, 2 in., formerly held by Warburg, consist of printed and unpublished annual reports of the Emergency Committee, financial statements, lists of names and curricula vitae of refugee psychoanalysts, published materials on refugee physicians, and other related items.

Photocopies of these materials are at the *Research Foundation for Jewish Immigration.

The case files originally held by Warburg have been destroyed.

35. AMERICAN PSYCHOLOGICAL ASSOCIATION, INC.
1200 17 St., N.W., Washington, DC 20036

A scientific and professional society of psychologists and educators founded in 1892.

Established a Committee on Displaced Foreign Psychologists in 1938 "to survey the problem of psychologists displaced from their positions and livelihoods in other countries and seeking asylum and professional opportunities elsewhere." The Committee operated under the leadership of Dr. Barbara S. Burks. When she died in 1943, most of the Committee's work was completed, and it was dissolved.

Literature. Jean Matter Mandler and George Mandler, "The Diaspora of Experimental Psychology: The Gestaltists and Others." In *The Intellectual Migration: Europe and America, 1930–1960,* Donald Fleming and Bernard Bailyn, eds. Cambridge, MA: Harvard Univ. Press, 1969, pp. 380-385.

Jeffrey Whitmore, "American Psychology Responds to Nazi Germany." Unpublished master's thesis, Univ. of Akron, 1969.

Records. Univ. of Akron, Archives of the History of American Psychology: materials relating to the Committee, ca. 0.5 in., consist primarily of documents from the files of Dr. Willard C. Olson, secretary of the Association at the time, including correspondence, reports of the Committee, financial reports, and resolutions.

Library of Congress, Manuscript Div.: records of the Association, 1912-72, ca. 96 ft (ca. 80,000 items), include files on Jewish psychologists in Germany, 1933, and on a Committee on Refugee Children, 1939-41. *NUCMC* MS 69-2027, 76-141. Finding aid: unpublished inventory.

36. ASSOCIATION OF FORMER CENTRAL EUROPEAN REFUGEES FROM SHANGHAI (GEMEINSCHAFT EHEMALIGER SHANGHAIER)
c/o Heinz Levinson (president), 55-16 96 St., Corona, NY 11368

Founded in 1948 as a fraternal organization of postwar immigrants from Central Europe who had spent the war years as refugees in *Shanghai, China.

Published souvenir journals: *15th Anniversary*, 1964; *20th Anniversary*, 1969; and *25th Anniversary*, 1974.

Literature. David Kranzler, *Japanese, Nazis & Jews: The Jewish Refugee Community of Shanghai 1938-45*. New York: Yeshiva Univ. Press, 1976.

Records. Records, consisting of minutes, publications, and materials on the Jewish refugee community of Shanghai, are with the president and other officers.

37. *AUFBAU*
2121 Broadway, New York, NY 10023

German-language periodical that became a major influence on German-Jewish immigrant opinion in the U.S.A. It first appeared in December 1934 as a 12-page "Bulletin of the German-Jewish Club, Inc., New York." In 1936, it became a regular newspaper with subscriptions and advertising fees; since December 1939 it has been published weekly by the *New World Club, New York. From the spring of 1939 until his death in December 1965, Manfred George (Cohn) was editor. He was succeeded by Hans J. Steinitz. A special biweekly supplement, *Die Westküste*, has appeared in *Aufbau* since 1941, reporting on the activities of the refugee community on the West Coast.

Literature. *International Biographical Dictionary*, vol. I (M. George and H. Steinitz).

Lessing, *Oral History*.

Will Schaber, ed., *Aufbau (Reconstruction); Dokumente einer Kultur im Exil*. Woodstock, NY: Overlook Press, 1972.

Records. *Aufbau* office: records include editorial files, indexes to articles, bound volumes and microfilm copies of *Aufbau*, and business records.

Copies of *Aufbau*, in part on microfilm, are available in major libraries in the U.S.A.

38. AXIS VICTIMS LEAGUE, INC.   *Defunct*

"An association for restitution and compensation of rights and interests to Axis victims." Founded by *Bruno Weil in New York City in 1943 and incorporated in 1944. Officers included both German-Jewish refugee lawyers and native Americans. Active in lobbying for postwar restitution legislation in the Federal Republic of Germany, and in improving the administration of those laws. Inactive since the early 1960s.

Literature. Lessing, *Oral History.*

Records. Records are with Fritz Moses (formerly a vice-president of the League), 113-14 72 Rd., Forest Hills, NY 11375.

Leo Baeck Institute Archives: Weil's papers include some documentation about the League.

39. BARON DE HIRSCH FUND, INC./JEWISH AGRICULTURAL SOCIETY, INC.
386 Park Ave. S., New York, NY 10016

The Fund was established by Baron Maurice de Hirsch, financier and philanthropist, to improve the social and economic condition of East European Jews. In 1889, de Hirsch allocated the proceeds of a $2.4 million fund to agricultural colonies and trade schools in the U.S.A. With the cooperation of American-Jewish leaders, the Fund was incorporated in 1891. That same year, de Hirsch founded the Jewish Colonization Association (ICA).

In 1900, the Fund's agricultural department was incorporated as the Jewish Agricultural Society. The Society continued to be supported by the Fund. The Society emphasized self-supporting agricultural activities, extended loans to farm cooperatives and individuals, and offered placement services and advice to potential farmers. In 1972, the Society was merged with the Fund. *Lewis L. Strauss was a director of the Society 1920-51 and its president.

Beginning in the middle 1930s, the Society offered guidance to Jewish refugees from Germany and other Axis-controlled countries, and assisted an estimated 2500 Jewish Nazi victims to establish and successfully operate cattle and chicken farms in 12 states of the U.S.A., especially New York, New Jersey, and Connecticut. The settlers, in turn, assisted friends and relatives to immigrate to the U.S.A. and to resettle on their farms. To prepare settlers for U.S. conditions, training courses of several weeks' duration were offered at the Society's Training Farm at Bound Brook, NJ.

Literature. Gabriel Davidson, *Our Jewish Farmers and the Story of the Jewish Agricultural Society.* New York: L. B. Fischer, 1943.
Lessing, *Oral History.*
Herman J. Levine and Benjamin Miller, *The American Jewish Farmer in Changing Times.* New York: Jewish Agricultural Society, 1966.
Romanofsky, *Social Service Organizations*, pp. 373-379.

Records. American Jewish Historical Society: records of the Fund, 1870-1935, 30 ft, contain some material on refugees for 1933, including correspondence with *Max J. Kohler. *NUCMC* MS 72-1365.

YIVO Institute for Jewish Research: records, 1890s-1960s, 1.25 ft, consist primarily of photographs of Jewish farm settlements in the U.S.A. Finding aid: unpublished inventory (6 pp.).

Records of the Fund since 1935, and records of the Society, are scanty and are at the Fund's office.

40. BERMUDA CONFERENCE ON REFUGEES, 1943

The Anglo-American Conference on Refugees, held in the Bermuda Islands April 19-28, 1943, was attended by British and U.S. government delegations to discuss steps to assist refugees from Axis-occupied Europe. It was called in response to growing public criticism in England and the U.S.A. of Allied inaction in saving refugees from Nazi control and the threat of extermination. The U.S. delegation consisted of Representative *Sol Bloom of New York, Senator Scott Lucas of Illinois, and Harold W. Dodds, president of Princeton University. George Backer, president of the *American ORT Federation, spoke for Jewish organizations pressing for increased rescue efforts on the part of the Allied governments.

Although the results of the Conference were entirely negligible, it helped to dramatize the failure of the American and British governments to act decisively in the rescue of Jews outside Axis control, and to act in any way to save Jews in Nazi-occupied Europe from extermination. A report on the meager results of the Conference was released November 19, 1943, following public clamor and criticisms in the *U.S. Congress of the policies of the *Roosevelt administration.

Literature. Feingold, *Politics of Rescue*, passim.

World Jewish Congress, *Memorandum Submitted to the Bermuda Refugee Conference by the World Jewish Congress.* New York, 1943.

Records. Records relating to the Conference are found in various collections, including the records of the *U.S. Dept. of State at the National Archives, and of the *U.S. War Refugee Board at the Franklin D. Roosevelt Library. Bloom's papers at the New York Public Library may contain some relevant material.

41. BLACK MOUNTAIN COLLEGE   *Defunct*

An experimental school in Black Mountain, North Carolina, 1933-56. In its early years, its faculty included a number of refugee scholars.

Literature. Martin Duberman, *Black Mountain: An Exploration in Community.* New York: Dutton, 1972.

Records. North Carolina Dept. of Cultural Resources, Div. of Archives and History: records, 1933-56, 100,000 items, include material on refugees teaching at the College, and correspondence with organizations aiding refugees. Finding aid: unpublished inventory.

42. BLUE CARD, INC.
2121 Broadway, New York, NY 10023

Founded in 1940 by German-Jewish immigrants as a mutual aid society; incorporated in 1943. Provides small cash contributions to needy immigrants from Central Europe. Receives financial support from *United Help, *New World Club, New York, and through donations from immigrants from Central Europe.

Literature. Blue Card, *Annual Reports*, 1941-date. Lessing, *Oral History.*

Records. Blue Card: records consist of minutes since 1940, financial statements, scrapbooks, publicity materials, and restricted case files.

43. B'NAI B'RITH HILLEL FOUNDATIONS, INC.
1640 Rhode Island Ave., N.W., Washington, DC 20036

Founded in 1923 and devoted to religious, cultural, and counseling activities among Jewish students at colleges and universities. Sponsored by *B'nai B'rith International.

Assisted in programs to aid refugee students beginning in 1939. Following World War II, Hillel's Foreign Student Service sponsored the admission to the U.S.A. of about 120 students from displaced persons camps, and supported them until graduation.

Literature. Alfred Jospe, ed., *The Test of Time: A Commemoration and Celebration of Hillel's Fiftieth Anniversary.* Washington, DC: B'nai B'rith Hillel Foundations, 1974, pp. 3, 101-103, 115.

Records. Minutes of the B'nai B'rith Hillel Commission, at the agency's office, include discussion on aid to refugee students and on the Foreign Student Service.

44. B'NAI B'RITH INTERNATIONAL
1640 Rhode Island Ave., N.W., Washington, DC 20036

International fraternal order and social service organization founded in 1843 in New York by Jewish immigrants from Germany. Engaged in educational, public affairs, community relations, and civic and social welfare programs. Sponsors *B'nai B'rith Hillel Foundations.

National officers cooperated with other American Jewish leaders from 1933 to 1945 on questions regarding immigration and refugees. Local lodges in the U.S.A. provided various forms of aid to members in Germany, Austria, and Czechoslovakia, and to immigrants following their arrival. German, Austrian, and Czech Jewish refugees founded lodges and chapters (B'nai B'rith Women) in the U.S.A. and in other countries of resettlement, including *Israel Lodge, Los Angeles, *Golden Gate Lodge and Chapter, San Francisco, *Heinrich Graetz Lodge, Philadelphia, *Joseph Popper Lodge and Chapter, *Leo Baeck Lodge and Chapter, and *Liberty Lodge and Chapter, New York City. Following World War II, B'nai B'rith filed claims against the German Federal Republic for indemnification of German-Jewish B'nai B'rith property confiscated by the Nazis and obtained a settlement. Although the *American Federation of Jews from Central Europe gave substantial assistance to B'nai B'rith in preparing its claims, B'nai B'rith failed to offer financial assistance to the Federation in pursuit of its social and cultural activities later on.

Literature. Edward E. Grusd, *B'nai B'rith: The Story of a Covenant.* New York: Appleton-Century, 1966.

Records. B'nai B'rith: records were not accessible in 1978. Although not completely catalogued, records were reported to include minutes of national governing bodies, material on persecution of European Jews during the 1930s, and documentation on restitution claims filed after the war.

American Jewish Historical Society: papers of *Label A. Katz include B'nai B'rith material concerning refugees and restitution.

45. BOOKS ABROAD
Univ. of Oklahoma, Norman, OK 73069

International literary quarterly published by the Univ. of Oklahoma.

Under the editorship of Roy Temple House, the journal maintained contact during the late 1930s with refugee and exile writers from Germany and Spain, including Ernst Bloch, Ferdinand Bruckner, Thomas Mann, Hans Marchwitza, Otto Strasser, and Alfred Werner.

Records. Univ. of Oklahoma Library, Western History Collections: the *Books Abroad* collection includes several dozen letters to House from the refugee writers listed above (box 1, section 7).

46. BRITH SHOLOM, INC.
1235 Chestnut St., Philadelphia, PA 19107

Jewish fraternal society founded in 1905. Brith Sholom and its Council of Women sponsored the immigration of fifty refugee children from Germany in the late 1930s, and placed them in foster homes until they were reunited with their parents. Temporary shelter was provided at Brith Sholomville camp near Collegeville, Pennsylvania.

Records. Brith Sholom: records include minutes and published reports of annual conventions, containing information on the refugee situation and Brith Sholom's efforts to aid refugee children. A large part of the organization's records has been lost or destroyed.

47. CARL NEUBERG SOCIETY FOR INTERNATIONAL SCIENTIFIC RELATIONS, INC.   *Defunct*

Founded in New York City in the late 1930s as the American Society of European Chemists and Pharmacists, an association of scientists graduated from European universities. Membership was composed of refugees. The organization was initially concerned with finding jobs for members. After World War II, it sponsored lectures and other academic activities. The Carl Neuberg Medal was established in 1947 in honor of the seventieth birthday of the renowned chemist who had been a founder and active member of the Society. Within a few years after Neuberg's death in 1956, the organization became known as the Society for International Scientific Relations, and then as the Carl Neuberg Society. . . . The Society ceased activities in the late 1960s, following the deaths of Bruno Kisch and Gustav Martin, the last presidents of the Society.

Records. Records, ca. 6 ft, formerly with Bruno Kisch and other officers, are with the last secretary, Isidore Greenberg, 471 E. 26 St., Brooklyn, NY 11226. Consist of correspondence, minutes of meetings, membership lists, biographical information on members, proceedings of symposia, and other materials.

48. CARNEGIE CORPORATION OF NEW YORK
437 Madison Ave., New York, NY 10022

A grant-making educational foundation established in 1911. Awards grants chiefly to colleges, universities, and educational organizations to finance research and experimental programs in certain aspects of education at all levels. Functions in the U.S.A. and in certain areas of the British Commonwealth, excluding the United Kingdom, India, and Pakistan. *Frederick P. Keppel was its president 1923-41.

Awarded scholarships to German refugee university teachers and scholars who had a good knowledge of English, for three, later two, years in British Commonwealth universities outside the United Kingdom. Applications for grants, which paid the salaries of grantees, had to be initiated by university presidents and vice-presidents in the Dominions and colonies. The program was in operation from 1934 to 1940.

Literature. *Annual Reports of the Carnegie Corporation.* 1933-1945.
Robert M. Lester, "A Thirty Year Catalog of Grants." *Carnegie Corporation of New York Review Series No. 33*, July 1942.

Records. Carnegie Corporation of New York: records relating to the Commonwealth grants program.

49. CARNEGIE ENDOWMENT FOR INTERNATIONAL PEACE
11 DuPont Circle, N.W., Washington, DC 20036

A program foundation established in 1910 which conducts research, communications, publishing, and training programs relevant to war/peace issues.

Devoted some of its attention to refugees during the 1930s and 1940s. Received inquiries from, and on behalf of, refugees seeking to immigrate to the U.S.A. and to secure positions. Some of these requests were received through *Nicholas Murray Butler, president of the Endowment and of Columbia Univ. Late in 1938, the Endowment helped to establish the American Committee for Relief in Czechoslovakia to raise funds for the relief and the resettlement of refugees from the Sudeten area. The Endowment's Visiting Carnegie Professors program provided funds for professors from abroad to come to the U.S.A. Although this program was not designed to aid refugee scholars, some of the individuals who had been Visiting Carnegie Professors preferred not to return to Germany after the Nazis seized power. The Endowment also gave financial support to several student service organizations active in relief and resettlement of refugee students in the U.S.A. and abroad.

Literature. John F. Greco, "A Foundation for Internationalism: The Carnegie Endowment for International Peace, 1931–1941." Unpublished Ph.D. dissertation, Syracuse Univ., 1971.

Records. Columbia Univ., Rare Book and Manuscript Library: extensive records, 1910-54, include files of the American offices of the Endowment and of the European Centre in Paris. Relevant materials include correspondence on aid to refugees, documentation on Czech relief, Visiting Carnegie Professors, and student service groups. *NUCMC* MS 61-2925. Finding aid: unpublished guide.

Recent records are at the Endowment's office.

50. CENTRAL CONFERENCE OF AMERICAN RABBIS, INC. (CCAR)
790 Madison Ave., New York, NY 10021

National organization of Reform rabbis established in 1889. The CCAR adhered to "classic" German Reform positions for more than 40 years until its membership gradually came under the influence of Zionism and Eastern European traditionalism. The CCAR pioneered rabbinical engagement in such areas as social action, church-state and interfaith relations, and religious education.

A Committee on Refugee Rabbis, subsequently renamed the Committee on Refugee Relief, was formed in 1939 under the chairmanship of Rabbi Felix A. Levy of Chicago. In 1942, this Committee's work was merged into the CCAR Committee on Relief and Subventions. The CCAR cooperated with the National Committee on Refugee Jewish Ministers of the *National Refugee Service.

Literature. CCAR, *Yearbook*, 1939-45.

Records. American Jewish Archives: records, 1889-1960s, 41 ft. It has not been determined whether the records include material on aid to refugee rabbis. *NUCMC* MS 68-14.

Recent records are at the organization's office.

51. CENTRAL LOCATION INDEX, INC. *Defunct*

Founded in 1944 in New York City by American social service agencies for the purpose of centralizing the search for survivors of Nazi persecution and the Holocaust in Europe and for relatives of such survivors in the U.S.A. Cooperated with the Central Tracing Bureau of the United Nations Relief and Rehabilitation Administration (UNRRA), later known as the International Tracing Service (ITS), at Arolsen, West Germany. In 1949, activities and archives of the Index were transferred to the ITS.

The ITS was founded in Europe in 1945 by the Supreme Headquarters, Allied Expeditionary Forces (SHAEF). That same year, after SHAEF had been dissolved, UNRRA established the Central Tracing Bureau. Its aims were to trace missing military and civilian nationals of the member states of the United Nations, to collect and preserve documents concerning non-Germans and displaced persons in Germany, and to assist in reuniting families that had been separated. In 1947, the Central Tracing Bureau was transferred to the International Refugee Organization, which changed the Bureau's name to International Tracing Service in 1948. In 1951, the ITS was transferred to the Allied High Commission for Germany (HICOG). Since 1955, ITS has been directed by the International Committee of the Red Cross, Geneva (*American National Red Cross), and its activities financed by the Federal Republic of Germany.

Literature. Etta Deutsch, *History of the Central Location Index.* New York, 1949.

International Tracing Service, *30 Years in the Service of Humanity.* Arolsen, 1975.

Records. Records of the Central Location Index, which were originally transferred to the ITS, are now at the Yad Vashem Archives, Israel. The records, 1944-48, ca. 400 ft, include a 900,000-card index on the search for survivors and relatives and ca. 330 ft of correspondence with Jewish and non-Jewish institutions.

Records of the ITS at Arolsen, West Germany, consist of more than 10 million documents with over 40 million reference cards in the Master Index. Finding aids: *Catalogue of Records Held by the International Tracing Service....* 4 vols. Arolsen, 1954. Subsequent accessions are listed in the annual ITS *Operations Report.* Much of the ITS material is on microfilm at Yad Vashem.

52. CHURCH OF THE BRETHREN, BRETHREN SERVICE COMMITTEE
1451 Dundee Ave., Elgin, IL 60120

The Brethren Service Committee was founded in 1939 as a permanent organization to offer relief to the needy in the U.S.A. and overseas. Renamed the Brethren Service Commission in 1947, it was later dissolved as a result of a reorganization of the church.

The Brethren Service Committee cooperated with the *American Friends Service Committee in resettling refugees in the U.S.A., and maintained an office in Spain to assist refugees in leaving Europe.

Literature. Romanofsky, *Social Service Organizations*, pp. 191-195.

Roger E. Sappington, *Brethren Social Policy 1908-1958.* Elgin, IL: Brethren Press, 1961, pp. 102-103.

Records. Church of the Brethren Archives: records include minutes of meetings of the Committee and correspondence regarding aid to refugees.

53. CITIZENS' COMMITTEE ON DISPLACED PERSONS   *Defunct*

Founded in New York in 1946 to lobby for legislation that would permit an adequate number of displaced persons into the U.S.A. independent of existing immigration quotas. Following an intensive publicity effort aimed at Congress and the public about the plight of postwar refugees in Europe, the Committee helped to secure passage of the Displaced Persons Act of 1948 and, later, its revision in 1950. By 1947, the Committee had 38 affiliated chapters in 19 states. It ceased to function ca. 1953.

Records. Univ. of Minnesota, Immigration History Research Center: records, 1946–53, consist of general correspondence, 1946-53, minutes of executive committee meetings, 1946-50, and financial records. A significant part of the Committee's records is presumed destroyed.

54. COMMITTEE FOR THE STUDY OF RECENT IMMIGRATION FROM EUROPE *Defunct*

Sponsored 1944–47 by *American Christian Committee for Refugees, *American Friends Service Committee, Catholic Committee for Refugees (*U.S. Catholic Conference), *National Refugee Service, and *United States Committee for the Care of European Children. Maurice R. Davie, professor of sociology at Yale Univ., directed the study, and *Alvin Johnson chaired the Committee.

Literature. Maurice R. Davie, *Refugees in America: Report of the Committee for the Study of Recent Immigration from Europe.* New York: Harper, 1947. Reprint, Westport, CT: Greenwood Press, 1975.

Records. YIVO Institute for Jewish Research: records, 1940-47, microfilm (22 reels). The original materials (105 files) were destroyed after microfilming. Consist of minutes of meetings, correspondence with refugees, refugee organizations, and agencies aiding refugees, questionnaire replies, interviews with outstanding refugees, drafts of various chapters of the published study, and other documentation generated by the study. Finding aid: unpublished inventory (14 pp.).

American Institute of Physics, Center for the History of Physics, Niels Bohr Library: biographical files on refugee scholars, 1.7 ft (photocopies of ca. 2000 items). These data were gathered in 1945 by Betty Drury, a staff member of the Committee. The original materials are with B. Drury, River Edge, NJ.

55. CONFERENCE ON JEWISH MATERIAL CLAIMS AGAINST GERMANY, INC. (CLAIMS CONFERENCE)
15 E. 26 St., New York, NY 10010

Founded in October 1951 by 23 Jewish organizations to obtain "funds for the relief and resettlement of Nazi victims, to aid the rebuilding of Jewish communities and institutions devastated by the Nazis, and to gain indemnification for the damages inflicted upon individuals by Nazi persecution." Participated in diplomatic negotiations with the Federal Republic of Germany, engaged in a wide variety of political and other activities to lend weight to the claims of Nazi victims, and developed programs of allocations for social, medical, communal, and cultural educational purposes that contributed substantially to the rebuild ing of Jewish life and the rehabilitation of individual Nazi victims, following World War II, in all countries of major Jewish settlement. In 1964, the Claims Conference organized the *Memorial Foundation for Jewish Culture in New York to promote Jewish learning in all fields and countries in the post-Holocaust period.

Literature. Twenty Years Later, Activities of the Conference on Jewish Material Claims Against Germany, 1952-1972. New York, n.d.

Records. Central Archives for the History of the Jewish People, Israel: records, ca. 660 ft, concerning cultural and research activities initiated or supported by the Conference. This material reflects the condition of Jewish educational, scientific, and cultural institutions inside and outside Europe after the Holocaust, and documents their reconstruction.

Records still at the Claims Conference's office will be transferred to the Central Archives.

Records relating to the Claims Conference, 18 transfiles, which were formerly in the Geneva, Switzerland, office of the *American Jewish Joint Distribution Committee, are also at the Central Archives.

56. CONFERENCE ON JEWISH SOCIAL STUDIES, INC.
250 W. 57th St., New York, NY 10019

Initiated in 1933 and incorporated in 1936 as the Conference on Jewish Relations by Salo W. Baron, Morris R. Cohen, *Koppel S. Pinson, and others to apply the methods and approaches of the social sciences and history to recent and contemporary Jewish subjects. Its quarterly periodical, *Jewish Social Studies*, 1939 to date, includes studies on Jewish migration, immigration, demography, and other subjects concerning the immigration and resettlement of Jews from Central Europe. The Conference adopted its present name in the 1950s.

Delegated two Jewish scholars, Oscar I. Janowsky and Melvin M. Fagen, to Geneva to assist *James G. McDonald, *League of Nations High Commissioner for Refugees. The results of their research were published, with the aid of the Conference, as *International Aspects of German Racial Policies*, New York: Oxford Univ. Press, 1937.

Assembled an almost complete list of Jewish physicians practicing in the U.S.A. during the 1930s, together with their backgrounds and qualifications. On the basis of this research, the Conference presented to the *National Refugee Service a list of American cities and towns with populations of over 10,000 which, at that time, had no Jewish doctors, and where new arrivals could be placed without increasing tensions with non-Jewish neighbors.

Established the Commission on European Jewish Cultural Reconstruction in 1944, which led to the founding of *Jewish Cultural Reconstruction, Inc., in 1947.

Literature. Salo W. Baron, "The Journal and the Conference of Jewish Social Studies." In *Emancipation and Counter-Emancipation: Selected Essays from Jewish Social Studies*, Abraham G. Duker and Meir Ben-Horin, eds. New York: Ktav, 1974, pp. 1-11.

Leonora Cohen Rosenfield, *Portrait of a Philosopher: Morris R. Cohen in Life and Letters.* New York: Harcourt, Brace & World, 1962.

Records. Records, 1933–?, were stored in a warehouse in 1978 and were inaccessible. Their ultimate disposition had not been determined by the Conference.

Recent records are at the Conference's office.

57. CORNELL UNIVERSITY, GERMAN DEPARTMENT
Ithaca, NY 14853

Records. Cornell Univ. Libraries, Dept. of Manuscripts and University Archives: records, 1933–44, 2 boxes (1371 items), include scattered letters concerning the placement of German scholars, both Jewish and non-Jewish, in American universities and colleges.

58. COUNCIL OF JEWISH FEDERATIONS AND WELFARE FUNDS, INC. (CJFWF)
575 Lexington Ave., New York, NY 10022

Founded in 1932. Provides national and regional services to associated Jewish community organizations in the U.S.A. and Canada, aiding in fund raising, community organization, health and welfare planning, personnel recruitment, and public relations. In 1935, CJFWF absorbed the activities of the Bureau of Jewish Social Research (BJSR), established in 1919 to promote Jewish social and communal services.

In late 1933, BJSR provided information which assisted in the placement of German-Jewish children in the U.S.A. In late 1936, CJFWF helped to resolve the competitive fund raising of two overseas relief agencies, the *American Jewish Joint Distribution Committee and the United Palestine Appeal, and helped to establish the *United Jewish Appeal in the late 1930s. Beginning in the early 1940s, CJFWF worked for about a decade to promote coordination among such overseas agencies as the *United Service for New Americans and *Hebrew Sheltering and Immigrant Aid Society (HIAS). In the late 1940s, CJFWF recommended the creation of the *New York Association for New Americans.

Literature. CJFWF, *The Council's First Quarter Century.* New York, 1956. Romanofsky, *Social Service Organizations,* pp. 195–198, 262–266.

Records. American Jewish Historical Society: records, 1916–71, 177 ft, include reports, budgets, and correspondence of and with numerous organizations in aid of refugees, both Jewish and non-Jewish, in the "Agency Files," as well as material on immigration and refugees in the "Subject Files." *NUCMC* MS 72-4. Finding aid: unpublished inventory.

Additional restricted materials and recent records are at the Council's office.

59. COUNCIL OF JEWS FROM GERMANY
c/o Dr. Werner Rosenstock (honorary secretary), 8 Fairfax Mansions,
London NW3, England

Founded in 1945 as the Council for the Protection of Rights and Interests of
Jews from Germany. The Council is composed of the central coordinating
organizations of Jews from Germany in Israel, the U.S.A., Latin America, continental Europe, and the United Kingdom. The *American Federation of Jews
from Central Europe is a founding member of the Council and its U.S. representative.

As the central, worldwide representation of Jewish émigrés from Germany,
the Council promotes the social, cultural, and legal interests of its constituents.
It took part in negotiations with the government of the Federal Republic of
Germany for comprehensive legislation providing for the restitution and indemnification of Nazi victims for the damages inflicted by the Nazi regime on individual and communal property, and monitors the execution of the relevant laws.
As a member of the *Conference on Jewish Material Claims Against Germany, it
distributes funds earmarked for the social and cultural needs of the worldwide
émigré community, and proposes policy guidelines to its affiliates in areas of
common concern.

Literature.   *Council Correspondence.*

Records.   Council of Jews from Germany, London Secretariat: records, 1945-
date. Restricted.

American Federation of Jews from Central Europe: records, 1945-date,
concerning the Council's activities in the U.S.A. and its representation on the
Conference on Jewish Material Claims Against Germany (through the American
Federation). Restricted.

60. DELAWARE VALLEY COLLEGE OF SCIENCE AND AGRICULTURE
Doylestown, PA 18901

Founded under Jewish auspices in 1896 as the National Farm School, the college
became a three-year junior college in 1945. Changed its name to National Farm
School and Junior College in 1946; became a four-year college and changed its
name to National Agricultural College in 1948. Present name adopted in 1960.

The School trained refugee students for agricultural work.

Records.   Records of the School are presumed to be at the College. No information has been obtained about the contents of such materials.

American Jewish Historical Society: records, 1902-67, ca. 420 items, consist of correspondence, primarily 1951-67, relating to finances and activities,
mimeographed minutes of meetings of the board of trustees 1952-61, catalogues
1934-37, 1941-43, 1946-47, 1952-53, 1957-59, and annual reports 1902-45.
This collection is reported to contain some information about refugee students
at the School. *NUCMC* MS 69-597.

61. DOMINICAN REPUBLIC SETTLEMENT ASSOCIATION, INC. (DORSA)
c/o American Jewish Joint Distribution Committee, 60 E. 42 St.,
New York, NY 10017

Founded in 1939 to settle European refugees at Sosúa in the Dominican Republic. It was funded mainly by *Agro-Joint, a subsidiary of the *American Jewish Joint Distribution Committee (JDC). *James N. Rosenberg was president of DORSA, and *Arthur M. Lamport was one of the principals in the creation of the colony. DORSA and the settlement at Sosúa continue their activities on a small scale (1978).

Literature. DORSA, *Pamphlet*, nos. 1-6, New York.
——, *Sosúa, Haven for Refugees* (account of a meeting held in New York City concerning the Sosúa undertaking, Sept. 24, 1941). New York, 1941.
Siegfried Kätsch and Elke Maria Kätsch, with the collaboration of Henry P. David, *Sosúa, verheissenes Land? Eine Dokumentation zu Adaptionsproblemen deutsch-jüdischer Siedler in der Dominikanischen Republik.* Dortmund: Univ. Münster, 1970.
Samuel T. Samuels, "Moshav in the Caribbean—Sosúa Revisited." *American Jewish Year Book* 73 (1972): 452-457.
Richard Symanski and Nancy Burley, "The Jewish Colony of Sosúa." *Annals of the Association of American Geographers* 63 (Sept. 1973): 366-378.

Records. Uncatalogued records of DORSA and related materials on the colony at Sosúa are with the American Jewish Joint Distribution Committee.

62. EMERGENCY COMMITTEE IN AID OF DISPLACED FOREIGN MEDICAL SCIENTISTS *Defunct*

Founded in 1933 as the Emergency Committee in Aid of Displaced Foreign Physicians. Adopted above name in 1939, when the *National Committee for the Resettlement of Foreign Physicians was founded. Cooperated with the *Emergency Committee in Aid of Displaced Foreign Scholars and other agencies serving refugees in the placement of refugee medical scientists. Disbanded in 1946.

Literature. Emergency Committee . . . Foreign Physicians, *Report*, Oct. 15, 1933 to Apr. 15, 1937. *Statement*, Jan. 1, 1937 to Dec. 31, 1937; Jan. 1, 1938 to Dec. 31, 1938.
Emergency Committee . . . Foreign Medical Scientists, *Statement*, 1939, 1940, 1941, 1942.
Genizi, "American Non-Sectarian," pp. 185-193.
Wetzel, "American Rescue," pp. 172-176.

Records. *American Council for Émigrés in the Professions, Medical Division: minute books, 1933-36 and 1937-42, and a list of grants made by the Committee, 1934-42.

Copies of minutes, 1933-46, are included among the papers of *Alfred E. Cohn (a founder and member of the Executive Committee of the Emergency Committee).

63. EMERGENCY COMMITTEE IN AID OF DISPLACED FOREIGN
SCHOLARS, INC. *Defunct*

Founded in 1933 in New York City as the Emergency Committee in Aid of Displaced German Scholars, through the efforts of *Felix M. Warburg, *Alfred E. Cohn, and others. Adopted above name in 1938. Assumed major responsibility in the U.S.A. for the placement of refugee scholars; cooperated and corresponded with virtually all agencies aiding refugees in this country and abroad. Dissolved in 1945. The Committee's work was carried on by the newly formed American Committee for Refugee Scholars, Writers and Artists (*American Council for Émigrés in the Professions).

Literature. Stephen Duggan and Betty Drury, *The Rescue of Science and Learning, The Story of the Emergency Committee in Aid of Displaced Foreign Scholars.* New York: Macmillan, 1948.
Emergency Committee . . . , *Reports.* 1934-38, 1940-42.
Wetzel, "American Rescue."

Records. New York Public Library, Manuscripts and Archives Div.: records, 1933-45, 90 ft, consist of administrative files and biographical data on refugee scholars, including case files. A collection of primary importance, containing materials bearing on the work of all major and many smaller agencies engaged in aid to refugees. *NUCMC* MS 76-1507. Finding aid: unpublished inventory (125 pp.).
    Cornell Univ. Libraries, Dept. of Manuscripts and Univ. Archives: records, 1933-36, 1 box, consist of minutes and correspondence between Edward R. Murrow, assistant secretary of the Committee, and Livingston Farrand, chairman of the agency's Executive Committee and president of *Cornell Univ. *NUCMC* MS 66-423.

64. EMERGENCY COMMITTEE TO SAVE THE JEWISH PEOPLE OF
EUROPE *Defunct*

Zionist-Revisionist group, formerly the Committee for an Army of Stateless and Palestinian Jews, organized ca. 1943 by Peter H. Bergson, to rescue and resettle European Jews in Palestine. Similar goals were pursued by the American Friends of a Jewish Palestine, American League for a Free Palestine, and Hebrew Committee of National Liberation, which aimed at assembling an independent Jewish army to fight against the Axis powers, and at reestablishing the Jewish nation in an independent Palestine.

Records. Yale Univ. Library, Dept. of Manuscripts and Archives: records, 1933-72, ca. 13 ft, of the organizations listed above, under the designation Palestine Statehood Committee Papers, include correspondence, memoranda, reports, publications, advertisements, scrapbooks, and clippings. Also on microfilm (20 reels, negative). *NUCMC* MS 74-1198.
    Institute for Mediterranean Affairs, the donor of the above Palestine Statehood Committee collection: photocopies of all records in the collection, and material not deposited at Yale Univ. Library.

Jabotinsky Institute, Israel: microfilm (positive) of the collection at Yale Univ. Library, and the larger part of the records of the Palestine Statehood Committees which are not included in the collections at Yale Univ. Library or are located at the Institute for Mediterranean Affairs.

65. EPISCOPAL COMMITTEE FOR EUROPEAN REFUGEES   *Defunct*

Founded by the National Council of the Protestant Episcopal Church in 1938 as the Episcopal Committee for German Refugees in the Dept. of Christian Social Relations. Above name was adopted in 1939. Cooperated with other agencies aiding refugees and encouraged parishes to provide assistance to refugees. Prepared refugee aid poster stamps to finance its efforts. Published pamphlets: *German Refugees Need Your Help, The Émigré Among Us*, and *Resettlement of Refugees: A Program for Parish Communities.*

Literature.   "Call to Aid German Refugees." *The Spirit of Missions* 104 (Mar. 19, 1939): 24.
Hertz, "Joint and Concurrent."
Romanofsky, *Social Service Organizations*, pp. 286-290.

Records.   Archives and Historical Collections of the Episcopal Church: records of the Dept. of Christian Social Relations do not include the records of the Episcopal Committee for European Refugees, which are presumed to have been destroyed.

Executive Council of the Protestant Episcopal Church (Episcopal Church Center, 815 Second Ave., New York, NY 10017): minutes of the National Council reflect policy decisions concerning the Episcopal Committee for European Refugees.

66. EUROPEAN JEWISH CHILDREN'S AID, INC.   *Defunct*

Established in 1934 as the German Jewish Children's Aid, a project of the *National Council of Jewish Women, to implement plans for the immigration to the U.S.A. of a limited number of unaccompanied German-Jewish children. The Committee on German Jewish Immigration Policy of the Joint Consultative Council was largely responsible for the formation of the agency, which was directed by *Cecilia Razovsky. In 1941, the *National Refugee Service assumed responsibility for the agency's operation. Cooperating committees throughout the U.S.A. assisted in resettlement efforts. The name European Jewish Children's Aid was adopted in 1942. The organization was dissolved in 1952, having assisted in the resettlement of children who had survived the Holocaust and immigrated to the U.S.A. Cooperated with the *U.S. Children's Bureau and the *United States Committee for the Care of European Children.

Records.   YIVO Institute for Jewish Research: records, 1933-53, microfilm (34 reels). (The originals [621 files] were discarded after microfilming.) A primary archival collection relating to the selection, transportation, placement, and naturalization of Jewish children from Central Europe in the U.S.A. Consist of correspondence with American social service agencies, foreign Jewish institutions, and individuals, minutes of meetings, memoranda, reports, financial records, surveys, printed items, lists of names, photographs, and other materials. Finding aid: unpublished inventory (25 pp.).

Case files, 1934–52, 64 file drawers, are included in the records of *United HIAS Service (HIAS-HICEM Collection IV) at YIVO.

67. ÉVIAN CONFERENCE ON REFUGEES, 1938

On March 23, 1938, President *Franklin D. Roosevelt reacted to the atrocities committed by Austrians against Jews following the *Anschluss*, and by the unregulated flight of Jews from Austria that followed, by instructing U.S. Secretary of State *Cordell Hull to call an international conference of immigration countries to "facilitate the emigration from Austria and presumably from Germany of political refugees." The resulting meeting of representatives from 32 nations in Évian-les-Bains, France, July 6–15, 1938 (the "Évian Conference") was attended also by observers from Poland, Romania, and Nazi Germany, and by the representatives of 39 organizations (20 of which were Jewish) concerned with assistance to refugees, including representatives of the Reichsvertretung der Juden in Deutschland and a spokesman for Austrian Jews.

During the Conference, the delegates of the represented countries reiterated the basically restrictionist immigration policies of their governments. The American delegation, headed by *Myron C. Taylor, also included *George L. Warren and *James G. McDonald. Their contribution to the Conference consisted of an announcement that the Austrian and German immigration quotas of the U.S.A. would be combined (to a total of about 28,000). However, already before the Conference, President Roosevelt had instructed the Consular Service (*U.S. Dept. of State) to ease formal restrictions on the admission of refugees from Germany and Austria.

Among the organizations whose delegates were heard (for a few minutes each!) by a subcommittee of the Conference were the Jewish Colonization Association, *International Migration Service, *International Student Service, *Agudath Israel World Organization, HICEM (*HIAS-ICA-Emigration Association), The Society of Friends (London), *World Jewish Congress, *Freeland League, *ORT, *Jewish Agency for Palestine, and other groups.

The Conference did not justify the high hopes raised by its agenda. Its main effect was the creation of the *Intergovernmental Committee on Refugees to give substance to the resolution of the Conference to place the emigration of "political refugees" from Germany and Austria on a planned basis. Nazi aggression against Czechoslovakia, the *Kristallnacht* in Germany, the disturbances in Palestine, and the coming of World War II changed the international atmosphere, and rendered the internationally planned resettlement of refugees from Nazism illusory.

Literature. S. Adler-Rudel, "The Évian Conference on the Refugee Question." In *Leo Baeck Institute Year Book* XIII (1968), pp. 235–273.

Records. Records relating to the Conference are found in various collections, including the records of the State Dept. at the National Archives and the papers of Roosevelt and of Taylor at the Franklin D. Roosevelt Library.

68. FREELAND LEAGUE FOR JEWISH TERRITORIAL COLONIZATION
200 W. 72 St., New York, NY 10023

When the rise of Nazism in Germany called for a solution to the problem of re-settling large numbers of Jewish refugees, and the absorptive capacity of Palestine appeared to be limited by internal and political circumstances, Isaac Nahman Steinberg (1888-1957), in cooperation with *T. B. Herwald and others, founded the Freeland League in London in 1935. Its aim was "to find and obtain large-scale room in some sparsely populated area for the Jewish masses where they could live and develop according to their own views and culture and religion."

Steinberg, a Russian-born Jewish lawyer, writer, and communal leader, had participated in pre-Soviet revolutionary activities as a member of the Social-Revolutionary Party, and had served as People's Commissar for Justice in Lenin's cabinet. Following the breakup of the coalition with the communists, Steinberg left Russia for Germany in 1923 and settled in Berlin. He left Germany in 1933 and settled first in London and, from 1943, in New York.

In pursuit of the Freeland League's program, Steinberg promoted settlement plans in Australia, 1938-44, and in Surinam. In 1938, the League was established in New York, where its headquarters have been since 1941. Steinberg edited the League's publication, *Oyfn Shvel* (On the Threshold) 1943-56. The League continues to issue various publications.

Literature. *International Biographical Dictionary*, vol. I (I. N. Steinberg). *News of the YIVO* 65 (July 1957): 6*.

Records. YIVO Institute for Jewish Research: Steinberg's papers, 1919-56, 25 ft, containing part of the League's records, 1935-56, include material about various plans for the resettlement of refugees. Finding aid: unpublished inventory (95 pp.).
Other records of the League are at its office.

69. GUSTAV WURZWEILER FOUNDATION, INC.
c/o Fred Grubel (executive secretary), Leo Baeck Institute, 129 E. 73 St., New York, NY 10021

Established in 1950 by Gustav Wurzweiler, a German-Jewish immigrant banker and philanthropist. The Foundation aids Jewish cultural, social, and educational institutions in the U.S.A. and Israel, with emphasis on higher education, research in Jewish history, religious education, hospitals, aid to the handicapped, and support for congregations. By 1970, about 100 institutions had received grants, with the *Leo Baeck Institute a major beneficiary. *United Help also received support. Rabbi *Max Gruenewald is cochairman.

Records. Records are with the executive secretary and are restricted.

70. HIAS-ICA-EMIGRATION ASSOCIATION, INC. (HICEM)   *Defunct*

European Emig-Direkt (Emigrations-Direktion, United Commitee for Jewish Emigration) was founded in Berlin in 1921 by the *Hebrew Sheltering and Immigrant Aid Society (HIAS) and the World Relief Conference (Carlsbad, 1920, which raised funds for relief and reconstruction in Central, Eastern, and Southeastern Europe). Emig-Direkt drew its major financial support from the *American Jewish Joint Distribution Committee (JDC), the Jewish Colonization Association (ICA), and other organizations, and assisted in the emigration of Jews from Eastern Europe.

HICEM was organized in Berlin in 1927 by HIAS and ICA. It moved to Paris in 1928 and was joined by Emig-Direkt in 1934. HICEM assisted Jews to emigrate from Europe and be admitted in various countries. After 1933, most of HICEM's efforts were devoted to financing and assisting the emigration of Jews from Nazi Germany, and to gaining admission for refugees from Eastern and Central Europe in Western Europe and South America. JDC continued to support HICEM during the Nazi period.

During that time, HICEM opened offices in New York, Prague, and Belgium. The central office in Paris was to be evacuated to Bordeaux in May 1940, but following the fall of France, the office was transferred to locations in Marseilles and Lisbon. Later, the Marseilles office was moved to Brive-la-Gaillarde. In 1941, HICEM headquarters were transferred to New York. After the war, the HICEM branch offices in Lisbon and Brive-la-Gaillarde were closed.

*Max Gottschalk was president of HICEM 1938–46. *Ilja M. Dijour was executive secretary of HICEM, New York. *Meyer Birman managed the HICEM office in the Far East. In 1945, HIAS dissolved its partnership with HICEM, and HICEM was officially dissolved that same year. HICEM's work was continued through an office set up by HIAS in Paris.

Literature. *News of the YIVO* 61 (June 1956): 1*-2*.
Mark Wischnitzer, *Visas to Freedom: The History of HIAS.* Cleveland: World, 1956.

Records. YIVO Institute for Jewish Research:
- Records of the New York office of HICEM are included in the HIAS-HICEM records, series I, on microfilm (100 reels), and consist of minutes of meetings, reports, correspondence (with HIAS, individuals, and other organizations), and other materials.
- Records of the European offices of HICEM, 1935-53, are included in the HIAS-HICEM records, series II, on microfilm (306 reels), and consist of records of the Paris office, 1930s–40, general material of HICEM in France during World War II, and partial records of the Lisbon office during the war.
- Additional records of the HICEM office in Lisbon, 1939-51, 565 files on microfilm (originals destroyed), form a part of the JDC-HICEM Lisbon collection.

- Materials regarding HICEM in Prague, 1933-39, are included in the Prague Committee for German Refugees collection.
- Papers of M. Gottschalk, I. M. Dijour, and M. Birman, in HIAS-HICEM records, series I, include materials on HICEM.

Finding aids: unpublished inventories (Yiddish) for all HIAS-HICEM collections.

71. HADASSAH, THE WOMEN'S ZIONIST ORGANIZATION OF AMERICA, INC.
65 E. 52 St., New York, NY 10022

Principal Zionist organization of women, founded in 1912 by *Henrietta Szold. Largest Zionist organization in the world. Provides maintenance and education for young newcomers in Israel through Youth Aliyah, of which Hadassah is the principal supporting agency in the U.S.A. Participates in fund-raising and educational activities, and sponsors medical research, training, and care in Israel.

Hadassah aided German refugees through its support of Youth Aliyah, established in 1934 to rescue and rehabilitate Jewish youth from Nazi persecution by resettling them in "youth villages" in Palestine.

Literature. Marlin Levin, *Balm in Gilead: The Story of Hadassah.* New York: Schocken Books, 1973.

Records. Hadassah: records include extensive documentation on Youth Aliyah since its founding, and some of Szold's papers.

72. HEBREW SHELTERING AND IMMIGRANT AID SOCIETY OF AMERICA, INC. (HIAS)   *Defunct*

Formed in New York City in 1909 through the merger of the Hebrew Sheltering House Association (founded 1884) and the Hebrew Immigrant Aid Society (founded 1902). Responding to the growing needs of Jewish immigrants from Eastern Europe, HIAS soon grew to national dimensions, providing help in legal entry, basic subsistence, employment, citizenship instruction, and location of relatives for nearly one-half million newcomers to the U.S.A. during the organization's first decade. Between 1917 and 1926, HIAS opened offices in Eastern Europe and the Far East. In 1927, HIAS joined the Jewish Colonization Association (ICA) to form HICEM (*HIAS-ICA-Emigration Association). Most of HICEM's efforts were subsequently devoted to assisting refugees from Nazi-occupied Europe.

HIAS services to refugees included assistance in locating relatives who might provide affidavits of support to prospective immigrants to the U.S.A., negotiations with U.S. and foreign governments to ease the admission of refugees (including assistance to the refugees traveling on the *S.S. *St. Louis* in 1939), reception and housing placement services, providing transportation funding and facilities for émigrés abroad (including transportation funds for Palestine), and a variety of related services in cooperation with other agencies during the Nazi and immediate postwar periods. The office in Marseilles, which it directed jointly with ICA, was forced out of Marseilles during World War II and moved to New York.

In 1945, HIAS dissolved its partnership with HICEM. In 1949, it cooperated with the *American Jewish Joint Distribution Committee (JDC) in forming the Displaced Persons Coordinating Committee, continued to fight against restrictive U.S. immigration laws, and cooperated with Israel and with other Jewish immigrant services.

In 1954, HIAS merged with the *United Service for New Americans (USNA) and the JDC Migration Dept. to form the *United HIAS Service. HIAS branches had existed in *Boston, *Baltimore, *Chicago, *Philadelphia, San Francisco, and Seattle.

Literature. Romanofsky, *Social Service Organizations*, pp. 342-345.
Mark Wischnitzer, *Visas to Freedom: The History of HIAS.* Cleveland: World, 1956.

Records. YIVO Institute for Jewish Research: records are included in the HIAS-HICEM records, series I, on microfilm (100 reels), and contain minutes, correspondence, reports, and a wide variety of other materials. There are also records of individual migration cases of the European HIAS office, 1945-60s, 253 boxes (partly on microfilm—261 reels); HIAS search material, 1915-23, microfilm (23 reels); HIAS legal briefs, 1905-23; and records of the HIAS office in Chile, 1939-70, 30 ft.

United HIAS Service (200 Park Ave. S., New York, NY 10003): minutes of meetings, 1913-54, and records since 1911 of Jewish immigrants who arrived at the Port of New York and were assisted by HIAS. The minutes of meetings, 1913-48, are on microfilm (6 reels) at YIVO.

73. HEBREW UNION COLLEGE-JEWISH INSTITUTE OF RELIGION
3101 Clifton Ave., Cincinnati, OH 45220

Postbaccalaureate school of Reform Jewish and Semitic studies, and rabbinical seminary, founded in Cincinnati in 1875 as the Hebrew Union College. The Jewish Institute of Religion, founded in New York in 1922 by Rabbi *Stephen S. Wise, was merged with the Hebrew Union College in 1950.

Under the guidance of Rabbi Julian Morgenstern, president of the College 1921-47, plans were made in 1934 to establish a "Jewish College in Exile" (similar to the University in Exile of the *New School for Social Research in New York). As a result of his efforts, the College placed 11 refugee scholars on its teaching, research, or library and archives staff.

Literature. Samuel E. Karff, ed., *Hebrew Union College-Jewish Institute of Religion at One Hundred Years.* Cincinnati: Hebrew Union College Press, 1975.
Michael A. Meyer, "The Refugee Scholars Project of the Hebrew Union College." In *A Bicentennial Festschrift for Jacob Rader Marcus*, Bertram W. Korn, ed. New York: Ktav, 1976, pp. 359-375.

Records. American Jewish Archives: Morgenstern's papers 1905-70, 5 ft, and records of Hebrew Union College, 1875-1950, include correspondence and other materials concerning the refugee scholars project. (See Meyer, *op. cit.*)

74. IMMIGRATION RESTRICTION LEAGUE, INC.   *Defunct*

Organizations under this name existed in Boston (from 1894), New York (from 1909), and elsewhere in the U.S.A. The Leagues took strong positions in opposing unrestricted immigration to the U.S.A., and were most active prior to the passage of the U.S. Immigration Law of 1924.

Although the League's influence and membership had diminished by the late 1930s, the surviving members voiced strong opposition to the admission of refugees from Europe.

Literature. Barbara Miller Solomon, *Ancestors and Immigrants: A Changing New England Tradition.* Cambridge, MA: Harvard Univ. Press, 1956. (Includes the history of the League through the 1920s.)

Records. Boston Public Library: scrapbooks, 1894-1957, relating to the Boston League and to immigration restrictions in general, are on microfilm (6 reels). Scrapbook 18 (on reel 6) consists of newspaper clippings, 1934-36, on activities directed against immigration.

Harvard Univ., Houghton Library: records of the Boston League, 1894-1921, are among the papers of its secretary, Prescott F. Hall.

Records of the New York League have not been located.

75. INSTITUTE FOR ADVANCED STUDY
Princeton, NJ 08540

Chartered in 1930 and opened in 1933 as a postgraduate school and research and experimental center. The founding director, *Abraham Flexner 1930-39, and his successor, *Frank Aydelotte 1939-47, were active in the *Emergency Committee in Aid of Displaced Foreign Scholars, as was *Oswald Veblen, head of the Institute's School of Mathematical Sciences. The Institute appointed leading refugee scholars to its faculty.

Literature. Frances Blanshard, *Frank Aydelotte of Swarthmore.* Middletown, CT: Wesleyan Univ. Press, 1970.
Abraham Flexner, *I Remember.* New York: Simon and Schuster, 1940. "Finding Men," chap. 28.
——, *Abraham Flexner: An Autobiography.* New York: Simon and Schuster, 1960. "Finding Men," chap. 28.
Beatrice M. Stern, unpublished history of the Institute, prepared ca. 1964, in a "locked vault" at the Institute.

Records. According to information received, the Institute has retained very few of its records. Most of the files for the period until 1947 are believed to be included in the papers of its directors, Flexner at the Library of Congress, and Aydelotte at Swarthmore College, Friends Historical Library.

76. INSTITUTE OF DESIGN (NEW BAUHAUS), Chicago *Defunct*

László Moholy-Nagy, a German refugee artist, established the New Bauhaus in Chicago in 1937 as a school for the education of designers and architects. The Institute was sponsored by the Association of Arts and Industries. It was planned to transplant the artistic tradition of the German *Bauhaus* movement to the U.S.A. The leader of this movement, Walter Gropius, who had immigrated to the U.S.A. in 1937 following his emigration to England in 1933, served as adviser to the Institute. It closed after one year as a result of financial difficulties, but was reconstituted in 1939 as the Chicago School of Design, and subsequently exerted significant influence on art education in the U.S.A. Later, it was renamed the Institute of Design, and eventually incorporated in the Illinois Institute of Technology.

Literature. *International Biographical Dictionary*, vol. II (L. Moholy-Nagy and W. Gropius).

William H. Jordy, "The Aftermath of the Bauhaus in America: Gropius, Mies, and Breuer." In *The Intellectual Migration: Europe and America, 1930–1960*, Donald Fleming and Bernard Baylin, eds. Cambridge, MA: Harvard Univ. Press, 1969, pp. 485–543.

Records. Univ. of Illinois, Chicago Circle Library, Dept. of Special Collections: records, 1927–72, 5 ft, consist of personal and business correspondence of the Institute's members, 1939–67, articles about the Institute and its members, publications of the Institute, minutes of meetings, financial reports, and other documents, photographs of exhibitions, course lists and descriptions, and speeches and essays by members of the Institute and others. Finding aid: unpublished inventory.

The primary repository for documentation on the *Bauhaus* movement is the Berlin Bauhaus-Archiv, Schloss-Strasse 1, D-1 Berlin 19, West Germany.

77. INTERCOLLEGIATE COMMITTEE TO AID STUDENT REFUGEES, INC. *Defunct*

Founded in December 1938 by the delegates to the first Intercollegiate Conference to Aid Student Refugees, held at International House in New York. The Conference had been called by the Harvard Committee to Aid German Student Refugees, one of the first such college committees organized in the U.S.A.

The Intercollegiate Committee was incorporated in June 1939 in New York City to stimulate students at U.S. colleges to collect money for scholarships for refugee students. Such committees had been formed already on some American campuses in spontaneous response to the burning of the synagogues and the mistreatment of Jews in Germany on November 9–10, 1938 (*Kristallnacht*).

The Intercollegiate Committee was sponsored by several student organizations and agencies aiding refugees, including the *Menorah Association, *National Coordinating Committee, and Public Affairs Committee of the *Society for Ethical Culture, New York. In September 1939, the Intercollegiate Committee merged with the *United States Committee of International Student Service.

Records. *Research Foundation for Jewish Immigration: several folders of material (partly photocopies) on the Intercollegiate Committee, Harvard Committee, and Yale Committee, deposited by Robert E. Lane, New Haven, and William W. Brill, New York, who had been students at Harvard and Yale, respectively, and leaders of the Intercollegiate Committee, in 1938-39.

Harvard Univ. Archives: one folder of documents relating to the Harvard Committee.

Similar materials may be found in the archives of other colleges and universities where students had organized groups to support refugee students.

78. INTERGOVERNMENTAL COMMITTEE ON REFUGEES   *Defunct*

The Intergovernmental Committee on Refugees (ICR) was established in London in 1938 by governments participating in the *Évian Conference on Refugees (July 1938) to give effect to its resolution to plan the emigration of "political refugees" from Germany and Austria in an orderly fashion. The ICR was headed by George Rublee, an American, and subsequently by Sir Herbert Emerson, the *League of Nations High Commissioner for Refugees. Negotiations with German representatives and plans to place Jewish emigration from Germany on a sound and more humane basis failed in the atmosphere of approaching war and German radical anti-Semitic measures and aggressive foreign policies.

Thus, the ICR's main achievements were small: an international agreement on travel papers for refugees who had been refused passports by the Nazi government, assistance to a group of refugees to settle in the Dominican Republic and some Latin American countries, and establishment of a refugee camp in North Africa.

To assist the ICR, an Anglo-American private corporation, the Coordinating Foundation, was established in 1939 to raise funds should the financial plans for the orderly transfer of refugees from Germany materialize. It was presided over by Paul van Zeeland of Belgium. Its American trustees included *Paul Baerwald, John W. Davis, Rufus M. Jones, Nathan L. Miller, Dave Hennen Morris, Judge Joseph M. Proskauer, Lessing J. Rosenwald, *Lewis L. Strauss, Rabbi *Stephen S. Wise, and Owen D. Young. Following the outbreak of the war in Europe, the money collected by the Foundation was returned to subscribers and the Foundation was liquidated when the ICR proved unable to fulfill its assigned tasks.

The ICR was reestablished for a short time by the Anglo-American Conference on Refugees of 1943 (*Bermuda Conference), and it received an allocation of $25 million to take part in the postwar rescue of displaced persons. In 1947, the functions of the ICR were assumed by the International Refugee Organization (IRO) of the United Nations, which in 1951 was replaced by the United Nations High Commissioner for Refugees.

Literature. Feingold, *Politics of Rescue*, passim.

Records. Records of the ICR's office in London were taken over by the IRO. They are believed to have been transferred to the IRO's headquarters in Geneva, Switzerland, and may now be at the headquarters of the U.N. High Commissioner in Geneva. Records of the Washington, DC, representative of the ICR were transferred to the Washington office of the IRO. The present location of these records has not been ascertained. Finding aid: U.S. National Archives, *Federal Records of World War II.* Washington, 1950. Vol. I: Civilian Agencies, pp. 1056–1057.

Records relating to the ICR are found in various collections, including the records of the *U.S. Dept. of State at the National Archives and the papers of *Myron C. Taylor, the ICR's vice-chairman, at the Franklin D. Roosevelt Library.

79. INTERNATIONAL INSTITUTES

International Institutes were founded by the *Young Women's Christian Association (YWCA). The first such Institute, established in New York City in 1910 as an experiment under the direction of settlement worker Edith Terry Bremer, was followed by the formation of other local Institutes under the guidance of the YWCA's War Work Council (whose initial task had been to assist immigrant women and girls in the U.S.A.). Following World War I, this Council was transformed by the YWCA's National Board into the Dept. of Immigration and Foreign Communities. Proliferating during World War I, 55 International Institutes had been established by 1920 across the country. In 1933, the Dept. of Immigration and Foreign Communities, which had supervised the International Institutes, was replaced by the National Institute of Immigrant Welfare as an independent national organization, and a number of local Institutes affiliated with that body.

According to Bremer, who owed her inspiration to the Progressive Movement of the period, the purpose of the International Institutes was to substitute ethnic pluralism and internal self-help democracy for the missionary and Americanization programs that had characterized social work for immigrants up to that time. The International Institutes expanded their programs to include work in settlement houses, casework and family care, and naturalization and language instruction, in the framework of fostering the immigrant's identification with his native culture as an aspect of his acculturation. As a result, a variety of cultural programs with ethnic content became standard activities for the Institutes.

In the 1930s, they provided advice concerning naturalization, citizenship, and—following 1940—alien legislation. The Institutes included refugees in their activities, mainly those who were not affiliated with a religious denomination, or were Christians.

In 1943, the National Institute of Immigrant Welfare changed its name to the American Federation of International Institutes. In 1959, the Federation merged with the Common Council for American Unity to form the *American Council for Nationalities Service, with which the then-existing local International Institutes became affiliated.

Literature. Romanofsky, *Social Service Organizations*, pp. 59–63.

Records. Univ. of Minnesota, Immigration History Research Center: extant records of the American Federation of International Institutes and its predecessor agencies are a part of the records of the American Council for Nationalities Service.

Records of affiliated International Institutes are with the local agencies. Some local records have been deposited in archives. The Immigration History Research Center of the Univ. of Minnesota completed a survey in 1978 to locate and describe the records of all International Institutes, past and present.

For a list of the Institutes discussed in this publication, see the Index.

80. INTERNATIONAL RESCUE COMMITTEE, INC.
386 Park Ave. S., New York, NY 10016

The International Rescue and Relief Committee was formed in 1942 by a merger of the International Relief Association and the Emergency Rescue Committee.

In 1933, the American branch of the International Relief Association was established as the International Relief Committee by a group of clergymen, journalists, and others including *Reinhold Niebuhr, who were concerned about Nazi atrocities. Renamed the International Relief Association, it provided financial assistance overseas and helped with the rescue and resettlement of opponents of Nazism.

In 1940, the Emergency Rescue Committee (ERC) was established by a group of prominent American liberals under the leadership of *Frank Kingdon to coordinate the rescue of political and literary refugees displaced by the fall of France. *Varian M. Fry was one of the ERC's representatives in Europe and assisted in the rescue efforts in France.

After 1942, the merged Committee continued the activities of its predecessors. Following the war, it participated in postwar rehabilitation of survivors in Europe. Known since 1951 as the International Rescue Committee, it is a major agency engaged in refugee aid activities today.

Literature. International Rescue Committee, *They Chose Freedom: Thirty Years of the IRC, 1933–1963.* New York, 1963.
Romanofsky, *Social Service Organizations*, pp. 362–367.
Wetzel, "American Rescue."

Records. State Univ. of New York at Albany, Dept. of Germanic Languages and Literatures: photocopies of case files of more than 175 refugees aided from 1940 to 1946, 8 ft, include biographical materials, correspondence, affidavits, and other documents. The original materials are at the Deutsche Bibliothek, Frankfurt am Main, Federal Republic of Germany, from whom permission must be obtained to examine the photocopies. Finding aid: unpublished list of individuals represented in the collection.

Records at the agency's office contain little material for the period prior to about 1950.

81. JEWISH CULTURAL RECONSTRUCTION, INC. (JCR)   *Defunct*

In 1944, the Conference on Jewish Relations (now the *Conference on Jewish Social Studies) established the Commission on European Jewish Cultural Reconstruction to investigate the changes wrought in Jewish cultural life by World War II. The Commission prepared a number of studies surveying the Jewish cultural treasures preserved in libraries, museums, and archives, Jewish educational institutions, the Jewish press, and the Jewish publishing firms which had existed in Nazi-occupied Europe before the war. These studies, which appeared as supplements to *Jewish Social Studies*, demonstrated the vast and irretrievable losses suffered by the world Jewish community.

Since there was an imminent danger, immediately after the war, that the remaining cultural treasures in private and public possession would be further destroyed or at least vanish from sight, the Commission organized Jewish Cultural Reconstruction, Inc. (JCR) in 1947, with the major Jewish national and international organizations as active members. JCR became a virtual arm of the *Jewish Restitution Successor Organization (JRSO) for the recovery of cultural objects. In 1949, it won government recognition as the trustee of all Jewish cultural objects stored at the book depot in Offenbach, Germany. Over 10,000 ceremonial objects were recovered and distributed to synagogues and museums around the world, and to congregations founded by immigrants from Central Europe. Over 250,000 books, pamphlets, and other writings were also distributed to libraries and archives.

Inactive since the mid-1950s, JCR was dissolved in 1976 and its remaining assets liquidated and distributed.

Literature. Salo W. Baron, "The Journal and the Conference of Jewish Social Studies." In *Emancipation and Counter-Emancipation: Selected Essays from Jewish Social Studies*, Abraham G. Duker and Meir Ben-Horin, eds. New York: Ktav, 1974, pp. 8–10.

Jewish Restitution Successor Organization, *Report on the Operations . . . 1947–1972.* "The Recovery of Cultural Property," pp. 30–32.

Records. Records are with the Conference on Jewish Social Studies (250 W. 57 St., New York, NY 10019). In 1978, they were stored in a warehouse and inaccessible. Their ultimate disposition has not been determined by the Conference.

82. JEWISH LABOR COMMITTEE, INC.
25 E. 78 St., New York, NY 10021

Founded in 1934 to represent Jewish interests in the American labor movement, and labor interests in the Jewish community. During the first five years of its existence, the Committee concentrated on supporting the activities of the U.S. labor movement directed against Nazism and fascism, and gave financial and other assistance to Jewish labor organizations in Europe. Organized mass demonstrations against Nazism and conducted a boycott of German goods and services through the *Joint Boycott Council. After the outbreak of World War II, the emphasis shifted to efforts to save labor and liberal leaders facing certain death at the hands of the Nazis. With the help of the American Federation of Labor, the Committee succeeded in bringing hundreds of such leaders, Jewish and non-Jewish, to the U.S.A.

Literature. George L. Berlin, "The Jewish Labor Committee and American Immigration Policy in the 1930s." In *Studies in Jewish Bibliography, History and Literature in Honor of I. Edward Kiev*, Charles Berlin, ed. New York: Ktav, 1971, pp. 45-73.

Records. Records, 1934-date, are at the Committee's office and include material relating to its anti-Nazi boycott and rescue activities. Some documentation regarding the Committee is at the Bund Archives of the Jewish Labor Movement, which also has material regarding East European Jewish refugees and the Holocaust.

83. JEWISH NAZI VICTIMS ORGANIZATION OF AMERICA, INC.

c/o Lew Shulgasser (corresponding secretary), 373 Fifth Ave., New York, NY 10016

Founded ca. 1956 by survivors of the Holocaust to assist and advise its members on problems concerning *Wiedergutmachung*, the health care of concentration camp survivors, and similar issues. Concerned also with locating Nazi war criminals.

Records. Records are with various officers.

84. JEWISH PHILANTHROPIC FUND OF 1933, INC.

570 Seventh Ave., New York, NY 10018

Founded by German-Jewish immigrants in 1953 as the Charity Fund of the *American Federation of Jews from Central Europe. Reorganized as an independent organization under the present name in 1960. Raises funds for the social and cultural needs of the immigrant community and its agencies mainly through a program of legacies.

Literature. Lessing, *Oral History.*

Records. Records, including minutes, since 1953, of meetings of the board of directors and the executive committee, as well as financial statements and printed materials, are with the Fund's secretary. Restricted. Additional records are included in the files of the American Federation of Jews from Central Europe. Restricted.

85. JEWISH RESTITUTION SUCCESSOR ORGANIZATION, INC. (JRSO)

15 E. 26 St., New York, NY 10010

Founded in 1947 to discover, claim, receive, and assist in the recovery of Jewish heirless or unclaimed property in the American Zone of Occupation in Germany, and to utilize such assets for the relief, rehabilitation, and resettlement of surviving victims of Nazi persecution. Developed into the central U.S. agency for the recovery of heirless properties of all kinds, including communal property confiscated, despoiled, or destroyed by the Nazi regime, and cultural objects, and the safeguarding of the pension rights of former employees of Jewish communities and agencies in Germany.

Appointed the Jewish Agency for Israel (*World Zionist Organization–American Section), the *American Jewish Joint Distribution Committee, and the *Council of Jews from Germany as operating agents for the conduct of relief, rehabilitation, and reconstruction on behalf of Nazi victims. Recipients of funds in the U.S.A. distributed for the Council of Jews from Germany by the *American Federation of Jews from Central Europe include *United Help, the *Leo Baeck Institutes (Jerusalem, London, New York), and other social agencies, homes for the aged, and religious or cultural organizations. JRSO also distributed funds directly or through the Council of Jews from Germany to groups in Israel, France, Belgium, Latin America, and other countries.

Cooperated with the other two organizations that also claimed heirless Jewish property in the occupied areas of Germany: the Jewish Trust Corp. Ltd., London (British Zone) and the Jewish Trust Corp., Branche Française, of Paris (French Zone).

Literature. *Report on the Operations of The Jewish Restitution Successor Organization 1947-1972.* Prepared by Saul Kagan and Ernest H. Weismann. New York, n.d.

Records. Records of the New York office include financial, administrative, and other materials. Restricted.

Central Archives for the History of the Jewish People, Israel: records from the JRSO offices in Berlin and Frankfurt am Main, from the Jewish Trust Corp. office in Hamburg, and from the Jewish Trust Corp., Branche Française, office in Paris. The files of claims for Jewish property left without heirs contain data on the economic condition of Jews in Germany, their communities and institutions before the Holocaust, and their despoilation. The administrative files of the organizations describe the negotiations with German authorities concerning the restitution of confiscated property, or payment of reparations for it.

86. JEWISH WAR VETERANS OF THE UNITED STATES OF AMERICA, INC. (JWV)
1712 New Hampshire Ave., N.W., Washington, DC 20009

Founded in 1896 by ex-servicemen to combat bigotry, and to prevent or stop the defamation of Jews.

In 1933, JWV formed an Anti-Nazi Boycott Committee and became the first Jewish organization to declare such a boycott. Did not show much interest in immigration or refugee matters prior to 1945 on the national level; some local posts formed refugee committees. Following World War II, JWV petitioned Congress to transfer quotas not used for immigration during wartime to displaced persons. Instituted aid programs for survivors of the Holocaust.

Literature. Gloria R. Mosesson, *The Jewish War Veterans Story.* Washington, DC, 1971.

Records. Relevant records at the headquarters of JWV have not been identified, although it is assumed that such documentation exists.

American Jewish Historical Society: collection of 277 items concerning primarily JWV's Anti-Nazi Boycott Committee. *NUCMC* MS 69-605.

American Jewish Archives: clippings and correspondence regarding the work of JWV in the anti-Nazi economic boycott, 1933-41, 2.5 ft.

87. *THE JEWISH WAY* Defunct

Published in New York until 1965 under the editorship of Max and Alice Oppenheimer primarily for German-Jewish refugees. In 1940, *The Way in America* and the *Neues jüdisches Gemeindeblatt* of the Synagogengemeinde Washington Heights (*Congregation Shaare Hatikvah, Ahavath Torah V'Tikvoh Chadoshoh) merged into *The Way in America and Neues jüdisches Gemeindeblatt*, 1940-41. It changed its name to *The Way in America* in 1942 and appeared as *The Jewish Way*, 1942-65. *The Way in America* was originally published as *Our Way in America, Zeitschrift für die Interessen der Einwanderer in U.S.A.*, 1939-40; it was edited by Aaron J. Weiss and others.

Literature. *International Biographical Dictionary*, vol. I (M. Oppenheimer and
    A. Oppenheimer).
Lessing, *Oral History*.

Records. New York Public Library, Jewish Div.: copies of *Our Way in America*, 1939-40, *The Way in America*, 1940, *The Way in America and . . .* , 1940-41, *The Way in America*, 1942, and *The Jewish Way*, 1942-46.

Leo Baeck Institute Library: copies of *The Way in America and . . .* , 1940-41, *The Way in America*, 1942, and *The Jewish Way*, 1942-65.

YIVO Institute for Jewish Research: copies of *The Way in America and . . .*, 1941, and *The Jewish Way*, 1942-45 and 1948-52 (scattered issues).

88. JEWISH WELFARE AGENCIES

Immigrants of the Nazi period arriving in the U.S.A. were served by a large network of voluntary Jewish social service agencies. These service organizations had their roots in the religious obligation of each Jew to care for the poor, the widow and orphan, and the migrant. Such efforts had expanded in the U.S.A., where voluntarism and mutual aid were dictated as much by frontier conditions as by the Calvinist and Quaker traditions.

Immigration had always been a major social concern in the U.S.A. When Jewish immigrants arrived in considerable numbers between 1880 and 1924, Jewish social assistance, like its nonsectarian or Christian counterparts, turned from lay to professional staffing. The new professional social worker developed a variety of specialized approaches to his tasks, and concerned himself with the role voluntary social agencies should play in an advanced industrial society characterized by considerable government activity in public assistance, unemployment compensation, or family service. Jewish welfare agencies, prior to the advent of the refugees of the 1930s, were also concerned with such specific Jewish problems as anti-Semitism, job opportunities for American Jews, and the restructuring of American-Jewish vocational services to "normalize" the occupational structure of the Jewish community in America. The professionals' approach to client–social worker relations had been influenced, since the 1920s, by the dynamic psychology then finding intellectual acceptance as popularized Freudianism in the U.S.A.

Imbued with the defensive philosophy of quick and complete Americanization for the arriving immigrant, often staffed by professionals committed to social and political change rather than Jewish ethnicity, Jewish professional social agencies cooperated with the large number of small, ad hoc "refugee committees" formed by religious, fraternal, cultural, and other communal groups to welcome the refugee. In small communities, most "refugee committees" remained ephemeral. In large communities, they were either absorbed, or, responding to need, developed into major refugee service agencies.

Some agencies were constituents or affiliates of such national organizations as the *Hebrew Sheltering and Immigrant Aid Society (HIAS), the *National Council of Jewish Women, the *National Coordinating Committee for Aid to Refugees and Emigrants Coming from Germany, the *National Refugee Service, and similar agencies documented in this publication. Other agencies, regional or local in origin and policy, grouped together to meet the needs of the immigrant from Germany.

Local committees mounted fund-raising drives to help finance social service activities. The funds would be allocated to local and regional professional agencies, serving such needs of the arriving refugee as initial financial assistance, job placement, language and citizenship classes, continued education, assistance to the sick, aged, or economically maladjusted, prenatal care and hospitalization, general child care, counseling, or family services.

After World War II, most of these agencies (now often called "Jewish Family Service") expanded the scope of their services to the Jewish community. The postwar generation of immigrants, preferring the identification of "New American" to "displaced person," "refugee," or "immigrant," benefited from the experience gained by these agencies in serving the refugee from Nazi Germany and Austria, and entered the American mainstream like other immigrants before them. For the refugee of the Nazi period, service to the aged in his community became the main social concern of the postwar years.

In addition to these social service agencies (which could not be documented in their entire geographic range in this publication), the arriving refugees created social service agencies on their own, staffed primarily by volunteers or leaders not trained in American social work schools. These organizations reflected the need of the new arrival to be received by fellow refugees who understood the psychological and social difficulties created by his uprooting, language difficulties, dependence on public assistance, or placement in an "entry job" unrelated to his past experience and training. They also reflected the middle-class background of the German-Jewish immigrant whose perceptions of his social situation and whose economic and occupational aspirations did not include an understanding of the philosophy of American-Jewish social welfare and its financial and political limitations.

The names adopted by such refugee-created agencies (Selfhelp, Selfaid, Mutual Aid Society, etc.) reflected their determination to seek strength in nativist unity. With the passage of time, such agencies either turned themselves into professional social agencies serving new clienteles while providing for the increasing number of aged and infirm among the earlier refugee group, or diminished with the declining needs of the group they were created to serve. Since the 1950s, their activities have been supported to a considerable extent by funds made available by the government of the Federal Republic of Germany via the *Conference on Jewish Material Claims Against Germany as "collective reparations" (*Wiedergutmachung*), and by contributions collected from the community of former refugees.

For a list of the local agencies discussed in this volume, see the Index.

Records. The records of social welfare agencies include information on organization, fund-raising, local–national relations, the realization of national directives on relocation and placement of refugee newcomers, minutes of boards and committees concerned with aid to refugees, and the case files established by social workers charged with professional assistance to the refugees. Like the records of other professionals such as lawyers, case files are considered confidential and privileged, and not subject to inspection on the part of persons, even qualified scholars, not professionally concerned with the individual seeking assistance. Overall, the records created by social welfare agencies that served immigrants from Nazi Germany represent a comprehensive documentation on the resettlement and acculturation and integration of that segment of the group that sought the help of social welfare agencies.

The nationwide mail inquiry conducted by the compiler of this volume, and the numerous personal inquiries and visits made in the greater New York area, where most refugees of the Nazi period settled either initially or permanently, have shown that Jewish welfare agencies in the U.S.A. have failed to understand the significance of their files for the history of the period. Most casework agencies wrote that they routinely destroy "closed case files" after a stated interval of years, generally 5 or 10 years. Other agencies, including some national agencies of considerable significance for the resettlement and acculturation of immigrants from Central Europe, destroyed large parts of their records when the end of postwar mass migration forced them to shrink their staffs and/or move to (often considerably) smaller premises.

In this manner, basic primary documentation for the history of the Holocaust period, and the history of the immigration, resettlement, and acculturation of Nazi victims in their manyfold aspects, has been lost. The compiler and the Research Foundation for Jewish Immigration consider it their obligation to note the disappearance or destruction of such records wherever appropriate under each of the entries in question.

89. JOINT BOYCOTT COUNCIL OF THE AMERICAN JEWISH CONGRESS AND JEWISH LABOR COMMITTEE   *Defunct*

Formed in 1935 by a merger of the Boycott Committee of the *American Jewish Congress, established in 1933, and the boycott organization of the *Jewish Labor Committee. The Council, which existed until 1941, had an impact on public attitudes toward refugees through its anti-Nazi propaganda activities. *Joseph L. Tenenbaum was chairman of the Boycott Committee of the American Jewish Congress 1933-35. Tenenbaum and *B. Charney Vladeck were cochairmen of the Joint Boycott Council.

Literature. Moshe Gottlieb, "The Anti-Nazi Boycott Movement in the American Jewish Community 1933-41." Unpublished Ph.D. dissertation, Brandeis Univ., 1967.
Hanns G. Reissner, "The American Anti-Nazi Boycott." In *Jubilee Volume Dedicated to Curt C. Silberman*, Herbert A. Strauss and Hanns G. Reissner, eds. New York: American Federation of Jews from Central Europe, 1969, pp. 60-79.

Records. New York Public Library, Manuscripts and Archives Div.: records, 1933-41, 30 ft, include material on the export of German goods by German refugees (*Nir-Haavarah* schemes, Rublee-Schacht negotiations), boycott movements in Europe and Latin America, relations with American business, labor, and Jewish organizations, and anti-Nazi activities. *NUCMC* MS 70-1747. Finding aid: unpublished inventory.

90. LABOR ZIONIST ALLIANCE, INC.
575 Sixth Ave., New York, NY 10011

Formed in 1972 by merger of the Labor Zionist Organization of America-Poale Zion (LZO, founded in 1905) and the Farband-Labor Zionist Order (Jewish National Workers Alliance, founded in 1912). In 1914, LZO, the U.S. branch of the Socialist–Zionist party Poale Zion, launched a movement to establish a democratic organization, representative of U.S. Jewry, to deal with Jewish problems growing out of World War I. The movement led to the establishment of the first *American Jewish Congress. At the same time, LZO played a leading role in forming the People's Relief Committee, which merged with the *American Jewish Joint Distribution Committee (JDC).

In the 1930s and 1940s, the LZO fought Nazism and Fascism, aided victims of Nazi persecution and the Holocaust, and propagated the establishment of a Jewish state in Palestine.

The Martin Buber Branch of the Jewish National Workers Alliance was founded in 1937 by German-Jewish refugees in New York City as a fraternal Zionist-Labor organization.

Literature. C. Bezalel Sherman, *Labor Zionism in America: Its History, Growth and Program.* New York, 1957.

Records. Archives and Museum of the Jewish Labor Movement, Israel: records of LZO and related groups, 1904-54, include materials on the rehabilitation of Jewish refugees, 1920-53, and minutes, correspondence, and program, policy, and financial materials.

American Jewish Archives (AJA) and YIVO Institute for Jewish Research: microfilm copies of above records, 126 reels. (AJA had custody of the records before they were microfilmed and transferred to Israel. Other records formerly at AJA were transferred to YIVO without being filmed.) *NUCMC* MS 65-1735.

YIVO Institute for Jewish Research: records, 1916-67, ca. 66 ft, include ca. 5 ft, 1916-44. Finding aid: unpublished inventory (82 pp.).

Recent records of Labor Zionist Alliance and other materials of the predecessor organizations are at the organization's office.

91. LEAGUE OF NATIONS HIGH COMMISSION FOR
REFUGEES   *Defunct*

In 1921, the League of Nations first created a High Commission for Refugees, which in 1930 was replaced by the Nansen International Office for Refugees. In 1933, the High Commission for Refugees (Jewish and Other) Coming from Germany was established, and *James G. McDonald was named High Commissioner. McDonald's agency, which was supported primarily by funds from Jewish sources, had aided in the resettlement of approximately 65,000 refugees by 1935.

The High Commission was not an integral part of the League of Nations. Since McDonald was unable to negotiate directly with the Nazis and to persuade governments to adopt more liberal admission policies, he resigned in 1935. His resignation was given wide publicity to arouse world opinion to the situation in Germany. In spite of this, the High Commission continued to be a relatively ineffective body. Sir Neill Malcolm assumed McDonald's post 1936-38.

In 1938, the *Intergovernmental Committee on Refugees was created as a result of the *Évian Conference on Refugees. That year, the former Nansen Office was merged with the High Commissioner for Refugees from Germany to create a new High Commissioner's post. Sir Herbert Emerson, who was appointed to this position and also director of the Intergovernmental Committee, served until 1946 when the League of Nations was dissolved.

Literature. Haim Genizi, "James G. McDonald: High Commissioner for Refugees, 1933-35." *The Wiener Library Bulletin*, Vol. 30, n.s. nos. 43/44 (1977), pp. 40-52.

George Scott, *The Rise and Fall of the League of Nations*. London: Hutchinson, 1973.

Records. Official records of the several High Commissions for Refugees and of the Nansen Office are contained in the archives of the League of Nations, at the United Nations Library in Geneva, Switzerland. Finding aid: Yves Pérotin, "The League of Nations." In *The New Guide to the Diplomatic Archives of Western Europe*, Daniel H. Thomas and Lynn M. Case, eds. Philadelphia: Univ. of Pennsylvania Press, 1975, pp. 383-389, 398-399.

A part of the League of Nations Archives, consisting of over 25,000 published and unpublished documents, 1919-46, is available on microfilm from Research Publications, Inc., New Haven, CT. Finding aid: Edward A. Reno, Jr., ed., *League of Nations Documents, 1919-1946: A Descriptive Guide and Key to the Microfilm Collection*. New Haven, CT: Research Publications, Inc., 1973-75. Volume 3 includes subject category XIII, "Refugees."

McDonald's papers include a substantial amount of documentation on his service as High Commissioner 1933-35.

92. LEO BAECK INSTITUTE, INC. (LBI)
129 E. 73 St., New York, NY 10021

Founded in 1955 by the *Council of Jews from Germany in Jerusalem, London, and New York to collect material and sponsor research on the history of the Jewish community in Germany and other German-speaking countries. Concerned primarily with the period from the emancipation to the destruction and dispersion of the Jewish community of Central Europe. Named in honor of Leo Baeck (1873-1956), the last recognized representative and spokesman of German Jewry in Germany during the Nazi period.

The *American Federation of Jews from Central Europe assisted in establishing the Institute in New York, which houses a library and archives documenting the history of Central European Jewry.

For its publications, see Leo Baeck Institute, *List of Publications*, Jan. 1978.

Literature. Max Kreutzberger, "The Library and Archives of the Leo Baeck Institute in New York." *Jewish Book Annual* 29 (5732/1971-72): 47-54.
LBI News, 1960–date.
Lessing, *Oral History.*

Records. Leo Baeck Institute: records since 1955, documenting the activities of the New York branch and its sister institutes. For materials in the Leo Baeck Institute Archives and Library on the immigration and resettlement of refugees, see List of Repositories and Archival Holdings.

93. "LIFE IN GERMANY" CONTEST

In 1940, Professors Gordon W. Allport and Sidney B. Fay of Harvard Univ., with the cooperation of Dr. Edward Y. Hartshorne, organized a contest for the best essays on the theme "My Life in Germany Before and After January 30, 1933." The purpose of the contest was to obtain information for a study of totalitarian propaganda, and of the psychology and sociology of Nazi Germany. The competition resulted in 253 autobiographical essays submitted by refugees from Nazi Germany.

The entries were evaluated and resulted in several studies:

Gordon W. Allport, Jerome S. Bruner, and Ernest M. Jandorf, "Personality under Social Catastrophe: An Analysis of 90 Life-Histories of the Nazi Revolution." *Character and Personality* 10 (Sept. 1941): 1-22. Reprinted, without appendices describing the contest, in *Personality in Nature, Society and Culture*, Clyde Kluckhohn and Henry A. Murray, eds., with the collaboration of David M. Schneider. 2nd ed. revised and enlarged. New York: Knopf, 1953, pp. 436-455.

Jerome and Katherine Bruner, "The Impact of the Revolution." *Saturday Review of Literature* 24 (Dec. 27, 1941): 3-4, 20-21.

Edward Y. Hartshorne, "Reactions to the Nazi Threat: A Study of Propaganda and Culture Conflict." *Public Opinion Quarterly* 5 (Winter 1941): 625-639.

Evelyn Ruth Kravitz, "A Comparison of the Autobiography and the Interview." Unpublished psychology honors thesis, Harvard Univ., 1941. (Ten life histories were analyzed and the results compared with data obtained by an independent interviewer.)

Records. Harvard Univ., Houghton Library: records, consisting of the autobiographies (some on microfilm), correspondence, and the judging committee's analyses. Finding aid: index of entries in the Library's *Accession Records, 1957-58.*

94. LUTHERAN COUNCIL IN THE U.S.A., LUTHERAN IMMIGRATION AND REFUGEE SERVICE
360 Park Ave. S., New York, NY 10010

Traces its origin to the founding of the Lutheran Refugee Service in 1938, an agency of the Dept. of Welfare of the National Lutheran Council. Provided assistance for Lutheran refugees and cooperated with other committees aiding refugees. About 1800 refugees were resettled in America by 1946.

Literature. Hertz, "Joint and Concurrent."
Romanofsky, *Social Service Organizations*, pp. 396-399.

Records. Lutheran Council in the U.S.A., Archives of Cooperative Lutheranism: records, 1938-51, 1 ft, include case files of refugees, correspondence, and general material on refugees. The minutes of the American Section of the Executive Committee of the Lutheran World Convention, 1938-43, also contain material on the Lutheran Refugee Service.

95. "M" [MIGRATION] PROJECT, 1943-1945

A secret project undertaken by the anthropologist *Henry Field on the initiative of President *Franklin D. Roosevelt, to study the feasibility of resettling refugees around the world. Financed by unvouchered funds of the White House, "M" Project resulted in 666 studies. *Isaiah Bowman, geographer and president of Johns Hopkins Univ., cooperated in this venture.

"M" Project issued these publications: *Studies of Migration and Settlement.* Washington, 1943-45. Administrative series. A. nos. 1-18. Lecture series. L. nos. 1-47. Memorandum series. M. nos. 1-345. Report series. R. nos. 1-169. Translation series. T. nos. 1-122. Special. F. nos. 1-2.

Literature. Henry Field, *"M" Project for FDR, Studies on Migration and Settlement.* Ann Arbor, MI, 1962.

Records. According to Field, *op. cit.*, no notes were kept on orders of the President, and the first copy of each study was delivered to him.

Franklin D. Roosevelt Library, Harry S. Truman Library, Library of Congress, and New York Public Library, General Research and Humanities Div., have incomplete sets of the *Studies.*

96. MEMORIAL FOUNDATION FOR JEWISH CULTURE, INC.
15 E. 26 St., New York, NY 10010

Founded in 1964 by the *Conference on Jewish Material Claims Against Germany to encourage and assist Jewish scholarship and education as a living memorial to Nazi victims. Its basic endowment of $10 million was provided by the Conference from funds obtained from the Federal Republic of Germany in partial satisfaction of the claims for material damages suffered by the Jewish people during the Nazi regime. It was increased subsequently. Its allocations totaled about $1.25 million per annum. The original policy of limiting grants to Nazi victims was changed subsequently in favor of research and publication in the field of Jewish studies in general, the training of rabbis and communal workers, and cultural programs, primarily in Israel.

Records. Records, at the Foundation's office, are restricted.

97. MENORAH ASSOCIATION, INC.   *Defunct*

The Menorah movement was founded in 1906 by Henry Hurwitz to promote academic study of Jewish culture in U.S. universities. The Intercollegiate Menorah Association was founded in 1913. By the 1920s, membership had begun to decline. The group was reorganized in 1929 as the Menorah Association, but interest continued to fade through the next decade. Hurwitz guided the Association's activities throughout. In 1915 he founded the *Menorah Journal* which he edited until his death in 1961. The Association was dissolved in 1963.

The Association assisted refugees in the late 1930s and received over $3500 in grants to aid scholars, writers, and artists. When the U.S.A. entered World War II, the Association's activities on behalf of refugees ended.

Records. American Jewish Archives: records, 1911–63, 30.8 ft (ca. 30,800 items), the "Henry Hurwitz/Menorah Association Memorial Collection," consist mostly of Hurwitz's files, 1911–63, and some records of the Association, 1911–32. Correspondence regarding the refugee project is included in 8 folders; one additional folder consists of correspondence, 1939–42, with the *National Refugee Service. NUCMC* MS 65-1726. Finding aid: unpublished inventory (42 pp.).

98. MUSICIANS EMERGENCY FUND, INC.
35 W. 4 St., New York, NY 10003

Organized in 1931 primarily to aid American musicians, the Fund cooperated with placement agencies for refugees by evaluating proficiency levels of refugee musicians, and advising them about job openings.

Records. Musicians Emergency Fund: records consist of minutes of meetings of the board of directors. Restricted.

99. NATIONAL COMMITTEE FOR THE RESETTLEMENT OF FOREIGN
PHYSICIANS, INC. *Defunct*

Founded in 1939 by American physicians as an expansion of the Boston Committee on Medical Émigrés, formed in 1938. It evaluated the eligibility of individual émigré physicians to practice in the U.S.A., assisted physicians to prepare for examinations and for American licensing requirements, and furthered their resettlement in those parts of the U.S.A. where medical services were needed. The Committee operated under the aegis of the *National Coordinating Committee (NCC) in 1939 (under the name Central Committee for the Resettlement of Foreign Physicians); *National Refugee Service (NRS), 1939-46; *United Service for New Americans (USNA), 1946-49; and *New York Association for New Americans (NYANA), 1949-53. From 1953 to 1963, the Committee was an independent agency. After it was dissolved in 1964, its functions were carried on by the newly founded Medical Div. of the *American Council for Émigrés in the Professions (ACEP).

Dr. *Ernst P. Boas and Dr. *Lawrence S. Kubie were founders and officers of the Committee; Dr. *Alfred E. Cohn was a member of the general advisory council of the Committee.

Literature. David L. Edsall and Tracy J. Putnam, "The Émigré Physician in
America, 1941; A Report of the National Committee for Resettlement of
Foreign Physicians." *Journal of the American Medical Association* 117 (Nov.
29, 1941): 1881-1888.
Genizi, "American Non-Sectarian," pp. 185-193.
Report of the National Committee . . . 1938-1940.

Records. Univ. of Minnesota, Immigration History Research Center: case files,
1938-54, 112.5 ft.
ACEP Medical Div.: case files after 1954 and a minute book for the reorganized Committee, 1953-63.
YIVO Institute for Jewish Research: some administrative records, 1939-49, are found among the records of NCC, NRS, and USNA.
Administrative records, 1949-53, may be among the records of NYANA (information not verified).
The papers of Boas, Cohn, and Kubie include documentation about the Committee.

100. NATIONAL COORDINATING COMMITTEE FOR AID TO
REFUGEES AND EMIGRANTS COMING FROM GERMANY (NCC)
Defunct

On March 9, 1934, Professor *Joseph P. Chamberlain and *James G. McDonald, the *League of Nations High Commissioner for Refugees, convened a meeting of leaders of social agencies and concerned individuals in New York to establish a coordinating agency to aid refugees and immigrants coming from Germany. As a result of the meeting, the National Coordinating Committee was established on June 7, 1934 by the major Jewish and nonsectarian social agencies active in assisting refugees from Germany, with *Cecilia Razovsky as its executive secretary. Its original nonsectarian membership became nearly exclusively Jewish by the late 1930s. In 1938, it established the National Coordinating Committee Fund, Inc., an entirely Jewish organization, to develop national support for its work. The Greater New York Coordinating Committee was an affiliated agency which specialized in activities in New York.

The NCC lobbied with government agencies and Congressional committees on behalf of individual refugees or legislation aimed at liberalizing immigration provisions (for example, the *Wagner-*Rogers bill of 1939), relocated refugees in communities other than New York City, and engaged in various forms of relief and assistance. In 1939, in response to an evaluation by *Harry Greenstein issued in May 1939, the NCC merged with its Fund and the Greater New York Committee, and assistance to refugees was transferred to its successor, the *National Refugee Service.

Literature. Genizi, "American Non-Sectarian," pp. 169-182.

Harry Greenstein, *Reorganization Study of the NCC and Its Affiliated Agencies.* New York, 1939.

Romanofsky, *Social Service Organizations*, pp. 492-494.

Lyman C. White, *300,000 New Americans: The Epic of a Modern Immigrant-Aid Service.* New York: Harper, 1957.

Records. YIVO Institute for Jewish Research: records, 1932-40, 105 files on microfilm (6 reels), include minutes, reports, correspondence, and other documentation. Many records of the NCC were taken over by the National Refugee Service and are found among that agency's records, as well as among those of its successor, the *United Service for New Americans, at YIVO. Finding aid: unpublished inventory (5 pp.).

101. NATIONAL COUNCIL OF JEWISH WOMEN, INC. (NCJW)
Headquarters: 15 E. 26 St., New York, NY 10010
Washington Office: 1346 Connecticut Ave., N.W., Washington, DC 20036

Founded in 1893 to offer community services and educational and social action programs principally for children, youth, the aged, and the poor. Upon request of the U.S. government began assisting unattached immigrant women, and single girls traveling alone, at the Port of New York in 1903. This activity developed into the Dept. of Immigrant Aid, subsequently known as the Committee on Service to Foreign Born (SFB).

With the arrival of refugees from Nazi Germany, SFB advised the local sections of NCJW on a variety of immigration services to be provided in local communities by the sections, or in cooperation with other agencies. NCJW's Triennial Conventions of 1937 (Pittsburgh), 1940 (New York), and 1943 (Chicago) devoted sessions to work with the foreign born, and an All-Day Institute on Immigration was held in Chicago on April 26, 1939. *Fanny Brin was president 1932-38, and *Cecilia Razovsky, secretary of the Dept. of Immigrant Aid, became associate director of NCJW in 1932. In 1946, the national SFB merged with the *National Refugee Service to form the *United Service for New Americans. Local sections continued to provide assistance to newly arrived immigrants in communities across the U.S.A.

The Washington office, established in 1944, is concerned with legislative activities and relations with U.S. government agencies and other organizations. Prior to 1944, members of the *District of Columbia Section, NCJW, often testified before Congressional committees on behalf of the national office of NCJW in New York.

Literature. Monroe Campbell and William Wirtz, *The First Fifty Years, A History of the National Council of Jewish Women, 1893-1943.* New York, 1943.

Bernice Graziani, *Where There's a Woman: 75 Years of History as Lived by the National Council of Jewish Women.* New York: McCall, 1967.

NCJW, *Proceedings—Triennial Convention.* 1937, 1940, 1943.

Records. Records (incomplete), 1893–date, at the organization's New York office, include some materials relating to SFB activities, minutes of meetings of governing bodies and committees, and other administrative records.

Library of Congress, Manuscript Div.: records of the Washington office, 1944–date, ca. 118,000 items.

Records of local sections are with each section's officers and/or office. Some local records have been placed in archival repositories. For a list of the sections discussed in this publication, see the Index.

102. NATIONAL COUNCIL OF THE CHURCHES OF CHRIST IN THE U.S.A.
475 Riverside Dr., New York, NY 10027

Formed in 1950 by the merger of 12 organizations, including the Federal Council of the Churches of Christ in America, to coordinate the Protestant denominations in the U.S.A.

The Federal Council, founded in 1908 and representing 24 Protestant denominations, "cultivated through the churches an interest in refugees and an understanding of their problems, and enlisted active cooperation of local congregations in attempting to resettle them."

The *American Christian Committee for Refugees (ACCR, earlier known as the American Committee for Christian German Refugees and as the American Committee for Christian Refugees) cooperated with the Federal Council without formal affiliation. Samuel McCrea Cavert, general secretary of the Federal Council, was a member of the *U.S. President's Advisory Committee on Political Refugees.

Records. Presbyterian Historical Society: records of the Federal Council, 1908–50, constituting a part of the records of the National Council, include materials regarding the activities of the ACCR and other Christian and nonsectarian agencies on behalf of refugees.

103. NATIONAL FEDERATION OF SETTLEMENTS AND NEIGHBORHOOD CENTERS, INC.
232 Madison Ave., New York, NY 10016

Social service agency, founded in 1911, to improve the services offered by settlement houses in the U.S.A.

Literature. Romanofsky, *Social Service Organizations*, pp. 533-540.

Records. Univ. of Minnesota Libraries, Social Welfare History Archives Center: records, 1891-1968, 75 ft and 6 microfilm reels, include material on refugee resettlement and alien legislation, 1938-43, in folders 6 (Alien Legislation Committee, 1939-42), 67 (*Good Neighbor Committee, New York, 1938-43), and 198 (Work for Refugees Committee, 1938-40). Finding aid: detailed inventory in *Descriptive Inventories of Collections in the Social Welfare History Archives Center.* Westport, CT: Greenwood Press, pp. 403-480.

Other materials and recent files are at the Federation's office.

104. NATIONAL JEWISH WELFARE BOARD, INC. (JWB)
15 E. 26 St., New York, NY 10010

National association of Jewish community centers and YM-YWHAs, founded in 1917, JWB also provides religious and social services to Jews in the U.S. armed services.

Cooperated with organizations aiding refugees in offering services to refugees through the Div. (Committee) for Social and Cultural Adjustment of Jewish Refugees, organized in 1938. Conducted a survey in 1938-39 among Jewish community centers on their activities for refugee adjustment. In New York City, the Committee on Jewish Activities of the Metropolitan Section of JWB developed programs for refugee adjustment. JWB assisted at the *U.S. Emergency Refugee Shelter at Ft. Ontario, NY 1944-46.

In 1945, JWB's Bureau of War Records conducted a study of refugees in the armed forces in cooperation with the *National Refugee Service. Of 3593 refugees surveyed, 10% had entered the service as compared to 8.9% for the total population. *Samuel C. Kohs directed the Bureau 1942-47.

Literature. *Adjustment of Recent Jewish Immigrants Through the Jewish Center.* New York: Jewish Welfare Board, May 1939 and 1940.
Isidor Kaufman, *American Jews in World War II.* New York: Dial Press, 1947, pp. 23-24.
Samuel C. Kohs, "Jewish War Records of World War 2 [sic]." *American Jewish Year Book* 47 (1945-46): 153-172, esp. p. 167.
Romanofsky, *Social Service Organizations*, pp. 562-568.

Records. JWB Archives: records include one folder on social and cultural activities for Jewish refugees, 1938-42 (box 1076), and one folder on the Emergency Refugee Shelter, 1944-46 (box 869).

American Jewish Historical Society: records of the JWB Bureau of War Records, 1942-47, 672 boxes, include correspondence with the National Refugee Service, and 4 ft of materials relating to the study of refugees in the armed forces. Finding aid: unpublished inventory.

105. NATIONAL REFUGEE SERVICE, INC. (NRS)   *Defunct*

Formed in June 1939 in New York as the successor to the *National Coordinating Committee (NCC) to coordinate the resettlement of newcomers in every part of the U.S.A. where opportunities were favorable for economic and social adjustment. This resettlement was carried out in cooperation with other national organizations (Jewish, Christian, and nonsectarian), and more than 750 local committees which absorbed refugees on a prepledged quota basis.

Supported by the *United Jewish Appeal, NRS developed a broad program of service to refugees aided by a substantial staff. These services included case work, financial aid and loans, English and citizenship training, service to children including the placement of refugee children in foster homes, placement services, aid to physicians and other professionals, family services, summer camps, care for the aged, and a wide variety of related services. NRS also was consulted by the U.S. government when President *Harry S. Truman's directive on displaced persons in Europe was being prepared in 1945.

The *National Committee for the Resettlement of Foreign Physicians, National Committee on Refugee Jewish Ministers (founded 1938), and National Committee for Refugee Musicians (founded 1938, *Mark Brunswick, chairman) served as special committees of NRS. *European Jewish Children's Aid, *Emergency Committee in Aid of Displaced Foreign Scholars, *Emergency Committee in Aid of Displaced Foreign Medical Scientists, Committee for Displaced Foreign Social Workers (founded 1937), and *National Council of Jewish Women, New York and Brooklyn Sections received funds from NRS.

The president of NRS at its inception was William Rosenwald (*Rosenwald Family Association). *Joseph P. Chamberlain was its chairman. *Cecilia Razovsky was assistant to the executive director, William Haber. In 1946, NRS merged with the National Service to Foreign Born of National Council of Jewish Women to form the *United Service for New Americans.

Literature. Genizi, "American Non-Sectarian," pp. 164–220.
Romanofsky, *Social Service Organizations*, pp. 592–595.
Lyman C. White, *300,000 New Americans: The Epic of a Modern Immigrant-Aid Service*. New York: Harper, 1957.

Records. YIVO Institute for Jewish Research: records, 1921–47, 1407 files on microfilm (69 reels—originals destroyed), constitute a major archival source about aid to refugees. The collection consists of material on many aspects of immigration and resettlement, including documentation concerning the special committees and funded agencies noted above. Some records of NRS and NCC, including individual case files, are found among the records of the United Service for New Americans at YIVO. Finding aid: unpublished inventory (67 pp.).

American Jewish Historical Society: records, 1935–46, 7 boxes, consist of correspondence and published materials relating to NRS and NCC. *NUCMC* MS 72-1382.

106. NATIONAL WAR FUND, INC.   *Defunct*

Organized in New York on December 15, 1942, at the request of the *U.S. President's War Relief Control Board, by representatives of the national community chest body, Community Chests and Councils, Inc., to coordinate the raising of funds for social services and overseas relief. Thirty-one voluntary agencies received support from the Fund, including *Refugee Relief Trustees (*American Christian Committee for Refugees, *International Rescue and Relief Committee, and *Unitarian Service Committee), *United States Committee for the Care of European Children, and World Student Service Fund (*U.S. Committee of International Student Service). The National War Fund ceased to operate in 1947 and was formally dissolved in 1957.

The president of the Fund, Winthrop W. Aldrich, of New York, also headed the Allied Relief Fund and the British War Relief Society during World War II.

Literature. Arthur Menzies Johnson, *Winthrop W. Aldrich: Lawyer, Banker, Diplomat.* Boston: Harvard Univ. Grad. School of Business Administration, 1968. Especially chap. X, "The War Relief Years, 1939-1946," pp. 253-278.
Harold J. Seymour, *Design for Giving: The Story of the National War Fund, Inc., 1943-1947.* New York: Harper, 1947.

Records. Harvard Univ., Graduate School of Business Administration, Baker Library, Manuscripts and Archives Dept.: Aldrich's papers 1918-62, 126 ft, include 2 ft of material pertaining to the Fund, 1942-48. Finding aid: unpublished inventory (22 pp.).

The records of the Fund were not kept in one location, and other materials may still be deposited elsewhere.

107. NEW SCHOOL FOR SOCIAL RESEARCH, GRADUATE FACULTY OF POLITICAL AND SOCIAL SCIENCE
65 Fifth Ave., New York, NY 10003

The Graduate Faculty, founded in 1933 as the University in Exile by *Alvin Johnson, president of New School (founded in 1919), was established to resettle displaced German scholars, and to transplant German-style graduate teaching to the U.S.A. In addition, from 1933 to 1945, Johnson and Else Staudinger sought to find positions for refugees in other American institutions, and to assist refugees to obtain visas under the nonquota provisions of the U.S. Immigration Act of 1924. In 1945, their work was institutionalized by the establishment of the American Committee for Refugee Scholars, Writers and Artists, later renamed *American Council for Émigrés in the Professions (ACEP). In 1940, the New School organized the École Libre des Hautes Études to aid displaced French and Belgian scholars.

Literature. Alvin Johnson, *Pioneer's Progress: An Autobiography.* New York: Viking Press, 1952.
Wetzel, "American Rescue," pp. 182-236.

Records. New School for Social Research, Office of the Dean of the Graduate Faculty: records of the University in Exile, 1933-45, 10 ft, located in Professor Saul Padover's office at 65 Fifth Ave. in 1978, consist of biographical files of displaced or dismissed European scholars, many of whom joined the New School or other U.S. colleges and universities. Include correspondence to and from Johnson and others interested in assisting and placing refugees. A small number of the documents originally included in this collection were removed and deposited with the Johnson papers at Yale Univ. Library. Photocopies of the removed documents have been retained in the collection at the New School.

108. NEW YORK FOUNDATION, INC.
4 W. 58 St., New York, NY 10019

Philanthropic foundation established in 1909 by prominent American Jews to deal with social problems in New York City. From 1930 until his death in 1937, *Felix M. Warburg was president of the Foundation.

Granted more than one million dollars to various agencies in aid of refugees from Nazi Germany, including *National Coordinating Committee and *National Refugee Service $373,500, *Emergency Committee in Aid of Displaced Foreign Scholars $317,000, *Emergency Committee in Aid of Displaced Foreign Medical Scientists $96,600, *American Friends Service Committee $97,000, International Migration Service (*Travelers Aid-International Social Service of America) $52,500, and *American Christian Committee for Refugees $32,500.

Literature. New York Foundation, *Forty Year Report, 1909-1940.* New York, n.d.
Wetzel, "American Rescue," pp. 334-337.

Records. New York Foundation: records, 1909-date, include files on grants given by the Foundation, arranged by name of recipient organization.

109. NON-SECTARIAN ANTI-NAZI LEAGUE TO CHAMPION HUMAN RIGHTS *Defunct*

Founded in 1933 as the American League for the Defense of Jewish Rights. The above name was adopted later that year. Led by Samuel Untermyer, a prominent Jewish lawyer, the League was organized to promote the boycott directed against Nazi Germany. It also analyzed the relationship of Nazi policies to the emigration problem of Jews in Germany, and was generally concerned with fighting anti-Semitism. After World War II, the League developed a broad interest in civil rights and discrimination matters. With the death of its last chairman, James H. Sheldon, in 1976, the League ceased its activities.

Literature. Moshe Gottlieb, "The Anti-Nazi Boycott Movement in the American Jewish Community 1933-41." Unpublished Ph.D. dissertation, Brandeis Univ., 1967.
Hanns G. Reissner, "The American Anti-Nazi Boycott." In *Jubilee Volume Dedicated to Curt C. Silberman*, Herbert A. Strauss and Hanns G. Reissner, eds. New York: American Federation of Jews from Central Europe, 1969, pp. 60-79.

Records. Columbia Univ., Rare Book and Manuscript Library: records, consisting of correspondence and printed and other materials, include documentation concerning the boycott and its relation to refugee problems. The large collection was being processed in 1978.

Columbia Univ., School of International Affairs, Herbert H. Lehman Papers: published materials collected by the League, including anti-Semitic, hate, and civil rights literature.

American Jewish Archives: clippings and correspondence concerning the work of the League in the anti-Nazi economic boycott, 1933-41, 2.5 ft.

110. THE OBERLAENDER TRUST   *Defunct*

Charitable foundation established in 1931 in Pennsylvania by Gustav Oberlaender. Administered by The Carl Schurz Memorial Foundation, Philadelphia, until the Trust was dissolved in 1953.

Among the Trust's activities was a program established in 1936 to aid refugee scholars, similar to the program of the *Emergency Committee in Aid of Displaced Foreign Scholars. Approximately 330 persons were helped by the Trust. In September 1940, the Trust, assisted by a grant from *The Rockefeller Foundation, began a study of refugees. A follow-up study was conducted in 1947; its results were published by Donald P. Kent as *The Refugee Intellectual: The Americanization of the Immigrants of 1933-1941*, New York: Columbia Univ. Press, 1953.

Literature.   Carl Schurz Memorial Foundation, *Annual Reports.*
Hanns Gramm, *The Oberlaender Trust, 1931-1953.* Philadelphia: The Carl Schurz Memorial Foundation, 1956.

Records.   YIVO Institute for Jewish Research: records concerning refugees, ca. 1935-47, 14 boxes (also on microfilm, 6 reels), consist of ca. 2000 data forms from the 1940 study, with an alphabetical list of the refugees participating in the study; correspondence of the Trust, ca. 1935-47, concerning refugees and organizations, aiding refugees, and a small amount of material concerning the 1947 follow-up study. Finding aid: unpublished inventory (6 pp.).

The 1947 follow-up questionnaires have not been located and are presumed destroyed.

National Carl Schurz Association (successor, since 1962, to The Carl Schurz Memorial Foundation): official records of the Trust, 1931-53, include minute books and other documents, some of which concern programs in aid of refugees.

111. ORGANIZATION OF THE JEWS FROM WÜRTTEMBERG (GEMEINSCHAFT DER WÜRTTEMBERGISCHEN JUDEN)
c/o Walter Strauss (chairman), 41 E. 42 St., New York, NY 10017

Founded in 1939 by Jewish immigrants from the South German state of Württemberg to assist Jewish Nazi victims overseas to prepare for their immigration to the U.S.A. After the war, the Organization raised funds for survivors in Germany. Engaged in social and cultural activities, which declined after 1949.

Literature.   Lessing, *Oral History.*

Records.   Records, consisting of correspondence and printed materials, are with the chairman.

112. PEC ISRAEL ECONOMIC CORPORATION
511 Fifth Ave., New York, NY 10017

Founded in 1926 under the name Palestine Economic Corp. (PEC) by American non-Zionists to provide financial aid to the Jewish settlement in Palestine in the form of investments in productive enterprises. Through subsidiaries in Palestine, PEC helped individuals of limited means, particularly immigrants, to secure a financial foothold. PEC also organized companies with the goal of developing basic industries and natural resources in Palestine. PEC's present name was adopted ca. 1963.

One of PEC's subsidiaries, the Central Bank of Cooperative Institutions in Palestine Ltd., aided in establishing hundreds of cooperative societies, some of which were founded by German-Jewish refugees during the 1930s.

Literature. *Annual Reports*, since 1933, include references to immigrants from Germany.

Records. New York Public Library, Manuscripts and Archives Div.: records, 1926-41, 22 cartons, include material on aid to German-Jewish refugees and refugee-founded cooperatives. Finding aid: unpublished inventory.

Records since 1941 are at the Corporation's office.

113. P.E.N. AMERICAN CENTER
156 Fifth Ave., New York, NY 10010

An association of poets, playwrights, editors, essayists, and novelists founded in 1922 as the American equivalent of the London P.E.N. Club, organized in 1921.

Formed a Foreign Writers' Committee to assist refugee literary figures. *Dorothy Thompson took an active part in this work.

Literature. Marchette Chute, *P.E.N. American Center: A History of the First Fifty Years*. New York, 1972, pp. 14-46.

Records. P.E.N. American Center: records, 1922-date, include materials on aid to refugees and refugee writers in the U.S.A., primarily in the "war period" file drawer.

114. [PASSENGER LISTS]

Records. Genealogical Society of Utah: microfilm copies of lists of passengers departing from Hamburg, Germany, through Dec. 1934. The lists include refugees leaving Nazi Germany, 1933-34. The copies for 1933 and 1934 each occupy 7 reels and one index reel. Original records are at the Staatsarchiv, Hamburg.

Lists for departures from Hamburg after 1934 and passenger lists for Bremerhaven, Germany, were destroyed during World War II.

Records of passengers arriving in the U.S.A. are described with the records of the *U.S. Immigration and Naturalization Service.

115. PHI EPSILON PI FRATERNITY   *Defunct*

A Greek-letter organization of college students with predominantly Jewish membership, founded in 1904 and absorbed by Zeta Beta Tau Fraternity in 1970.

Formed a Refugee Committee to aid refugee students, and to cooperate with the refugee committees of other fraternities.

Records. American Jewish Historical Society: records, 1912-69, 26 ft, include material on the Refugee Committee, on aid to refugee students by other fraternities, and on anti-Semitism and the Holocaust. *NUCMC* MS 72-1383.

116. [PUBLIC OPINION POLLS]

In 1938-39, *Fortune* magazine and the American Institute of Public Opinion (AIPO) conducted polls to assess American attitudes toward refugees from Central Europe. In May 1938, *Fortune* asked, "What is your attitude toward allowing German, Austrian, and other political refugees to come into the United States?" In November 1938, AIPO asked, "Should we allow a larger number of Jewish exiles from Germany to come to the United States to live?" and "Should our government contribute money to help Jewish and Catholic exiles from Germany settle in lands like Africa and South America?" In January 1939, *Fortune* asked, "If you were a member of the incoming Congress, would you vote yes or no on a bill to . . . open the doors of the U.S. to a larger number of European refugees than now admitted under our immigration quotas?" and AIPO asked, "Do you favor a plan that the government permit 10,000 refugee children from Germany to be brought into this country and taken care of in American homes?"

AIPO also conducted polls in July 1940 concerning the admission of English women and children to the U.S.A., and other polls were conducted from 1944 to 1948 regarding the admission of displaced persons to the U.S.A.

Literature. Hadley Cantril, ed., *Public Opinion, 1935-1946.* Princeton: Princeton Univ. Press, 1951.

Records. Roper Public Opinion Research Center: original data from these and other surveys.

117. REFUGEE ECONOMIC CORPORATION   *Defunct*

Founded in 1934 in New York as the Refugee Rehabilitation Committee to give economic aid to émigrés from Germany and other countries, to assist in the financing and management of banking, credit, industrial, mercantile, agricultural, or utility enterprises, and to promote colonization and rural settlements by émigrés. The Refugee Assistance Fund, Inc. (Émigré Charitable Fund, Inc. 1934-47), the philanthropic arm of the Corporation, gave grants in 1938 and 1941 to the Walter Hines Page School of International Relations, Johns Hopkins Univ., for research on the resettlement of refugees directed by *Isaiah Bowman. In 1938-39, a grant was given to the Alvin Corp. (*Alvin Johnson, president) for establishing a farm settlement for refugees in North Carolina. Sponsored survey commissions to explore resettlement possibilities in the Philippine Islands, British Guiana, and the Dominican Republic. *Felix M. Warburg was president 1934-37; Charles J. Liebman was president 1937-50. The Corporation and its philanthropic affiliate were liquidated in 1950 and the assets transferred to the *American Jewish Joint Distribution Committee (JDC).

Literature. Refugee Economic Corp., *Annual Reports*, 1936-46.

Records. The JDC has surviving records, 1934-50.

118. REFUGEE RELIEF TRUSTEES, INC. *Defunct*

Founded in 1943 in New York by the American Committee for Christian Refugees (*American Christian Committee for Refugees), *Unitarian Service Committee, and International Rescue and Relief Committee (*International Rescue Committee) as a joint fund-raising agency of those organizations. Co-operated with Jewish social agencies assisting refugees. Was one of 17 major recipients of support from the *National War Fund. Supported the Special Labor Aid Project to help elderly refugee labor leaders. *James G. McDonald was chairman 1945-46. In general, the officers were affiliated with one of the three constituent agencies. Ceased its activities in late 1946.

Records. Records have not been located and are presumed lost. Records of the Unitarian Service Committee and records of the *National Refugee Service may contain documentation about Refugee Relief Trustees, Inc. Records of the American Christian Committee have been destroyed and early records of the International Rescue Committee are missing. Surviving records of the National War Fund are among the papers of its president, Winthrop W. Aldrich.

119. RESEARCH FOUNDATION FOR JEWISH IMMIGRATION, INC.
570 Seventh Ave., New York, NY 10018

Incorporated in 1971 by leading personalities of the *American Federation of Jews from Central Europe upon the initiative of its executive vice-president, Herbert A. Strauss. The goal of the Research Foundation is to engage in all phases of scholarly research, documentation, and writing concerning the history of Jewish immigrants from Central Europe since 1933, especially their resettlement and acculturation, and to stimulate scholarly interest in the national or comparative aspects of this history. The Foundation cooperates with the immigration history project sponsored by the *Council of Jews from Germany (London-Jerusalem-New York) and has conducted an interview project (oral history) among Jewish immigrants from Nazi Germany in the U.S.A.

Projects and publications in progress include the series *Jewish Immigrants of the Nazi Period in the U.S.A.* (New York: K. G. Saur, 1979-81): Volume I: *Archival Resources*; Volume II: *Annotated Bibliography of Books and Articles*; Volume III: *Guide to the Oral History Collection of the Research Foundation for Jewish Immigration*; Volumes IV and V: source histories of the emigration and immigration of Jews from Nazi Germany and Austria; Volume VI: a social and intellectual history of the Jewish immigrant from Nazi Germany in the U.S.A.

The Foundation has cooperated since 1972 with the Institut für Zeitgeschichte, Munich, Federal Republic of Germany, in assembling an archives of biographical data on about 25,000 émigrés and exiles from Central Europe, consisting of printed sources, archival material, questionnaire replies, interview data, and other material assembled in or about the major countries of resettlement and continental Europe, including returnees to countries of origin. The biographical archives includes émigrés independent of religion, national origin, age, sex, or country of settlement or return. The three-volume *International Biographical Dictionary of Central European Émigrés 1933-1945*, which documents the life histories of about 8000 émigrés, is being published in 1979-81 by K. G. Saur, Munich. Funding for this project, in addition to assistance provided by the Research Foundation for Jewish Immigration and the Institut für Zeitgeschichte, was obtained from the Deutsche Forschungsgemeinschaft, Bad Godesberg, Federal Republic of Germany, the PSC–CUNY Research Foundation, New York, NY, and the National Endowment for the Humanities, Washington, DC.

Records.   Records of the Foundation, of its research projects, and of the International Biographical Archives and Dictionary of Central European Émigrés, are at the Foundation's office. An archival collection, now being organized, includes miscellaneous materials pertaining to the immigration and resettlement of Jewish immigrants from Nazi Germany. The biographical data file is maintained in duplicate at the Institut für Zeitgeschichte, Munich. For the oral history collection, see *Research Foundation for Jewish Immigration, Oral History Collection. Access to the collections is by permission of the Foundation.

120. THE ROCKEFELLER FOUNDATION, INC.
1133 Avenue of the Americas, New York, NY 10036

Philanthropic foundation established in 1913 to promote public health and further the natural and social sciences throughout the world. To this end, it has established research programs of its own and has financed the research programs of other agencies and individual scholars through grants and fellowships.

Between 1933 and 1945, the Foundation spent nearly $1.5 million to aid displaced scholars. It assisted 303 qualified refugees to find new positions in the U.S.A., Europe, and Latin America, and granted financial support to the *Emergency Committee in Aid of Displaced Foreign Scholars, University in Exile (*New School for Social Research, Graduate Faculty of Political and Social Science), *The Oberlaender Trust, Notgemeinschaft deutscher Wissenschaftler im Ausland, and other agencies. The Foundation's European office, which was moved from Paris to Lisbon in 1940-41, helped refugees to secure visas and make travel arrangements.

Literature.   Raymond B. Fosdick, *The Chronicle of a Generation: An Autobiography.* New York: Harper, 1958.
——, *The Story of the Rockefeller Foundation.* New York: Harper, 1952.

Rockefeller Foundation, *Annual Reports*, 1933-1945.
Wetzel, "American Rescue," pp. 319-327.

Records. Rockefeller Archive Center: records, 1913-75, 1655 ft. Materials relating to displaced scholars, 1933-45, 6 ft, comprise the following:

- Projects Files—Series 200: Emergency Committee in Aid of Displaced Foreign Scholars, 1940-41, 9 folders; Oberlaender Trust, deposed scholars study, 1939-41, one folder; Refugee Scholars, 1935-41, ca. 2 ft. Series 200S: Graduate Faculty of Political and Social Science (New School), 1933-41, 8 folders. Series 400S: Royal Institute of International Affairs (United Kingdom), refugee problem, 1936-40, 4 folders. Series 717: German Exiles, special research aid, 1933-40, 10 folders; Notgemeinschaft der deutschen Wissenschaft (Forschungsgemeinschaft), 1936-38, 4 folders.
- General Correspondence—Series 200: Refugee Scholars, 1939-41, 51 folders. Series 401: Refugee Scholars (England), 1940-41, 2 folders. Series 717: German Exiles, 1933-40, 29 folders.

Finding aid: unpublished inventory.

121. ROSENWALD FAMILY ASSOCIATION   *Defunct*

Charitable trust established under the will of Julius Rosenwald (1862-1932), merchant, industrialist, and founder of Sears, Roebuck and Co. The Association supported intellectuals and artists, museums, libraries, scholarly publications, and related activities.

Provided financial support for agencies aiding refugees, including: *Emergency Committee in Aid of Displaced Foreign Scholars $159,000, *American Jewish Joint Distribution Committee (JDC) $54,000, Graduate Faculty of Political and Social Science, *New School for Social Research $110,000, *American Friends Service Committee $80,000, Rosenwald Fellowship Program (through the Emergency Committee) $50,000, *Emergency Committee in Aid of Displaced Foreign Medical Scientists $70,000, and *United Jewish Appeal for Refugees and Overseas Needs (UJA) $108,000. The Association ended its activities in 1943 and distributed its assets among Rosenwald's five children, who made the following contributions:

- William Rosenwald: president, Rosenwald Family Association; vice-chairman, *National Coordinating Committee 1936-39; president, *National Refugee Service 1939-44; national chairman, UJA 1942-63.
- Lessing J. Rosenwald: member of management council, Coordinating Foundation (*Intergovernmental Committee on Refugees); in 1950, the Lessing J. Rosenwald Foundation gave $100,000 to the Resettlement Campaign for Exiled Professionals, organized by the *International Rescue Committee.
- Marion Rosenwald (Mrs. Max Ascoli): gave $101,000 to the New School for Social Research.
- Adele Rosenwald (Mrs. David M. Levy): gave $105,000 to the New School for Social Research.
- Edith Rosenwald (Mrs. Edgar B. Stern): through the Edgar Stern Family Fund, provided financial support to the Emergency Committee in Aid of Displaced Foreign Scholars.

Literature. Wetzel, "American Rescue," pp. 164-172, 210-213, 339-340.

Records. Records, 1931-40s, with the Starwood Corp. (100 Park Ave., New York, NY 10017), include materials on the Association's support of agencies aiding refugees, general documentation on aid to refugees, and files concerning support to German relatives of the Rosenwald family, some of whom were helped to emigrate to the U.S.A.

122. S.S. *ST. LOUIS*, May-June, 1939

The S.S. *St. Louis*, a passenger ship owned by the Hamburg-America Line, left Germany for Havana, Cuba, on May 13, 1939, with 930 Jewish immigrants. By the time the ship reached Cuba, the visas of all but 22 persons aboard had been declared i..valid, and the refugees were not permitted to land. Negotiations for the validation of their visas in exchange for ransom money, conducted by the *American Jewish Joint Distribution Committee (JDC), were unsuccessful, and the vessel headed back to Europe on June 6, 1939. The passengers were resettled in Holland, Great Britain, Belgium, and France through the efforts of the JDC, which agreed to support the refugees in these countries.

Literature. Gordon Thomas and Max Morgan Witts, *Voyage of the Damned.* New York: Stein & Day, 1974.

Records. For a listing of archival materials concerning the *St. Louis*, see Thomas and Witts, *op. cit.*, bibliography. Some of these materials are in the possession of the authors.

Documents gathered by Josef Joseph, who was head of the passenger committee aboard the *St. Louis*, are with Mrs. Lilli Kamin, New Rochelle, NY.

123. SELFHELP COMMUNITY SERVICES, INC.
   44 E. 23 St., New York, NY 10010

Founded by German intellectual and professional immigrants in 1936 as Selfhelp of German Émigrés, and incorporated in 1937. In 1939, the name was changed to Selfhelp of Émigrés from Central Europe, Inc. Present name was adopted in 1969. Had branches in England, France, Switzerland, and Shanghai before 1939, and sister agencies in *Chicago and *San Francisco.

This nonsectarian agency was established to assist refugees in Europe, care for aged refugees in the U.S.A., find jobs, and place refugees or their children in resort camps. Its welfare and homemaker services were expanded in 1938-39 to respond to increasing demands.

Originally staffed exclusively by volunteers or administrative personnel, Selfhelp became a professional social work agency in the 1950s and provided a wide range of services, mainly care for the aged, building two apartment complexes (Kissena I and Kissena II in Flushing, Queens, New York), offering homemaker services, and developing outreach programs in upper Manhattan and Queens.

In the late 1960s, Selfhelp expanded its program for the aged and extended its services to the general community in New York, while maintaining its services to Nazi victims. Receives financial support from *United Help and participates in the Nehemiah Robinson Memorial Scholarship Fund (for students) of United Help.

Literature. Michael N. Dobkowski, "The Social Service System of German-Jewish Immigrants from Central Europe" (ms. title). To be published by Michael N. Dobkowski and Herbert A. Strauss, *A Social and Intellectual History of the German-Jewish Immigrant of the Nazi Period in the U.S.A.* (in preparation as Volume VI of this series).

Lessing, *Oral History.*

Selfhelp, *Annual Reports,* 1963-date.

Selfhelp–20 Years of Service, 1956.

Herbert A. Strauss, "The Immigration and Acculturation of the German Jew in the United States of America." *Leo Baeck Institute Year Book,* XVI (1971): 63-94.

Records. Selfhelp office: records include minutes since 1937, case files, financial statements, correspondence, and committee reports. Restricted.

124. [SHANGHAI REFUGEE COMMUNITY]

Shanghai, China, was a major intermediate settlement for Jewish refugees from Germany, Austria, and other countries between 1937 and 1945. A large number of these refugees resettled in the U.S.A. following the armistice with Japan in 1945. The *Association of Former Central European Refugees from Shanghai was founded in New York by such immigrants.

Literature. David Kranzler, *Japanese, Nazis & Jews: The Jewish Refugee Community of Shanghai 1938-1945.* New York: Yeshiva Univ. Press, 1976.

Records. YIVO Institute for Jewish Research: collection of documents concerning the Shanghai refugee community, most of which were gathered in connection with an exhibition mounted at YIVO in 1948 on "Jewish Life in Shanghai." Finding aids: unpublished catalog; Z. Szajkowski, comp., *Catalogue of the Exhibition Jewish Life in Shanghai.* New York, 1948.

David H. Kranzler, 729 Avenue N, Brooklyn, NY 11230: collection of over 10,000 documents on the Jewish refugee community of Shanghai consists primarily of photocopies or microfilm reproductions of materials in institutions and private hands, and some original documents. Taped oral history interviews conducted by Kranzler with former residents of the Shanghai "ghetto" constitute "The Jewish Community in China" project of the Hebrew Univ. of Jerusalem, Institute of Contemporary Jewry, Oral History Div., described separately in this publication under Oral History Collections.

125. SIGMA ALPHA MU FRATERNITY (National Office)
7 E. 21 St., Indianapolis, IN 46202

A Greek-letter organization of college students with predominantly Jewish membership, founded in 1909.

Provided assistance to refugee students during the late 1930s through 12 of its more than 36 chapters.

Records. Sigma Alpha Mu: records include correspondence on the background of, and assistance to, refugee students.

126. SOCIETY FOR THE HISTORY OF CZECHOSLOVAK JEWS, INC.

c/o Lewis Weiner (president), 87-08 Santiago St., Holliswood, NY 11423

Founded in 1961 by Jewish immigrants from Czechoslovakia who were members of the *Joseph Popper Lodge and *Joseph Popper Chapter of *B'nai B'rith in New York. Successor to the Society for the History of the Jews in the Czechoslovak Republic, which existed from 1928 to 1939 in Czechoslovakia. Sponsors the publication of *The Jews of Czechoslovakia, Historic Studies and Surveys:* vol. I, 1968; vol. II, 1971; vol. III to be published in 1979.

Records. Records are with the Society's officers and members.

127. SURVEY ASSOCIATES, INC. *Defunct*

Nonprofit publishing organization founded in 1912 to issue *The Survey*, after 1933 *The Survey Graphic*, a leading journal of social service and reform, edited by Paul Underwood Kellogg until it ceased publication in 1952. Chairmen of the board of directors were *Julian W. Mack 1938-43, and *Joseph P. Chamberlain 1943-52.

Survey Graphic carried frequent articles on refugees and on the activities of the agencies which served them. In February 1939, a special issue, "Calling America: The Challenge to Democracy Reaches Over Here," focused on the refugee problem by carrying articles on Jews and other persecuted groups in Europe, and by discussing the mounting harassment of Catholics, Protestants, trade unionists, and liberals in Europe and other parts of the world.

Literature. Clarke A. Chambers, *Paul U. Kellogg and The Survey: Voices for Social Welfare and Social Justice.* Minneapolis: Univ. of Minnesota Press, 1971.

Romanofsky, *Social Service Organizations*, pp. 677-684.

Records. Univ. of Minnesota Libraries, Social Welfare History Archives Center: records, 1891-1952, 125 ft, include correspondence regarding refugees in folders 382 (Jacob Billikopf of the *National Coordinating Committee), 424-425 (Chamberlain), 504 (John L. Elliott of the *Society for Ethical Culture in the City of New York), 719 (*James G. McDonald, *League of Nations High Commissioner for Refugees), 846 (Raymond Gram Swing, radio commentator and editor of the special "Calling America" issue), 895 (Rabbi *Stephen S. Wise), and 580 (Mary W. Glenn, prominent social worker). Kellogg's papers, 1891-1952, 17 ft, also in this repository, include editorial correspondence, 1935, on McDonald's resignation as High Commissioner (folder 142). *NUCMC* MS

70-1652. Finding aids: detailed inventories in *Descriptive Inventories of Collections in the Social Welfare History Archives Center.* Westport, CT: Greenwood Press, 1970, pp. 111-166, 533-614.

128. SYNAGOGUE COUNCIL OF AMERICA, INC.
432 Park Ave. S., New York, NY 10016

Central coordinating agency and representation of Orthodox, Conservative, and Reform Judaism in the U.S.A., founded in 1926.

Its Committee on Religious Objects, 1950-51, distributed ritual objects rescued in Europe after World War II on behalf of *Jewish Cultural Reconstruction primarily to immigrant congregations in the U.S.A.

Records. American Jewish Historical Society: records, 1935-74, 53 cartons, include several folders concerning the Committee on Religious Objects.

Recent records are at the organization's office.

129. TRAVELERS AID-INTERNATIONAL SOCIAL SERVICE OF AMERICA, INC.
345 E. 46 St., New York, NY 10017

Nonsectarian social agency formed in 1972 by a merger of the Travelers Aid Association of America and the American Branch of the International Social Service.

Travelers Aid was founded in 1917 as a national organization to serve people in transit. As the National Travelers Aid Association, it cooperated with organizations aiding refugees, including the *National Refugee Service.

The International Migration Service (IMS), with headquarters in Geneva, Switzerland, was founded in 1924 and renamed International Social Service in 1947. The American Branch (AB) was organized in 1924 and incorporated in New York in 1926. In 1934, the AB cooperated with other national organizations in the *National Coordinating Committee. By 1939, the AB had organized a children's project to provide homes for refugee children. It supported the *Wagner-*Rogers bill of 1939 and liberalized immigration laws. The AB and the IMS continued through the war and postwar periods to assist refugees in the U.S.A. and in Europe. *Joseph P. Chamberlain was chairman, and *George L. Warren general director of the AB 1928-40.

Literature. Romanofsky, *Social Service Organizations*, pp. 367-373, 684-692.

Records. Univ. of Minnesota Libraries, Social Welfare History Archives Center: records of Travelers Aid, 1915-64, 3 ft and microfilm (36 reels), and of International Social Service, 1923-59, 80 ft and microfilm (2 reels of minutes of meetings). Case files prior to 1945 for IMS are presumed to have been destroyed.

Recent records are at the agency's office.

Additional documentation may be located in the archives of the General Secretariat, International Social Service, 15 Rue Charles Galland, 1206 Geneva, Switzerland.

130. UNION OF ORTHODOX RABBIS OF THE UNITED STATES AND CANADA, INC. (AGUDATH HARABBONIM)
235 E. Broadway, New York, NY 10002

Founded in 1902, the Union is the oldest organization of Orthodox rabbis in the U.S.A. In 1914, it set up the Central Relief Committee, which was absorbed by the *American Jewish Joint Distribution Committee (JDC). The Union tends to be militantly Orthodox in its policies and opposes formal cooperation between Orthodox and non-Orthodox rabbis.

Organized the Vaad Hahatzala (Rescue Council) in 1939 as the principal rescue committee of the Union of Orthodox Rabbis (and of the Orthodox community) to aid leading Orthodox personalities and rabbis in Europe. During World War II, the Vaad Hahatzala engaged in a variety of negotiations and activities designed to ransom Orthodox Jews and rabbis, or to save them from internment and extermination. Cooperated with the *World Jewish Congress, the JDC, Swiss intermediaries, and others to achieve these ends. The Union provided more than $1 million to the *U.S. War Refugee Board. After the War, the Vaad Hahatzala became known as the Vaad Hahatzala Rehabilitation Committee.

Literature. Moshe Prager, *Churbn un Rettung (Disaster and Salvation: The History of "Vaad Hahatzala" in America).* (Yiddish.) New York, 1957. Efraim J. Zuroff, "Rabbis, Relief, and Rescue: American Vaad Hahatzala 1939-1945," Ph.D. dissertation in progress, Hebrew Univ. of Jerusalem.

Records. Yeshiva Univ. Archives: records of Vaad Hahatzala, 1939-?, ca. 60 ft, include primarily correspondence with Jewish organizations, government agencies and the Vaad's overseas branches, and materials dealing with the immigration of groups and individuals.

Union of Orthodox Rabbis: records concerning rescue attempts of the Union both before and after the founding of the Vaad Hahatzala, and other materials relating to the Vaad Hahatzala.

131. UNITARIAN-UNIVERSALIST SERVICE COMMITTEE
78 Beacon St., Boston, MA 02108

Formed in 1963 by a merger of the Unitarian Service Committee (USC) and the Universalist Service Committee. The USC was established in 1940 by the American Unitarian Association (AUA–since 1961, Unitarian Universalist Association) as an outgrowth of the activities of the AUA's Department of Social and Foreign Relations, whose executive secretary was Dr. *Robert Dexter. In 1939, the Department founded the Commission for Service in Czechoslovakia, a joint venture with the *American Friends Service Committee, to rescue intellectuals in Prague. As a result of this effort, the USC was formed.

In response to news of Nazi persecutions, the USC joined with other liberal social service organizations in establishing relief and rescue services abroad. Following the fall of France in 1940, the USC provided food and medical services for refugees and refugee children in France, including medical services and educational facilities in internment camps and a clinic at Marseilles, France, and coordinated medical relief activities with other agencies. Its European office, headed by Dr. Charles R. Joy, assisted refugee children to escape from France across the Pyrenees and to immigrate to the U.S.A.

The USC's activities were continued through its social services in other war and postwar areas such as Italy, Vietnam, Korea, and Africa, and in a variety of community and self-help projects in the U.S.A. *Ernst Papanek was director of USC Child Projects 1945-47.

Literature. Howard L. Brooks, *Prisoners of Hope, Report on a Mission.* New York: L. B. Fischer, 1942.

James Ford Lewis, "The Unitarian Service Committee." Unpublished Ph.D. dissertation, Univ. of California, 1952.

Romanofsky, *Social Service Organizations*, pp. 692-698.

Wyman, *Paper Walls.*

Records. Harvard Univ., Divinity School, Andover-Harvard Theological Library: records of the USC, although incomplete for the early years, do include significant materials about the USC's efforts to aid refugees.

Recent records are at the agency's office, and other materials may be at the Unitarian Universalist Association (25 Beacon St., Boston, MA 02108).

132. UNITED HELP, INC.
44 E. 23 St., New York, NY 10010

Founded in 1953 as the Help and Reconstruction Fund for the Aged, Inc. Present name was adopted in 1955. Cosponsored by the *American Federation of Jews from Central Europe (AFJCE) and the *Gustav Wurzweiler Foundation. United Help is the main planning and disbursing agency for funds, including German *Wiedergutmachung* payments, available for social services for Nazi victims. Funds received from the *Conference on Jewish Material Claims Against Germany, via the *Council of Jews from Germany and the AFJCE, and from private sources, are allocated to social service agencies for Nazi victims, especially the aged, across the U.S.A. Beneficiaries include *Selfhelp Community Services, *Help and Reconstruction, New York, *Blue Card, *Selfhelp Home for the Aged, Chicago, and Beth Abraham Home, Bronx, New York.

Assisted in establishing two apartment complexes for the aged (Kissena I and Kissena II in Flushing, Queens, New York) which were built by Selfhelp Community Services and house a substantial number of Nazi victims.

United Help founded, supports, and administers the Nehemiah Robinson Memorial Scholarship Fund, which provides supplementary assistance to Nazi victims and the children of Nazi victims studying for a vocational or professional career in U.S. institutions of higher learning.

Literature. Kurt G. Herz, "United Help, Inc." In American Federation of Jews from Central Europe, *Twenty Years 1940-1960.* New York, 1961, pp. 27-35.

Lessing, *Oral History.*

Records. United Help: records include minutes since 1953, committee files, and documentation on beneficiary agencies and projects. The records of the Scholarship Fund include minutes of the Scholarship Committee, statistical studies, and case files. Restricted.

133. UNITED HIAS SERVICE, INC. (HIAS)
200 Park Ave. S., New York, NY 10003

Formed in 1954 by a merger of the *Hebrew Sheltering and Immigrant Aid Society (HIAS), the *United Service for New Americans, and the Migration Dept. of the *American Jewish Joint Distribution Committee (JDC). Its assistance to immigrants, while primarily concentrated on post-World War II émigrés from Eastern Europe, North Africa, Cuba, and the Soviet Union, included aid to refugees from Germany arriving in the U.S.A. from countries of intermediate settlement.

Literature. Romanofsky, *Social Service Organizations*, pp. 708-710.

Records. YIVO Institute for Jewish Research: records, 1951-67, 17 ft, include some material for the pre-1954 period.
   Most of the records of United HIAS Service are at the agency's office.

134. UNITED JEWISH APPEAL (UJA) (National Office)
1290 Avenue of the Americas, New York, NY 10019

Founded in 1939 as the United Jewish Appeal for Refugees and Overseas Needs for 1939, to combine the fund-raising efforts of the *American Jewish Joint Distribution Committee (JDC), the United Palestine Appeal, and the *National Coordinating Committee Fund. Subsequently became the United Jewish Appeal for Refugees and Overseas Needs and Palestine. Later, the present name was adopted. UJA became the central fund-raising agency of American Jews for overseas aid, including Palestine/Israel.
   From 1939 through 1966, the UJA distributed $924 million to the United Israel Appeal and to its predecessor, United Palestine Appeal; $582 million to the JDC; $55 million to the *United Service for New Americans and its predecessor, the *National Refugee Service; $29 million to the *New York Association for New Americans; and $4 million to *United HIAS Service. The chairmen of the UJA included Rabbi *Abba Hillel Silver and *Henry Morgenthau, Jr.

Records. United Jewish Appeal: archival and noncurrent records are in a warehouse undergoing processing and are not accessible to researchers. Recent records are at the organization's office.

135. UNITED PRESBYTERIAN CHURCH IN THE U.S.A.
475 Riverside Dr., New York, NY 10027

Formed in 1958 by a merger of the Presbyterian Church in the U.S.A. and the United Presbyterian Church of North America.

The Board of National Missions of the Presbyterian Church in the U.S.A., through its Dept. of Jewish Evangelization, assisted refugees with a view to converting Jews to Protestantism. Published *German Refugees 1939-1940* and *Emergency*, two pamphlets concerning aid to German refugees.

Literature. Hertz, "Joint and Concurrent."

Records. Presbyterian Historical Society: records of the Dept. of Jewish Evangelization, 1923-48, 2 ft (ca. 4000 items), include material on refugee relief. Restricted. *NUCMC* MS 77-1709. Finding aid: unpublished inventory.

136. UNITED RESTITUTION ORGANIZATION (URO)
570 Seventh Ave., New York, NY 10018

Worldwide Jewish welfare agency organized in 1948 to assist Nazi victims in preparing claims under West German *Wiedergutmachung* legislation. The central office of URO is in Frankfurt am Main, Federal Republic of Germany (Wiesenau 53), with a head office in London, England. The American branch was founded in 1948 in New York by the *American Federation of Jews from Central Europe (AFJCE), under whose charter it operates as part of AFJCE's mission to assist victims of Nazi persecution to obtain redress of damages inflicted upon them by the Third Reich. In 1955, a West Coast branch office of URO was founded in *Los Angeles. Many Jewish and nonsectarian social welfare agencies in the U.S.A. cooperated with URO. *National Council of Jewish Women, Greater Miami Section, *Jewish Family and Children's Service, Baltimore, and *Legal Aid Society of Philadelphia were especially active in this regard and maintained separate units for *Wiedergutmachungs*-cases.

Literature. Lessing, *Oral History.*

Records. URO, New York: ca. 300,000 claims were filed since 1948 with the assistance of this office, for ca. 80,000 clients. The open case files for these claims are at the agency's office; closed files are routinely destroyed by the agency. A substantial amount of closed and semi-closed files were destroyed by fire at 1241 Broadway, New York. See also *Jewish Welfare Agencies.

URO, New York, and AFJCE: administrative files, financial records, and other materials concerning the New York office and worldwide URO activities. Restricted.

Stanford Univ., Hoover Institution on War, Revolution, and Peace: URO collection, 6 boxes, comprises URO *Rundschreiben*, 1957-67, 3 folders of mimeographed directives on legal procedures for *Wiedergutmachungs*-claims, 1957-58, and one draft for the revision of West German *Wiedergutmachungs*-laws. *NUCMC* MS 77-1106.

Records of the West Coast branch office of URO in Los Angeles are with that agency.

The central file of claims from around the world is located at the central URO office in Frankfurt am Main. Case files are also at the various German *Wiedergutmachungsämter* (restitution offices) and in the local branches of URO in West Germany and worldwide. In some instances, German *Wiedergutmachungs-ämter* have deposited files at the State Archives of various German states.

137. UNITED SERVICE FOR NEW AMERICANS, INC. (USNA)   *Defunct*

Formed in 1946 in New York by a merger of the *National Refugee Service (NRS) and the National Service to Foreign Born of the *National Council of Jewish Women. One of the principal agencies assisting in the migration and re-settlement of immigrants. In 1954, USNA joined with the *Hebrew Sheltering and Immigrant Aid Society (HIAS) and the Migration Dept. of the *American Jewish Joint Distribution Committee (JDC) to form the *United HIAS Service.

USNA's clients consisted primarily of postwar immigrants from Europe, the survivors of the Holocaust arriving in the U.S.A. as displaced persons, for whom it offered a full range of social services through a staff of over 600 people (1947). Persons arriving in the U.S.A. following World War II included Jewish refugees from Germany coming from countries or places of intermediate settle-ment (Great Britain, Switzerland, Latin America, *Shanghai, etc.).

Literature.   Romanofsky, *Social Service Organizations*, pp. 716-717.
Lyman C. White, *300,000 New Americans: The Epic of a Modern Immigrant-Aid Service.* New York: Harper, 1957.

Records.   YIVO Institute for Jewish Research: records, ca. 1943-54, ca. 3600 files, consist of minutes, correspondence, reports, and a variety of other materials concerning USNA and its predecessor agencies, including individual case files, many of which were opened by the NRS and its predecessor, the *National Coordinating Committee. Much of this collection pertains to postwar displaced persons. Finding aid: unpublished inventory.

American Jewish Historical Society: records, ca. 1947-54, ca. 13 ft, consist of correspondence and published materials concerning USNA and its predeces-sors. Much of the collection relates to postwar displaced persons. *NUCMC* MS 77-46.

138. U.S. CATHOLIC CONFERENCE, DIVISION OF MIGRATION AND REFUGEE SERVICES

Headquarters: 1312 Massachusetts Ave., N.W., Washington, DC 20005
New York Branch Office: 1250 Broadway, New York, NY 10001

The Conference unites all Catholic bishops in the U.S.A. for corporate action on matters affecting Catholics in America. The Div. of Migration and Refugee Services was formerly the Bureau of Immigration of the National Catholic Wel-fare Conference.

The Division assumed the responsibility for aiding Catholic refugees which was previously exercised by the Committee for Catholic Refugees from Ger-many, 1936-41, the Catholic Committee for Refugees, 1941-47, and the Catholic Committee for Refugees and Displaced Persons, 1947-?. The Com-mittee was formed in 1936 in response to a petition addressed to the four American cardinals by the Archbishop of Breslau on behalf of the German hierarchy. An International Catholic Office for Refugee Affairs also existed during the 1930s and 1940s. Cooperated with other refugee aid agencies. Msgr. Joseph Francis Rummel, Archbishop of New Orleans, chairman of the Commit-tee and of the International Office, was a member of the *U.S. President's Advisory Committee on Political Refugees.

Literature. Romanofsky, *Social Service Organizations*, pp. 212–216.

Report of The Committee for Catholic Refugees from Germany: Covering the Period from Jan. 1, 1937 to Sept. 30, 1938.

Tenth Annual Report of Catholic Committee for Refugees, Oct. 1, 1945 to Sept. 30, 1946.

Twenty-Fifth Annual Report of Catholic Committee for Refugees, Oct. 1, 1960 to Sept. 30, 1961.

Records. Center for Migration Studies of New York: records of the headquarters, 1917–70, 52.5 ft, and of the New York branch office, 2 ft. The files of the New York branch office include some original records of the Catholic Committee, but the case files for 1933–45 are presumed to have been destroyed. Finding aid: Center for Migration Studies of New York, *A Guide to the Archives.* Vol. 1, 1974, pp. 36–38.

139. UNITED STATES COMMITTEE FOR THE CARE OF EUROPEAN CHILDREN, INC. *Defunct*

The Non-Sectarian Committee for German Refugee Children was organized in December 1938 as a lobbying group to urge passage of Congressional legislation that would permit the admission to the U.S.A. of German refugee children outside existing quotas. The Committee had state branches in Ohio, Michigan, Texas, Illinois, Minnesota, Colorado, Utah, and California. Clarence Pickett, executive secretary of the *American Friends Service Committee (AFSC), headed the Committee.

The *Wagner–*Rogers Child Refugee Bill of 1939 was never reported out of committee in the *U.S. Congress, and a Non-Sectarian Foundation for Refugee Children was formed in April 1940 to care for unaccompanied German and Austrian refugee children in the U.S.A.

The United States Committee for the Care of European Children (USCCEC) was organized in June 1940 in New York City to coordinate the nationwide effort to promote the immigration of refugee children. The Foundation was soon absorbed by USCCEC as its Child Care Div. Until 1953, when USCCEC was disbanded, it was the foremost agency in the U.S.A. for the care of child refugees. USCCEC had local cooperating committees in 172 cities. Marshall Field III, Chicago business executive, was president 1940–53. *Eleanor Roosevelt was honorary president of USCCEC and honorary vice-president of the Foundation.

Literature. Kathryn Close, *Transplanted Children: A History* [of USCCEC]. New York, 1953.

Genizi, "American Non-Sectarian," pp. 204–213.

Romanofsky, *Social Service Organizations*, pp. 731–734.

Records. In 1953, case files were transferred to the five cooperating national child care agencies: *European Jewish Children's Aid, Catholic Committee for Refugees (*U.S. Catholic Conference), National Lutheran Council (*Lutheran Council in the U.S.A.), Church World Service (*American Christian Committee for Refugees), and American Hellenic Educational Progressive Association,

Administrative records of USCCEC have not been located and are presumed destroyed. Copies of minutes of meetings of the Non-Sectarian Committee and Non-Sectarian Foundation are located among the records of the AFSC. Materials relating to USCCEC are found among the records of European Jewish Children's Aid and presumably among the records of other major refugee aid organizations.

140. UNITED STATES COMMITTEE OF INTERNATIONAL STUDENT SERVICE *Defunct*

The U.S. Committee was established in 1926 as a national committee of the International Student Service (ISS), which had been founded in 1920 to assist needy students following World War I. By agreement with the *League of Nations High Commissioner for Refugees, ISS accepted the financial responsibility for students displaced by Nazism after 1933 from Germany and, later, from Axis-occupied Europe.

The U.S. Committee of ISS absorbed the *Intercollegiate Committee to Aid Student Refugees in 1939 as its Student Refugee Dept. During the years of World War II, activities of the U.S. Committee included direct aid to refugee students, support for the World Student Service Fund, work and summer encampments, conferences and leadership institutes, publicity, and publications.

The U.S. Committee was dissolved in July 1943, and its functions assumed by the newly formed Student Service of America, Inc. By then, the U.S. Committee had helped about 700 refugee students. Following a period of inactivity, Student Service of America was reactivated in 1945. It aided students until it was dissolved in 1947 and its programs were continued by the Institute of International Education.

In 1950, World University Service was created in Europe to assume the former functions and activities of ISS. Its headquarters are at 5 Chemin des Iris, 1216 Geneva, Switzerland. In 1953, World University Service was formed in the U.S.A. to carry on the activities of the former World Student Service Fund, which had been the American fund-raising agency for ISS overseas activities. The American office of World University Service is c/o Dr. Glen Nygreen, Dean of Students Office, Herbert H. Lehman College of CUNY, Bedford Park Blvd., Bronx, NY 10468.

Literature. World University Service, *World Student Relief 1940–1950.* Geneva, 1951.

Records. Records of the U.S. Committee of ISS, of Student Service of America, and of World Student Service Fund have not been located. There is pertinent documentation about the first two agencies among the papers of *Alfred E. Cohn, who served on their executive bodies.

Records of World University Service and its predecessor international organizations are at its headquarters in Geneva.

United States of America, Federal Agencies

141. U.S. BUREAU OF FOREIGN AND DOMESTIC COMMERCE   Defunct

Established in 1912 to promote the development of U.S. commerce and industry by compiling and distributing information on domestic and foreign trade, manufacturing, and markets. The Foreign Commerce Service, established within the Bureau in 1927 to investigate foreign commercial and industrial conditions, was transferred to the *U.S. Dept. of State in 1939, to be administered as part of the Foreign Service. In 1952, the Bureau, originally an agency of the U.S. Dept. of Commerce, was integrated into the Department's administrative structure.

Commercial attachés serving in Europe reported on conditions affecting the business activities of Jews in areas under Nazi control.

Literature. Douglas Miller, *Via Diplomatic Pouch.* New York: Didier, 1944. (Miller was a commercial attaché in the U.S. Embassy in Berlin during the 1930s. This book consists of reports he made on business and economic subjects. Pages 227-235 cover expropriation of Jewish enterprises in 1935.)

Records. National Archives and Records Service, Civil Archives Div.: records comprise Record Group 151. Include reports of commercial attachés, 1932-40, arranged alphabetically by name of city where the official was stationed and thereunder chronologically. Finding aids: National Archives, *Guide,* pp. 486-488. National Archives, *Preliminary Inventory of the Records of the Bureau of Foreign and Domestic Commerce, Record Group 151.* PI NC-27. Washington, DC, May 1963. Mimeo., at National Archives Library.

142. U.S. CHILDREN'S BUREAU   Defunct

Established in 1912 by the *U.S. Dept. of Labor to study and report on all matters relating to children. In 1969, the Bureau's functions were transferred to the Office of Child Development in the U.S. Dept. of Health, Education and Welfare.

Set standards for the care of refugee children brought to the U.S.A. from Europe, and kept records of unaccompanied children. Worked closely with the *European (formerly German) Jewish Children's Aid and with the *United States Committee for the Care of European Children.

Literature. U.S. Children's Bureau, *Care of Children Coming to the United States for Safety Under the Attorney General's Order of July 13, 1940; Standards Prescribed by the Children's Bureau.* Bureau Publ. No. 268. Washington, DC, 1941.
——, *Five Decades of Action for Children, A History of the Children's Bureau.* Washington, DC, 1962.

Records. National Archives and Records Service, Civil Archives Div.: records comprise Record Group 102. The central file and index, 1912-40, are arranged in chronological segments, including 1933-36 and 1937-40. The latter segment includes 1.25 ft (boxes 592-594) on "Refugee Problems" under the file code

0-2-0-7-1[2]. There may be additional relevant material under other file codes for 1937–40 and for the period 1933–36. Finding aids: National Archives, *Guide*, p. 510. National Archives, *Preliminary Inventory of the Records of the Children's Bureau, Record Group 102.* PI 184. Washington, DC, 1976.

National Archives and Records Service, Washington National Records Center: records of the Children's Bureau for the period after 1941 are believed to include material on refugees similar to that found in the earlier records. Access to these records is obtained through the U.S. Dept. of Health, Education and Welfare, Office of Human Development Records Officer, Washington, DC 20201.

143. U.S. COMMITTEE ON FAIR EMPLOYMENT PRACTICE (FEPC) *Defunct*

First established by Executive Order 8802 of June 25, 1941, in the Office of Production Management (OPM). The FEPC was assigned to the War Production Board when that agency succeeded the OPM and was transferred in 1942 to the U.S. War Manpower Commission (WMC). Abolished by Executive Order 9346 of May 27, 1943, which created a new Committee on Fair Employment Practice in the Office for Emergency Management. The FEPC was dissolved in 1946 after issuing its final report to the President.

The FEPC formulated and interpreted policies to combat racial and religious discrimination in employment; received, investigated, and adjusted complaints of such discrimination; and assisted government agencies, employers, and labor unions with problems of discrimination. Liaison was maintained by the FEPC with the WMC through the WMC's Minority Groups Service in its Bureau of Placement. Of a total of 14,000 complaints of discrimination handled by the FEPC, those based on creed or religion amounted to 6% and originated primarily from Jewish sources; those based on national origin amounted to 14%. The FEPC also processed complaints involving aliens.

Literature. Louis Ruchames, *Race, Jobs, & Politics; the Story of FEPC.* New York: Columbia Univ. Press, 1953.

Records. National Archives and Records Service, Civil Archives Div.: records comprise Record Group 228. Records of the FEPC regional offices are with the regional archives branches of the National Archives. Finding aids: National Archives, *Guide*, pp. 616–618. National Archives, *Preliminary Inventory of the Records of the Committee on Fair Employment Practice, Record Group 228.* PI 147. Washington, DC, 1962.

FEPC Headquarters and Field records have been microfilmed almost completely on 213 reels by Microfilming Corp. of America (Glen Rock, NJ). Finding aid: *Guide to the Microfilm Record of Selected Documents of Records of the Committee on Fair Employment Practice in the Custody of the National Archives.* Glen Rock, NJ, 1970.

New York Public Library, General Research and Humanities Div.; Queens College Library; and Cornell Univ., School of Industrial and Labor Relations Library, have copies of all or part of the microfilm edition.

144. U.S. CONGRESS: HOUSE OF REPRESENTATIVES AND SENATE
Washington, DC

Congressional Representatives and Senators, as members of various committees and subcommittees, dealt with a variety of issues relating to refugees, aliens, and immigration.

In the House of Representatives, the following committees held hearings on such matters, 1933-45: Immigration and Naturalization, Foreign Affairs, Appropriations, Labor, Territories; the Special Committee on Un-American Activities (1934-35) and the Special Committee for the Investigation of Un-American Activities (1938-), predecessors of the Committee on Un-American Activities; and the Select Committee Investigating National Defense Migration (of the Committee on Migration).

In the Senate, the following committees held such hearings, 1933-45: Immigration, Foreign Relations, Labor, and Territories Insular Affairs.

Literature. U.S. Senate Historical Office, *The United States Senate: An Historical Bibliography.* Washington, DC, 1977.

Records. National Archives and Records Service, Civil Archives Div.: House of Representatives records comprise Record Group 233; Senate records comprise Record Group 46. Include committee records and reports, documents referred to committees, records of legislative proceedings, and bills and resolutions. Finding aids: National Archives, *Guide*, pp. 49-53. National Archives, *Preliminary Inventory of the Records of the United States House of Representatives, 1789-1946.* PI 113. 2 vols. Washington, DC, 1959. National Archives, *Preliminary Inventory of the Records of the United States Senate.* PI 23. Washington, DC, 1950. National Archives, *Printed Hearings of the House of Representatives Found Among Its Committee Records in the National Archives of the United States, 1824-1958.* Special List 35. Washington, DC, 1974. National Archives, *Preliminary Inventory of the Records of the Special Committee of the House of Representatives Investigating National Defense Migration, 1940-43.* PI 71. Washington, DC, 1954.

The papers of several Representatives and Senators include materials relating to Congressional activity on matters pertaining to immigration. See the Index.

145. U.S. DEPARTMENT OF JUSTICE
Washington, DC 20530

Administers the immigration and naturalization laws, the registration of aliens, and deportation proceedings through the *U.S. Immigration and Naturalization Service, which was transferred to the Department in 1940 from the *U.S. Dept. of Labor.

Supervises U.S. attorneys and marshals. Under Department regulations during World War II, U.S. attorneys regulated the travel of enemy aliens, and U.S. marshals had custody of radio transmitters, shortwave receivers, cameras, firearms, and other articles enemy aliens were not permitted to own in wartime.

Records. National Archives and Records Service, Civil Archives Div.: records of the Justice Dept. comprise Record Group 60. The classified subject files, 1914–41 and 1945–49, include materials on "Naturalization" in class 38 and on "Immigration" in class 39. Some records are restricted; additional records are still with the Department. Finding aid: National Archives, *Guide*, pp. 336-343.

Records of U.S. attorneys and marshals, which comprise Record Group 118, are partially with the National Archives and Records Service in its regional branches, but are primarily with the U.S. attorneys and marshals in each federal court district. Finding aid: National Archives, *Guide*, pp. 343-344.

146. U.S. DEPARTMENT OF LABOR
Washington, DC 20210

Has jurisdiction over matters relating to the welfare of American wage earners, including the improvement of their working conditions and the advancement of profitable employment opportunities. *Frances Perkins was Secretary of the Department 1933-45.

The *U.S. Immigration and Naturalization Service was administered by the Department from 1913 to 1940, when it was transferred to the *U.S. Dept. of Justice. The *U.S. Children's Bureau was a part of the Dept. of Labor until 1946.

Records. National Archives and Records Service, Civil Archives Div.: records comprise Record Group 174. The general files of the Office of the Secretary, 1907-42, which are arranged in a numerical classification plan, include materials on aliens. The general subject files of Perkins, 1933-44, are arranged alphabetically in two segments, 1933–40 and 1940-44. The earlier segment includes 3 ft (boxes 49-55) on "Immigration." The latter segment does not have a subject file on this topic. Finding aids: National Archives, *Guide*, pp. 491-493. National Archives, *Preliminary Inventory of the General Records of the Dept. of Labor, Record Group 174.* PI NC-58. Washington, DC, May 1964. Mimeo., at National Archives Library.

147. U.S. DEPARTMENT OF STATE
Washington, DC 20520

The State Dept. had a major influence on the admission of refugees to the U.S.A. through its Visa Div., the instructions issued to consuls around the world, its administration of restrictive policies such as the clause preventing future immigrants from becoming public charges ("LPC" clause), the distribution of visa quotas to the various consulates, and similar powers. From 1941 to 1945, it established a three-tiered review of visas to be issued, the Board of Appeals on Visa Cases.

*Breckinridge Long, the head of its Special Div. (Special War Problems Div.), an opponent of liberalized immigration practices, guided visa and admission policies during this period. *Cordell Hull was Secretary of State 1933-44. See also *Myron C. Taylor.

Literature. Feingold, *Politics of Rescue.*

Saul S. Friedman, *No Haven for the Oppressed: United States Policy Toward Jewish Refugees, 1938-1945.* Detroit: Wayne State Univ. Press, 1973.

Arthur D. Morse, *While Six Million Died; A Chronicle of American Apathy.* New York: Random House, 1967.

U.S. Dept. of State, *Foreign Relations of the United States* for pertinent years. Wyman, *Paper Walls.*

Records. National Archives and Records Service, Civil Archives Div.: records of the State Dept. comprise Record Group 59; records of the Foreign Service Posts comprise Record Group 84. The central files of the State Dept. constitute an extensive primary source relating to U.S. government policy and activity with respect to immigration of the 1933-45 period. Records of American consular posts abroad include material concerning the immigration of Central European refugees. Finding aids: National Archives, *Guide,* pp. 131–142. National Archives, *Preliminary Inventory of the General Records of the Department of State.* PI 157. Washington, DC, 1963. National Archives, *List of Foreign Service Post Records in the National Archives.* Special List 9. Washington, DC, 1967. National Archives, *Purport Lists for the Department of State Decimal File, 1910-44.* Microfilm publication M-973, 654 reels (the principal finding aid for the central files of the State Dept.).

Other State Dept. records may still be with the agency or with its subdivisions, including the Visa Office. Records relating to individuals are confidential.

148. U.S. DEPARTMENT OF THE INTERIOR
Washington, DC 20240

The *U.S. Div. of Territories and Island Possessions, a part of the Department, was involved in plans to resettle refugees in Alaska, the Virgin Islands, and the Philippine Islands, 1938-41. *Harold L. Ickes, Secretary of the Interior 1933-46, favored such plans and more liberal immigration policies. Felix S. Cohen, Assistant Solicitor in the Department, was coauthor of the King–Havenner Bill for Alaska Development in 1940.

The *U.S. Office of Education, which prepared educational programs for immigrants, was under the Department until 1939.

Literature. Claus-M. Naske, "Jewish Immigration and Alaskan Economic Development: A Study in Futility." *Western States Jewish Historical Quarterly* 7 (Jan. 1976): 139–157.

Wyman, *Paper Walls,* chap. 5.

Records. National Archives and Records Service, Civil Archives Div.: records comprise Record Group 48. The central files of the Office of the Secretary, 1907-53, are arranged according to a numeric-subject classification system, with a subject and name index. The central files include materials on the Div. of Territories and Island Possessions' activities relating to plans to resettle refugees (under file codes 9-0-12, 9-1-2, and 9-11-26), and on the Office of Education's role in the education of immigrants. The general subject file of the Office of the Solicitor includes four "large" files relating to refugee resettlement in

Alaska, 1939–40, and the Virgin Islands, 1940–41. Finding aid: National Archives, *Guide*, pp. 364–371.

National Archives and Records Service, Audiovisual Archives Div.: records of the Office of the Secretary of the Interior include sound recordings of the radio program, "Americans All, Immigrants All," produced by the Office of Education in 1939, and sound recordings concerning the contributions of civilians, including immigrants and Jews, to the war effort. Finding aid: National Archives, *Audiovisual Records in the National Archives of the U.S. Relating to World War II.* Reference Information Paper No. 70. Washington, DC, 1974, p. 15.

149. U.S. DISPLACED PERSONS COMMISSION   *Defunct*

Established in 1948 to administer the U.S. Displaced Persons Act of 1948. Its tasks included the selection and screening of applicants and their resettlement in the U.S.A. As a result of its activities, over 400,000 persons were resettled in the U.S.A. The Commission was liquidated in 1952. Ugo Carusi was chairman 1948–50; *John W. Gibson was chairman 1950–52.

Thirty-six states of the U.S.A. had Displaced Persons Committees or Commissions.

Literature.   U.S. Displaced Persons Commission, *Annual Reports.*
——, *Memo to America: The Displaced Persons Story; The Final Report of the . . . Commission.* Washington, DC, 1952.

Records.   National Archives and Records Service, Civil Archives Div.: records, 1948–52, ca. 50 ft, comprise Record Group 278. Consist of central subject files; Commissioners Edward M. O'Connor's and Harry N. Rosenfield's office files; files of the Legal Div., Editorial and Information Div., and Research and Statistical Div.; European history project files; and orphan correspondence files.

National Archives and Records Service, Federal Records Center, Bayonne: records showing the Commission's action on processed cases. Unavailable to researchers; will be retained until 2026. Records relating to individual cases were destroyed as having no value for historical or other research purposes.

150. U.S. DIVISION OF TERRITORIES AND ISLAND POSSESSIONS
Defunct

Established in 1934 by the *U.S. Dept. of the Interior, the Division was concerned with the development of the economic, social, and political life of the territories. The Office of Territories was founded in 1950 as the successor to the Division, which, after further reorganization in 1971 and 1973, became the Office of Territorial Affairs.

The Division prepared plans to resettle refugees in Alaska, the Virgin Islands, and the Philippine Islands, 1938–41. In 1939, Secretary of the Interior *Harold L. Ickes assigned Ernest H. Gruening, Director of the Division (later Territorial Governor of Alaska), the responsibility for developing a plan to establish colonies of refugees in Alaska. "The Problem of Alaskan Development," a report released in August 1939 under the auspices of Under Secretary of the Interior Harry Slattery, advocated such refugee settlements for Alaska.

In February 1940, the "Alaskan Development Bill" was introduced in Congress by Senator William H. King of Utah, and Representative Frank Havenner of California. It called for the resettlement of refugees and other measures to further the economic development of the territory. The bill was opposed by immigration restrictionists and Alaskan officials, and died in a subcommittee of the *U.S. Senate Committee on Territories and Insular Affairs.

Literature. Feingold, *Politics of Rescue.*

Claus-M. Naske, "Jewish Immigration and Alaskan Economic Development: A Study in Futility." *Western States Jewish Historical Quarterly* 7 (Jan. 1976): 139–157.

Wyman, *Paper Walls*, chap. 5.

Records. National Archives and Records Service, Civil Archives Div.: records comprise Record Group 126. The central files, 1907–51, are arranged according to a numeric–subject classification system, and are further subdivided by subject and arranged chronologically. The central files include materials relating to refugee resettlement plans (under file codes 9-1-60 and 9-11-21). Finding aids: National Archives, *Guide*, pp. 403–405. National Archives, *Preliminary Inventory to the Records of the Office of Territories, Record Group 126*. PI 154. Washington, DC, 1963.

National Archives and Records Service, Washington National Records Center: subject card indexes to the central files, 1907–51. Access to these indexes is obtained through the Office of Territorial Affairs, Washington, DC 20240.

151. U.S. EMERGENCY REFUGEE SHELTER AT FORT ONTARIO, OSWEGO, N.Y. *Defunct*

Established on June 8, 1944, by an Executive Order of President *Franklin D. Roosevelt announcing the decision to bring 1000 refugees from Europe to the U.S.A. outside the quota system. They were to be housed in a shelter in the U.S.A., Fort Ontario, which, for this purpose, was transferred from the administration of the Army to the *U.S. War Refugee Board, which was also charged with determining the policies that were to govern the administration of the shelter. Actual control of the shelter was transferred to the *U.S. War Relocation Authority (WRA), under whose authority the camps under the Japanese relocation scheme on the West Coast had been established.

On August 5, 1944, 982 refugees selected from internment camps in Italy arrived at Fort Ontario. They included members of 18 nationalities, the majority being Yugoslavs and Austrians, many of whom were of the Jewish religion. The regime under which they lived at the shelter was patterned after the regime of the Japanese relocation centers. On June 6, 1945, the shelter was transferred to the authority of the *U.S. Dept. of the Interior.

In spite of urgings by the WRA and citizens' groups and organizations in the U.S.A., the refugees were not permitted to leave the shelter or live with

American relatives until they could be admitted as quota immigrants to the U.S.A. In January 1946, the refugees were released from the camp, and on February 28, 1946, the WRA returned the shelter to the *U.S. War Dept.

Literature. U.S. Dept. of the Interior. War Relocation Authority, *Token Shipment, The Story of America's War Refugee Shelter.* Washington, DC, 1946.

Records. National Archives and Records Service, Civil Archives Div.: records of the Shelter, in Record Group 210 (Records of the War Relocation Authority), consist of subject-classified general files, 1944-46, 5 ft, and case files of refugees, 1944-46, 11 ft. Access to these records, part of the WRA field records, is restricted. WRA headquarters records also include materials on the Shelter. Finding aids: National Archives, *Guide,* pp. 689-691. National Archives, *Preliminary Inventory of the Records of the War Relocation Authority, Record Group 210.* PI 77. Washington, DC, 1955. Item nos. 55-56.

Columbia Univ., Rare Book and Manuscript Library: records of the Shelter, 1944-46, 6.7 ft, consist of official reports, manuals, correspondence, and various releases and memoranda tracing the history of the development, operation, and closing of the Shelter.

American Jewish Historical Society: the Jack Cohen (Rochester, NY) collection, ca. 900 pp., comprises papers and correspondence (mostly photocopies) concerning the administration of, and activities at, the Shelter. Included are minutes of meetings and reports, 1944-46, of the executive director of the Coordinating Committee for Fort Ontario; materials on the Friends of Fort Ontario; and the papers, 1944-60, of Mosco Tzechoval, who served as Rabbi at Fort Ontario. J. Cohen, who holds the original materials, was *B'nai B'rith War Service Chairman for New York State, and a member of the Coordinating Committee for Fort Ontario.

152. U.S. IMMIGRATION AND NATURALIZATION SERVICE
Washington, DC 20536

Administers laws relating to admission, exclusion, deportation, and naturalization of aliens, and alleged violations of those laws; patrols U.S. borders to prevent unlawful entry of aliens; supervises naturalization proceedings in designated courts; cooperates with public schools to provide textbooks on citizenship, and other services to prepare candidates for naturalization; and registers and fingerprints aliens in the U.S.A.

The Service was part of the *U.S. Dept. of Labor until 1940, when it was transferred to the *U.S. Dept. of Justice.

The National Citizenship Education Program (NCEP), for the education and assimilation of the foreign born, was conducted from 1941 to 1943 jointly by the Service and the *U.S. Work Projects Administration (WPA). When WPA ended in 1943, the Service continued NCEP by increasing its program and staff for the education of the foreign born.

Under the Alien Registration Act of 1940, aliens were obligated to register with the government. The Alien Enemy Control Unit was formed in 1941 to supervise aliens and to review cases of those apprehended by the Federal Bureau of Investigation. An Enemy Alien Hearing Board, composed of private citizens, was established in each Federal judicial district in 1941.

Records. National Archives and Records Service, Civil Archives Div.: records, comprising Record Group 85, include material on general immigration matters, alien registrations, passenger arrivals, naturalizations, "Americanization" activities, and internment of enemy aliens; and records of the Service's New York field office relating to citizenship education programs. Some records are restricted; additional records are still with the Service. Finding aids: National Archives, *Guide*, pp. 345-348. National Archives, *Preliminary Inventory of the Records of the Immigration and Naturalization Service, Record Group 85.* PI NC-87. Washington, DC, Jan. 1965. Mimeo., at National Archives Library.

Records of naturalizations of aliens, since 1906, are maintained in two locations. The Immigration and Naturalization Service has the closed master file on each case, while the court that conducted the naturalization proceedings has copies of the official documents, which are open to public search.

153. U.S. NATIONAL YOUTH ADMINISTRATION (NYA)   *Defunct*

Established by Executive Order 7086 of June 26, 1935, within the U.S. Works Progress (later *Work Projects) Administration. In 1939, NYA was transferred to the Federal Security Agency and, in 1942, to the U.S. War Manpower Commission. NYA conducted work programs for needy young people between the ages of 16 and 24. *Charles W. Taussig was chairman of the National Advisory Committee of NYA 1935-43. NYA was liquidated in 1944.

Refugee youths participated in NYA camps in 17 states, under the NYA Resident Center Program for Refugee Youth. The program, which began in 1938, was conducted jointly by NYA and the *National Refugee Service.

Literature. *Final Report of the National Youth Administration, Fiscal Years 1936-1943.* Washington, DC, 1944.

Tesse Rutberg, "A Study of an Experiment in Training of Refugee Youth in National Youth Administration Resident Centers." Unpublished master's thesis, New York School of Social Work, Columbia Univ., Dec. 1940.

Records. National Archives and Records Service, Civil Archives Div.: records, comprising Record Group 119, include records concerning the Resident Center Section of NYA. The nature and extent of material on refugee youth participating in NYA programs, presumed to be included in these records, have not been determined. Finding aids: National Archives, *Guide*, pp. 634-636. National Archives, *Preliminary Inventory of the Records of the National Youth Administration, Record Group 119.* PI NC-35. Washington, DC, Nov. 1963. Mimeo., at National Archives Library.

NYA records kept at state levels have not been identified.

154. U.S. OFFICE OF EDUCATION
Washington, DC 20202

Responsible for collecting and disseminating information on education in the

U.S.A. and abroad, and for promoting better education throughout the country. In 1939, the Office was transferred from the *U.S. Dept. of the Interior to the Federal Security Agency, which, in 1953, became the U.S. Dept. of Health, Education and Welfare.

Assisted with educational programs for immigrants, and cooperated with the *U.S. Work Projects Administration and the *U.S. Immigration and Naturalization Service in the National Citizenship Education Program. In 1939, the Office's Radio Education Project sponsored a series of radio programs, "Americans All, Immigrants All," each of which dealt with a group of different national origin in the U.S.A.

Records. National Archives and Records Service, Civil Archives Div.: records comprise Record Group 12. The "historical file" of the Office of the Commissioner, ca. 1870-1950, arranged in a numerical classification scheme, includes material on immigrant education (file code 420). Records of the Radio Education Project include documentation on the program series "Americans All, Immigrants All." Finding aids: National Archives, *Guide*, pp. 505-507. National Archives, *Preliminary Inventory of the Records of the Office of Education, Record Group 12.* PI 178. Washington, DC, 1974.

National Archives and Records Service, Audiovisual Archives Div.: sound recordings of the "Americans All, Immigrants All" series in Record Group 12 and Record Group 48 (Records of the Office of the Secretary of the Interior).

American Jewish Archives: one tape recording (reel no. 484) of the radio program "Americans All, Immigrants All."

155. U.S. PRESIDENT'S ADVISORY COMMITTEE ON POLITICAL REFUGEES (PACPR)   *Defunct*

Appointed by President *Franklin D. Roosevelt on April 30, 1938 to coordinate the activities of private organizations in the U.S.A. serving antifascist refugees, and to form a liaison between such organizations and the government. The PACPR assisted the U.S. delegate, *Myron C. Taylor, at the *Évian Conference on Refugees, May 1938. It served as the New York office for the *Intergovernmental Committee on Refugees (IGCR) located in London, which was established by the Conference. The PACPR prepared a preliminary screening of the names of persons submitted by private organizations as worthy of admission to the U.S.A. for humanitarian reasons; it then submitted its lists of approved names to the *U.S. Dept. of Justice for further clearance, and to the *U.S. Dept. of State for the issuance of visas. After the *U.S. War Refugee Board was established in 1944, the PACPR ceased to function.

*James G. McDonald served as chairman of the PACPR throughout its existence. Other members were: Hamilton Fish Armstrong, editor, *Foreign Affairs;* *Paul Baerwald; Samuel McCrea Cavert, general secretary, Federal (*National) Council of the Churches of Christ; *Joseph P. Chamberlain; Basil Harris, shipping executive and prominent Roman Catholic layman; Louis Kenedy, Roman Catholic publishing executive and lay leader; Archbishop Joseph F. Rummel, chairman, Catholic Committee for Refugees and Displaced Persons (*U.S. Catholic Conference); James M. Speers, president, American

Committee for Christian Refugees (*American Christian Committee for Refugees); and Rabbi *Stephen S. Wise. *George L. Warren was executive secretary of the PACPR.

Literature. Feingold, *Politics of Rescue.*
Wyman, *Paper Walls.*

Records. YIVO Institute for Jewish Research: records of the PACPR are included in the papers of Joseph P. Chamberlain.

American Jewish Historical Society: minutes of meetings of the PACPR are also found among the papers of Stephen S. Wise.

Franklin D. Roosevelt Library: Roosevelt's papers contain ca. 2000 pages relating to the IGCR and the PACPR.

156. U.S. PRESIDENT'S WAR RELIEF CONTROL BOARD   *Defunct*

In September 1939, all organized appeals for funds to be used in foreign relief were required to register with the *U.S. Dept. of State to allow close supervision of their links with belligerent countries. In 1941, President *Franklin D. Roosevelt established his Committee on War Relief Agencies, and Executive Order (EO) 9205 of July 25, 1942, established its successor, the President's War Relief Control Board. Board members were *Joseph E. Davies, *Charles P. Taft, and *Frederick P. Keppel; *Charles Warren took over Keppel's position upon the latter's death in 1943. The Board registered and dealt with many social welfare and relief organizations, including the *American Jewish Joint Distribution Committee, *American Friends Service Committee, and *American Federation of Jews from Central Europe. The Board was dissolved by EO 9723 of May 14, 1946. Its work was continued by the Advisory Committee on Voluntary Foreign Aid, whose functions were assumed, after several reorganizations, by the Agency for International Development of the U.S. Dept. of State.

Literature.   President's War Relief Control Board, *Compilation of Documents, President's Committee on War Relief Agencies and President's War Relief Control Board.* Washington, DC, 1946.
———, *Voluntary War Relief During World War II.* Washington, DC, 1946.

Records.   National Archives and Records Service, Washington National Records Center: records of and concerning the Board and its predecessor and successor committees are found in Record Group 286 (Records of the Agency for International Development) and in Record Group 220 (Records of Presidential Committees, Commissions, and Boards). Access to these records is obtained through the Agency for International Development, Freedom of Information Officer, Washington, DC 20523. Finding aid: National Archives, *Federal Records of World War II.* Washington, DC, 1950. Vol. I, Civilian Agencies, item no. 152.

157. U.S. PUBLIC HEALTH SERVICE
Rockville, MD 20852

In 1939, the Service was transferred from the U.S. Dept. of the Treasury to the

Federal Security Agency, which, in 1953, became the U.S. Dept. of Health, Education and Welfare.

Conducted the medical examination and inspection of arriving aliens and prospective immigrants.

Literature. Ralph Chester Williams, M.D., *The United States Public Health Service, 1798-1950.* Washington, DC, 1951.

Records. National Archives and Records Service, Civil Archives Div.: records comprise Record Group 90. The central files of general correspondence, 1897-1946, are grouped in chronological segments, including 1936-46. The nature and extent of materials on Central European arrivals, 1933-50, presumed to be contained in these records, has not been determined. Finding aids: National Archives, *Guide*, pp. 502-505. National Archives, *Preliminary Inventory of the Records of the Public Health Service, Record Group 90.* PI NC-34 (revised). Washington, DC, Jan. 1966. Mimeo., at National Archives Library.

158. U.S. WAR DEPARTMENT *Defunct*

Under the National Security Act of 1947, the U.S. War Dept. became the U.S. Dept. of the Army in the National Military Establishment (after 1949, the U.S. Dept. of Defense).

The Department was charged with issuing permits to aliens working in plants with government defense contracts during World War II. The Military Intelligence Div. of the Department was represented on the Interdepartmental Visa Committee, 1940-45, which passed judgment on political refugees seeking to enter the U.S.A. The Western Defense Command (WDC) was established in 1941 to provide for the defense of the U.S. West Coast. The Wartime Civil Control Administration (WCCA), organized in 1942 by the WDC, was initially responsible for the relocation of persons excluded from sensitive military areas, including German and Italian aliens. This function was subsequently assumed by the *U.S. War Relocation Authority (WRA). The Eastern Defense Command (EDC), formed in 1941, and the Southern Defense Command (SDC) were responsible for the defense of the American eastern and southern coasts. The SDC (after 1944, the Southwestern Sector of EDC) was involved in the alien exclusion program for U.S. areas adjacent to the Gulf of Mexico.

Records. National Archives and Records Service, Military Archives Div.: relevant records are in several Record Groups (RG). RG 165 (Records of the U.S. War Dept. General and Special Staffs) includes (among the records of the Office of the Director of Intelligence [G-2]) reports by military attachés, 1917-41, which contain information about German and Austrian refugees, and (among the records of the Civil Affairs Div.) messages relating to refugees, 1944-48.

RG 338 (Records of U.S. Army Commands, 1942-) contains material relating to the West Coast and southern coast exclusion programs. These programs, while affecting primarily the relocation of persons of Japanese ancestry, also concern some German enemy aliens.

Records of the WCCA are among the records of the WRA in RG 210. Other RGs concerning units and activities of the U.S. War Dept. may also contain documentation about refugees. Finding aid: National Archives, *Guide*, pp. 216-220, 278-280, etc.

159. U.S. WAR REFUGEE BOARD   *Defunct*

Established in the Executive Office of the President by Executive Order 9417 of January 22, 1944, the Board consisted of the Secretaries of State, the Treasury, and War. Its administrative functions were carried on by an Executive Director and by special attachés having diplomatic status. In cooperation with other federal agencies and with foreign governments, it sought to effect the rescue and relief of victims of Axis oppression and provide temporary refuge for them. In 1944, the Board formulated policies for the *U.S. War Relocation Authority's administration of the *U.S. Emergency Refugee Shelter at Fort Ontario, Oswego, NY. The Board was dissolved by Executive Order 9614 of September 14, 1945.

Literature. U.S. War Refugee Board, *Final Summary Report of the Executive Director.* Washington, DC, 1945.

Records. Franklin D. Roosevelt Library: records, 1944-45, 46 ft, consist of correspondence, memoranda, reports, history, petitions, vouchers, clippings, and other records. Restricted. *NUCMC* MS 75-584. Finding aids: unpublished inventories and indexes. National Archives, *Guide*, p. 107. National Archives, *Preliminary Inventory of the Records of the War Refugee Board.* PI 43. Washington, DC, 1952.

Zionist Archives and Library: minutes of the Board, 1944-45, on microfilm (one reel).

National Archives and Records Service, Civil Archives Div.: records of the Board, 1944-45, 1 ft, are in Record Group 210 (Records of the War Relocation Authority). Include correspondence, reports, statements, Executive Orders, and publicity material documenting the origin of the program for the establishment of emergency refugee shelters in the U.S.A., and the policies governing the Fort Ontario shelter. Finding aids: National Archives, *Guide*, pp. 689-691. National Archives, *Preliminary Inventory of the Records of the War Relocation Authority, Record Group 210.* PI 77. Washington, DC, 1955. Item no. 63.

160. U.S. WAR RELOCATION AUTHORITY   *Defunct*

Established in the Office for Emergency Management by Executive Order 9102 of March 18, 1942, to provide for the removal, relocation, maintenance, and supervision of persons excluded from strategic military zones. Initial assembling of evacuees had been undertaken by the Wartime Civil Control Administration, organized in 1942 by the Army's Western Defense Command (*U.S. War Dept.). Although the primary function of the Authority was to assist persons of Japanese ancestry who had been evacuated from the West Coast by military order, the Authority was also responsible for the relocation of other persons, particularly German and Italian aliens excluded from sensitive military areas. The Authority's responsibility for Germans and Italians was limited to providing financial aid for their transportation and relocation. It did not house them in relocation centers.

The Authority was transferred in February 1944 to the *U.S. Dept. of the Interior. In June 1944, President *Franklin D. Roosevelt directed the Authority to operate the *U.S. Emergency Refugee Shelter for European refugees at Fort Ontario, Oswego, NY, under policies formulated by the *U.S. War Refugee Board.

In December 1944, the West Coast general exclusion order was revoked, and the Supreme Court ruled certain of the detention features of the relocation program unconstitutional. Thereafter, the Authority largely engaged in the resettlement of evacuees. Terminated by Executive Order 9742 of June 25, 1946.

Literature. U.S. Dept. of the Interior, War Relocation Authority, *WRA: A Story of Human Conservation.* Washington, DC, 1946.

Records. National Archives and Records Service, Civil Archives Div.: records, comprising Record Group 210, consist of headquarters records, field records, and records of the Wartime Civil Control Administration and U.S. War Refugee Board. Headquarters records include records of the War Refugee Div., reports on the Shelter, and case files on individual exclusions, 1942–45, 6 ft (about persons of other than Japanese descent excluded from military areas). Field records include records of the Shelter at Fort Ontario. Restricted. Finding aids: National Archives, *Guide*, pp. 689–691. National Archives, *Preliminary Inventory of the Records of the War Relocation Authority, Record Group 210.* PI 77. Washington, DC, 1955.

161. U.S. WORK PROJECTS ADMINISTRATION (WPA)   *Defunct*

The U.S. Work Projects Administration (known as the Works Progress Administration until July 1, 1939) was established in 1935 to administer the government's work-relief program. In 1939, the WPA was made a part of the U.S. Federal Works Agency. The WPA was terminated in 1943 and its liquidation completed in 1944.

The National Citizenship Education Program (NCEP), for the education and assimilation of foreign-born, was conducted from 1941 to 1943 jointly by the WPA and the *U.S. Immigration and Naturalization Service (INS), with the cooperation of the *U.S. Office of Education. At the state level, WPA units in conjunction with state education departments offered programs in education for citizenship. When WPA ended in 1943, the INS continued NCEP by expanding its program and increasing its staff for the education of the foreign born. William F. Russell, Dean of Teachers College at Columbia Univ., was director of NCEP 1941–45.

Literature. U.S. Federal Works Agency, *Final Report on the WPA Program, 1935–43.* Washington, DC, 1947.

Records. National Archives and Records Service, Civil Archives Div.: records comprise Record Group 69. The WPA central files, 1935–44, are arranged according to a decimal classification plan. The "general subject" series includes 4 boxes on NCEP, 1941–43 (under file code 211.44). The "State" series includes material on state citizenship education programs, 1941–43 (under file code

651.3144 for each state). Records of the WPA Div. of Information include 2 boxes of press releases and newspaper clippings on NCEP (under file codes 814: literacy classes, and 815: citizenship classes) and 9 bound volumes of WPA publications that deal with WPA education programs and include samples of citizenship materials. Finding aid: National Archives, *Guide*, pp. 693-699.

162. WOMEN'S INTERNATIONAL LEAGUE FOR PEACE AND FREEDOM, INC.
1783 Pine St., Philadelphia, PA 19103

Founded in 1915 by Jane Addams, a pacifist and feminist social worker who drew national attention to the plight of immigrants through her activities at Hull House, one of the first settlement houses in Chicago.

The League established a National Committee to work on behalf of refugees, and an Educational Committee to influence public opinion on refugee questions.

Records. Swarthmore College Peace Collection: records include material on refugees.

163. WORLD JEWISH CONGRESS
North American Section: 15 E. 84 St., New York, NY 10028

The World Jewish Congress (WJC) was founded in Geneva, Switzerland, in 1936 under the leadership of *Stephen S. Wise and Nahum Goldmann by delegates representing 32 countries. The WJC is an association of "representative Jewish bodies, communities, and organizations" throughout the world, organized to "assure the survival, and to foster the unity of the Jewish people." Its international headquarters are in Geneva. The American branch of the WJC, established in 1939, has its head office in New York City.

During World War II, the WJC had a share in significant rescue attempts and relief and rehabilitation programs on behalf of victims of Nazi persecution. Dr. Gerhard Riegner, secretary of the WJC in Geneva, was the first Jewish official to inform American and British Jewish leaders and government agencies of the genocide perpetrated in Nazi-occupied Europe against the Jews.

The WJC played a central role in formulating Jewish policies with regard to the peace treaties, the prosecution and trials of Nazi war criminals, the adoption of a scheme of reparations for Jewish victims of the Holocaust by the occupying powers and the German Federal Republic, and the rehabilitation of Jewish communal and cultural life in the postwar years. On September 10, 1952, Goldmann signed the "Luxembourg Agreement" between the Federal Republic of Germany and the State of Israel on behalf of organized Jewries in the Diaspora, a representative function that had been prepared by the establishment of the WJC.

During the 1940s, the WJC's Advisory Council on European Jewish Affairs consisted of various Representative Committees, including the German Jewish, Austrian Jewish, and Czechoslovak Jewish Representative Committees composed of former refugees.

Literature. A. Leon Kubowitzki et al., eds., *Unity in Dispersion: A History of the World Jewish Congress.* New York, 1948.

Records. It was not possible to ascertain the scope and quantity of records in the custody of the North American Section in New York. Over the years, records of the WJC have been relocated several times, and it is believed that a significant amount of documentation is at the headquarters in Geneva.

Yad Vashem Archives, Israel: records, 1945-48, ca. 60 ft, of the Relatives Search Dept. of the WJC in the U.S.A., and records, 1945-46, ca. 60 ft, of the Relatives Search Dept. of the WJC in Stockholm.

164. WORLD UNION FOR PROGRESSIVE JUDAISM, LTD.
North American Board: 838 Fifth Ave., New York, NY 10021
Headquarters: Jerusalem, Israel

Founded in 1926 as a coordinating agency to promote Reform, Liberal, and Progressive Judaism throughout the world. Headquarters were located in London 1922-60, and New York 1960-73.

Participated in attempts to rescue Jews in Europe, especially by finding positions for rabbis, religious functionaries, and scholars in the field of Judaica. Its affiliated congregations assisted in the immigration and resettlement of refugees through social programs, financial aid, religious services, hospitality to newly established Reform congregations, and other activities.

Literature. World Union for Progressive Judaism, *Bulletin.* Issues of the 1930s and 1940s provide information on aid to refugees.

Records. American Jewish Archives: records, 1926-65, 5.4 ft (ca. 5400 items), consist of minutes of meetings of the executive committee and the governing body, conference programs, correspondence, and miscellaneous materials. The names of more than a dozen refugee rabbis appear in this collection. Also on microfilm (11 reels). Finding aid: unpublished inventory (12 pp.).

Recent records are at the Union's offices in New York and Jerusalem.

165. WORLD ZIONIST ORGANIZATION–AMERICAN SECTION
515 Park Ave., New York, NY 10022

Known until 1971 as the Jewish Agency–American Section, when the Jewish Agency for Israel (formerly Jewish Agency for Palestine) was reconstituted.

The policies of the Jewish Agency for Palestine had a major influence on the distribution of émigrés from Germany across the world. In 1933, the Central Bureau for the Settlement of German Jews in Palestine was formed by the Jewish Agency, with Dr. Chaim Weizmann heading its London office, and *Georg Landauer its director in Palestine. By 1936, the Bureau had become the German Dept. of the Jewish Agency. It assigned quotas of immigration certificates to various European countries in the 1930s.

The Jewish Agency's transfer agreements with Nazi Germany (*Haavara*) aided in transferring funds owned by German Jews to Palestine and indirectly to other immigration countries, including the U.S.A. Its policies on immigration to Palestine affected Jewish attitudes on immigration and resettlement in the U.S.A. in the 1940s. The Jewish Agency assumed responsibility for the Youth Aliyah program designed to bring children to Palestine from Nazi Germany.

Records. Central Zionist Archives, Israel: records of the American Section of the Jewish Agency, 1939–51, 162 ft. As the primary repository of archival materials relating to the Zionist movement, the Jewish Agency, and the World Zionist Organization, this repository has other collections which concern the emigration of the Nazi era, including records, 1933–37, ca. 4 ft, of the London office of the Central Bureau, and records, 1939–54, of the Jewish Agency's Dept. for Restitution of German Jewish Property.

Zionist Archives and Library: small amount of the American Section's records, including one box, 1933–39, relating to the Jewish Agency's Central Bureau for the Resettlement of German Jews in Palestine, consisting of correspondence with American Zionist Leaders, reports, and minutes of meetings.

Recent records of the American Section are at its office.

Landauer's papers, at the Leo Baeck Institute Archives, include material relating to the Jewish Agency.

166. YOUNG MEN'S CHRISTIAN ASSOCIATION, NATIONAL BOARD (YMCA)
291 Broadway, New York, NY 10007

The YMCA's declared purpose is the "moral, spiritual, intellectual, and physical improvement of the nation's youth." It was established in the U.S.A. in 1851. The YMCA serves foreign students upon their arrival in the U.S.A. and offers inexpensive accommodations in its hostels.

The YMCA's activities in Europe, including relief for refugees, were administered by the International Committee (now International Division) of YMCA in New York and by the World's Alliance of YMCAs in Geneva, Switzerland. Donald A. Lowrie, an American YMCA official who worked for the World's Alliance of YMCAs, was active in promoting YMCA European relief for refugees and prisoners of war. Lowrie was the chairman of the *Comité de Coordination pour l'Assistance dans les Camps* (CCAC), also known as the Nîmes Committee, which was comprised of Americans working in France during World War II on behalf of American relief and refugee aid agencies.

Literature. Donald A. Lowrie, *The Hunted Children.* New York: Norton, 1963. Chap. 8, "The Nîmes Committee," and chap. 9, "Emigration," are especially relevant.
Romanofsky, *Social Service Organizations*, pp. 758–764.

Records. Records are in the YMCA Historical Library and in the office of the International Div. at YMCA National Board headquarters. Files dealing with refugee work are not segregated from other records relating to the international activities of the YMCAs.

Additional documentation may be located in the archives of the World's Alliance of YMCAs, 37 Quai Wilson, 1201 Geneva, Switzerland.

Leo Baeck Institute Archives: the *Konzentrationslager Frankreich* (French concentration camp) collection, 1939-44, 3 in. (907 pp.), consists of records relating primarily to the activities of the CCAC and the *American Friends Service Committee in France. Included are minutes of CCAC meetings in Nîmes, 1940-42, and other documentation about aid to refugees in France. Finding aid: unpublished inventory (6 pp.).

167. YOUNG WOMEN'S CHRISTIAN ASSOCIATION, NATIONAL BOARD (YWCA)
600 Lexington Ave., New York, NY 10022

A coordinating agency of associations founded in 1871. YWCA's Dept. of Immigration and Foreign Communities, which supervised the *International Institutes, was replaced in 1933 by an independent National Institute of Immigrant Welfare, which was later known as the American Federation of International Institutes.

At its convention of April 28, 1938, the National Board adopted a resolution concerning refugees. In November 1938, the National Board authorized the appointment of a Committee on Refugees in the Laboratory Div. of the YWCA. Local units of the YWCA across the country were encouraged to participate in efforts to assist refugees. In March 1939, the National Board endorsed the *Wagner-*Rogers bill. At the request of the Committee on Refugees, the National Board issued two pamphlets, *Meet the Refugees*, 1940, and *Refugees in Wartime*, 1943. In 1940, the International Div. in New York, which provided assistance to overseas branches of the YWCA, formed a World Emergency Committee to administer relief overseas. This activity was coordinated with the World's Council of the YWCA in Geneva, Switzerland, whose general secretary was *Ruth F. Woodsmall.

Literature. Rhoda E. McCulloch, "The Dispossessed." *Woman's Press* 33 (Jan. 1939): 14-16.
Romanofsky, *Social Service Organizations*, pp. 764-772.
YWCA, National Board, Committee on Refugees, *Refugees Bulletin*, no. 1-2, 1938-39.

Records. YWCA Archives: comprehensive records, including microfilm, 1906-60, 300 reels, contain the minute book of the Committee on Refugees, 1941-45, and several microfilm reels on immigration and the International Institutes, including some documentation on aid to refugees. Finding aid: *Inventory to the National Board YWCA Records Files Collection.* New York, 1978.

Smith College Library, Sophia Smith Collection: records, 1889-1959, ca. 23 ft, comprising the original materials for part of the microfilm collection at the YWCA Archives, include materials on immigration, the International Institutes, and refugees. *NUCMC* MS 77-1842. Finding aid: unpublished inventory.

Additional documentation may be located in the archives of the World's Council of the YWCA, 37 Quai Wilson, 1201 Geneva, Switzerland.

168. ZIONIST ORGANIZATION OF AMERICA, INC. (ZOA)
4 E. 34 St., New York, NY 10016

Principal Zionist organization in the U.S.A., founded in 1897. Seeks to safeguard the integrity and independence of Israel by means consistent with the laws of the U.S.A., to assist in the economic development of Israel, and to foster the unity of the Jewish people and the centrality of Israel in Jewish life in the spirit of general Zionism.

Assisted with the migration and resettlement of European refugees, especially active Zionists. German refugee Zionists in New York organized District 81 of ZOA, the *Theodor Herzl Society, and Austrian refugee Zionists in New York established District 82, *Igul.

Literature. Melvin I. Urofsky, *American Zionism from Herzl to the Holocaust.* Garden City, NY: Anchor Press, 1975.

Records. A substantial part of ZOA's records was discarded during several moves of the national office. Remaining records, at Zionist Archives and Library, include one folder of correspondence regarding the Zionistische Vereinigung für Deutschland, between German Zionists and the ZOA, discussing cases of individual Jews who wished to emigrate to the U.S.A. and were asking assistance from ZOA.

Recent records are at ZOA's office.

Two

REGIONAL AND LOCAL ORGANIZATIONS

California

169. STATE OF CALIFORNIA, DIVISION OF IMMIGRATION AND HOUSING
Defunct

A state agency that provided assistance to the foreign born. The Division was administered by the Dept. of Industrial Relations until 1945, when the Department was reorganized. Then the Division of Immigration and Housing became the Dept. of Housing, now the Dept. of Housing and Community Development.

Direct service to immigrants from Central Europe of the Nazi period is presumed to have been limited, although the agency coordinated the activities of various organizations offering services to refugees.

Records. Univ. of California at Berkeley, Bancroft Library: records, 1910–34, ca. 100 ft. *NUCMC* MS 71-708.

Records, 1935–45, could not be found at the Dept. of Housing and Community Development, the Dept. of Industrial Relations, the California State Archives, or the State Records Service.

Los Angeles

170. B'NAI B'RITH, ISRAEL LODGE NO. 1793
c/o Ephraim Goldschneider (president), 1331 N. Gardner, Los Angeles, CA 90046

Lodge of *B'nai B'rith International, founded by German-Jewish immigrants in Los Angeles in 1949 for cultural and social purposes and mutual aid.

Records. Records are with various officers.

171. JEWISH CLUB OF 1933, INC.
8057 Beverly Blvd., Los Angeles, CA 90048

German-Jewish immigrant organization founded in 1933 as the German-Jewish Club of Los Angeles, and incorporated in 1936. Adopted present name in 1940.

Originally offering artistic and literary as well as social and religious programs, the Club concentrated on protecting the civil rights of German-Jewish émigrés with the outbreak of World War II, while continuing its cultural and mutual aid activities. Engaged in mutual aid, social welfare, and social and cultural activities. Affiliated with *American Federation of Jews from Central Europe.

After the Club's own efforts to create a "Southern California Home for Jewish Emigrants" were abandoned, it contracted with the Los Angeles Jewish Home for the Aged in Reseda in 1955 to establish a "Jewish Club of 1933 Wing" for aged immigrants from Germany. Cofounder, 1955, of West Coast branch office of the *United Restitution Organization.

Published a monthly bulletin, *Neue Welt*, from 1933, which in 1941 was incorporated into *Aufbau* (New York) and thereafter appeared as a special supplement, *Die Westküste*. Published *Mitteilungsblatt* monthly since 1948.

Literature. Lessing, *Oral History.*

Records. Records prior to 1946 are scanty and presumed lost. Records are principally at the Club's office and with various officers and members.

172. JEWISH FAMILY SERVICE OF LOS ANGELES
6505 Wilshire Blvd., Los Angeles, CA 90048

See *Jewish Welfare Agencies for general description.

The Coordinating Committee for Aid to Jewish Refugees and its successor, the Los Angeles Émigré Service of the Jewish Social Service Bureau (later renamed Jewish Family Service), assisted in the resettlement of refugees.

Literature. Anton Lourié, "Social Readjustment of German-Jewish Refugees in Los Angeles." Unpublished master's thesis in sociology, Univ. of Southern California, Los Angeles, Jan. 1953.

Records. As a matter of policy, the agency destroys the files of its clients five years after closing their case. Materials concerning refugee resettlement are included in the minutes of the Jewish Family Service, on file at its office. The minutes of the Émigré Service are with the Jewish Federation-Council, at the same address.

173. NATIONAL COUNCIL OF JEWISH WOMEN, LOS ANGELES SECTION
543 N. Fairfax Ave., Los Angeles, CA 90036

A section of the *National Council of Jewish Women.

The activities of its Service to Foreign Born were transferred in 1968 to the *Jewish Family Service of Los Angeles.

Records. Records at the agency's office are presumed to include materials concerning refugees. According to information received, the records of the Service to Foreign Born were transferred in 1968 to the Jewish Family Service of Los Angeles.

174. UNITED RESTITUTION ORGANIZATION (URO)
8230 Beverly Blvd., Los Angeles, CA 90048

West Coast branch office of the *United Restitution Organization, created in 1955.

Records. Records, restricted, consisting of client case files and administrative materials, are at the agency's office.

Oakland

175. EAST BAY FRIENDS
c/o Julius Lowenstein (president), 407 Perkins St., Oakland, CA 94610

German-Jewish immigrant organization founded in 1948 by postwar immigrants who had spent the war years as refugees in *Shanghai, South America, and other countries of intermediate settlement. Initially organized as the "Shanghai Group" of the *Jewish Council of 1933, San Francisco. Engaged in mutual aid, social welfare, and social and cultural activities. Conducts high holiday services. Affiliated with *American Federation of Jews from Central Europe.
Published a bulletin, *The Bay View.*

Literature. Lessing, *Oral History.*

Records. Records, including bylaws and minutes since 1960, are with the president and secretary.

176. JEWISH FAMILY SERVICE OF ALAMEDA AND CONTRA COSTA COUNTIES
3245 Sheffield Ave., Oakland, CA 94602

See *Jewish Welfare Agencies for general description.
Cooperated with social agencies in San Francisco in aiding the resettlement of refugees.

Records. Records at the agency's office concerning refugee resettlement include minutes of board and committee meetings, correspondence, and case files of refugees.

San Diego

177. NEW LIFE CLUB
c/o Yearl Schwartz (president), 4803 Lorraine Dr., San Diego, CA 92115

German-Jewish immigrant organization founded in 1952 for mutual aid, social, and cultural activities. Affiliated with *American Federation of Jews from Central Europe from 1956 to 1964.

Records. Records are with various officers.

San Francisco

178. B'NAI B'RITH, GOLDEN GATE LODGE NO. 2464
c/o Max Levi (president), 140 El Verano Way, San Francisco, CA 94127

Lodge of *B'nai B'rith International, founded by German-Jewish immigrants in San Francisco in 1945 for cultural and social purposes and mutual aid.

Records. Records are with various officers.

179. B'NAI B'RITH WOMEN, GOLDEN GATE CHAPTER NO. 1372
c/o Mrs. Lottie Rothschild (president), 446 Lawton St., San Francisco, CA 94122

Chapter of *B'nai B'rith International, founded by German-Jewish immigrants in San Francisco in 1970 for cultural and social purposes and mutual aid.

Records. Records are with various officers.

180. CONGREGATION B'NAI EMUNAH
3595 Taraval St., San Francisco, CA 94116

German-Jewish immigrant congregation founded in 1949 by postwar immigrants who had spent the war years as refugees in *Shanghai. Conducted high holiday services jointly with *Jewish Council of 1933. Affiliated with the United Synagogue of America.

Published quarterly *Newsletter*, and *10th Anniversary, 20th Anniversary, 21st Anniversary*, 1971, and *25th Anniversary* [journals].

Literature. Lessing, *Oral History.*

Records. Records, including minutes since 1949 and publications, are at the synagogue and with various officers and members.

181. HAKOAH ATHLETIC CLUB OF SAN FRANCISCO, INC.
c/o Alfred Laufer (vice-president), 263 Lakeshore Dr., San Francisco, CA 94132

Zionist-oriented sports club founded in 1945 by Central European Jewish immigrants for social, cultural, and sports activities. Modeled on the Jewish sports organization *Hakoah*, founded in Vienna in 1909.

Published *Hakoah News*, irregularly at present; and *10 Years Hakoah A.C. San Francisco 1945-1955, Hakoah's November Affair, 1963, Hakoah A.C. San Francisco 1965 Purim Dance Program Book,* and *Hakoah Athletic Club Celebrates Israel's Independence, 1969.*

Literature. *International Biographical Dictionary*, vol. I (J. Torczyner).

Records. Records are with the founder and past president, Joshua Torczyner, 3003 Hillside Dr., Burlingame, CA 94010, and with various officers.

182. HOMEWOOD TERRACE (A Jewish Child Care Agency)
540 Arguello Blvd., San Francisco, CA 94118

Principal child care agency for the San Francisco Jewish community.

Sponsored refugee children brought to San Francisco by the German Jewish Children's Aid (after 1942, *European Jewish Children's Aid). The children were placed in foster homes until they were reunited with their families, or became self-supporting.

Records. Records dealing with refugee children, 1937-63, 3 file drawers, consisting of case histories and correspondence, are at the agency's office.

183. JEWISH COUNCIL OF 1933, INC. *Defunct*

German-Jewish immigrant organization founded in 1938 as the Council of Jewish Émigrés. By 1943, the name had been changed to Jewish Council of San Francisco and the Bay Area. Present name adopted in 1944 and incorporated in 1946. Engaged in mutual aid and social and cultural activities. Conducted high holiday services, later combined with those of *Congregation B'nai Emunah. Provided advice on *Wiedergutmachung* through the good offices of attorney Dr. Helmut Erlanger. Unsuccessfully tried to form an "East Bay Group" in 1945. Assisted postwar immigrants; its "Shanghai Group," which first met in November 1948, became a separate organization, *East Bay Friends, Oakland. (Liberty Forum, an informal social organization of German-Jewish immigrants, also existed 1934-41.) Affiliated with *American Federation of Jews from Central Europe. Discontinued activities in October 1977 and legally dissolved in 1978.

Published *Jewish Council Bulletin* monthly from 1943 to 1977.

Literature. *International Biographical Dictionary*, vol. I (H. Erlanger). Lessing, *Oral History.*

Records. Western Jewish History Center: records, 1 ft, include minutes of meetings, copies of the *Jewish Council Bulletin*, correspondence, membership lists, bylaws, reports, and publicity material.

American Federation of Jews from Central Europe has a fairly complete set of the early issues of the *Jewish Council Bulletin*, including: vol. [1], nos. 1, 3-4, 9-12 (Nov. 1943, Feb.-Apr., Oct. 1944-Feb. 1945); vol. 2, nos. 13-14, 16, 19-28 (Apr.-May, Aug., Nov. 1945-Sept. 1946); vol. 3, nos. 1-12 (Oct. 1946-Sept. 1947); vol. 4, nos. 1-2, 4-5, 9, 11 (Oct.-Nov. 1947, Jan.-Feb., June, Aug. 1948); vol. 5 to end, scattered issues.

184. JEWISH FAMILY SERVICE AGENCY
1600 Scott St., San Francisco, CA 94115

See *Jewish Welfare Agencies for general description.

The San Francisco Committee for Service to Émigrés was established in 1936 by the Federation of Jewish Charities (later renamed Jewish Welfare Federation), and was subsequently incorporated in the Jewish Family Service Agency.

Literature. Lessing, *Oral History*.

San Francisco Committee for Service to Émigrés, *Report*, Jan. 1936–June 1941.

Records. Records at the Agency's office include case files, 1936–54 (ca. 1356 available out of an original 2660), dealing mostly with resettlement. They include cases of postwar refugees resettling in the U.S.A. via *Shanghai. Cases concerning the Agency's assistance to prospective immigrants in obtaining affidavits were mostly destroyed.

185. NATIONAL COUNCIL OF JEWISH WOMEN, SAN FRANCISCO SECTION
1825 Divisadero St., San Francisco, CA 94115

A section of the *National Council of Jewish Women.

Its Service to Foreign Born cooperated with the San Francisco Committee for Service to Émigrés (*Jewish Family Service Agency).

Records. Some records are at the agency's office. The bulk of the material relating to the Service to Foreign Born is with the former chairwoman of the Service to Foreign Born, Mrs. Oscar Geballe, 1880 Jackson, San Francisco, CA 94109.

186. SELFHELP OF ÉMIGRÉS FROM CENTRAL EUROPE, SAN FRANCISCO BRANCH   *Defunct*

Founded in 1940 by Central European immigrants (including Dr. *Leon Kolb) as the San Francisco branch of Selfhelp of Émigrés from Central Europe (*Selfhelp Community Services), following exploratory contacts of founder–member Professor *Carl Landauer with Selfhelp in New York, begun in 1937. Engaged in individual aid until 1941, then raised funds for Selfhelp and cooperated with local and national refugee aid and immigrant organizations.

Literature. Lessing, *Oral History*.

Records. Correspondence, 1937–41, one folder, concerning Selfhelp in San Francisco and Landauer's activities for Selfhelp is included in Landauer's papers.

Records of Selfhelp Community Services in New York are presumed to include information on Selfhelp, San Francisco.

Colorado

Denver

187. CLUB OF 1946
c/o Walter D. Loebl (president), 1191 Grape St., Denver, CO 80220

German-Jewish immigrant organization founded in 1946 and reorganized in 1972 for mutual aid and social and cultural activities. Formerly affiliated with *American Federation of Jews from Central Europe.

Records. Records are with the president and other officers.

188. JEWISH FAMILY AND CHILDREN'S SERVICE OF COLORADO
1375 Delaware St., Denver, CO 80204

See *Jewish Welfare Agencies for general description.
    Formed in 1947 by a merger of the Central Jewish Aid Society, founded in 1916, and the Denver Coordinating Committee for Immigrants, founded in the 1930s to assist in the resettlement of refugees.

Literature. Allen D. Breck, *The Centennial History of the Jews of Colorado, 1859-1959.* Denver: Univ. of Denver, 1960, pp. 194-195, 245.
Rosslyn E. Stewart (Univ. of Colorado), Ph.D. dissertation in progress on the Denver Jewish community's response to Jewish refugees who resettled there, 1933-40.

Records. American Jewish Archives: records, 1907-58, 34 ft, consist of correspondence, reports, and closed case files.
    American Jewish Historical Society: records, 1921-69, 27 ft, consist of more than 3000 case files, the majority of which were closed between 1948 and the 1960s. The early cases deal with new immigrants, including refugees, resettling in Denver. *NUCMC* MS 70-1009, MS 77-34.
    Later records are at the agency's office.

189. NATIONAL COUNCIL OF JEWISH WOMEN, DENVER SECTION
For current address, contact the headquarters of NCJW in New York.

A section of the *National Council of Jewish Women.

Records. Rocky Mountain Jewish Historical Society: minutes of meetings. Other records are with the agency's officers.

Connecticut

Bridgeport

190. JEWISH FAMILY SERVICE
2370 Park Ave., Bridgeport, CT 06604

See *Jewish Welfare Agencies for general description.
    The Jewish Welfare Bureau (later renamed Jewish Family Service) assisted in the resettlement of refugees.

Records. Records at the agency's office include case files of clients.

191. JEWISH UNITY CLUB
c/o Ernest Frohsinn, 38 Kalan Circle, Fairfield, CT 06430

German-Jewish immigrant organization founded in 1940 in Bridgeport for social welfare, mutual aid, and social and cultural activities. Formerly affiliated with *American Federation of Jews from Central Europe. Since ca. 1960, functions as a burial society. Maintains a cemetery plot for members.

Records. Records, including current membership lists and cemetery papers, are with Mr. Frohsinn. According to information received, the club kept no minutes of its meetings or activities.

Hartford

192. JEWISH FAMILY SERVICE OF GREATER HARTFORD
740 N. Main St., West Hartford, CT 06117

See *Jewish Welfare Agencies for general description.
   The Coordinating Committee for Refugees and subsequently the Refugee Service of Hartford assisted in the resettlement of refugees.

Records. The Service has no records concerning the resettlement of refugees.

New Haven

193. JEWISH FAMILY SERVICE
152 Temple St., New Haven, CT 06510

See *Jewish Welfare Agencies for general description.
   The Coordinating Committee for Aid to Émigrés assisted in the resettlement of refugees.

Records. No information was obtained following an inquiry about the agency's records.

Delaware

194. STATE OF DELAWARE, SERVICE FOR FOREIGN BORN
Delaware Technical and Community College, 333 Shipley St., Wilmington, DE 19801

A state agency that provided assistance to the foreign born. Formerly the Service Bureau for Foreign Born People of the Dept. of Public Instruction.

Records. Delaware Div. of Historical and Cultural Affairs: records, 1918–69, 80 ft, consist of inactive case files. Index cards to the files and annual reports since 1944 are at the Service's office.

District of Columbia (Washington)

195. ACHDUTH-CHEVRAH, INC.
c/o Eric Rapp (president), 2810 Spencer Rd., Chevy Chase, MD 20015

German-Jewish immigrant organization founded in 1949 and incorporated ca.

1953. Functions as a *chevra kadisha* (burial society) in the traditional manner. Affiliated with *American Federation of Jews from Central Europe.

Records. Records, consisting of brief minutes of annual meetings, 1949 to early 1960s, are with the president.

196. JEWISH SOCIAL SERVICE AGENCY
6123 Montrose Rd., Rockville, MD 20852

See *Jewish Welfare Agencies for general description.
    The Agency's Committee for Refugee Services assisted in the resettlement of refugees.

Literature. Ann R. Goldberg, "Jewish Social Service in Washington, D.C., 1890-1940." *The Record* (Publication of The Jewish Historical Society of Greater Washington) 4 (May 1969): 22-32.

Records. Records at the agency's office include minutes of meetings and case files of clients.

197. NATIONAL COUNCIL OF JEWISH WOMEN, DISTRICT OF COLUMBIA SECTION
For current address, contact the headquarters of NCJW in New York.

A section of the *National Council of Jewish Women (NCJW), founded 1895.
    In addition to the social assistance offered to refugees by the Council's Service to Foreign Born, this Section's members often testified before Congressional committees on immigration and related issues on behalf of the NCJW, which did not have a permanent office in Washington until 1944.

Literature. Leona H. Hacke, "Early History of the D.C. Section of the National Council of Jewish Women (1915-1957)." *The Record* (Publication of The Jewish Historical Society of Greater Washington) 5 (May 1970): 33-41.

Records. No information was obtained following an inquiry about the agency's records.

Florida

Miami

198. CHEVRA FELLOWSHIP OF MIAMI, INC.
c/o Eric Tichauer (vice-president), 7735 Abbott Ave., Miami Beach, FL 33141

German-Jewish immigrant organization incorporated in 1963 for social, cultural, and religious activities. Provides burials for deceased members in the traditional manner.

Records. Records, including minutes of annual meetings, are with various officers.

199. CONTINENTAL FRIENDSHIP CLUB OF MIAMI BEACH
c/o Arthur Brodtmann (president), 245 18 St., Miami Beach, FL 33139

German-Jewish immigrant organization founded in 1966 for social activities.

Records. Records are with various officers.

200. JEWISH FAMILY AND CHILDREN'S SERVICE
1790 S.W. 27 Ave., Miami, FL 33145

See *Jewish Welfare Agencies for general description.

The Refugee Coordinating Committee was established in Miami in November 1938 by several agencies including the Jewish Welfare Bureau (later renamed Jewish Family and Children's Service) and the Greater Miami Section of *National Council of Jewish Women. A State Resettlement Committee was formed in March 1939. Miami was a major port of entry for refugees arriving via the Caribbean and Latin America.

Literature. Gertrude D. Pinsky, "Community Organization for Refugee Work— A Descriptive Analysis of the Factors and Problems Involved in the Organization of Social Service Facilities for Refugees in a Southern Community [Miami] Whose Work Is of National Significance Since It Is a Port of Entry." Unpublished master's thesis, New York School of Social Work, Columbia Univ., Aug. 1941.

Records. No information was obtained following an inquiry about the agency's records.

201. MIAMI SOCIAL CLUB   *Defunct*

German-Jewish immigrant organization founded ca. 1950 for social and cultural activities. Ceased to function ca. 1970 after the death of its president, Dr. Oscar D. May. Affiliated with *American Federation of Jews from Central Europe.

Records. Records, consisting of programs, photographs, clippings, and attendance lists, are with Dr. May's son, John E. May, 1500 Bay Rd., Miami Beach, FL 33139.

202. NATIONAL COUNCIL OF JEWISH WOMEN, GREATER MIAMI SECTION
4200 Biscayne Blvd., Miami, FL 33137

A section of the *National Council of Jewish Women.

Cooperated with the Jewish Welfare Bureau (*Jewish Family and Children's Service) and other groups in forming the Refugee Coordinating Committee in 1938. Provided "Port and Dock" service and maintained a Service to Foreign Born. From 1953 to 1970, the Section operated a branch office of the *United Restitution Organization, processing approximately 1000 cases and recovering about $500,000 of *Wiedergutmachungs*-payments for Nazi victims residing in south Florida. In 1970, the program was phased out, and Mrs. Alexandra Selden, who had previously served as the Section's caseworker, continued to advise claimants on pending cases. The Section is the local representative of *United HIAS Service and cooperates with it in all matters concerning overseas migration.

Literature. Gertrude D. Pinsky, "Community Organization for Refugee Work— A Descriptive Analysis of the Factors and Problems Involved in the Organization of Social Service Facilities for Refugees in a Southern Community [Miami] Whose Work Is of National Significance Since It Is a Port of Entry." Unpublished master's thesis, New York School of Social Work, Columbia Univ., Aug. 1941.

Records. Records at the agency's office include minutes since the 1930s, reports on immigration prepared in the 1940s, and some general correspondence on *Wiedergutmachung.* Case files on immigration and *Wiedergutmachung* have been destroyed. According to information received, Mrs. Selden has the card index to all *Wiedergutmachungs*-cases processed by the Section.

Georgia

Atlanta

203. JEWISH FAMILY AND CHILDREN'S BUREAU
1753 Peachtree Rd., N.E., Atlanta, GA 30309

See *Jewish Welfare Agencies for general description.

Records. Records at the agency's office include minutes of meetings and files concerning resettlement and claims for *Wiedergutmachung* from the Federal Republic of Germany.

204. NEW WORLD CLUB OF ATLANTA   *Defunct*

German-Jewish immigrant social club founded in 1947 as an outgrowth of the "Tuesday Night Group," which was organized ca. 1939 by the Service to Foreign Born of the *National Council of Jewish Women, Atlanta Section. The "Group's" purpose had been to promote Americanization. Published a bulletin in 1958. Ceased to exist ca. 1960.

Records. Records have not been located, according to information received from the last president of the Club, William H. Sachs, Atlanta, GA.

Illinois

Chicago

205. CHEWRA KADISHA ESRAS NIDOCHIM, INC.
c/o Theo Straus (president), 1607 E. 50 Pl., Chicago, IL 60615

Burial society founded in 1938 by German-Jewish immigrants who rejected

"American style" Jewish funeral customs and instituted traditional "European" burial customs for deceased members. A voluntary organization supported by members' dues, the Chewra owns its own cemetery and invests its surplus funds in Israel Bonds.

Records. Records, including minutes, charter, membership files, and financial statements, are with the president.

206. CONGREGATION EZRA HABONIM
2620 W. Touhy Ave., Chicago, IL 60645

German-Jewish immigrant congregation formed in 1973 by a merger of Ezra Congregation and Congregation Habonim. Affiliated with United Synagogue of America.

Ezra Congregation was founded by German-Jewish immigrants in 1937 as the North Center of Jewish Youth. The North Center was initially the North Side "chapter" of the Jewish Center (Center of Jewish Youth), which had been formed by German-Jewish immigrants in 1936. Ezra Congregation was known as Jewish North Center 1941–44, Jewish North Center Congregation 1944–47, Temple Ezra 1947–67, and Ezra Congregation 1967–73.

Congregation Habonim, founded in 1939 as the Friday Evening Congregation, adopted the name Habonim in 1944. In 1946, it joined with the Jewish Center (Center of Jewish Youth) to form Congregation Habonim Jewish Center. In 1957, the name was shortened to Congregation Habonim.

Literature. Lessing, *Oral History.*

Records. Records of the congregation and of its predecessors, including minutes since 1938 and publications, are at the synagogue and with various officers and members.

Some publications at Spertus College of Judaica, Asher Library, include Temple Ezra *10th Anniversary* [Yearbook], 1948 and *25th Anniversary* [Yearbook], 1963, which includes "A Chronology" by Dr. Kurt Schwerin; Ezra Congregation *Bulletin*, 1970–73; Congregation Habonim *Bulletin*, 1967–73, and a typewritten history, ca. 1966; Congregation Ezra Habonim *Bulletin*, 1974–date, and a copy of its constitution, 1974.

207. HEBREW IMMIGRANT AID SOCIETY
130 N. Wells St., Chicago, IL 60606

Formerly the Chicago branch of the *Hebrew Sheltering and Immigrant Aid Society (HIAS), now an independent agency. Provided services to immigrants overseas and following their arrival in Chicago.

Records. Records are at the agency's office. No details have been obtained about their scope.

208. JEWISH CHILDREN'S BUREAU
1 S. Franklin St., Chicago, IL 60606

Principal child care agency for the Chicago Jewish community.

Sponsored refugee children brought to Chicago by the German Jewish Children's Aid (renamed *European Jewish Children's Aid in 1942). The children were placed in foster homes until they were reunited with their families, or became self-supporting.

Records. No information was obtained following an inquiry about the agency's records.

209. JEWISH FAMILY AND COMMUNITY SERVICE
1 S. Franklin St., Chicago, IL 60606

See *Jewish Welfare Agencies for general description.

The Refugee Dept. of the Jewish Social Service Bureau (later renamed Jewish Family and Community Service) assisted in the resettlement of refugees. Its activities were coordinated with those of other agencies and organizations by the Chicago Committee for Jewish Refugees.

Records. Records at the agency's office include minutes of board meetings, case files of clients, and materials concerning claims for *Wiedergutmachung* from the Federal Republic of Germany.

210. JEWISH VOCATIONAL SERVICE
1 S. Franklin St., Chicago, IL 60606

Provided vocational counseling and placement to the Chicago Jewish community.

The Refugee Dept. of the Jewish Vocational Service and Employment Center specialized in the vocational integration of refugees, many of whom had been referred to it by the Refugee Dept. of the Jewish Social Service Bureau (*Jewish Family and Community Service).

Literature. Jimmy Stern Fuerst, "Placement of Refugees by Jewish Vocational Services of Chicago." Unpublished master's thesis, Univ. of Chicago, School of Social Service Administration, 1941.

Records. Records at the agency's office include minutes of meetings of the board of directors beginning in 1936, and some printed materials regarding aid to refugees.

211. NATIONAL COUNCIL OF JEWISH WOMEN, CHICAGO SECTION
185 N. Wabash Ave., Chicago, IL 60601

A section of the *National Council of Jewish Women, founded 1893.

Its Dept. of Service to the Foreign Born cooperated with other Chicago agencies in resettling immigrants.

Literature. Harriet S. Aries, "National Council of Jewish Women, Chicago Section, Department of Service to the Foreign Born: Its Development, Function and Progress." Unpublished master's thesis, Loyola Univ., 1946.

Records. Chicago Historical Society, Manuscript Div.: records, 3.5 ft, include minutes, annual reports, correspondence and other materials, and some documents relating to the Service to Foreign Born and refugees.
Recent records are at the agency's office.

212. SELFHELP OF CHICAGO, INC./SELFHELP HOME FOR THE AGED, INC.
908 W. Argyle St., Chicago, IL 60640

Founded in 1938 by German-Jewish immigrants as the Chicago chapter of Selfhelp of Émigrés from Central Europe (*Selfhelp Community Services); incorporated as a separate organization in 1949 for mutual aid and social welfare activities, especially for the aged.

Selfhelp Home for the Aged was founded in 1949 as the Chicago Home for Aged Immigrants, aided by a grant from *United Help and local contributions. Present name was adopted in 1955.

Literature. Lessing, *Oral History.*

Records. Records, including minutes since 1949 and newsletters since 1948, are at the agency's office.

213. TEMPLE B'NAI YEHUDA
1424 W. 183 St., Homewood, IL 60430

German-Jewish immigrant congregation founded in 1944 in Chicago as the Hyde Park Liberal Congregation. Adopted present name in 1957. Affiliated with Union of American Hebrew Congregations.

Records. Records, including minutes, correspondence, photographs, plaques, and awards are at the synagogue and with various officers and members.

Copies of its *Bulletin*, 1945–date, *Silver Anniversary Jubilee Book*, 1969, and *Dedication Ad Book*, 1961, are with Mrs. Edith Strauss, 8754 S. Euclid Ave., Chicago, IL 60617.

Some publications are at Spertus College of Judaica, Asher Library, including several one-page histories of the congregation and copies of the *Bulletin*, 1974–75.

214. TRAVELERS AID SOCIETY OF METROPOLITAN CHICAGO–IMMIGRANTS' SERVICE LEAGUE
22 W. Madison St., Chicago, IL 60602

Formed in 1967 by a merger of the Travelers Aid Society of Chicago and the Immigrants' Service League, formerly known as the Immigrants' Protective League. Member agency of the *American Council for Nationalities Service.

The League has provided primarily legal and technical service to the foreign born in the Chicago area since 1908.

Literature. Romanofsky, *Social Service Organizations*, pp. 357–360.

Records. Univ. of Illinois, Chicago Circle Library, Dept. of Special Collections: records of the League, 1904-67, 17.5 ft, consist of case files, administrative records, and other materials. Records of the Travelers Aid Society, 1914-61, 6.5 ft, are also in this repository. Finding aids: unpublished inventories.

Recent records are at the agency's office.

215. UNITED CHARITIES OF CHICAGO
64 E. Jackson Blvd., Chicago, IL 60604

Social agency serving the Chicago community.

Its Family Service Bureau formed a Refugee Service to provide counseling and job placement for Christian refugees primarily of Jewish descent.

Records. Chicago Historical Society, Manuscript Div.: records, 1867-1971, consist of correspondence, minutes, reports, and printed materials. Include one folder of correspondence, reports, surveys, and minutes of its Refugee Service, and of the Chicago branch of the *American Christian Committee for Refugees. *NUCMC* MS 75-422. Finding aid: unpublished inventory.

Other materials and recent files are at the agency's office.

Indiana

Indianapolis

216. JEWISH FAMILY AND CHILDREN'S SERVICES
1475 W. 86 St., Indianapolis, IN 46260

See *Jewish Welfare Agencies for general description.

The Indiana Coordinating Committee (later renamed the Indiana Refugee Service) assisted in the resettlement of refugees.

Records. Records concerning the resettlement of refugees, including minutes of meetings and case files of clients, are at the agency's office and with the Jewish Welfare Federation, 615 N. Alabama St., Indianapolis, IN 46204.

Kentucky

Louisville

217. JEWISH SOCIAL SERVICE AGENCY
118 S. Second St., Louisville, KY 40202

See *Jewish Welfare Agencies for general description.

The Kentucky Refugee Service Committee was established by the Louisville

Conference of Jewish Organizations (later renamed Jewish Community Federation of Louisville) to assist in the resettlement of refugees.

Literature. Clarence F. Judah, *Unity in Community: Four Decades of Federation in Louisville, 1934–1974.* Louisville, 1974.

Records. Records at the Agency's office include minutes of meetings and case files of clients. Materials concerning the Federation's assistance in the resettlement of refugees are with the Federation at 702 Marion E. Taylor Bldg., Louisville, KY 40202.

Louisiana

New Orleans

218. JEWISH FAMILY AND CHILDREN'S SERVICE
211 Camp St., New Orleans, LA 70130

See *Jewish Welfare Agencies for general description.

The New Orleans Committee for Refugee Service and the Louisiana Coordinating Committee for Refugees cooperated with the Jewish Welfare Federation and the *New Orleans Section of National Council of Jewish Women in the resettlement of refugees.

Records. No information was obtained following an inquiry about the agency's records.

219. NATIONAL COUNCIL OF JEWISH WOMEN, GREATER NEW ORLEANS SECTION
4747 Earhart Blvd., New Orleans, LA 70125

A section of the *National Council of Jewish Women.

Provided "Port and Dock" service for immigrants arriving in New Orleans by boat.

Records. Records relating to "Port and Dock" activities, including minutes of meetings, memos, and the correspondence of the committee charged with this work, are at the agency's office.

Maryland

Baltimore

220. BALTIMORE YOUNG WOMEN'S CHRISTIAN ASSOCIATION (YWCA), INTERNATIONAL DIVISION
128 W. Franklin St., Baltimore, MD 21201

Known as the YWCA International Center until 1971, it was one of several dozen *International Institutes and a member agency of the *American Council for Nationalities Service.

Records. Baltimore YWCA: records of the International Center, ca. 9 ft, include some material relating to local aid to (primarily non-Jewish) refugees, 1933–45.

Univ. of Minnesota, Immigration History Research Center: microfilm copies of the International Center records.

221. CHEVRA AHAVAS CHESED, INC.
c/o Walter Lichtenauer (president), 3621 Rusty Rock Rd., Randallstown, MD 21133

German-Jewish immigrant religious organization founded in 1941 in Baltimore by leaders of *Holiday Services, Inc. Engaged in mutual aid, social welfare, and Jewish communal activities. Its *chevra kadisha* (burial society) arranges burials in the traditional manner; it maintains two cemeteries. Affiliated with *American Federation of Jews from Central Europe.

Literature. Gertrude Hirschler, *To Love Mercy: The Story of the Chevra Ahavas Chesed of Baltimore.* Baltimore, 1972.

Records. Records, including minutes since 1942, minutes of the ladies' auxiliary, printed materials, and an unpublished history 1943, are with the president and with other officers and members.

222. HIAS OF BALTIMORE, INC.
5750 Park Heights Ave., Baltimore, MD 21215

An independent agency, formerly the Baltimore branch of the *Hebrew Sheltering and Immigrant Aid Society (HIAS), aided immigrants overseas and following their arrival in Baltimore.

In the 1950s, HIAS of Baltimore established the Baltimore Emergency Committee as its Indemnification Project, with the participation of the Refugee Adjustment Committee of the *Jewish Family and Children's Service of Baltimore and the Baltimore Section of the *National Council of Jewish Women. Its purpose was to advise Nazi victims on filing claims for *Wiedergutmachung* against the Federal Republic of Germany. The Committee was affiliated with the *United Restitution Organization.

Literature. Eugene Kaufmann, *A Half-Century of HIAS in Baltimore, 1903–1953.* Baltimore, 1953.

Records. HIAS of Baltimore: records, including ca. 1000 case files, minutes of meetings, correspondence, and other materials.

223. HOLIDAY SERVICES, INC.   *Defunct*

German-Jewish immigrant religious organization founded in 1940 in Baltimore to conduct high holiday services. Its leaders founded *Chevra Ahavas Chesed in 1941. In 1951, donated to Chevra Ahavas Chesed a monument to the 6 million victims of the Nazi Holocaust, which was erected in its cemetery. Ceased to exist in 1961.

Literature. Gertrude Hirschler, *To Love Mercy: The Story of the Chevra Ahavas Chesed of Baltimore.* Baltimore, 1972, pp. 13-15, 46-47.

Records. Records have not been located, according to information from the former president, Fred Baer, Baltimore.

224. JEWISH FAMILY AND CHILDREN'S SERVICE
5750 Park Heights Ave., Baltimore, MD 21215

See *Jewish Welfare Agencies for general description.

The Refugee Adjustment Committee was established in 1937 as a separate agency which cooperated with the Jewish Family and Children's Bureau (later renamed Jewish Family and Children's Service). In 1938, a local coordinating committee in aid to refugees was established by the Bureau, *HIAS of Baltimore, the Service to Foreign Born of the Baltimore Section of *National Council of Jewish Women, the local committee of German Jewish Children's Aid (*European Jewish Children's Aid), and members of the community. In 1940, placement services for refugees were transferred to the Associated Placement and Guidance Bureau. The Refugee Adjustment Committee subsequently became a part of the Jewish Family and Children's Service.

Literature. Louise A. Alpert, "The Economic and Vocational Adjustment of Refugees in Baltimore." Unpublished master's thesis, New York School of Social Work, Columbia Univ., Sept. 1941.

Records. Records of the Refugee Adjustment Committee from 1940 on, in several notebooks, consist of minutes of meetings, financial reports, and statistics. These materials and minutes of the board of the Jewish Family and Children's Service are at the agency's office. Most case files have been destroyed.

225. NATIONAL COUNCIL OF JEWISH WOMEN, BALTIMORE SECTION
7241 Park Heights Ave., Baltimore, MD 21215

A section of the *National Council of Jewish Women.

Its Service to Foreign Born Division cooperated with the Baltimore Refugee Adjustment Committee (*Jewish Family and Children's Service). The Section also operated a shop which sold products that were homemade by refugees for the most part.

Literature. Louise A. Alpert, "The Economic and Vocational Adjustment of Refugees in Baltimore." Unpublished master's thesis, New York School of Social Work, Columbia Univ., Sept. 1941.

Records. No information was obtained following an inquiry about the agency's records.

Massachusetts

226. COMMONWEALTH OF MASSACHUSETTS, DIVISION OF IMMIGRATION AND AMERICANIZATION
73 Tremont St., Boston, MA 02108

Established in 1917 "to bring into sympathetic and mutually helpful relations the Commonwealth and its residents of foreign origin."

Offered assistance to refugees arriving at the port of Boston and/or settling in Massachusetts.

Literature. *Annual Report of the Division . . . for the Year Ending November 30, 1938,* pp. 12–15, "The Refugee Situation."
Annual Report . . . November 30, 1939, p. 4.

Records. Records of the Division are reportedly destroyed after seven years, and therefore no materials for the 1930s and 1940s are presumed to be with the agency. However, it is possible that the Dept. of Education, of which the Division is a part, may have relevant documentation. The board of the Division, which established policy for the agency, met monthly in 1940; its minutes would offer primary documentation about the Division's activities.

Boston

227. AUSTRO-AMERICAN ASSOCIATION OF BOSTON, INC.
c/o Dr. Martha Brunner-Orne (president), 88 Marlborough St., Boston, MA 02116

Organization founded by Austrian immigrants of the Nazi period ca. 1940 for social activities. Promotes interest in Austrian culture and Austro-American friendship in cooperation with the local Austrian consulate. Published a bulletin, *AAA News.*

Literature. Lessing, *Oral History.*

Records. Records are with various officers.

228. HEBREW IMMIGRANT AID SOCIETY   *Defunct*

An independent agency, formerly the Boston branch of the *Hebrew Sheltering and Immigrant Aid Society (HIAS), aided immigrants overseas and following their arrival in Boston. Ceased operations in 1978.

Records. American Jewish Historical Society: records, 1930–78, ca. 150 ft, consist largely of case files of European refugees who were assisted in emigrating to the U.S.A. and Israel. Include correspondence with institutions and agencies, files on persons sought by relatives overseas, copies of regulations affecting immigrants, and other materials regarding the Society. *NUCMC* MS 77-31.

229. IMMIGRANTS MUTUAL AID SOCIETY (CLUB OF NEW AMERICANS 1938), INC. (IMAS)
c/o Frederic T. Poras (treasurer), 76 Verndale St., Brookline, MA 02146

German-Jewish immigrant organization founded in Boston in 1938 and incorporated in 1956. Engaged in social welfare, mutual aid, and social and religious activities. Its *chevra kadisha* (burial society) provides burials in the traditional manner. Maintains a cemetery and conducts high holiday services. Affiliated with *American Federation of Jews from Central Europe. Published a bulletin, *IMAS News*, 1941-date, and journals: *10th Anniversary*, 1948, *15th Anniversary*, 1953, *25th Anniversary*, 1963, and *35th Anniversary*, 1973.

Literature. Lessing, *Oral History.*

Records. American Jewish Historical Society: records, 1949-75, 2 cartons (ca. 1100 pp.), consist of minutes, bylaws, bulletins, reports, programs, correspondence, and special announcements. *NUCMC* MS 77-32.

American Jewish Periodicals Center: copies of *IMAS News*, 1941-42, on microfilm.

Records may also be with various officers and members.

230. INTERNATIONAL INSTITUTE OF BOSTON
287 Commonwealth Ave., Boston, MA 02115

One of several dozen *International Institutes and a member agency of the *American Council for Nationalities Service.

Cooperated with the *Austro-American Association of Boston and with the *Immigrants Mutual Aid Society (IMAS).

Records. Univ. of Minnesota, Immigration History Research Center: records, 1920-late 1950s, ca. 35 ft, consist of case studies on the Institute's work with immigrants of virtually all ethnic backgrounds, copies of the Institute's publication, *The Beacon*, 1922-73, and other material relating to the Institute's activities in the Boston area.

Recent records are at the Institute's office.

231. JEWISH FAMILY AND CHILDREN'S SERVICE
31 New Chardon St., Boston, MA 02114

See *Jewish Welfare Agencies for general description.

The Boston Refugee Committee and the Service to Foreign Born Dept. of the *National Council of Jewish Women, Greater Boston Section, assisted in the resettlement of refugees in cooperation with the Associated Jewish Philanthropies of Boston.

Literature. Miriam Segal Rubin, "Boston Meets the Refugee; the Organization of Community Resources in Greater Boston to Aid Refugees from Nazi-Dominated Lands, 1934-45." Unpublished master's thesis, Simmons College, Boston, 1946.

Barbara Miller Solomon, *Pioneers in Service: The History of the Associated Jewish Philanthropies of Boston*. Boston, 1956.

Florence Shari Stern, "Services Extended to New Americans Under Auspices of the Associated Jewish Philanthropies." Unpublished master's thesis, Simmons College, Boston, 1950.

Records. Records at the agency's office include case files of clients, files on *Wiedergutmachungs*-claims, and newspaper articles on resettlement of immigrants.

232. NATIONAL COUNCIL OF JEWISH WOMEN, GREATER BOSTON SECTION
1407 Beacon St., Brookline, MA 02146

A section of the *National Council of Jewish Women.

Its Service to Foreign Born cooperated with other Boston agencies in resettling immigrants.

Records. No information was obtained following an inquiry about the agency's records.

233. THE WINDOW SHOP, INC., SCHOLARSHIP FUND
56 Brattle St., Cambridge, MA 02138

The Window Shop was organized in May 1939 by the wives of Harvard Univ. faculty members as a small dress-making and gift shop selling textiles, hats, fashion accessories, and baked goods to help German and Austrian refugees in the Boston area. In 1940, it grew into a bakery, tea room, and restaurant, and functioned as a placement, referral, and retraining center for refugee women. Some of the merchandise sold was produced by refugee families and enterprises. In 1943, the Window Shop established Friendship House, a lecture and language center to foster mutual understanding between immigrants and native Americans. The Shop cooperated with, and was assisted by, other local organizations aiding refugees, including the New England Christian Committee for Refugees (founded ca. 1936, later renamed the New England Div. of the *American Christian Committee for Refugees).

The Shop became a landmark in Cambridge and continued, with less success, to aid displaced persons after the war and Hungarian and Cuban refugees during the 1950s and 1960s. The Elsa Brändström-Ulich Assistance Fund was created by the Shop to provide scholarships for immigrant students in the Boston area. (It honors a founder and leader of the Shop, herself a refugee, who died in 1948.) In 1972, the directors closed the Shop, sold the building at 56 Brattle St. to the Cambridge Adult Education Center, and used the proceeds to enlarge the Assistance Fund, which is now the Shop's only activity.

Literature. Mrs. Oliver Cope, "The Story of the Window Shop." Unpublished address, Cambridge Historical Society, Nov. 17, 1974.

Mrs. William A. Muller, "The Window Shop." Unpublished paper, Mother's Study Club, Cambridge, Apr. 1959.

Records. Records are with various officers and board members, and will eventually be deposited at Radcliffe College, Schlesinger Library on the History of Women in America.

Lynn

234. JEWISH FAMILY SERVICE
564 Loring Ave., Salem, MA 01970

See *Jewish Welfare Agencies for general description. The Jewish Social Service Agency, formerly located in Lynn, Massachusetts, was renamed the Jewish Family Service.

Records. Records at the agency's office include case files of refugees resettled in the area around Lynn (northeast of Boston).

Springfield

235. JEWISH FAMILY SERVICE OF GREATER SPRINGFIELD
184 Mill St., Springfield, MA 01108

See *Jewish Welfare Agencies for general description.

The Springfield Coordinating Committee for Refugees cooperated with the Jewish Social Service Bureau (later renamed Jewish Family Service) in resettling refugees.

Records. Records have been destroyed.

Worcester

236. JEWISH FAMILY SERVICE
646 Salisbury St., Worcester, MA 01609

See *Jewish Welfare Agencies for general description.

The Worcester Coordinating Committee for Émigrés and its successor, the Worcester Refugee Committee, assisted in the resettlement of refugees, in cooperation with the Jewish Social Service Agency (later renamed Jewish Family Service) and the Worcester Section of *National Council of Jewish Women.

Records. No information was obtained following an inquiry about the agency's records.

237. NATIONAL COUNCIL OF JEWISH WOMEN, WORCESTER SECTION
633 Salisbury St., Worcester, MA 01609 (Immigration and Naturalization Office)

A section of the *National Council of Jewish Women.

The Section's Immigration and Naturalization Office cooperated with the local *Jewish Family Service in assisting refugees in matters concerning immigration, naturalization, and *Wiedergutmachung.*

Records. Records, 10 ft, at the Section's Immigration and Naturalization Office, consist of confidential case files arranged in alphabetical order.

Michigan

238. MICHIGAN COMMISSION ON DISPLACED PERSONS AND REFUGEES
Defunct

After the passage of the Displaced Persons Act of 1948, the Michigan Commission on Displaced Persons was established in 1949 by Executive Order of the Governor. Prior to 1948, various volunteer agencies in Michigan had been active in resettling immigrants. The Michigan Committee on Displaced Persons, a state chapter of the *Citizens' Committee on Displaced Persons, had campaigned for the passage of legislation to admit displaced persons as nonquota immigrants.

The Commission cooperated with Michigan sponsors, volunteer agencies, and the federal and state governments, including the *U.S. Displaced Persons Commission, in resettling displaced persons and refugees. Its main functions were to collect and coordinate information in such areas as housing, transportation, employment, legislation, and education. It also investigated the suitability of individuals and organizations sponsoring displaced persons.

The name of the Commission was changed to the Michigan Commission on Displaced Persons and Refugees after the passage of the Refugee Relief Act of 1953. In 1960, the Commission recommended to the Governor that he establish a Michigan Commission on Refugees on a standby basis.

Records. Wayne State Univ., Archives of Labor History and Urban Affairs: records, 1937–65, 24 ft, comprising the "Displaced Persons Collection," include 1 ft, 1939–47, relating to special projects involving aliens and recently naturalized citizens; *Interpreter Releases*, 1937–64, published by the *American Council for Nationalities Service and its predecessors; *National Refugee Service Bulletin*, 1944–46; *U.S. Immigration and Naturalization Service *Monthly Review*, 1943–52; and materials relating to displaced persons and refugees, 1946–65. Finding aid: unpublished inventory (14 pp.).

Detroit

239. CONGREGATION BETH HILLEL
Defunct

Chevrath Gemiluth Chassodim was organized in 1939 in Detroit by recent German-Jewish immigrants, to serve primarily as a burial society. With the arrival in 1941 of a rabbi from Germany, Chevrath Gemiluth Chassodim was incorporated as an Orthodox congregation under the name Congregation Gemiluth Chassodim.

In 1964, the more traditional members withdrew from the Congregation to join other Orthodox congregations, and the remaining members reorganized as Congregation Beth Hillel and affiliated with the United Synagogue of America. Congregations Gemiluth Chassodim and Beth Hillel were affiliated with the *American Federation of Jews from Central Europe.

In the early 1970s, Congregation Beth Hillel decided to move to a suburban location and, for economic reasons, to merge with Congregation Beth Abraham, which was also planning to move. The new congregation took the name Congregation Beth Abraham-Hillel-Moses and is located at 5075 W. Maple Rd., West Bloomfield, MI 48033.

Records. Records of Congregations Gemiluth Chassodim and Beth Hillel are believed to be with Congregation Beth Abraham-Hillel-Moses, although this information has not been verified.

240. JEWISH FAMILY AND CHILDREN'S SERVICE
24123 Greenfield Rd., Southfield, MI 48075

See *Jewish Welfare Agencies for general description.

A merger of the Jewish Social Service Bureau (founded in 1899 as United Jewish Charities), the Jewish Children's Bureau, and the Resettlement Service. (The Children's Bureau became a department of the Social Service Bureau in 1944.)

The Jewish Social Service Bureau and the Jewish Child Placement Bureau (later renamed Jewish Children's Bureau) assisted in the resettlement of refugees. In 1937, their activities were taken over by the Resettlement Service organized by the Jewish Welfare Federation in collaboration with the Social Service Bureau.

Literature. Samuel Lerner and Rose Kaplan, "A Brief History of the Detroit Jewish Family and Children's Service: An Overview." *Michigan Jewish History* 16 (July 1976): 22–26.
Harold Silver, "Jewish Child Placement Services in Detroit, 1933–1944." *Michigan Jewish History* (Nov. 1960).

Records. YIVO Institute for Jewish Research: records, 1924–63, microfilm (121 reels). The original materials (777 files) were destroyed after microfilming. Consist of case files, general correspondence, minutes of staff and committee meetings, and other materials. Include files of the Resettlement Service concerning aid to refugees and correspondence with *European Jewish Children's Aid, *Hebrew Sheltering and Immigrant Aid Society (HIAS), and other immigrant aid agencies. Among the several thousand case files are some for refugee clients who were assisted by the Resettlement Service. Finding aid: unpublished inventory (32 pp.).

Recent records are at the agency's office.

241. NATIONAL COUNCIL OF JEWISH WOMEN, GREATER DETROIT SECTION
16400 W. 12 Mile Rd., Southfield, MI 48076

A section of the *National Council of Jewish Women.

Its Service to Foreign Born cooperated with other Detroit agencies in resettling immigrants.

Records. Records are at the agency's office.

Minnesota

242. INTERNATIONAL INSTITUTE OF MINNESOTA
1694 Como Ave., St. Paul, MN 55108

One of several dozen *International Institutes and a member agency of the *American Council for Nationalities Service.

Records. Univ. of Minnesota, Immigration History Research Center: records, 1920-71, 48 ft, consist of case files, correspondence, minutes, and other materials relating to the Institute's activities in Minnesota.
Recent records are at the Institute's office.

Minneapolis

243. JEWISH FAMILY AND CHILDREN'S SERVICE OF MINNEAPOLIS
811 LaSalle Ave., Minneapolis MN 55402

See *Jewish Welfare Agencies for general description.
The Minneapolis Refugee Service Committee and the St. Paul Refugee Service Division coordinated activities in aid to refugees in the region.

Records. Minnesota Historical Society, Div. of Archives and Manuscripts: records, 1910-63, ca. 2 ft, consist of minutes and reports. *NUCMC* MS 76-2057.
Case files of clients and other records are at the agency's office.

244. NATIONAL COUNCIL OF JEWISH WOMEN, MINNEAPOLIS SECTION
For current address, contact the headquarters of NCJW in New York.

A local section of the *National Council of Jewish Women.
Its Service to Foreign Born cooperated with other Minneapolis agencies in resettling immigrants.

Records. Minnesota Historical Society, Div. of Archives and Manuscripts: records, 1917-67, 1 ft (1000 items). *NUCMC* MS 69-1717. Finding aid: unpublished inventory.
Recent records are with the agency's officers.

245. NEW WORLD CLUB OF MINNEAPOLIS, INC.   *Defunct*

German-Jewish immigrant organization, 1938-57 (incorporated in 1949), which offered mutual aid, social welfare, and social and cultural activities. Affiliated with *American Federation of Jews from Central Europe.

Records. Research Foundation for Jewish Immigration: records, 1946-57, 2 in., formerly with the Club's last president, Leo Wallach, Minneapolis.

Missouri

Kansas City

246. JEWISH FAMILY AND CHILDREN'S SERVICES
1115 E. 65 St., Kansas City, MO 64131

See *Jewish Welfare Agencies for general description.

The Kansas City Placement Council was organized in 1937 to assist in the resettlement of refugees, in cooperation with the United Jewish Social Services (later renamed Jewish Family and Children's Services).

Records. No information was obtained following an inquiry about the agency's records.

St. Louis

247. INTERNATIONAL INSTITUTE OF METROPOLITAN ST. LOUIS
4484 W. Pine Blvd., St. Louis, MO 63108

One of several dozen *International Institutes and a member agency of the *American Council for Nationalities Service.

Records. Univ. of Minnesota, Immigration History Research Center: records, 1919–61, consist of organizational materials and records of activities in the St. Louis area.

Recent records are at the Institute's office.

248. JEWISH EMPLOYMENT AND VOCATIONAL SERVICE
1727 Locust St., St. Louis, MO 63103

Provided vocational placement and counseling to the St. Louis Jewish community.

The agency served refugees referred to it by the Jewish Social Service Bureau (*Jewish Family and Children's Service).

Literature. Shirley A. Melcher, "A Follow-Up Study of the Jewish Immigrants Who Had Been Clients of the Jewish Employment and Vocational Service Between 1939–45." Unpublished master's thesis, Washington Univ., St. Louis, School of Social Work, 1955.

Records. Records at the agency's office concerning refugees include the registration master file dating from 1940. As a matter of policy, the agency destroys the case files of clients five years after closing their case.

249. JEWISH FAMILY AND CHILDREN'S SERVICE
9385 Olive Blvd., St. Louis, MO 63132

See *Jewish Welfare Agencies for general description.

The St. Louis Committee for Service to Emigrants, in cooperation with the Jewish Social Service Bureau (later renamed Jewish Family and Children's Service), assisted in the resettlement of refugees. Resettlement in the region was aided by the Resettlement Committee of Southern Illinois and Eastern Missouri.

Records. Records at the agency's office include case files of clients and minutes of meetings.

250. NATIONAL COUNCIL OF JEWISH WOMEN, ST. LOUIS SECTION
8630 Delmar Blvd., St. Louis, MO 63124

A section of the *National Council of Jewish Women.
Its Service to Foreign Born assisted in the resettlement of refugees.

Records. Records at the agency's office include material relating to the Service to Foreign Born.

251. SELF AID OF ST. LOUIS *Defunct*

German-Jewish immigrant organization, 1937–ca. 1950, which offered mutual aid, cultural and social activities, and assistance to newcomers, including post-1945 arrivals from *Shanghai. Affiliated with *American Federation of Jews from Central Europe.
Published a bulletin ca. 1940.

Records. Records have not been located, according to information from a former board member, Ludwig M. Priebat, Walnut Creek, CA.

Nebraska

Omaha

252. JEWISH FEDERATION OF OMAHA
333 S. 132 St., Omaha, NE 68154

See *Jewish Welfare Agencies for general description.
The Omaha Coordinating Committee and Nebraska Coordinating Committee assisted in the resettlement of refugees.

Records. Records of the Federation's Family Service Dept. include case files of clients.

New Jersey

Camden

253. JEWISH FAMILY SERVICE
2393 W. Marlton Pike, Cherry Hill, NJ 08034

See *Jewish Welfare Agencies for general description.

Records. Records concerning refugee resettlement were destroyed.

Elizabeth

254. JEWISH FAMILY SERVICE AGENCY OF CENTRAL NEW JERSEY
500 Westfield Ave., Elizabeth, NJ 07208

See *Jewish Welfare Agencies for general description.

The Elizabeth Refugee Coordinating Committee and its successor, the Elizabeth Refugee Service, assisted in the resettlement of refugees.

Records. No information was obtained following an inquiry about the agency's records.

Newark

255. DERECH JESCHOROH, INC.–CHEVROH KADISCHAH
c/o D. Lowenstein (president), 64 Union Ave., Irvington, NJ 07111

German-Jewish immigrant organization founded in Newark, NJ, in 1946 to offer social welfare, mutual aid, and social and cultural activities. Provides burials in the traditional "European" manner, maintains cemetery plots, and conducts services on the Jewish high holidays.

Records. Records are with the president and the secretary.

256. JEWISH COUNSELING AND SERVICE AGENCY
161 Millburn Ave., Millburn, NJ 07041

See *Jewish Welfare Agencies for general description.

A countywide social agency, providing services rendered previously by the Jewish Family Service of Essex County, the Bureau of Service to Foreign Born of the *National Council of Jewish Women, Essex County Section, and the Jewish Child Care Association of Essex County.

The Essex County Émigré Service and its successor, the Émigré Service Bureau of New Jersey, assisted in the resettlement of refugees.

Records. Records concerning the resettlement of refugees, consisting of administrative materials and case files of clients, are located at the Jewish Community Federation of Metropolitan New Jersey, 60 Glenwood Ave., East Orange, NJ 07017. This Federation also has administrative files on this subject.

257. JEWISH UNITY CLUB OF NEW JERSEY
c/o Sigfried Mayer (president), 723 Stuyvesant Ave., Irvington, NJ 07111

German-Jewish immigrant organization founded in 1935 in Newark, NJ, as the German-Jewish Club of Newark, later known as the Jewish Unity Club of Newark. Engaged in mutual aid, social, and cultural activities; maintained youth and sports groups during early years. Has active women's group. Affiliated with *American Federation of Jews from Central Europe.

Literature. Lessing, *Oral History.*

Records. Records, including bulletins, newsletters, and souvenir journal, are with the president and with various officers and members.

258. NATIONAL COUNCIL OF JEWISH WOMEN, ESSEX COUNTY SECTION
321 Millburn Ave., Millburn, NJ 07041

A section of the *National Council of Jewish Women, formerly known as Newark Section.

Its Service to Foreign Born merged with the *Jewish Counseling and Service Agency.

Records. No information was obtained following an inquiry about the agency's records.

Passaic

259. JEWISH FAMILY SERVICE OF PASSAIC-CLIFTON AND VICINITY
199 Scoles Ave., Clifton, NJ 07012

See *Jewish Welfare Agencies for general description.

The *National Council of Jewish Women, Passaic Section, assisted in the resettlement of refugees, and provided family counseling services until 1948 when the Jewish Social Service Agency (later renamed Jewish Family Service) was established.

Records. Records at the agency's office include case files of clients and other materials for the period since 1948. No information was obtained on earlier records.

Paterson

260. JEWISH FAMILY SERVICE OF NORTH JERSEY
1 Pike Dr., Wayne, NJ 07470

See *Jewish Welfare Agencies for general description.

The Jewish Community Council guided the resettlement of refugees in Paterson, NJ, prior to the establishment of the Jewish Social Service Bureau (later renamed Jewish Family and Children's Service, now the Jewish Family Service of North Jersey).

Records. No information was obtained following an inquiry about the agency's records.

Trenton

261. JEWISH FAMILY SERVICE
51 Walter St., Trenton, NJ 08628

See *Jewish Welfare Agencies for general description.

The Trenton Refugee Service cooperated with the Jewish Family Welfare Bureau (later renamed Jewish Family Service) in the resettlement of refugees.

Records. Records at the agency's office include minutes of meetings and case files of clients.

New York

Albany

262. JEWISH FAMILY SERVICES
291 State St., Albany, NY 12210

See *Jewish Welfare Agencies for general description.

The Albany Refugee Committee cooperated with the Albany Jewish Social Service (later renamed Jewish Family Services) in aiding the resettlement of refugees.

Records. No information was obtained following an inquiry about the agency's records.

Buffalo

263. INTERNATIONAL INSTITUTE OF BUFFALO
864 Delaware Ave., Buffalo, NY 14209

One of several dozen *International Institutes and a member agency of the *American Council for Nationalities Service.

Records. International Institute: records consist primarily of case files.

264. JEWISH FAMILY SERVICE OF ERIE COUNTY
775 Main St., Buffalo, NY 14203

See *Jewish Welfare Agencies for general description.

The German Jewish Committee and its successors, the Buffalo Coordinating Committee and the Buffalo Refugee Service, were established by the Jewish Welfare Society (later renamed Jewish Family Service) to assist in the resettlement of refugees.

Records. Records, 1930s–date, including minutes of meetings and case files of clients and of claimants for *Wiedergutmachung* from the Federal Republic of Germany, are at the agency's office.

New York City

265. AGUDATH ISRAEL OF UPPER MANHATTAN
617 W. 179 St., New York, NY 10033

Founded in 1939 in Washington Heights by Jewish immigrants from Central Europe as a branch of *Agudath Israel of America.

Literature. Max T. Braunfeld, *A Short History of Agudath Israel in Washington Heights.* Presented at the Occasion of "The Annual Dinner" of Agudath Israel of Upper Manhattan on March 19, 1972, Parkside Plaza, N.Y.

Records. Records are with various officers.

266. AMERICAN CONGREGATION OF JEWS FROM AUSTRIA
118 W. 95 St., New York, NY 10025

Austrian-Jewish immigrant congregation founded ca. 1940 on the west side of Manhattan under the spiritual leadership of Rabbi Julius M. Bach, formerly of Vienna. Known as the Austrian Jewish Congregation until 1946, when the present name was adopted. During the early 1940s, this congregation and *Congregation Kehillath Jawne cooperated as the Vereinigte Gemeinden. Affiliated with *American Federation of Jews from Austria.

Records. Records are at the synagogue and with various officers.

267. AMERICAN JEWISH CONGREGATION   *Defunct*

German-Jewish immigrant congregation on the west side of Manhattan which traced its origin to the German Jewish Center and the subsequent German Jewish Congregation (Deutsch-Israelitische Kultusgemeinde), founded in 1927. The name American Jewish Congregation was adopted in 1939, after many recent immigrants had joined the congregation. Ceased to exist in 1970.

Literature. Max Malina, *Deutsche Juden in New York nach dem Weltkriege.* New York, 1931.
——, ed., *Jüdisches Familienblatt.* New York, 1937–39. Includes data on the early history of this congregation and on the pre-1933 German-Jewish immigration of the twentieth century. Max Malina was rabbi of the congregation from 1927 until his death in 1940. Copies of *Jüdisches Familienblatt* are at New York Public Library, Jewish Div.
Malina also published and edited a monthly, *Jüdischer Zeitgeist*, 1930–37, copies of which have not been located.

Records. Records have not been located and are presumed lost, according to information from James Jacks, New York, the last president of the congregation.

268. AUSTRIAN FORUM, INC.
c/o Dr. Margaret Bush (president), 305 West End Ave., New York, NY 10023

Founded in 1942 as the Austrian Institute for Science, Art and Economics to unite, and offer cultural and social programs to, Austrian refugees in the U.S.A. Provided German-speaking audiences for writers, actors, musicians, and lecturers of all kinds. In 1963, the name was changed to Austrian Forum.

Records. Records are with various officers.

269. B'NAI B'RITH, JOSEPH POPPER LODGE NO. 1525
c/o Robert Eisner (president), 121 81 Ave., Kew Gardens, NY 11415

Lodge of *B'nai B'rith International, founded by Czech-Jewish immigrants in 1944 for overseas relief, aid to Israel, and social and cultural purposes. Sponsor of annual memorial service for Nazi victims. Founded *Society for the History of Czechoslovak Jews.

Records. Records, consisting of a quarterly *Newsletter* published jointly with *B'nai B'rith Women, Joseph Popper Chapter, are with the editor, Hugh Colman, 109-23 71 Rd., Forest Hills, NY 11375.

270. B'NAI B'RITH, LEO BAECK LODGE NO. 1531
c/o Congregation Habonim, 44 W. 66 St., New York, NY 10023

Lodge of *B'nai B'rith International, founded by German-Jewish immigrants in 1944 for overseas relief, aid to Israel, and social and cultural purposes.

Publications include the semiannual *Voice*, the monthly *Young Couples Bulletin*, and souvenir journals for special occasions.

Literature. Lessing, *Oral History.*

Records. Records are with various officers.

271. B'NAI B'RITH, LIBERTY LODGE NO. 1533
c/o Stefan G. Koref, 39 W. 28 St., New York, NY 10001

Lodge of *B'nai B'rith International, founded by Austrian-Jewish immigrants in 1944 for overseas relief, aid to Israel, and social and cultural purposes.

Records. Records, consisting of bulletins issued every 2 to 3 months, are with the president.

272. B'NAI B'RITH WOMEN, JOSEPH POPPER CHAPTER NO. 628
c/o Rose Abeles (president), 102-30 62 Rd., Forest Hills, NY 11375

Chapter of *B'nai B'rith International, founded by Czech-Jewish immigrants in 1948 for social, cultural, and charitable purposes. Sponsors annual memorial service for Nazi victims. Founded *Society for the History of Czechoslovak Jews.

Records. Records, consisting of a quarterly *Newsletter* published jointly with *B'nai B'rith, Joseph Popper Lodge, are with the editor, Hugh Colman, 109-23 71 Rd., Forest Hills, NY 11375.

273. B'NAI B'RITH WOMEN, LEO BAECK CHAPTER NO. 450
c/o Congregation Habonim, 44 W. 66 St., New York, NY 10023

Chapter of *B'nai B'rith International, founded by German-Jewish immigrants in 1944 for social, cultural, and charitable purposes.

Records. Records are with various officers.

274. B'NAI B'RITH WOMEN, LIBERTY CHAPTER NO. 452
c/o Stefan G. Koref, 39 W. 28 St., New York, NY 10001

Chapter of *B'nai B'rith International, founded by Austrian-Jewish immigrants in 1944 for social, cultural, and charitable purposes.
Published a 30th anniversary souvenir booklet, 1974.

Records. Records, consisting of bulletins issued every 2 to 3 months since 1944, are with Mrs. Fritzi Ekstein, 137-47 45 Ave., Flushing, NY 11355.

275. CHEVROH GEMILUS CHESED, INC.
c/o B. Dublon (president), 43-30 44 St., Long Island City, NY 11104

German-Jewish immigrant congregation founded in 1941. Was given hospitality and a place to meet by the Woodside Jewish Center in Queens. Conducts high holiday services and maintains cemetery plots for members.

Records. Records are with various officers.

276. COMMITTEE FOR REFUGEE EDUCATION, INC. *Defunct*

Founded in 1939 in New York by 21 social agencies and educational institutions upon the initiative of the New York Adult Educational Council. Provided programs for English-language classes and appointed teachers who would be more suitable for instructing refugees, and displaced persons following World War II, than routine public school personnel. The Committee published several guides and manuals for use in English-language instruction for adults, and maintained special classes for rabbis and displaced rabbinical students in its nonsectarian program after 1945. The Committee had taught 17,000 foreign-born students (1939–49) when it disbanded ca. 1951.

Literature. Committee for Refugee Education, *Progress Reports*, 1939/40–1948/49.

Records. Records could not be located, despite numerous interviews with persons formerly associated with the Committee. Records of the *New York Association for New Americans and its predecessor agencies may contain pertinent documentation on the Committee for Refugee Education.

277. CONFERENCE OF JEWISH IMMIGRANT CONGREGATIONS *Defunct*

Founded in 1940 by German-Jewish immigrant congregations in New York City to represent their common interests. Comprised 20 congregations in 1950. Ceased to function in 1955. Chairmen were Rabbis Hugo Hahn 1940-48, Siegmund Hanover 1948–55, and Ralph Neuhaus 1955. In 1951, the Conference distributed to immigrant congregations throughout the U.S.A. ritual objects recovered from Europe and made available by *Jewish Cultural Reconstruction.

Literature. *International Biographical Dictionary*, vol. I (H. Hahn, S. Hanover, R. Neuhaus).
Lessing, *Oral History.*

Records. Research Foundation for Jewish Immigration: records, 1945–55, ca. 1 ft, include minutes, correspondence, publicity materials, and files concerning the distribution of recovered ritual objects.
Records, 1940–44, have not been located.

278. CONGREGATION ADATH JESHURUN OF WEST BRONX   *Defunct*

German-Jewish immigrant congregation founded in 1939 as Synagogengemeinde Bronx. Affiliated with *American Federation of Jews from Central Europe. Inactive since 1970.

Records. Records have not been located and are presumed lost, according to information received from the congregation's last president and secretary, Morris Wolff and Milton Samis, New York.

279. CONGREGATION ADATH MACHSIKE HADATH   *Defunct*

German-Jewish immigrant congregation founded in 1940 on the west side of Manhattan. Inactive since the death of its founder, Rabbi Joshua Grunwald, in 1969. Affiliated with *American Federation of Jews from Central Europe.

Records. Records have not been located and are presumed lost, according to information received from Mrs. Joshua Grunwald, New York.

280. CONGREGATION AGUDAS YESHORIM   *Defunct*

German-Jewish immigrant congregation founded in 1939 on the upper west side of Manhattan under the spiritual leadership of Rabbi Philipp Biberfeld, formerly of Frankfurt am Main. Established a branch in Washington Heights ca. 1950. Inactive since 1972 except for maintenance of cemetery plots. Affiliated with *American Federation of Jews from Central Europe.

Literature. *Jewish Way*, Dec. 30, 1945.

Records. Records, consisting of a memorial book with names of deceased members of the congregation, a few bulletins, and files regarding the congregation's cemetery plots, are with its last president, Walter Heymann, 729 W. 186 St., New York, NY 10033. Some bulletins are also with Rabbi Biberfeld, 621 W. 172 St., New York, NY 10032.

281. CONGREGATION BETH HILLEL OF WASHINGTON HEIGHTS
571 W. 182 St., New York, NY 10033

German-Jewish immigrant congregation founded in 1940 in Washington Heights primarily by Jewish immigrants from Munich under the spiritual leadership of

Rabbi Leo Baerwald, formerly of Munich. In 1941, a group of Jewish immigrants from Nuremberg, under the spiritual leadership of Rabbi Isak Heilbronn, formerly of Nuremberg, joined Beth Hillel after an organizational connection with an American congregation had proved unsatisfactory. Maintains a *chevra kadisha* (burial society), sisterhood, and family club. Formerly had a religious school, parent association, youth group, and young people's league. Affiliated with *American Federation of Jews from Central Europe.

Published a *Bulletin* since 1941. Issued *20th* and *25th Anniversary Journals*, 1961 and 1966.

Literature. *Festschrift in Honor of the 36th Anniversary of Congregation Beth Hillel of Washington Heights, New York, New York, 1940-1976.*
Lessing, *Oral History.*

Records. Records, including minutes since 1940, publications, and files concerning the *chevra kadisha*, sisterhood, school, and family club, are at the synagogue and with various officers.

Copies of the *Bulletin* are at the Leo Baeck Institute Library.

282. CONGREGATION BETH ISRAEL OF WASHINGTON HEIGHTS
562 W. 181 St., New York, NY 10033

German-Jewish immigrant congregation founded in 1949 in Washington Heights.
Published *Hakohol*, congregational bulletin and magazine, quarterly since 1953, and *Rabbi's Newsletter for Young Adults*, monthly since 1962.

Records. Records, including publications and minutes since 1949, are at the synagogue and with various officers.

283. CONGREGATION B'NAI JACOB   *Defunct*
German-Jewish immigrant congregation founded in 1945 in the Bronx. Ceased to exist ca. 1973.

Records. Records, consisting of minutes of meetings, are with the last president, Isidore Levy, 124-16 84 Rd., Kew Gardens, NY 11415.

284. CONGREGATION CHEVRA GEMILUTH CHESED
771 McDonald Ave., Brooklyn, NY 11218

German-Jewish immigrant congregation founded in 1939. Affiliated with *American Federation of Jews from Central Europe.

Records. Records are at the synagogue and with various officers.

285. CONGREGATION EMES WOZEDEK
560 W. 166 St., New York, NY 10032

German-Jewish immigrant congregation founded in 1939 in Washington Heights by Rabbi Max Koppel, who had earlier served the Synagogengemeinde Washington Heights (*Congregation Shaare Hatikvah, Ahavath Torah V'Tikvoh Chadoshoh).

Published *Gemeinde Anzeiger*, 1940-?.

Literature. *International Biographical Dictionary*, vol. I (M. Koppel). Lessing, *Oral History.*

Records. Records are at the synagogue and with various officers.

286. CONGREGATION HABONIM
44 W. 66 St., New York, NY 10023

German-Jewish immigrant congregation founded in 1939 under the spiritual leadership of Rabbi Hugo Hahn. Met for its first four years at Central Synagogue, New York, then rented quarters for its services in Manhattan and Queens, New York, until it had built its own temple in 1958. Maintains a religious school and conducts services also in Queens, where many members of the congregation reside.

Continued the religious liberalism and *Lehrhaus* (adult education) tradition of German Jewry, and maintains religious school, musical services, lecture programs, senior citizens' group, sisterhood, brotherhood, and youth group. Affiliated with Union of American Hebrew Congregations and *American Federation of Jews from Central Europe.

Published a *Bulletin* since 1940. Issued *Anniversary Year Book 1939–1949* and *Past–Present–Future 1939–1959* [Twentieth Anniversary Year Book].

Literature. Sam Cauman, *Jonah Bondi Wise, A Biography.* New York: Crown, 1966, pp. 132-135. (Wise was rabbi of Central Synagogue, New York.)
Michael N. Dobkowski, "'The Fourth Reich'–German-Jewish Religious Life in America Today." *Judaism* 27 (Winter 1978): 80-95.
Gleanings: Sermons Preached by Rabbi Hugo Hahn. New York, 1974.
International Biographical Dictionary, vol. I (H. Hahn).
Lessing, *Oral History.*
Living Legacy: Essays in Honor of Hugo Hahn. New York, 1963.

Records. Records are at the synagogue and with various officers.
American Jewish Archives: photocopies of typed minutes, 1941–45, 44 pp.
New York Public Library, Jewish Div., and Leo Baeck Institute Library have copies of the *Bulletin.*

287. CONGREGATION KEHILATH JACOB
305 W. 79 St., New York, NY 10024

German-Jewish immigrant congregation founded in 1941 on the west side of Manhattan. Rabbi Naphthali H. Carlebach, formerly of Berlin and Baden near Vienna, was its spiritual leader 1945-57.

Literature. *International Biographical Dictionary*, vol. I (N. H. Carlebach).

Records. Records are at the synagogue and with various officers.

288. CONGREGATION KEHILLATH JAWNE   *Defunct*

German-Jewish immigrant congregation founded in 1939 under the spiritual leadership of Rabbi Dr. Adolf Kober, formerly of Cologne. During the early 1940s, this congregation and the *Austrian Jewish Congregation cooperated as the Vereinigte Gemeinden. The congregation met for high holiday services at Congregation B'nai Jeshurun Community Center. Kober's death in 1958 led to its disbandment. Affiliated with *American Federation of Jews from Central Europe.

Records. Records have not been located.

289. CONGREGATION KEHILLATH YAAKOV
390 Fort Washington Ave., New York, NY 10033

German-Jewish immigrant congregation founded in 1942 in Washington Heights under Rabbi Leo Breslauer, formerly of Fürth, Germany.

Records. Records are at the synagogue and with various officers.

290. CONGREGATION K'HAL ADATH JESHURUN
85 Bennett Ave., New York, NY 10033

German-Jewish immigrant congregation founded in October 1938 in Washington Heights as a *minyan* of former members of the Orthodox *Agudas Jisroel* (secessionist Orthodoxy) in Germany, mainly Frankfurt am Main, under the spiritual leadership of Rabbi Joseph Breuer, formerly of Frankfurt am Main. Developed into largest German-Jewish Orthodox immigrant congregation in U.S.A. Operates *mikveh* (ritual bath), burial society, and free loan and charity funds; established a school system ranging from a kindergarten to advanced Jewish studies (Yeshiva Rabbi Samson Raphael Hirsch and Rika Breuer Teachers' Seminary for Girls).

Literature. Michael N. Dobkowski, "'The Fourth Reich'—German-Jewish Religious Life in America Today." *Judaism* 27 (Winter 1978): 80-95.
International Biographical Dictionary, vol. I (J. Breuer).
Dan Landsman, "K'hal Adath Jeshurun, Inc. (A Frankfurt-on-the-Main–Oriented Kehillah)—Its Schools and Institutions." Unpublished master's thesis, Yeshiva Univ., 1969.
Lessing, *Oral History*.

Records. Records are at the synagogue and schools.

291. CONGREGATION MACHANE CHODOSH
c/o Rabbi Manfred Gans, 108-42 67 Rd., Forest Hills, NY 11375

German-Jewish immigrant congregation founded in 1939 in Brooklyn as the

Jüdische Kultusgemeinde. Maintained a synagogue in Brooklyn until 1977, when the congregation sold its property and relocated to Forest Hills, Queens, where many members reside. The congregation worshiped in temporary quarters in 1978 and expected to occupy a new building in 1979 at 67-39 108 St., Forest Hills. Affiliated with the *American Federation of Jews from Central Europe.

Published *Kehillah News, 10 Years 1939-1949*, and *Anniversary Journals*, 1959 and 1974.

Records. Records are with the congregation's officers.

292. CONGREGATION NODAH BIYEHUDAH
392 Fort Washington Ave., New York, NY 10033

German-Jewish immigrant congregation founded in 1940 in Washington Heights under Rabbi Ezekiel Landau, formerly of Berlin.

Literature. *Jewish Way*, Mar. 21, 1945, p. 6.

Records. Records are at the synagogue and with various officers.

293. CONGREGATION OHAV SHOLAUM
4624 Broadway, New York, NY 10040

German-Jewish immigrant congregation founded in 1940 in Washington Heights. Affiliated with *American Federation of Jews from Central Europe. Published *Ohav Sholaum News* since 1942(?).

Literature. Lessing, *Oral History.*

Records. Records are at the synagogue and with various officers.

294. CONGREGATION OHEL JACOB   *Defunct*

German-Jewish immigrant congregation, founded in 1944 on the west side of Manhattan under the spiritual leadership of Rabbi Leo Munk. Inactive since 1971; maintains cemetery plots for former members.

Records. Records have not been located and are presumed destroyed, according to information from the last president, Max Haas, New York. Ritual objects were donated to *Congregation K'hal Adath Jeshurun, New York.

295. CONGREGATION RAMATH ORAH
550 W. 110 St., New York, NY 10025

Immigrant congregation founded in 1942 by Jewish immigrants from Luxembourg under the spiritual leadership of Rabbi Robert Serebrenik, who, in 1941, set up the Luxembourg Jewish Information Bureau in New York to assist in the rescue of Jews in Luxembourg. The Luxembourg Jewish Society is affiliated with the congregation. Published a *Bulletin.* Affiliated with *American Federation of Jews from Central Europe.

Records. Records are at the synagogue and with various officers.

296. CONGREGATION SHAARE HATIKVAH, AHAVATH TORAH V'TIKVOH CHADOSHOH
711 W. 179 St., New York, NY 10033

German-Jewish immigrant congregation formed in 1975 by a merger of Congregation Shaare Hatikvah and Congregation Ahavath Torah V'Tikvoh Chadoshoh of Washington Heights. Affiliated with *American Federation of Jews from Central Europe.

Shaare Hatikvah (Gates of Hope) was founded in 1935 in Washington Heights by Jews from Würzburg. Rabbi Siegmund Hanover, formerly of Würzburg, served as spiritual leader from 1940 to 1963.

Ahavath Torah V'Tikvoh Chadoshoh was formed ca. 1960 by a merger of Congregation Ahavath Torah of Washington Heights and Congregation Tikvoh Chadoshoh.

Ahavath Torah was founded in 1938 by German-Jewish immigrants as Synagogengemeinde Washington Heights. The name was changed in 1941 to Ahavath Torah. Its first rabbi was Max Koppel, who founded his own congregation, *Emes Wozedek in 1939. Rabbi Herman Lieber was spiritual leader from 1939 to 1958.

Tikvoh Chadoshoh was founded in 1938 under the auspices of the *Prospect Unity Club, at whose clubhouse the congregation met until 1953, when the congregation moved to Washington Heights. Until ca. 1956, the spiritual leader was Rabbi Henry M. Shotland. Rabbi Mendel Lewkowitz served from ca. 1956 to ca. 1960.

Synagogengemeinde Washington Heights published *Jüdisches Gemeindeblatt für den Zusammenschluss zur Einheitsgemeinde*, 1938-39, and *Neues jüdisches Gemeindeblatt*, 1939-40. The latter merged in 1940 with *The Way in America* to form *The Way in America and Neues jüdisches Gemeindeblatt*, 1940-41, *The Way in America*, 1942, and **The Jewish Way*, 1942-65, all published privately under the editorship of Max and Alice Oppenheimer.

Literature. *International Biographical Dictionary*, vol. I (M. Koppel, H. Lieber, S. Hanover, M. Oppenheimer, and A. Oppenheimer).
Jewish Way, Dec. 2, 1945 (on Shaare Hatikvah), Jan. 13, 1946 (on Ahavath Torah), Feb. 10, 1946 (on Tikvoh Chadoshoh).
Lessing, *Oral History*.

Records. Records are at the synagogue and with various officers.
Copies of *Jüdisches Gemeindeblatt . . .* are at New York Public Library, Jewish Div.

297. CONGREGATION SHAARE TEFILLAH   *Defunct*

German-Jewish immigrant congregation in the Bronx 1938-ca. 1952. Affiliated with *American Federation of Jews from Central Europe.

Records. Records have not been located and are presumed lost.

298. CONGREGATION SHAARE ZEDEK OF ASTORIA   *Defunct*

German-Jewish immigrant congregation founded in 1942. In 1957, members joined the newly formed Astoria Heights Jewish Center in Queens. Inactive since then except for maintenance of cemetery plots. Affiliated with *American Federation of Jews from Central Europe.

Records. Records on the Congregation's cemetery plots are with the last president, William Aron, 31-64 36 St., Long Island City, NY 11106.

299. COUNCIL OF CHURCHES OF THE CITY OF NEW YORK
475 Riverside Dr., New York, NY 10027

A predecessor agency, the Greater New York Federation of Churches, cosponsored *Friendship House for Refugees 1940–41, and cooperated with organizations in assisting refugees in New York City.

Records. Records of the Council and its predecessor units are stored in a warehouse. They are inaccessible and uncatalogued. It is presumed that they contain relevant information regarding the agency's assistance to refugees. Recent records are at the Council's office.

300. ELMHURST JEWISH CENTER
37-53 90 St., Jackson Heights, NY 11372

A religious congregation founded in 1950 largely by German-Jewish immigrants and composed primarily of immigrants from Central Europe and their children (1978).

Literature. Lessing, *Oral History.*

Records. Records are at the synagogue and with various officers.

301. FEDERATION OF JEWISH PHILANTHROPIES OF NEW YORK, INC.
130 E. 59 St., New York, NY 10022

The centralized New York City Jewish welfare fund-raising and disbursing agency, which was formed in 1944 by a merger of the Federation for the Support of Jewish Philanthropic Societies of New York City and the Brooklyn Federation of Jewish Charities.

In 1934, the New York Federation joined the *American Jewish Joint Distribution Committee in organizing a local campaign for the relief of German Jews. From 1937 to 1944, the New York and Brooklyn Federations engaged in joint fund raising and provided some financial support for refugee aid. In 1939, the New York Federation assisted the *National Coordinating Committee with a major fund-raising drive for German-Jewish refugees.

Literature. *The Golden Heritage: A History of the Federation of Jewish Philanthropies of New York from 1917 to 1967.* New York, 1969, p. 72.

Records. Federation of Jewish Philanthropies: records are not organized in such a way as to permit ready identification of documents concerning refugees. A significant portion of the Federation's records has presumably been destroyed.

302. FREE SONS OF ISRAEL, FREEDOM LODGE NO. 182
c/o Julius Frohsinn (president), 102-55 67 Dr., Forest Hills, NY 11375

This Lodge, a member of the fraternal order Free Sons of Israel founded in 1849, was founded in 1939 by German-Jewish immigrants. Engaged in social, cultural, and charitable activities. The Ladies' Auxiliary merged with the Lodge in 1974.

Literature. Fred O. Baron, *The First Twenty Years*, 1959.

Records. Records, including minutes since 1970, are with the president.

303. FRIENDSHIP HOUSE FOR REFUGEES   *Defunct*

Organized in New York in 1940 by the American Committee for Christian Refugees (ACCR, *American Christian Committee for Refugees), the Greater New York Federation of Churches (*Council of Churches of the City of New York), and the Immigrants Conference of 1939 as a facility where refugees could meet for social and cultural activities. It opened in May 1940 at 1010 Park Ave. in the former Brick Presbyterian Church, and ceased its activities in August 1941. Eva Sanderson Child, secretary of the women's division of the ACCR, served as executive secretary of Friendship House.

Literature. *Aufbau Almanac, The Immigrant's Handbook.* New York: New World Club, 1941.

Records. The records of the Brick Presbyterian Church (62 E. 92 St., New York, NY 10028), 1940–41, contain documentation about Friendship House in Trustees Files, folders 32 and 32A, Trustees Minutes, Mar. 8, 1940, and June 6, 1941, and Session Minutes, Feb. 27 and Apr. 23, 1940.

304. GEMILUTH CHESSED OF GREATER NEW YORK, INC.
717 W. 177 St., New York, NY 10033

Orthodox Jewish organization founded in 1954 by German-Jewish immigrants as Gemiluth Chessed of Washington Heights, Inc. Present name adopted in 1960. A joint undertaking by various Orthodox congregations to dispense charity, provide *kosher* food in hospitals, send children to camps, arrange religious burials, and care for the elderly. Established the *Palisades Gardens Foundation in 1966 to build and operate an old age home in Palisades, NY.

Literature. Lessing, *Oral History.*

Records. Records are at the organization's office and with various officers.

305. GOOD NEIGHBOR COMMITTEE ON THE ÉMIGRÉ AND THE COMMUNITY *Defunct*

Founded in 1939, largely through the concern of Christian organizations aiding refugees, to bring refugees into contact with Americans in those parts of New York City where refugees were concentrated and where community centers and other social resources were sparse. The Good Neighbor Committee was located at the *Society for Ethical Culture's headquarters and cooperated with that agency.

The Committee sponsored conferences in May and November 1939 and published several studies dealing with the integration of the refugee into the community. There were subcommittees on Social Guidance and on American Orientation. In 1941, the Good Neighbor Committee was reorganized as the Central Good Neighbor Committee, Inc. to extend its activities to other areas in the U.S.A. The Committee ceased its activities in 1943.

Literature. Society for Ethical Culture, *Newsletter.*

Records. Mrs. May H. Weis, New York, NY, who was active in the Good Neighbor Committee and in the Women's Conference of the Ethical Culture Society, has materials relating to the Good Neighbor Committee, including copies of printed items, correspondence, and minutes of meetings.

The location of the Good Neighbor Committee's files has not been determined. Relevant materials may be with the uncatalogued archives of the Ethical Culture Society.

306. HEBREW SINGING AND SOCIAL SOCIETY OF WASHINGTON HEIGHTS, INC. *Defunct*

German-Jewish choral society founded by immigrants in 1939 as the Ehrenreich Singing Club. [Nathan Ehrenreich, its first conductor (later of Buffalo, NY) had been active as a choral conductor at Frankfurt am Main and with the *Jüdischer Kulturbund* in Germany.] Incorporated in 1946 under the above name. Ceased to exist ca. 1969.

Records. Records have not been located and are presumed lost, according to information from the last president, Beni Greenebaum, New York.

307. HELP AND RECONSTRUCTION, INC.
37 Hillside Ave., New York, NY 10040

Founded in 1940 by German-Jewish immigrants. Originally operated the "We for You" Day Nurseries primarily for children of immigrant families, and provided other social services. Currently raises funds to send needy children to summer camp. Receives financial support from *United Help.

Literature. Lessing, *Oral History.*
Bess Stein, "A Study of a German Day Nursery." Unpublished master's thesis, New York School of Social Work, Columbia Univ., Sept. 1941.

Ruth Vogel, "The Meaning of the Day Nursery to the Refugee Parent." Unpublished master's thesis, New York School of Social Work, Columbia Univ., June 1941.

Records. Records, consisting of minutes and scrapbooks, are at the organization's office and with various officers.

308. IGUL ALUMNI ASSOCIATION OF ZIONIST FRATERNITIES (*ZIONIST ORGANIZATION OF AMERICA, DISTRICT NO. 82)
c/o Saul Jecies (president), 41 E. 42 St., New York, NY 10017

Founded in 1939 by Austrian-Jewish refugees as an organization of former members of Austrian Zionist student organizations. Affiliated with *American Federation of Jews from Austria.

Records. Records have not been located, according to information received from the president.

309. INTERNATIONAL INSTITUTE OF NEW YORK CITY, INC.   *Defunct*

Founded in 1911 as the first *International Institute by the *Young Women's Christian Association, National Board (YWCA), to serve the foreign born. In 1912, the Institute was placed under the jurisdiction of the YWCA of the City of New York. In 1941, the name was changed to International Center of the YWCA. The Center separated in 1946 from the New York YWCA and was incorporated as the International Institute of New York City. It ceased to function in the early 1950s. An unsuccessful attempt was made during the late 1950s and early 1960s to continue the Institute under the auspices of the American Federation of International Institutes and its successor, the *American Council for Nationalities Service.

The Institute and the Center provided services to refugees from Nazism in New York, including language and citizenship classes, social services, and the "Fireside Group for New Americans."

Literature. Daniel Balsam and Joseph E. Klug, "The Role of Group Work in Refugee Adjustment—A Study of the Activities of a Select Number of Group Work Agencies in Manhattan." Unpublished master's thesis, New York School of Social Work, Columbia Univ., Oct. 1943.

Records. Records of the Institute and its predecessors were mostly destroyed following the agency's closing in the early 1950s.

Univ. of Minnesota, Immigration History Research Center: papers of Kyra Malkovsky, a former staff member of the Institute, include ca. 1 ft of material on the Institute, 1939-49. Records of the American Council for Nationalities Service may include some documentation on the Institute.

YWCA of the City of New York, Archives and Resource Center: some information about the International Institute/Center, 1911-46.

310. JACOB EHRLICH SOCIETY   *Defunct*

Founded in 1939 by Austrian and Czech Zionist refugees. Affiliated with *American Federation of Jews from Austria. Inactive since the late 1950s.

Records. Records have not been located, according to information received from former officers.

311. JEWISH BOARD OF FAMILY AND CHILDREN'S SERVICES, INC.
   33 W. 60 St., New York, NY 10023

Formed in 1978 by a merger of the Jewish Family Service (JFS) and the Jewish Board of Guardians. JFS had been established in 1946 by a merger of the Jewish Social Service Association of New York (JSSA) and the Jewish Family Welfare Society of Brooklyn (JFWS). See *Jewish Welfare Agencies for general description.

   JSSA established a German Department in 1934 to assist refugees (men and families) living in Manhattan, the Bronx, and Long Island. JFWS assumed responsibility for assistance to refugees in Brooklyn as part of its case load. Following World War II, JFS transferred all of its refugee cases to the *United Service for New Americans.

Literature.   Romanofsky, *Social Service Organizations*, pp. 379–391.

Records.   Records of JFS and its predecessors, at the agency's office, include minutes of board meetings, statistical and budgetary files, selected case records (1 out of 10 files was retained), and other administrative materials, some of which deal with service to refugees.

312. JEWISH CHILD CARE ASSOCIATION OF NEW YORK, INC.
   345 Madison Ave., New York, NY 10017

Principal child care agency for the New York Jewish community.

   Various units of the Association's predecessor agencies were responsible for supervising refugee children, primarily in New York City, who had been brought to the U.S.A. without their families. The Home Bureau of the Hebrew Sheltering Guardian Society and, later, the Foster Home Bureau of the New York Association for Jewish Children arranged for placement of the children. Some refugee children were placed in child care institutions under the Association's jurisdiction. Between 1934 and 1940, about 600 Jewish children from Germany were cared for by the Association, and adult refugees were employed by units of the Association in various social service jobs.

Literature.   Jacqueline Bernard, *The Children You Gave Us: A History of 150 Years of Service to Children.* New York, 1973.
   Florence S. Kaufman, "Refugee Children in Placement (A Study of Eighteen Evacuated Children Under the Care of the Foster Home Bureau)." Unpublished master's thesis, New York School of Social Work, Columbia Univ., June 1944.

Records. American Jewish Historical Society: records, 1855-1941, 30 ft (ca. 35,000 items) of the predecessor Hebrew Orphan Asylum, and part of the records, 1879-1940, 4 ft, of the predecessor Hebrew Sheltering Guardian Society. It has not been determined whether these records contain relevant material on aid to refugee children. *NUCMC* MS 69-602, 69-603.

The bulk of the agency's records, including case files, are at its office.

313. JEWISH FRIENDS SOCIETY, INC.
c/o Ernest Melamed, 701 W. 175 St., New York, NY 10033.

Founded in 1941 by Central European Jewish immigrants, under Rabbi Ezekiel Landau, formerly of Berlin, for social and cultural purposes and mutual aid.

Records. Records are with the officers of the Society.

314. JEWISH VACATION ASSOCIATION   *Defunct*

Coordinated the activities of summer camps sponsored by Jewish organizations. Its responsibilities were assumed by the Association of Jewish Sponsored Camps (founded in 1963, 130 E. 59 St., New York, NY 10022), the coordinating agency for summer camps sponsored by Jewish organizations in the New York area, which is supported by the *Federation of Jewish Philanthropies of New York.

In spring 1939, the Association established a separate department for refugee children which cooperated with the Committee for Summer Placement of Refugee Children of the *National Refugee Service.

Literature. Ida Oppenheimer, "Camp and the Refugee Child." Unpublished paper presented at New York State Conference on Social Work, Forty-First Annual Meeting, Oct. 1940. (On file at the New York State Welfare Conference, Albany, NY 12201.)

Records. Records of the Jewish Vacation Association prior to 1945 are not in the possession of the successor Association and are presumed to be lost or destroyed.

315. JEWISH VETERANS ASSOCIATION   *Defunct*

German-Jewish immigrant organization founded in 1938 as the Immigrant Jewish War Veterans by former members of the Reichsbund jüdischer Frontsoldaten, a civil defense organization of German-Jewish veterans of World War I, founded in 1918. The name Jewish Veterans Association was adopted in the 1950s. Dissolved and assets distributed in 1973. Affiliated with *American Federation of Jews from Central Europe. Rabbi Hugo Stransky, of *Congregation Beth Hillel of Washington Heights, was the last chaplain of the Association.

During its most active period, 1938-50s, the Association had four separate posts: Washington Heights 1938-?, Ludwig Frank, Bronx 1939-?, Manhattan Midtown 1939-?, Brooklyn 1940-?, and a Ladies Auxiliary 1940-?. Activities included participation in American Jewish veterans' affairs, meetings, religious events, a burial fund, mutual aid, and sociability.

Published monthly *Mitteilungen*, 1942-45; and a tenth-anniversary journal, *Immigrant Jewish War Veterans 1938-1948.*

Literature. Lessing, *Oral History.*

Records. Leo Baeck Institute Archives: records, 1938-75, 1.5 ft, including minutes, photographs, financial and burial-fund files, and a Memorial Book, 1972. The Rabbi Hugo Stransky Collection includes materials of, and about, the Association, 1960s–70s, such as memorial programs, letters, copies of articles, clippings, and memorial sermons by H. Stransky. Finding aid: unpublished inventory (2 pp.).

New York Public Library, Jewish Div.: copies of the Association's *Mitteilungen*, 1942-45.

International Synagogue Museum at JFK International Airport: flags and other objects.

316. KEW GARDENS ANSHE SHOLOM JEWISH CENTER
82-52 Abingdon Rd., Kew Gardens, NY 11415

Formed in 1948 by a merger of the Kew Gardens Jewish Center and Congregation Anshe Sholom. The Center was an American congregation founded in 1930. Anshe Sholom was founded in 1944 by German-Jewish immigrants, many of whom had formerly been members of the Kew Gardens Jewish Center. Affiliated with United Synagogue of America.

Records. Records of Anshe Sholom, consisting of printed journals, are at the synagogue.

317. K'HAL ADAS YEREIM and K'HAL ADAS YEREIM OF BORO PARK
27 Lee Ave., Brooklyn, NY 11211 and
5402 14 Ave., Brooklyn, NY 11219

Orthodox Jewish congregation founded in 1942 in Williamsburg, Brooklyn, by Austrian-Jewish immigrants who had formerly been members of the Orthodox Hungarian *Schiffschul* in Vienna. Since 1945, the Congregation's membership has consisted primarily of former Hungarian Jews, many of them postwar immigrants.

Literature. *25 Years Adas Yereim: Anniversary Journal. The "Wiener" Kehila in Vienna and in New York*, 1967.

Records. Records are at the synagogues and with various officers.

318. MACCABI ATHLETIC CLUB, INC.   *Defunct*

Founded in 1938 (incorporated in 1960) by German-Jewish refugees as a Zionist social and sports club. Affiliated with *American Federation of Jews from

Central Europe. The Club maintained clubrooms in Washington Heights until it dissolved ca. 1970.

Records. Records have not been located, according to information received from former officers.

319. MARGARET TIETZ CENTER FOR NURSING CARE, INC.
164-11 Chapin Pkwy., Jamaica, NY 11432

A nonprofit nursing home and health-related facility founded by Jewish immigrants from Nazi Germany. Provides 120 beds for patients, including Nazi victims. The Center was named Kew Gardens Nursing Home Co., Inc., from 1967 to 1975. Established by the *New York Foundation for Nursing Homes with the assistance of the *Jewish Philanthropic Fund of 1933.

Literature. Lessing, *Oral History.*

Records. Records, including minutes, financial files, correspondence, and bulletins, are at the Center's office and with its officers. Some case files are at *Selfhelp Community Services (44 E. 23 St., New York, NY 10010).

320. NATIONAL COUNCIL OF JEWISH WOMEN, BROOKLYN SECTION
1001 Quentin Rd., Brooklyn, NY 11223

A section of the *National Council of Jewish Women (NCJW).

The Section operated a Service to Foreign Born until 1955, when its activities were incorporated in the Service to Foreign Born of the *New York Section of NCJW. During the 1930s and 1940s, the Service had a German Division to assist refugees. Following World War II, a Search Dept. was formed to assist Jewish survivors to locate their relatives in the U.S.A.

Literature. NCJW, Brooklyn Section, *Annual Reports.*
——, *A History,* 1977.

Records. Records at the agency's office consist of minutes of board meetings and reports by the president, officers, and committees.

Yeshiva Univ. Archives: closed case files, ca. 1942-55, 85 boxes, which, in 1955, had been transferred to the New York Section's Service to Foreign Born. Restricted.

YIVO Institute for Jewish Research: "search and location" records, 1945-55, microfilm (4 reels), consist mostly of letters from Jewish survivors of the Holocaust and some reports on the progress of the search for relatives in the U.S.A. The original records (55 boxes), which were destroyed, included not only these microfilmed materials but also copies of replies and NCJW interoffice memoranda.

321. NATIONAL COUNCIL OF JEWISH WOMEN, NEW YORK SECTION
9 E. 69 St., New York, NY 10021

A section of the *National Council of Jewish Women (NCJW).

The Section operated a Service to Foreign Born until 1976, when the case-load was distributed to other Jewish agencies. In 1955, the Service to Foreign Born of the *Brooklyn Section of NCJW was incorporated in the New York Section's Service to Foreign Born.

In 1934, the Section started a placement service for unattached German refugee women and girls, which later developed into the Guidance and Placement Dept. Its activities included the retraining of refugee women for jobs as waitresses. Following World War II, a Search Dept. was formed to assist Jewish survivors in locating their relatives in the U.S.A.

Literature. Judith Lowenstein, "Vocational Adjustment of Jewish Immigrant Women and Girls Assisted by the New York Section of the National Council of Jewish Women." Unpublished master's thesis, New York School of Social Work, Columbia Univ., 1938.
NCJW, New York Section, *Bulletin.*

Records. Records at the agency's office include minutes of meetings of the executive committee since 1932, minutes of meetings of the board of directors since 1935, reports of annual meetings, information on the training program, and administrative materials relating to the Service to Foreign Born.

Yeshiva Univ. Archives: closed case files, ca. 1939-68, 194 boxes and 52 file drawers. Restricted.

*United HIAS Service: open and closed case files, 1969-76. Restricted.

YIVO Institute for Jewish Research: "search and location" records, 1945-58, microfilm (4 reels), consist mostly of letters from Jewish survivors of the Holocaust and some reports on the progress of the search for relatives in the U.S.A. The original records (39 boxes), which were destroyed after microfilming, included not only these microfilmed materials but also copies of replies and NCJW interoffice memoranda.

322. NEW JERSEY FELLOWSHIP FUND FOR THE AGED, INC.

c/o Mrs. Leni Thurnauer (secretary), 601 Winthrop Rd., Teaneck, NJ 07666

Founded in 1948 by German-Jewish immigrants as the successor to the Co-operative Residence Club, Inc. The Club had been established in New York in 1942 as a joint project of the *American Friends Service Committee and Self-help of Émigrés from Central Europe (*Selfhelp Community Services). Until 1948 the Club sponsored a residence home for Nazi victims at Christadora House in New York City. From 1948 to 1972, the Fellowship Fund sponsored Newark House, an old age home for Nazi victims in Newark, NJ, and provided financial support for aged Nazi victims in other institutions after Newark House was dissolved. *Hertha Kraus was president of the Cooperative Residence Club 1942-48, and of the Fellowship Fund 1948-52.

Literature. Daniel Balsam and Joseph E. Klug, "The Role of Group Work in Refugee Adjustment—A Study of the Activities of a Select Number of Group Work Agencies in Manhattan." Unpublished master's thesis, New York School of Social Work, Columbia Univ., Oct. 1943.

Marta Fraenkel, *Cooperative Residence Living for Aged Nazi Victims: Thirty Years of Service 1942 to 1972.* Teaneck, NJ, 1974.

Lessing, *Oral History.*

Records. Records of the Fellowship Fund and the Residence Club are with the president, Albert U. Tietz, Forest Hills, NY, with other officers, and with Selfhelp Community Services (44 E. 23 St., New York, NY 10010).

323. NEW WORLD CLUB, INC.
2121 Broadway, New York, NY 10023

German-Jewish immigrant organization tracing its origin to the German-Jewish Club founded in New York City in 1924. In 1933, it was merged with the German Jewish Center, founded in 1927. The present name was adopted in 1939, when many refugees had joined the organization and made it the largest organization of its kind among refugees of the Nazi period in the U.S.A. The Club engaged in social and cultural activities and formed numerous interest groups to serve its members. The sports activities of the Club were shifted in 1953 to the newly organized Blue Star Sport Club. The Club also owns cemetery plots through the New World Benevolent Association.

One of the Club's principal activities has been the publication of the weekly **Aufbau.* The Club also published *Aufbau Almanac,* 1941, and *International Science: A Bi-Monthly Devoted to the Study of Cultural Interaction,* vol. 1, no. 1, May 1941 (only issue).

Literature. *Aufbau,* passim.

Lessing, *Oral History.*

Max Malina, *Deutsche Juden in New York nach dem Weltkriege.* New York, 1931.

Records. Records are at the Club's office and with various officers.

324. NEW YORK ASSOCIATION FOR NEW AMERICANS, INC. (NYANA)
225 Park Ave. S., New York, NY 10003

Founded in 1949 to assume the responsibilities for the resettlement of arriving immigrants in New York City previously discharged by the *United Service for New Americans (USNA) and by the *Hebrew Sheltering and Immigrant Aid Society (HIAS). From 1949 to 1953, the *National Committee for the Resettlement of Foreign Physicians was directed by NYANA. In 1951, NYANA assumed the functions of the Westchester Committee for Refugees, which had been formed in 1944 to take over the activities of the Westchester County Coordinating Committee for Émigrés.

Records. NYANA: records consisting of case files and other materials, some of which are stored in a warehouse, include some pre-1949 documentation and records of the Westchester Committee. These records are unavailable to researchers.

325. NEW YORK FOUNDATION FOR NURSING HOMES, INC.
164-11 Chapin Pkwy., Jamaica, NY 11432

Founded in 1966 by German-Jewish immigrants to act as the planning and funding agency for the establishment of a nursing home for the care of Nazi victims. The Kew Gardens Nursing Home Co., Inc., formed in 1967 for this purpose, is now known as the *Margaret Tietz Center for Nursing Care.

Literature. Lessing, *Oral History.*

Records. Records, including minutes and financial files, are at the Foundation's office and with officers and committee chairpersons.

326. NEW YORK GENERAL COMMITTEE ON IMMIGRATION AND NATURALIZATION
c/o Lydia Savoyka (chairwoman), U.S. Catholic Conference, Div. of Migration and Refugee Services, 1250 Broadway, New York, NY 10001

Formed in 1966 by a merger of the General Committee of Immigrant Aid at Ellis Island and New York Harbor, and the New York Committee on Immigration and Naturalization.

The General Committee was founded in 1918 and included representatives from sectarian and nonsectarian agencies serving immigrants. It cooperated with the Ellis Island Committee, a nonpartisan group, in conducting a study of conditions at Ellis Island during the early 1930s. (The *Report* of the Ellis Island Committee was issued in 1934.)

The New York Committee on Naturalization, which was established prior to 1942, became the New York Committee on Immigration and Naturalization following World War II. It dealt with various problems concerning the naturalization of aliens.

The New York General Committee is a coordinating agency concerned with the protection of immigrants during the early stages of arrival and resettlement. It holds periodic conferences with staff members of the *U.S. Immigration and Naturalization Service. *Cecilia Razovsky chaired the General Committee during the 1930s and the New York Committee in 1943.

Records. Records of the New York Committee on Naturalization and the New York Committee on Immigration and Naturalization, 1942-66, and of the New York General Committee on Immigration and Naturalization since 1966, 1 ft, are with its chairwoman. They consist primarily of records of the New York Committee on Immigration and Naturalization, 1947-66. One folder concerns the New York Committee on Naturalization, 1942-44, and includes information on naturalization problems of Jewish refugees from Nazi-occupied countries. Another folder consists of correspondence of the General Committee of Immigrant Aid, 1948-56. The bulk of the General Committee's records has not been located.

327. PALISADES GARDENS FOUNDATION, INC.
Oak Tree Rd., Palisades, NY 10964

Founded in 1966 by the *Gemiluth Chessed of Greater New York, an organization of Orthodox German-Jewish refugees, to build and operate an Orthodox Jewish old age home, which opened at the above location in 1970.

Literature. Lessing, *Oral History.*

Records. Records are at the Foundation's office and at the office of Gemiluth Chessed (717 W. 177 St., New York, NY 10033).

328. PROSPECT UNITY CLUB, INC. *Defunct*

German-Jewish philanthropic, social, and cultural organization founded in 1925 as the Prospect Unity Club of Yorkville and incorporated in 1927.

During the 1930s and 1940s, the Club aided immigrants many of whom subsequently joined the organization. Established a synagogue, Congregation Tikvoh Chadoshoh, in 1938, which met in the organization's clubhouse at 558 W. 158 St. until 1953, and merged ca. 1960 with Congregation Ahavath Torah of Washington Heights (*Congregation Shaare Hatikvah, Ahavath Torah V'Tikvoh Chadoshoh).

Sponsored Henry Sander Post No. 357 of *Jewish War Veterans of the United States, ca. 1950. Sports activities were shifted in 1953 to the newly organized Blue Star Sport Club.

Activities ceased ca. 1953, although former members continued to hold semi-annual reunions. Affiliated with *American Federation of Jews from Central Europe. Published *25 Years Prospect Unity Club 1926–1951 Souvenir Journal*, 1951.

Literature. Max Malina, *Deutsche Juden in New York nach dem Weltkriege.* New York, 1931.

Records. Some records which had been kept in the clubhouse prior to 1953 are presumed to have been lost through vandalism. Other records are with a Club founder, Louis Reichenberg, 33-44 93 St., Jackson Heights, NY 11372, and with various former officers and members.

329. THE SOCIETY FOR ETHICAL CULTURE IN THE CITY OF NEW YORK
2 W. 64 St., New York, NY 10023

Founded in 1876 by Dr. Felix Adler as an ethical, educational, and social reform movement, with branches in other American cities and abroad.

Formed a Refugee Coordinating Committee in 1938, which offered lectures, language information, vocational guidance, and social programs for refugees. By 1942, its functions had been transferred to the Women's Conference of the Ethical Culture Society, which organized lecture series and after-school care programs for children, guidance classes, and other activities. About 85% of those aided were Jewish refugees. The *Good Neighbor Committee on the Émigré and the Community, while administratively separate from the Ethical Culture Society, was located at the Society's building and cooperated closely with it.

Literature. American Ethical Union, *Standard.*

Daniel Balsam and Joseph E. Klug, "The Role of Group Work in Refugee Adjust-ment—A Study of the Activities of a Select Number of Group Work Agencies in Manhattan." Unpublished master's thesis, New York School of Social Work, Columbia Univ., Oct. 1943.

Howard B. Radest, *Toward Common Ground: The Story of the Ethical Culture Societies in the United States.* New York: Ungar, 1969.

Society for Ethical Culture, *Newsletter.* For references to refugees, see vol. 36 (Dec. 1938) ff.

Records. The uncataloged archives of the Ethical Culture Society were inaccessible in 1978. It could not be determined whether there are materials bearing on aid to refugees in the collection.

330. SOCIETY OF FRIENDS FROM BRESLAU (GESELLSCHAFT DER BRESLAUER FREUNDE) *Defunct*

Founded by Jewish immigrants from Breslau, Germany, in 1940 for social, cultural, and charitable activities. Functions ceased in 1975.

Literature. Charlotte Weissbart, "Liebe Freunde in Israel." *Mitteilungen des Verbandes ehemaliger Breslauer und Schlesier in Israel E.V.*, no. 37 (Apr. 1975): 7 (an account of the Society's activities).

Records. Records have not been located and are presumed lost, according to information received from a former officer of the Society, Charlotte Weissbart, New York, NY.

331. THEODOR HERZL SOCIETY (ZIONIST ORGANIZATION OF AMERICA, DISTRICT NO. 81) *Defunct*

Founded by German-Jewish immigrants in 1934 as an affiliate of the *Zionist Organization of America for cultural purposes and political activities on behalf of Palestine/Israel. In 1948, it reached its peak membership of 500 members; inactive since 1970. Affiliated with *American Federation of Jews from Central Europe.

Literature. Lessing, *Oral History.*

Records. Records, consisting of membership lists and financial statements, are with the last secretary-treasurer, Mrs. Lucia Fluss, 717 W. 177 St., New York, NY 10033.

332. UNITED NEIGHBORHOOD HOUSES OF NEW YORK, INC.
101 E. 15 St., New York, NY 10003

A federation of New York City settlement houses operating neighborhood centers, primarily in the city's poverty areas.

Activities included concern with immigrants. Its League of Mothers' Clubs maintained a Refugees Fund 1938-40.

Records. Univ. of Minnesota Libraries, Social Welfare History Archives Center: records, 1898–1961, 136 ft, include one folder (#563) on the Refugees Fund and several folders (#307-311 and others) on immigration. Finding aid: detailed inventory in *Descriptive Inventories of Collections in the Social Welfare History Archives Center.* Westport, CT: Greenwood, 1970, pp. 637–743.

Recent records are at the agency's office.

333. VIRCHOW–PIRQUET SOCIETY
c/o Dr. Elizabeth D. Strauss (secretary), 315 Central Park West,
New York, NY 10025

An association of physicians most of whom were graduates of Central European universities. Formed in 1976 by a merger of the Rudolf Virchow Medical Society in the City of New York and the Pirquet Society of Clinical Medicine. A member of the Federation of American-European Medical Societies (along with Hungarian, Polish, and Yugoslav groups).

The Rudolf Virchow Medical Society, founded in 1860, was known until 1939 as the German Medical Society of the City of New York. By the 1940s, the membership consisted primarily of German refugee physicians who subsequently assumed the leadership of the organization.

The Pirquet Society of Clinical Medicine, founded ca. 1942 by graduates of European medical schools, largely refugees from Austria, was known until 1963 as the Medical Circle.

Literature. *Pirquet Bulletin of Clinical Medicine* (formerly *Medical Circle Bulletin*). 1954–date.
Rudolf Virchow Medical Society, *Jubilee Volume, 100th Anniversary; Festschrift zur 100-Jahr-Feier, Nov. 7, 1860-1960.* Basel: S. Karger, 1960.
——. *Proceedings* . . . . 1942-date, annual.

Records. New York Academy of Medicine Library: records of the Virchow Society on deposit include correspondence, applications for membership, announcements of meetings, and reports. Permission of the Society's Archivist-Historian must be obtained to use the records.

Additional records of the Virchow Society and records of the Pirquet Society are with various officers.

Rochester

334. JEWISH FAMILY SERVICE
456 E. Main St., Rochester, NY 14604

See *Jewish Welfare Agencies for general description.
The Rochester Coordinating Committee for Aid to German Refugees and its successor, the Rochester Refugee Committee, cooperated with the Jewish Social Service Bureau (later renamed Jewish Family Service) in aiding the resettlement of refugees.

Records. Records at the agency's office include case files of clients. As a matter of policy, the agency destroys the files of its clients 10 years after closing their case. Basic information from such files is preserved on index cards.

Syracuse

335. JEWISH FAMILY SERVICE BUREAU
316 S. Warren St., Syracuse, NY 13202

See *Jewish Welfare Agencies for general description.

The Syracuse Refugee Committee cooperated with the Jewish Social Service Bureau (later renamed Jewish Family Service Bureau) in assisting in the resettlement of refugees.

Records. No information was received following an inquiry about the agency's records.

Ohio

Akron

336. JEWISH FAMILY SERVICE
750 White Pond Dr., Akron, OH 44320

See *Jewish Welfare Agencies for general description.

The Jewish Social Service Federation (later renamed Jewish Family Service) assisted in the resettlement of refugees.

Records. No information was received following an inquiry about the agency's records.

Cincinnati

337. CONGREGATION NEW HOPE (TIKVOH CHADOSHOH)
1625 Cresthill Ave., Cincinnati, OH 45237

German-Jewish immigrant congregation founded in 1939. Affiliated with Union of Orthodox Jewish Congregations of America.

Published *New Hope Bulletin*, 1940-date, and *35th Anniversary Banquet* journal, 1974.

Literature. Lessing, *Oral History.*

Records. Records are at the synagogue and with various officers and members.

Hebrew Union College–Jewish Institute of Religion, Klau Library, has copies of some of the congregation's publications.

338. GATE CLUB   *Defunct*

German-Jewish immigrant organization founded ca. 1936 by rabbinical students from Germany at the *Hebrew Union College in Cincinnati. Engaged in social welfare, cultural and social activities, and conducted services on the Jewish high holidays during the early years. Ceased to exist ca. 1954.

Literature. Lessing, *Oral History.*

Records. Records have not been located, according to information from a former member, Richard J. Wise, Cincinnati, OH.

339. JEWISH FAMILY SERVICE
1710 Section Rd., Cincinnati, OH 45237

See *Jewish Welfare Agencies for general description.
The Cincinnati Committee for Refugees and the Ohio State Committee for Resettlement of Refugees were established by the United Jewish Social Agencies (later renamed Jewish Family Service) to assist in the resettlement of refugees.

Records. Records at the agency's office include minutes of meetings, correspondence, policy memoranda, and case files. Some of the case files are on microfilm.
American Jewish Archives: search records, 1936-52, 59 ft, consist of over 2200 cases which did not result in resettlement in Cincinnati. Consist of correspondence between Jews in Germany and Eastern European countries, and national and local rescue agencies in the U.S.A. *NUCMC* MS 68-40.

340. NATIONAL COUNCIL OF JEWISH WOMEN, CINCINNATI SECTION
For current address, contact the headquarters of NCJW in New York.

A section of the *National Council of Jewish Women.
Its Service to Foreign Born cooperated with other Cincinnati agencies in resettling immigrants.

Records. American Jewish Archives: records, 1908-17 and 1923-44, microfilm (7 reels), include minutes, reports, membership lists, newspaper articles, correspondence, and other materials.
The original records and later materials are with the agency's officers.

Cleveland

341. JEWISH CHILDREN'S BUREAU
21811 Fairmount Blvd., Cleveland, OH 44118

Principal child care agency for the Cleveland Jewish community.
Sponsored refugee children brought to Cleveland by the German Jewish Children's Aid (renamed *European Jewish Children's Aid in 1942). The children were placed in foster homes until they were reunited with their families or became self-supporting.

Records. As a matter of policy, the agency destroys the files of its clients 20 years after closing their case. Basic statistical data are preserved on microfilm.

342. JEWISH FAMILY SERVICE ASSOCIATION
2060 S. Taylor Rd., Cleveland Heights, OH 44118

See *Jewish Welfare Agencies for general description.

The Cleveland Coordination Committee for Immigrants, established by the Jewish Welfare Federation in 1936, and its successor, the Refugee Service Committee of the Jewish Social Service Bureau (later renamed Jewish Family Service Association), assisted in the resettlement of refugees.

Literature. Alice Florence Browne, "The Refugee Child's Dilemma. A Study of Four Refugee Families Who Have Been in the United States Two Years or More, with Emphasis on the Problems of Adolescent Children, and Their Adjustment to the American Culture." Unpublished master's thesis, Western Reserve Univ. School of Applied Social Sciences, 1945.

Jack Emmer, "Uprooted. A Study of the Adjustment to the U.S. of Four Refugee Families Known to the Jewish Social Service Bureau, Cleveland, Ohio, with Reference to the Differences in Adjustment of Children and Parents." Unpublished master's thesis, Western Reserve Univ. School of Applied Social Sciences, 1943.

Helen L. Glassman, *Adjustment in Freedom: A Follow-up Study of One Hundred Jewish Displaced Families.* Cleveland: United HIAS Service and Jewish Family Service Association, 1956.

Records. Western Reserve Historical Society, Cleveland Jewish Archives: records, 1895–1974, 20.5 ft, include Refugee Service Committee records, 1937–70, 36 folders, comprising financial ledgers, correspondence, minutes of meetings, and other materials. Restricted. Finding aid: unpublished register.

Records at the agency's office include case file master cards.

343. LEAGUE FOR HUMAN RIGHTS   *Defunct*

Organized in Cleveland in 1937 to combat anti-Semitism and counter local Nazi propaganda.

Concerned with the anti-Nazi boycott and the refugee problem.

Records. Western Reserve Historical Society, Cleveland Jewish Archives: records, 1936–47, 4 ft, consist of correspondence, reports, and publications concerning the League's operations and the cases of anti-Semitism which it investigated. Records are restricted.

344. MAYFIELD HILLCREST SYNAGOGUE
1732 Lander Rd., Mayfield Heights, OH 44124

Formed in 1970 by a merger of Mayfield Temple and Congregation B'nai Israel. Mayfield Temple was a German-Jewish immigrant congregation founded in 1940 in Cleveland as Congregation Gates of Hope, Shaare Hatikvah. The name Mayfield Temple was adopted in 1956. B'nai Israel was an American congregation founded in 1964. Affiliated with United Synagogue of America and *American Federation of Jews from Central Europe.

Literature. Lessing, *Oral History.*

Records. Records, 1940-date, including minutes, monthly bulletins, and annual journals, are at the synagogue and with various officers and members.

345. NATIONAL COUNCIL OF JEWISH WOMEN, CLEVELAND SECTION
3535 Lee Rd., Cleveland, OH 44120

A section of the *National Council of Jewish Women.

Its Service to Foreign Born cooperated with other Cleveland agencies in resettling immigrants.

Records. Western Reserve Historical Society, Cleveland Jewish Archives: records, 1894-1964, 23 ft, include minutes, correspondence, scrapbooks, clippings, publications, and visual materials.

Recent records are at the agency's office.

346. NATIONALITIES SERVICE CENTER
1001 E. Huron Rd., Cleveland, OH 44115

One of several dozen *International Institutes, as the Center was known until 1953, and a member agency of the *American Council for Nationalities Service.

Records. Western Reserve Historical Society: records, 1918-64, 130 ft, consist of case files of immigrants aided by the agency, minute books, and administrative materials relating to the Center's activities in the Cleveland area. Restricted.

Recent records are at the Center's office.

Columbus

347. JEWISH FAMILY SERVICE
1175 College Ave., Columbus, OH 43209

See *Jewish Welfare Agencies for general description.

The Columbus Coordinating Committee for Refugees was established by the Jewish Welfare Federation (later renamed Jewish Family Service) to assist in the resettlement of refugees.

Literature. A study of refugees in Columbus was in progress in 1978 at the Columbus Jewish History Project, Ohio Historical Society.

Records. Ohio Historical Society: records, 1954-72, 27 ft. *NUCMC* MS 75-1052. Finding aid: unpublished inventory (24 pp.).

The location of earlier records and of materials concerning refugees could not be ascertained.

348. NATIONAL COUNCIL OF JEWISH WOMEN, COLUMBUS SECTION
c/o Nearly New Shop, 1007 E. Livingston Ave., Columbus, OH 43209

A section of the *National Council of Jewish Women, founded 1917.

Its Committee on Service to Foreign Born assisted in the resettlement of refugees.

Records. Ohio Historical Society: records, 1920–72, 11 ft, are presumed to include material relating to the Section's Committee on Service to Foreign Born. *NUCMC* MS 75-1114. Finding aid: unpublished inventory.

Recent records are with the agency's officers.

Toledo

349. JEWISH FAMILY SERVICE
5151 Monroe St., Toledo, OH 43623

See *Jewish Welfare Agencies for general description.

Records. Records at the agency's office include case files of clients beginning in 1939, minutes of meetings, and other materials.

Oregon

Portland

350. JEWISH FAMILY AND CHILD SERVICE
1130 S.W. Morrison, Portland, OR 97205

See *Jewish Welfare Agencies for general description.

The Oregon Émigré Committee of the Federated Jewish Societies (later renamed Jewish Welfare Federation) coordinated the resettlement of refugees. After the war, the Émigré Committee became the Oregon Service for New Americans.

Records. Jewish Historical Society of Oregon: record book, 1936–49, of the Oregon Émigré Committee (formerly held by the Jewish Welfare Federation).

Records at the agency's office include client case files and correspondence.

Pennsylvania

Philadelphia

351. ASSOCIATION FOR JEWISH CHILDREN OF PHILADELPHIA
1301 Spencer St., Philadelphia, PA 19141

Principal child care agency serving the Philadelphia Jewish community, formed in 1941 by the merger of several established organizations, including the Juvenile Aid Society, founded 1901.

The Juvenile Aid Society and the Association sponsored refugee children brought to Philadelphia by the German Jewish Children's Aid (since 1942, *European Jewish Children's Aid). The German (European) Jewish Children's Aid Committee administered this program. The children were placed in foster homes until they were reunited with their families, or became self-supporting.

Records. Case records, including those for refugee children assisted by the agency, are at the Association's office. Restricted.

Philadelphia Jewish Archives Center: all other records, 1855-1974, 45 boxes and 28 volumes, include records of the European Jewish Children's Aid Committee, 1934-64, 26 folders and 1 volume, which consist of minutes, correspondence, budgets, statistics, and other materials. Finding aid: unpublished inventory (20 pp.).

352. B'NAI B'RITH, HEINRICH GRAETZ LODGE NO. 1877
c/o Julius Simon (president), Salem Harbour Apts., 104 Moorsgate, Andalusia, PA 19020

Lodge of *B'nai B'rith International, founded by German-Jewish immigrants in Philadelphia in 1951 for cultural and social purposes and mutual aid. Its honorary president was *William Graetz.

Literature. Lessing, *Oral History.*

Records. Records, including minutes since 1951 and monthly newsletters, are with the president and other officers.

353. CENTRAL CLUB OF PHILADELPHIA, INC.
4805 York Rd., Philadelphia, PA 19141

German-Jewish immigrant organization founded in 1935 as the German Jewish Club. Engaged in social welfare, mutual aid, and social and cultural activities. Its women's group was organized in 1942. Members of the Club founded *Congregation Tikvoh Chadoshoh in 1942. Affiliated with *American Federation of Jews from Central Europe.

Published a bulletin, and journals: *Tenth Anniversary* 1945, *Our Twentieth Year* 1955, *Twenty-Fifth Anniversary* 1960, *Thirtieth Anniversary* 1965, *Thirty-Fifth Anniversary* 1970, and *Fortieth Anniversary* 1975.

Literature. Lessing, *Oral History.*

Records. Records are at the Club House and with various officers and members. Copies of the bulletin, ca. 1938-47, are also with Mrs. Stefanie Perlstein, R.D. 6, Bridgeton, NJ 08302, who was secretary of the Club, 1942-47.

354. CONGREGATION AGUDATH ACHIM
c/o Edward Fleischmann (president), 1000 W. Olney Ave., Philadelphia, PA 19141

German-Jewish immigrant congregation founded in 1957, when Rabbi Helmut Frank resigned as spiritual leader of *Congregation Tikvoh Chadoshoh, Philadelphia. The new congregation was established to follow a more traditional ritual.

Literature. Helmut Frank, "As a German Rabbi to America." *Paul Lazarus Gedenkbuch.* Jerusalem: Jerusalem Post Press, 1961, pp. 135-142.

International Biographical Dictionary, vol. I (H. Frank).
Lessing, *Oral History*.

Records. Records are with Morris Mayer (secretary-treasurer), 4604 N. Hurley St., Philadelphia, PA 19126.

355. CONGREGATION TIKVOH CHADOSHOH/CHEVRATH TIKVOH CHADOSHOH
5364 W. Chew Ave., Philadelphia, PA 19138

German-Jewish immigrant congregation founded in 1942 as an outgrowth of high holiday services organized by members of the *Central Club of Philadelphia. Chevrath Tikvoh Chadoshoh (burial society), providing burials in the traditional "European" manner, was founded in 1943 as an auxiliary activity of the Congregation. Several years later the *chevrah* separated from the main congregation and was incorporated as an independent organization. Affiliated with United Synagogue of America and *American Federation of Jews from Central Europe. Published *25th Anniversary* [Journal] , 1967.

Literature. Helmut Frank, "As a German Rabbi to America." *Paul Lazarus Gedenkbuch.* Jerusalem: Jerusalem Post Press, 1961, pp. 135-142.
Lessing, *Oral History*.

Records. Records of the congregation, including minutes since 1945 and bulletins, are at the synagogue and with various officers and members.
Records of the *chevrah* are with its officers.

356. HIAS AND COUNCIL MIGRATION SERVICE OF PHILADELPHIA
1510 Chestnut St., Philadelphia, PA 19102

Formed in 1952 by a merger of the Philadelphia branch of the *Hebrew Sheltering and Immigrant Aid Society (HIAS) and the Service to Foreign Born of the Greater Philadelphia Section of the *National Council of Jewish Women (NCJW). (The HIAS branch was founded in 1884 as the Association for the Protection of Jewish Immigrants and joined national HIAS in 1913.) Prior to the merger, the two local agencies had shared office facilities and had rendered a partially overlapping range of services to immigrants overseas and following their arrival in Philadelphia.

HIAS and NCJW were member agencies of the Philadelphia Coordinating Committee for Refugees (*Jewish Family Service of Philadelphia).

Literature. Anna S. Petluck, "A Descriptive Study and Analysis of the Needs of the Foreign Born of the Jewish Community in Port City [Philadelphia]; of the Present Services Rendered by the Local Sections of the Two National Jewish Immigration Agencies [HIAS and NCJW] and of the Factors Involved in Planning for Future Community Service." Unpublished master's essay, New York School of Social Work, Columbia Univ., Aug. 1942.

Records. HIAS and Council Migration Service: pre-1952 (merger) records include Council card files on naturalization and port arrival assistance, HIAS card files on naturalization assistance, and combined HIAS–Council records and card files. The minutes of board and committee meetings for the period prior to 1957, with the exception of the material at the American Jewish Archives (described below), are presumed lost or destroyed.

American Jewish Archives: HIAS records, 1884–1952, ca. 2 ft, comprise mostly pre-1935 material and include microfilm copies of arrival records, 1884–1921.

Philadelphia Jewish Archives Center: HIAS records, 1884–1948, 45 vols., comprise mostly pre-1934 arrival records, passage orders, and ticket purchase records.

The Greater Philadelphia Section of NCJW (1601 Walnut St., Philadelphia, PA 19103) may also have material about the Council's pre-1952 activity.

357. JEWISH FAMILY SERVICE OF PHILADELPHIA
   1610 Spruce St., Philadelphia, PA 19103

See *Jewish Welfare Agencies for general description.

Founded in 1869 as the United Hebrew Charities. In 1921 the name was changed to Jewish Welfare Society, and in 1949 to the present name.

Assisted in the resettlement of refugee families in the Philadelphia area. The Philadelphia Refugee Resettlement Committee functioned under the auspices of the Jewish Welfare Society, and was one of the cooperating agencies in the Philadelphia Coordinating Committee, which also included the International Institute (*Nationalities Service Center), HIAS (*HIAS and Council Migration Service of Philadelphia), National Council of Jewish Women, and the *Legal Aid Society, among others. After World War II, the Committee was called the Philadelphia Committee for New Americans.

Literature. Alma Cantor, "Establishing Eligibility for Financial Assistance with the Refugee Client: A Case Work Process." Unpublished practice paper for master's degree, Univ. of Pennsylvania, School of Social Work, 1940.
Jewish Family Service, *The Birth and Growth of the Jewish Family Service of Philadelphia: A History of One Hundred Years of Service to Individuals and Families.* Philadelphia, 1969.

Records. The case records of clients, including refugees resettled by the agency, are on microfilm at the agency's office. Restricted.

Philadelphia Jewish Archives Center: administrative records, including minutes of the board of directors, 1921–63, and a few financial statements of the Refugee Resettlement Committee, 1939–46.

358. LEGAL AID SOCIETY OF PHILADELPHIA   *Defunct*

Organized in 1901 and re-organized in 1933, the Society was dissolved in 1976. Gave advice on legal matters to Philadelphia area residents, including assistance with naturalizations and name changes.

Member agency of the Philadelphia Coordinating Committee for Refugees

(*Jewish Family Service of Philadelphia). From the 1950s until 1968, the Society maintained a Restitution Cases Dept. which cooperated with the *United Restitution Organization (URO), New York, in assisting persons in preparing claims for *Wiedergutmachung* against the West German government. *William Graetz was a special assistant for this service.

Records. Temple Univ., Urban Archives Center: records, 1933-76, 18 ft, consist of administrative and financial files and reports of other agencies. It is not known to what extent the records relate to the administration of the Restitution Cases Dept. Finding aid: *Guide to Philadelphia Social Service Collections at the Urban Archives Center.* Philadelphia, 1976, pp. 41-42.

All case files on *Wiedergutmachung* were transferred to URO, New York, after the Department closed in 1968.

359. NATIONALITIES SERVICE CENTER
1300 Spruce St., Philadelphia, PA 19107

One of several dozen *International Institutes, as the Center was known until 1963, and a member agency of the *American Council for Nationalities Service.

Member agency of the Philadelphia Coordinating Committee for Refugees (*Jewish Family Service of Philadelphia).

Records. Temple Univ., Urban Archives Center: records, 1920-75, 38 ft, consist of case files, statistical and social surveys of immigrants, and administrative materials relating to the Center's activities in the Philadelphia area. Finding aid: *Guide to Philadelphia Social Service Collections at the Urban Archives Center.* Philadelphia, 1976, pp. 42-43.

Recent records are at the Center's office.

Pittsburgh

360. AMERICAN SERVICE INSTITUTE OF ALLEGHENY COUNTY
Defunct

Was one of several dozen *International Institutes and a member agency of the *American Council for Nationalities Service.

Records. Univ. of Pittsburgh Library, Archives of Industrial Society: records, 1941-61, 50 ft, consist of case files, publications, correspondence, and other materials relating to the Institute's activities in the Pittsburgh area. Only a small part of the material relates to refugees of the Nazi period. *NUCMC* MS 65-1746. Finding aid: unpublished inventory.

361. FRIENDSHIP CLUB OF PITTSBURGH, INC.
5857 Forbes Ave., Pittsburgh, PA 15217

German-Jewish immigrant organization founded in 1936 and incorporated in 1951. Engaged in social welfare, mutual aid, social, cultural, and religious activities, and conducts high holiday services. Affiliated with *American Federation of Jews from Central Europe. Published two monthlies, *Friendship Club Gossip*, 1953-56 and *Friendship Club Recorder*, 1957-date.

Literature. Lessing, *Oral History.*
"20 Years of Aiding Newcomers Help Ex-Refugees Forget Past." *The Pittsburgh Press*, Oct. 7, 1956.

Records. Univ. of Pittsburgh Libraries, Archives of Industrial Society: records, 1935-76, 6 boxes, include minutes, correspondence, financial records, publications, and other documentation, primarily of the period since 1950. Finding aid: unpublished inventory (5 pp.).
   Records may also be with various officers and members.

362. JEWISH FAMILY AND CHILDREN'S SERVICE
234 McKee Pl., Pittsburgh, PA 15213

See *Jewish Welfare Agencies for general description.
   The Tri-State Coordinating Council cooperated with the Jewish Social Service Bureau (later renamed Jewish Family and Children's Service) in the resettlement of refugees.

Literature. Phyllis Swick, "Vocational Placement of New Americans: An Analysis of the Vocational Placement of New Americans Accepted for Case Work Service by the Jewish Family and Children's Service of Pittsburgh During 1947 and 1948." Unpublished master's thesis, Univ. of Pittsburgh, 1950.

Records. Records at the agency's office include client case files.

363. NATIONAL COUNCIL OF JEWISH WOMEN, PITTSBURGH SECTION
1620 Murray Ave., Pittsburgh, PA 15217

A section of the *National Council of Jewish Women.

Records. Univ. of Pittsburgh Library, Archives of Industrial Society: records, 1893-1967, 15 ft, include correspondence, minutes of meetings of the executive board, reports by officers and committees, membership records, miscellaneous scrapbooks and clippings, and material relating to specific activities of the Section such as the Service to Foreign Born. Box 13 includes materials on the Relief Campaign for Jews in Germany, 1933, and German Jewish Children's Aid (*European Jewish Children's Aid), 1934-35. Box 14 includes information on the Committee on Service to Foreign Born, 1933-36, 1939-45, 1948-56. Box 3/suppl. includes material on the Committee on Service to Foreign Born. Box 5/suppl. contains material on Service to Foreign Born and correspondence on immigration and naturalization. *NUCMC* MS 65-1752. Finding aid: unpublished inventory.
   Recent records are at the agency's office.

Rhode Island

Providence

364. INTERNATIONAL INSTITUTE OF PROVIDENCE
104 Princeton Ave., Providence, RI 02907

One of several dozen *International Institutes and a member agency of the *American Council for Nationalities Service.

Records. Rhode Island College Library, Special Collections Dept.: records, 1921–70, consist of case files, reports, correspondence, and other material relating to the Institute's activities in the Providence area. Restricted.
Recent records are at the Institute's office.

365. JEWISH FAMILY AND CHILDREN'S SERVICE
229 Waterman Ave., Providence, RI 02906

See *Jewish Welfare Agencies for general description.
The Rhode Island Refugee Service assisted in the resettlement of refugees.

Records. No information was received following an inquiry about the agency's records.

366. RHODE ISLAND SELFHELP
c/o Bruno Hoffman (president), 137 Woodbine St., Providence, RI 02906

German- and Austrian-Jewish immigrant organization founded in 1944 as an outgrowth of the "new immigrants" group which had met informally at the Jewish Community Center beginning in early 1940. Engaged in social welfare, mutual aid, and social and cultural activities. Affiliated with *American Federation of Jews from Central Europe.

Records. Records are with various officers.

Tennessee

Memphis

367. JEWISH SERVICE AGENCY
· 6560 Poplar Ave., Memphis, TN 38138

See *Jewish Welfare Agencies for general description.

Records. Records at the agency's office include minutes of meetings and case files of clients dealing with the resettlement of refugees.

Texas

Dallas

368. JEWISH FAMILY SERVICE
11333 N. Central Expy., Dallas, TX 75231

See *Jewish Welfare Agencies for general description.
    The Émigré Service Committee was established by the Jewish Welfare Federation to assist in the resettlement of refugees.

Records. Records at the agency's office include case files of clients.

369. SELF HELP, INC.
c/o Manfred Marx, 6548 Lafayette Way, Dallas, TX 75230

German-Jewish immigrant organization founded in 1946 and incorporated in 1959. Engaged in mutual aid and social and cultural activities. Affiliated with *American Federation of Jews from Central Europe.

Records. Records, including minutes since 1959 and membership lists, are with the president and other officers.

Houston

370. JEWISH FAMILY SERVICE
4131 S. Braeswood, Houston, TX 77025

See *Jewish Welfare Agencies for general description.
    The Refugee Service Committee of the Jewish Community Council assisted in the resettlement of refugees.

Records. Records at the agency's office include case files of clients dealing with the resettlement of refugees.

Virginia

Norfolk

371. JEWISH FAMILY SERVICE OF TIDEWATER
7300 Newport Ave., P.O. Box 9503, Norfolk, VA 23505

See *Jewish Welfare Agencies for general description.
    The Norfolk Refugee Committee cooperated with the Jewish Family Welfare Bureau (later renamed Jewish Family Service) in assisting in the resettlement of refugees.

Records. Records at the agency's office include case files of clients and claimants for *Wiedergutmachung* from the Federal Republic of Germany.

Richmond

372. JEWISH FAMILY SERVICES
4206 Fitzhugh Ave., Richmond, VA 23230

See *Jewish Welfare Agencies for general description.

The Richmond Jewish Community Council assisted in the resettlement of refugees before the Jewish Family Services were established in the 1950s to provide services to immigrants.

Literature. Anne Fischer, "A Study of the Problem of the Refugee in Richmond, Va." Unpublished master's thesis, Richmond School of Social Work of the College of William and Mary [now Virginia Commonwealth Univ., Richmond], May 1944.

Selma Levenson, "A Study of the Richmond Jewish Community Council." Unpublished master's thesis, Richmond School of Social Work . . . , Apr. 1947.

Records. The files of the Jewish Community Council were destroyed by fire ca. 1947. Although the case records of the Jewish Family Services are destroyed 10 years following their closing, a number of files dealing with immigrants have been retained at the agency's office.

373. NEW AMERICAN JEWISH CLUB
c/o John J. Newmont (president), 7009 Coachman Lane, Richmond, VA 23228

German-Jewish immigrant organization founded in 1947 for mutual aid, social welfare, and social and cultural purposes. Cooperates with Emek Sholom Cemetery Co., a related but independent organization founded in 1950, which owns a cemetery. Affiliated with *American Federation of Jews from Central Europe.

Records. Congregation Beth Ahabah Archives: records include minutes of the Club and the Cemetery Co., correspondence, clippings, lists of immigrants to Richmond 1935–41 and 1947–50, and documentation on the Holocaust.

Washington

Seattle

374. JEWISH CLUB OF WASHINGTON
c/o Klaus L. Stern (president), 4531 Purdue Ave., N.E., Seattle, WA 98105

German-Jewish immigrant organization founded in 1945 to provide social welfare, mutual aid, and social and cultural activities. Preceded by informal but regular meetings of Jewish refugees in Seattle, 1937–41, which were discontinued during the U.S. involvement in World War II. During this time, the Washington Émigré Bureau (*Jewish Family and Child Service, Seattle) maintained contacts with and among the refugees. Affiliated with *American Federation of Jews from Central Europe.

Literature. Lessing, *Oral History.*

Records. Records are with various officers.

375. JEWISH FAMILY AND CHILD SERVICE
1110 Harvard Ave., Seattle, WA 98102

See *Jewish Welfare Agencies for general description.

The Washington Émigré Bureau was established in 1939 by several agencies, including the Jewish Welfare Society (later renamed Jewish Family and Child Service) and the *National Council of Jewish Women, Seattle Section, to assist in the resettlement of refugees.

Records. Univ. of Washington Libraries, Archives and Manuscripts Div.: some records, including 6 folders concerning the resettlement of refugees. Most inactive case files of clients have been destroyed.

376. NATIONAL COUNCIL OF JEWISH WOMEN, SEATTLE SECTION
For current address, contact the headquarters of NCJW in New York.

A section of the *National Council of Jewish Women.

Operated a settlement house for refugees, and cooperated with the Jewish Welfare Society (*Jewish Family and Child Service) and other agencies in forming the Washington Émigré Bureau in 1939.

Records. Univ. of Washington Libraries, Archives and Manuscripts Div.: records, 1900-58, consist of minutes and related materials.

Recent records are with the agency's officers.

Wisconsin
377. WISCONSIN JEWISH MILITARY SERVICE RECORDS

Records. State Historical Society of Wisconsin: records, 1941-57, 8 boxes, concern Wisconsin Jewish servicemen in World War II, including lists of refugees, casualties, officers, and honor rolls compiled from various sources. Finding aid: Lindsay B. Nauen, ed., *Guide to the Wisconsin Jewish Archives at The State Historical Society of Wisconsin.* Madison, 1974, p. 22.

Madison

378. MADISON CITIZENS' COMMITTEE FOR DISPLACED PERSONS
Defunct

A chapter of the *Citizens' Committee on Displaced Persons (CCDP), founded after World War II.

Records. State Historical Society of Wisconsin: records consist of correspondence and primarily of printed materials, including a few dispatches from CCDP's New York headquarters.

Manitowoc

379. MANITOWOC COORDINATING COMMITTEE   *Defunct*

A branch of the *National Coordinating Committee for Aid to Refugees and Emigrants Coming from Germany. The local committee gave affidavits of support to prospective immigrants wishing to resettle in the Manitowoc area and raised funds for their support after their arrival.

Records. Univ. of Wisconsin, Green Bay Area Research Center: records, 1939-41, one box, include correspondence, affidavits, financial materials, and minutes of national, state, and local committees, meetings, and conferences. Finding aids: unpublished register; Lindsay B. Nauen, ed., *Guide to the Wisconsin Jewish Archives at The State Historical Society of Wisconsin.* Madison, 1974, p. 15.

American Jewish Archives: microfilm of the material described above.

Milwaukee

380. JEWISH FAMILY AND CHILDREN'S SERVICE
1360 N. Prospect Ave., Milwaukee, WI 53202

See *Jewish Welfare Agencies for general description.

The Milwaukee Committee for Refugees and the Jewish Social Service Association (later renamed Jewish Family and Children's Service) assisted in the resettlement of refugees.

Records. Records at the agency's office include minutes of meetings and case files of clients.

381. NEW HOME CLUB, INC.
c/o Walter Jacobsohn (president), 4428 N. Sheffield Ave., Milwaukee, WI 53211

German-Jewish immigrant organization founded in 1937 as Gesellschaft der Freunde (Society of Friends). Present name adopted in 1940 and incorporated in 1948. Engaged in social welfare, mutual aid, and social, cultural, and religious activities. Affiliated with *American Federation of Jews from Central Europe.

Published a newsletter, *Nachrichtenblatt*, during its early years (two copies are included in the records).

Literature. Herman Weil, "New Home Club, Refugees from W. Europe, Blended into Fabric of US Life." *Wisconsin Jewish Chronicle*, Oct. 6, 1972.

Records. Records, including minutes since 1963 and published items, are with the president, with Professor Herman Weil, historian of the Club, 2027 E. Lake Bluff Blvd., Milwaukee, WI 53211, and with other officers and members.

Three

INDIVIDUALS

382. AYDELOTTE, FRANK, 1880-1956

Lawyer; president, Swarthmore College 1921-39. Director 1939-47 (successor to *Abraham Flexner), director emeritus 1947-56, trustee 1930-56, *Institute for Advanced Study, Princeton, NJ.

Appointed refugee scholars to Swarthmore and the Institute for Advanced Study. Member of executive committee, *Emergency Committee in Aid of Displaced Foreign Scholars 1940-45. Frequently consulted by *American Friends Service Committee (AFSC) on its aid to refugees. In August 1939, traveled to Mexico with a group attempting to arrange resettlement of Jewish refugees. Member, Anglo-American Committee of Inquiry on Jewish Problems in Palestine and Europe 1945-46.

Literature. Frances Blanshard, *Frank Aydelotte of Swarthmore.* Middletown, CT: Wesleyan Univ. Press, 1970.

Papers. Swarthmore College, Friends Historical Library: papers, 53 file drawers and 15 boxes. Correspondence concerning the Institute for Advanced Study (20 drawers) includes 2 folders on the Emergency Committee, 1935-47, correspondence with the AFSC, and other materials on resettlement of refugees. There is also ca. 1 ft on the Anglo-American Committee of Inquiry.

Univ. of Iowa Libraries, Manuscripts Dept.: papers on the Anglo-American Committee of Inquiry, 1945-48, ca. 250 items. *NUCMC* MS 72-171. Finding aid: unpublished inventory.

383. BAERWALD, PAUL, 1871-1961

Banker and philanthropist. Member of a family of German-Jewish immigrant bankers. Close friend of *Herbert H. Lehman. Associate treasurer 1917-20, treasurer 1920-32, chairman 1932-45 (successor to *Felix M. Warburg), honorary chairman 1945-61, *American Jewish Joint Distribution Committee (JDC).

Active in farm resettlement organizations for Jews during 1920s. Trustee, Palestine Economic Corp. (*PEC Israel Economic Corp.).

Member of management council, Coordinating Foundation (*Intergovernmental Committee on Refugees). Member of board of directors, *Refugee Economic Corp. Supervised JDC rescue work during World War II.

Literature. Yehuda Bauer, *My Brother's Keeper, A History of the American Jewish Joint Distribution Committee 1929-1939.* Philadelphia: Jewish Publication Society, 1974.

Papers. Columbia Univ., School of International Affairs, Herbert H. Lehman Papers: papers, 1925-61, 2 ft (3000 items), include material concerning Baerwald's involvement with JDC and other refugee aid activities. *NUCMC* MS 74-290. Finding aids: unpublished index; Columbia Univ. School of International Affairs, *The Herbert H. Lehman Papers: An Introduction, Checklist, and Guide.* By William B. Liebmann. New York, 1968, p. 17.

384. BARUCH, BERNARD MANNES, 1870-1965

Financier, philanthropist, statesman, and economic adviser to President *Franklin D. Roosevelt.

Developed a plan with *Herbert Hoover in 1939 for resettling refugees in Africa (Baruch-Hoover Resettlement Plan). Participated in the first meeting of the *U.S. President's Advisory Committee on Political Refugees, April 13, 1938.

Literature. Bernard Mannes Baruch, *Baruch: My Own Story.* New York: Holt, 1957.

——, *Baruch: The Public Years.* New York: Holt, Rinehart and Winston, 1960.

Papers. Princeton Univ., Manuscript Library: papers, 1905-1965, ca. 221 ft and 521 vols., include some correspondence regarding refugee matters with Hamilton Fish 1939; *Alvin Johnson 1939, 1942-43; *Herbert H. Lehman 1939-40; *Eleanor Roosevelt 1939, 1945; Franklin D. Roosevelt 1938-39, 1944; *Abba Hillel Silver 1945; and Herbert Bayard Swope 1945. *NUCMC* MS 71-378. Finding aid: unpublished guide.

385. BECKER, CARL LOTUS, 1873-1945

Professor of European history, *Cornell University 1917-45.

Literature. *D.A.B.*, suppl. 3, pp. 46-48.

Burleigh Taylor Wilkins, *Carl Becker: A Biographical Study in American Intellectual History.* Cambridge, MA: M.I.T. Press, 1961.

Papers. Cornell University Libraries, Dept. of Manuscripts and University Archives: papers, 1898-1956, ca. 7 ft, include letters from two German refugee historians: Hans Baron, 1938-39, 1942, 1944 and Hans W. Rosenberg, 1935-37, 1944, concerning their difficulties in finding teaching positions in the U.S.A. *NUCMC* MS 62-2359. Finding aid: unpublished index.

386. BERGMANN, MAX, 1886-1944

German biochemist, immigrated to the U.S.A. in 1933. Associate member, Rockefeller Institute for Medical Research 1934-37; after *P. A. Levene's retirement in 1937, Bergmann was promoted to full membership and appointed head of the chemistry laboratory.

Assisted in finding positions for refugee scientists. Wife, Martha Bergmann, was active in *Selfhelp Community Services.

Literature. *D.A.B.*, suppl. 3, pp. 60-61.
Burckhardt Helferich, "Max Bergmann, 1886-1944." *Chemische Berichte* 102, Heft 1 (1969): i-xxvi.
International Biographical Dictionary, vol. II.
Lessing, *Oral History.*

Papers. American Philosophical Society Library: papers, 1930-44, 10 ft (ca. 8500 items), include material concerning the rescue and resettlement of Nazi-period immigrants, especially scientists. *NUCMC* MS 68-1465. Finding aids: unpublished list of file headings (11 pp.) and unpublished inventory (24 pp.); *Survey of Sources* [for the History of Biochemistry and Molecular Biology] *Newsletter*, vol. 1, no. 4 (Dec. 1976): 7-8.

387. BERLE, ADOLF AUGUSTUS, JR., 1895-1971

Lawyer; professor of law, Columbia Univ. Prominent in politics and government in the New Deal period. Assistant Secretary of State 1938-44.

In the *U.S. Dept. of State, Berle had little influence on the actual conduct of foreign affairs, but was given numerous planning assignments. His presence smoothed relations between his disharmonious superiors, *Cordell Hull and *Sumner Welles. An advocate of neutrality and a united Western hemisphere, he was concerned with government policy on immigration legislation, refugees, and Palestine.

Literature. Beatrice B. Berle and Travis B. Jacobs, eds., *Navigating the Rapids: 1918-1971. From the Papers of Adolf A. Berle.* New York: Harcourt Brace Jovanovich, 1973. [A compilation from Berle's personal diaries.]

Papers. Franklin D. Roosevelt Library: papers, 1912-74, 92 ft, include correspondence with *Alvin Johnson concerning refugee scholars on the staff of the *New School's Graduate Faculty, with individual refugees, and organizations concerned with immigration. Berle's subject files and diaries also contain relevant materials. *NUCMC* MS 77-252. Finding aid: unpublished inventory.

388. BIRMAN, MEYER, 1891-1955

Russian-born Jewish organization executive, who directed Jewish migration and relief activities in the Far East from 1918 until his emigration to the U.S.A. in 1949.

In 1918, appointed director of the newly organized Far Eastern Jewish Central Information Bureau (DALJEWCIB) in Harbin, China, which was taken over in 1919 by the *Hebrew Sheltering and Immigrant Aid Society (HIAS), with Birman continuing as its head. In 1939, when DALJEWCIB had become a division of HICEM (*HIAS-ICA-Emigration Association), the office was transferred to *Shanghai, where Birman continued to direct its migration and relief work until 1949.

Literature. *News of the YIVO* 61 (June 1956): 6*.

Papers. YIVO Institute for Jewish Research: papers, 1918–55, ca. 2 ft, also on microfilm (5 reels), consist of correspondence, reports, financial records, minutes of meetings, statistical surveys, printed material, newspaper clippings, photographs, and invitations; include materials concerning immigration to, and refugee resettlement in, China and other Far Eastern locations. Finding aid: unpublished inventory (11 pp., Yiddish and English).

389. BLAINE, ANITA (McCORMICK), 1866-1954

Philanthropist, daughter of the inventor Cyrus H. McCormick, Chicago.

Member of executive committee, Emergency Rescue Committee (ERC) and its successor, International Rescue and Relief Committee (IRRC–*International Rescue Committee).

Literature. *D.A.B.*, suppl. 5, pp. 60–61.
Wetzel, "American Rescue," pp. 117–119.

Papers. State Historical Society of Wisconsin: papers, 1828-1958, 1117 boxes, include materials on her activities for ERC and IRRC. Finding aid: Margaret R. Hafstad, ed., *Guide to the McCormick Collection of the State Historical Society of Wisconsin.* Madison, 1973, p. 32.

390. BLOOM, SOL, 1870-1949

U.S. Representative from New York City (Lower East Side of Manhattan) 1923-49. Chairman, *House Committee on Foreign Affairs 1938–49. Supported the New Deal and the United Nations.

Delegate to the *Bermuda Conference on Refugees, April 1943. Active in refugee and immigration matters.

Literature. Sol Bloom, *The Autobiography of Sol Bloom.* New York: Putnam, 1948.
D.A.B., suppl. 4, pp. 87–89.

Papers. New York Public Library, Manuscripts and Archives Div.: papers, 1920s–49, 58 ft, consist primarily of correspondence with constituents and with the U.S. Departments of *Justice, *Labor, and *State, on immigration problems of constituents. *NUCMC* MS 68-1066. Finding aid: unpublished inventory.

391. BOAS, ERNST PHILIP, 1891-1955

Physician. Son of *Franz Boas.
Officer, *Emergency Committee in Aid of Displaced Foreign Medical Scientists. Founder and officer, *National Committee for the Resettlement of Foreign Physicians.

Literature. *Journal of the American Medical Association* 157 (Apr. 16, 1955): 1425.

Papers. Several file drawers of correspondence are with Boas' son, Norman F. Boas, M.D., Old Ridgefield Road, P.O. Box 398, Wilton, CT 06897. Include minutes of meetings 1943-45 of the Emergency Committee; correspondence with the National Committee and with the *United Service for New Americans; miscellaneous correspondence and reports relating to the placement of foreign scientists, including letters from recipients of aid.

392. BOAS, FRANZ, 1858-1942

German-born and -trained anthropologist, immigrated to the U.S.A. in 1887. Professor of anthropology, Columbia Univ. Became a leading liberal intellectual and student of biometrics, in opposition to racist thought. Father of *Ernst P. Boas.
Chairman and guiding influence, American Committee for Democracy and Intellectual Freedom, whose work included efforts on behalf of refugees. Member of Faculty Fellowship Fund, Columbia Univ., which raised money to support refugee scholars.

Literature. *D.A.B.*, suppl. 3, pp. 81-86.
Dictionary of Scientific Biography, vol. II, pp. 207-213.

Papers. American Philosophical Society Library: papers, 1862-1942, ca. 10,000 items, include correspondence concerning assistance to refugee scholars and resettlement efforts in the U.S.A. and Great Britain. *NUCMC* MS 63-4.
Also on microfilm (44 reels): Scholarly Resources, Inc., *The Professional Papers of Franz Boas.* Wilmington, 1972. Copies at Balch Institute, Columbia Univ. Library, and New School for Social Research Library. Finding aid: Scholarly Resources, Inc., *Guide to the Microfilm Collection of the Professional Papers of Franz Boas.* 2 vols. Wilmington, 1972.

393. BOWMAN, ISAIAH, 1878-1950

Geographer. Chairman, U.S. National Research Council 1933-35. President, Johns Hopkins Univ., Baltimore 1935-49. His *Limits of Land Settlement: A Report on Present-Day Possibilities*, an important discussion of resettlement issues, was published in New York, 1937.
Adviser on geographic questions and consultant on the resettlement of refugees to President *Franklin D. Roosevelt. Directed research on refugee resettlement at Walter Hines Page School of International Relations, Johns

Hopkins Univ. 1938-41, financed by *Refugee Economic Corp. with grants of $25,000 in 1938 and 1941. Cooperated with *Henry Field on *"M" [Migration] Project 1943-45.

Papers. D.A.B., suppl. 4, pp. 98-100.
Dictionary of Scientific Biography, vol. II, pp. 373-374.
Geoffrey J. Martin, *The Life and Thought of Isaiah Bowman*. Publication expected 1979.

Records. Johns Hopkins Univ. Library, Dept. of Special Collections: papers, 6 file drawers (unrestricted) and ca. 35 ft (restricted), include scattered correspondence on refugees and migration problems with Roosevelt and Charles J. Liebman, president of the Refugee Economic Corp. *NUCMC* MS 63-217.

Johns Hopkins Univ. Archives: records of the Walter Hines Page School include 14 items, 1938-39 and 1941, on the grants received from the Refugee Economic Corp. These items were originally part of the records of the Office of the President of Johns Hopkins Univ.

394. BRANDEIS, LOUIS DEMBITZ, 1856-1941

Jurist and social reformer. Associate Justice of the U.S. Supreme Court 1916-39. Zionist leader, especially during World War I. By the 1930s, Brandeis had become the respected elder statesman of all Jewish groups in the U.S.A.

Literature. D.A.B., suppl. 3, pp. 93-100.
Alpheus Thomas Mason, *Brandeis: A Free Man's Life*. New York: Viking Press, 1946.
Ezekial Rabinowitz, *Justice Louis D. Brandeis: The Zionist Chapter of His Life*. New York: Philosophical Library, 1966.

Papers. Univ. of Louisville, Law Library: papers, 1870-1938, 140 ft (ca. 25,000 items). Those papers which relate to Brandeis' Jewish activities are on microfilm (31 reels) at Zionist Archives and Library, American Jewish Archives, Brandeis Univ. Library, and Central Zionist Archives, Israel. *NUCMC* MS 61-945 (Univ. of Louisville), 68-1137 (American Jewish Archives). Finding aid: unpublished index.

395. BRESLAUER, WALTER, 1890-

German-Jewish lawyer and communal leader, emigrated to England in 1936. *Verwaltungsdirektor* (chief executive), Berlin Jewish Community 1931-36.
Cofounder and executive board member, Association of Jewish Refugees (AJR), Great Britain. Vice-president, *Council of Jews from Germany. Leading expert on legal aspects of *Wiedergutmachungs*-laws for damages suffered by victims of Nazi persecution.

Literature. International Biographical Dictionary, vol. I.

Papers. Leo Baeck Institute Archives: collection of Breslauer's publications, 1938-73, includes articles concerning emigration and *Wiedergutmachung* in

AJR Information (London) and other periodicals. Finding aid: unpublished inventory (7 pp.).

396. BRIN, FANNY (FLIGELMAN), 1884-1961

Civic leader in Minneapolis, active in social welfare, pacifist, and women's causes. National president, *National Council of Jewish Women 1932-38.

Active participant in the Minneapolis Committee for Refugee Service (whose work was continued by the *Jewish Family and Children's Service, Minneapolis).

Literature. Barbara Stuhler, "Fanny Brin, Woman of Peace." In *Women of Minnesota: Selected Biographical Essays*, Barbara Stuhler and Gretchen Kreuter, eds. St. Paul: Minnesota Historical Society, 1977, pp. 284-300.

Papers. Minnesota Historical Society, Div. of Archives and Manuscripts: papers, 1896-1958, 10 ft (ca. 12,500 items), include materials concerning Brin's efforts on behalf of the National Council of Jewish Women, aid to refugees from Germany, German (*European) Jewish Children's Aid, and cooperation with other Jewish organizations concerned with immigration and resettlement. Also one box of "Refugee Letters," consisting of correspondence, 1933-51, with and about refugees; and correspondence, 1933-46, on the work of a committee appointed in 1933 by the president of the Univ. of Minnesota, Lotus D. Coffman, to aid displaced German scholars. *NUCMC* MS 63-232. Finding aid: unpublished inventory.

397. BROWN, DAVID ABRAHAM, 1875-1958

Business executive and Jewish communal leader, Detroit and New York.

Active in various relief programs. Member of executive committee, *American Jewish Joint Distribution Committee 1915-36.

Literature. *Who's Who in World Jewry*, 1955, p. 110.

Papers. American Jewish Archives: papers, 1891-1959, 1.3 ft (ca. 1200 items), include material on Committee for the Assistance of European Jewish Refugees in *Shanghai, *National Coordinating Committee, and *Non-Sectarian Anti-Nazi League, 1934. *NUCMC* MS 68-11. Finding aid: unpublished inventory (12 pp.).

398. BRUNSWICK, MARK, 1902-1971

Composer; professor of music and department chairman, The City College, New York.

Responsible for the placement of hundreds of European musicians and university teachers in the U.S.A. Chairman, National Committee for Refugee Musicians (former name: Placement Committee for German and Austrian Musicians), affiliated with the *National Refugee Service. Author of "Refugee Musicians in America," *Saturday Review*, Jan. 26, 1946, pp. 9, 50-51.

Literature. Genizi, "American Non-Sectarian," pp. 202–204.

Papers. New York, City College Library, Dept. of Archives and Special Collections: photocopies of mimeographed materials, 1938–45, 50 pages, consist mostly of reports on the Committee's activities. The original materials are with Brunswick's widow, Mrs. Natasha Artin-Brunswick, Princeton, NJ.

399. BUTLER, NICHOLAS MURRAY, 1862–1947

President, Columbia Univ. 1902–45. President, *Carnegie Endowment for International Peace 1925–45. Cowinner of Nobel Peace Prize 1931.

Because of his positions, Butler received numerous inquiries relating to refugees. Corresponded with the political refugees Hubertus Prinz zu Loewenstein and Richard N. Coudenhove-Kalergi, and with *Dorothy Thompson and *Leslie C. Dunn. Chairman, American Committee for Relief in Czechoslovakia, ca. 1939 (the Committee raised funds for relief and forwarded the money to the Czechoslovakian Red Cross and other local organizations).

Literature. D.A.B., suppl. 4, pp. 133–138.
Albert Marrin, *Nicholas Murray Butler.* Boston: Twayne, 1976.

Papers. Columbia Univ., Rare Book and Manuscript Library: papers, ca. 1900–1947, ca. 200 ft, include correspondence and other material dealing with refugees, immigration, and related topics. *NUCMC* MS 61-2922. Finding aid: unpublished index.

Many of the inquiries which Butler received asking for help for refugee scholars were forwarded to the Carnegie Endowment, in whose records they are found.

400. CELLER, EMANUEL, 1888–

Lawyer; U.S. Representative from Brooklyn, NY 1923–72; chairman, *House Judiciary Committee 1948–72.

Advocate of liberalized immigration legislation since 1923 and a leading critic of the restrictive immigration practices of the *U.S. Dept. of State during the *Roosevelt era. Proposed a liberalized immigration bill following the Austrian Anschluss of March 12, 1938; urged rescue efforts in Congress for Nazi victims in occupied Europe during World War II, and supported U.S. policies favoring the establishment of a Jewish state in Palestine since the 1940s.

Literature. Emanuel Celler, *You Never Leave Brooklyn: The Autobiography of Emanuel Celler.* New York: J. Day Co., 1952.

Papers. Library of Congress, Manuscript Div.: papers, 1924–72, ca. 183,000 items, include correspondence, notes, clippings, memoranda, speeches, printed matter, and materials concerning refugees, immigration, Jewish affairs, and Israel. *NUCMC* MS 70-942. Finding aid: unpublished inventory.

401. CHAMBERLAIN, JOSEPH PERKINS, 1873-1951

Author and diplomat. Professor of public law, Columbia University 1923-51. Chairman, *Survey Associates 1943-51. Special Assistant to Secretary of the Treasury on the problem of blocked funds of nationals of enemy countries 1941. Member, Advisory Committee on Voluntary Foreign Aid, *U.S. Dept. of State 1949-51.

Chairman, *National Coordinating Committee for Aid to Refugees and Emigrants Coming from Germany (NCC) 1934-39. Chairman of the board, *National Refugee Service (NRS—successor to NCC) 1939-46. Honorary chairman of the board, *United Service for New Americans (USNA—successor to NRS) 1946-51. Member of governing board, *League of Nations High Commission for Refugees (Jewish and Other) Coming from Germany 1933-35. Member, *U.S. President's Advisory Committee on Political Refugees (PACPR). Chairman, International Migration Service, American Branch (*Travelers Aid–International Social Service of America). Founder 1943, chairman 1943-50, honorary chairman 1951, *American Council of Voluntary Agencies for Foreign Service.

Literature. D.A.B., suppl. 5, pp. 107-108.

Papers. YIVO Institute for Jewish Research: papers, 1933-51, ca. 1.7 ft, also on microfilm (4 reels), consist of the files of the PACPR, 1938-43, and other materials on Chamberlain's activities on behalf of refugees. Include correspondence with individuals and organizations working to aid refugees, and correspondence with and about individual refugees who sought Chamberlain's assistance in finding jobs or obtaining funds.

Some materials on Chamberlain's activities in aid to refugees, especially activities connected with the American Council of Voluntary Agencies for Foreign Service, are with that agency.

402. COHEN, ISRAEL, 1879-1961

British writer; secretary, Zionist Organization, London. Toured Poland and Hungary after World War I to investigate the position of Jews, and reported on current pogroms and discrimination.

Literature. Israel Cohen, *A Jewish Pilgrimage: The Autobiography of Israel Cohen.* London: Vallentine, Mitchell, 1956.
News of the YIVO 83 (July 1962): 3*, 6*.

Papers. YIVO Institute for Jewish Research: papers, 1930s, 1.25 ft, consist of manuscripts, reports, clippings, and correspondence relating to European Jewish life, the Nazi persecution of Jews, the *Évian Conference, and refugee problems.

403. COHN, ALFRED EINSTEIN, 1879-1957

Physician and medical researcher, Rockefeller Institute for Medical Research, New York.

Assistant treasurer, *Emergency Committee in Aid of Displaced Foreign Scholars. Member, *Emergency Committee in Aid of Displaced Foreign Medical Scientists. Member of general advisory council, *National Committee for the Resettlement of Foreign Physicians. Member of executive committee, *United States Committee of International Student Service, and director, Student Service of America. Treasurer, *American Council for Émigrés in the Professions. Sponsored a resolution in support of aid to refugees at the New York Academy of Medicine. Author of "Exiled Physicians in the United States," *The American Scholar* 12 (Summer 1943): 352-361.

Literature. *Journal of the American Medical Association* 165 (Sept. 28, 1957): 380.
Who's Who in American Jewry, 1938-39, p. 185.

Papers. Rockefeller Univ. Archives: papers, ca. 40 ft, include 4 ft of correspondence, placement reports, and minutes of various committees in aid of refugees, reflecting Cohn's involvement in such activities.

404. COOK, FANNIE (FRANK), 1893-1949

Author and lecturer, St. Louis, MO, active in the field of race relations.

Literature. *Current Biography*, 1946, pp. 129-130.

Papers. Missouri Historical Society: papers, 1881-1949, ca. 4 ft, include correspondence with relatives in Germany concerning the possibilities of bringing some to the U.S.A. Also include formal immigration documents and eleven "case histories" of unnamed immigrants, which form part of the background for one of her novels, *Storm Against the Wall*, Garden City, NY: Doubleday, 1948. *NUCMC* MS 64-323.

405. CORSI, EDWARD, 1896-1965

Association executive, government official, and author. Special Assistant to Secretary of State for Refugee and Minority Problems 1954-55.

U.S. Commissioner of Immigration at Ellis Island 1931-33, and Commissioner of the *U.S. Immigration and Naturalization Service 1933-34. Chairman, Enemy Alien Hearing Board, Southern District of New York 1941-44. Took an interest in work with immigrants and participated in organizations concerned with immigration, such as the American Federation of *International Institutes.

Literature. *Collier's Encyclopedia Yearbook*, 1956, pp. 517-518.

Papers. Syracuse Univ. Library, Manuscript Div.: papers, 1918-65, 25 ft, include correspondence with individuals, organizations, and government agencies, published and unpublished speeches and articles, and materials relating to Corsi's activities in the immigration and naturalization field. *NUCMC* MS 70-708. Finding aid: unpublished inventory.

406. CRONBACH, ABRAHAM, 1882-1965

Rabbi and professor of Jewish social studies, *Hebrew Union College, Cincinnati 1922-50.

Called for a conference in Philadelphia in 1935 between Jews and Americans sympathetic to Nazism, to bring about a reconciliation. Worked with the *American Friends Service Committee (AFSC) in 1935 to raise $5000 for an Austrian Relief Fund to aid persecuted Austrians as well as German Jews and Nazis who had fled to Austria from Germany. During World War II, supported conscientious objectors and, in 1942, helped to found the Jewish Peace Fellowship.

Literature. Abraham Cronbach, "Autobiography." *American Jewish Archives* 11 (Apr. 1959): 3-81.

Papers. American Jewish Archives: papers, 1902-65, 4.2 ft (ca. 4200 items), consist of correspondence, manuscripts, and printed material relating to Cronbach's publications, career, and involvement in Jewish and pacifist organizations. Include material on the AFSC, aid to refugees, the 1935 conference, and the National Conference of Christians and Jews. *NUCMC* MS 67-978. Finding aid: unpublished inventory (11 pp.).

407. DAVIES, JOSEPH EDWARD, 1876-1958

U.S. Ambassador to USSR 1937-41 (succeeded by *Laurence A. Steinhardt). Author of *Mission to Moscow*, New York: Simon and Schuster, 1941.
Chairman, *U.S. President's War Relief Control Board 1942-46.

Literature. *Current Biography*, 1942, pp. 177-180.
Keith D. Eagles, "Ambassador Joseph E. Davies and American-Soviet Relations, 1937-1941." Unpublished Ph.D. dissertation, Univ. of Washington, 1966.

Papers. Library of Congress, Manuscript Div.: papers, 1860-1957, 65 ft (ca. 50,000 items). Subject and chronological files include one box of newspaper clippings on aid to refugees in the 1940s. *NUCMC* MS 62-4609.

408. DEXTER, ROBERT CLOUTMAN, 1887-1955, and DEXTER, ELIZABETH WILLIAMS (ANTHONY), 1887-1972

Robert Dexter: Organization executive. As director, Depts. of Social and Foreign Relations, American Unitarian Association (AUA) 1927-40, he did relief work in Czechoslovakia, 1938. Executive director, *Unitarian Service Committee (USC) of the AUA 1940-44; engaged in refugee relief work in Portugal 1941-44. Attaché, U.S. Embassy, Lisbon 1944, as representative of *U.S. War Refugee Board.

His wife, Elizabeth, author and educator, was a staff member of USC in Portugal.

Literature. *New York Times*, Oct. 13, 1955, p. 31.
An oral history interview with Elizabeth Dexter on her experiences in Portugal is with the Hebrew Univ. of Jerusalem, Institute of Contemporary Jewry, Oral History Div.

Papers. Brown Univ. Library, Univ. Archives: papers, 3 cartons, include materials relating to the Dexters' refugee aid activities, primarily correspondence between Robert and Elizabeth Dexter and between them and the home office of USC in Boston. Also several drafts of a manuscript by Elizabeth Dexter about their work in Portugal beginning in June 1941.

409. DIAMOND, DAVID, 1898-1968

Attorney, Buffalo, NY. Supreme Court Justice, State of New York 1941. Active in politics, civil rights matters, and Jewish philanthropies, including Israel, the anti-Nazi boycott movement, and aid for Jewish refugees. Chairman, Zionist Emergency Council, Buffalo. Delegate from Buffalo to *American Jewish Conference 1943. Member of national council, *United HIAS Service.

Literature. *National Cyclopaedia of American Biography*, vol. 54, pp. 573-574.

Papers. American Jewish Historical Society: papers, 1928-68, 3 ft, contain correspondence relating to Diamond's legal and political career, and his communal and philanthropic activities, including material concerning anti-Nazi activities and the *Emergency Committee to Save the Jewish People of Europe. *NUCMC* MS 69-598.

410. DICKSTEIN, SAMUEL, 1885-1954

U.S. Representative from New York City (Lower East Side of Manhattan) 1923-45; chairman, *House Committee on Immigration and Naturalization 1931-45; vice-chairman, *House Special Committee on Un-American Activities 1934-35. Supreme Court Justice, State of New York 1946-54.

Early Congressional opponent of the German-American Bund and other American Nazi organizations. Urged that the U.S.A. break off diplomatic relations with Nazi Germany. As chairman of the House Committee on Immigration and Naturalization, Dickstein first became aware of the great number of foreigners illegally residing in the U.S.A. and the vast amount of anti-Semitic and anti-American literature being distributed in this country. This interest led him to investigate independently the activities of American Nazi and fascist groups; his committee began official hearings on Nazi activities in the U.S.A. in November 1933. In 1934, Dickstein called for the formation of the House Special Committee on Un-American Activities, of which he was named vice-chairman. Following the Committee's report of February 1935, he continued his personal investigation into Nazi activities and propaganda in the U.S.A. In 1937, he called for a renewed House investigation which resulted in the formation of a new House Special Committee for the Investigation of Un-American Activities under the chairmanship of Martin Dies.

Dickstein was an outstanding proponent of liberalized immigration policies. His committee was responsible for the passage of most of the immigration bills passed by Congress between 1930 and 1945.

Literature. *National Cyclopaedia of American Biography*, vol. 42, pp. 122-123.

Papers. American Jewish Archives: papers, 1923–44, 12.1 ft, and tape recordings (3 reels), consist of correspondence, legislative records, and printed material relating primarily to Dickstein's investigation of fascist activities, including documentation on the impact of the refugee question on American Jewish life. *NUCMC* MS 65-1741. Finding aid: unpublished inventory (10 pp.).

The location of Dickstein's other papers has not been established.

411. DIJOUR, ILJA M., 1896–

Russian-born Jewish organization executive, author, educator, and immigration expert. Immigrated to the U.S.A. 1942.

Director, *Hebrew Sheltering and Immigrant Aid Society (HIAS) office, Berlin 1923–28; director, HICEM (*HIAS-ICA-Emigration Association) office, Paris 1928–40; director, HIAS office, Lisbon 1940–42; executive secretary, HICEM, New York 1942–45. HIAS director for Germany and Austria 1945–47, for Latin America 1947–51, and of research 1947–54. Director of research and statistics, *United HIAS Service 1954–60s.

Author of memoranda on Jewish migration, 1924 and 1928; *Modern Mass Migration*, 1929; *Dix Années d'Émigration Juive*, 1936; memorandum to the *Évian Conference 1938; and other publications on refugees and migration.

Literature. *News of the YIVO* 100 (Dec. 1966): 8*-9*.

Papers. YIVO Institute for Jewish Research: papers, pre-World War I–1964, ca. 1 ft, also on microfilm (3 reels), consist of correspondence, manuscripts, financial records, forms, reports, statistical surveys, printed materials, and notes concerning Dijour's HIAS/HICEM activities and family matters. Include his memoirs, "Jews Run from Poland: Memoirs of Twenty-Five Years of Migration Activities," 1918–43 (in Yiddish), and extensive correspondence about immigration between HIAS/HICEM and other agencies. Finding aid: unpublished inventory (2 pp.).

412. DODD, WILLIAM EDWARD, 1869-1940

Professor of history, Univ. of Chicago; president, American Historical Association 1934; U.S. Ambassador to Germany 1933–37 (succeeded by *Hugh R. Wilson). A bitter critic of the Nazi regime.

Literature. *D.A.B.*, suppl. 2, pp. 152–154.

Robert Dallek, *Democrat and Diplomat: The Life of William E. Dodd.* New York: Oxford Univ. Press, 1968.

Martha Dodd, *Through Embassy Eyes.* New York: Harcourt, Brace, 1939.

William Dodd, Jr., and Martha Dodd, *Ambassador Dodd's Diary, 1933-1938.* New York: Harcourt, Brace, 1941.

Papers. Library of Congress, Manuscript Div.: papers, 1900–40, 26 ft (ca. 20,000 items), include 4 boxes of correspondence (nos. 49-52) concerning refugees. *NUCMC* MS 60-576. Finding aid: unpublished inventory.

413. DOUGLAS, JUDITH HYAMS, 1875-1955

Lawyer and organization leader, New Orleans.

Papers. Louisiana State Univ. Library, Dept. of Archives and Manuscripts: papers, 1897-1955, 700 items and 3 vols., include 13 manuscript items concerning Douglas' interest in establishing a local refugee aid committee [probably the New Orleans Committee for Refugee Service (*Jewish Family and Children's Service, New Orleans)], including correspondence with *Joseph P. Chamberlain. *NUCMC* MS 75-736.

414. DUNN, LESLIE CLARENCE, 1893-1974

Geneticist. Professor of zoology, Columbia Univ. 1928-62. Director, Institute for the Study of Human Variation 1952-58.

Member of executive committee, *Emergency Committee in Aid of Displaced Foreign Scholars; member of refugee subcommittee, *United States Committee of International Student Service; secretary of Faculty Fellowship Fund, Columbia Univ., which raised money to support refugee scholars.

Literature. *National Cyclopaedia of American Biography*, vol. J, pp. 506-507.
Charles Weiner, "A New Site for the Seminar: The Refugees and American Physics in the Thirties." In *The Intellectual Migration: Europe and America, 1930-1960*, Donald Fleming and Bernard Bailyn, eds. Cambridge, MA: Harvard Univ. Press, 1969, pp. 212-213.

Papers. American Philosophical Society Library: papers, 1920s-74, 15 ft (ca. 8000 items), contain materials on European refugee scientists and refugee aid activities, including 15 files on the Emergency Committee and files on individual refugees whom Dunn assisted. *NUCMC* MS 69-1371. Finding aids: unpublished inventory (56 pp.); American Philosophical Society Library, *Mendel Newsletter*, no. 12 (July 1976).

415. EZEKIEL, MORDECAI, 1899-1974

Agricultural economist in the U.S. Dept. of Agriculture. Economic adviser to the Secretary of Agriculture 1933-46.

Literature. *Encyclopaedia Judaica*, vol. 6, col. 1100.

Papers. Franklin D. Roosevelt Library: papers, 1920-70, 40 ft, include one small subject file on resettlement of refugees, consisting of memoranda by various authors regarding Jewish immigration to Mexico and British Guiana.

416. FERMI, LAURA (CAPON), 1907-

Author of *Illustrious Immigrants: The Intellectual Migration from Europe, 1930-41*, Chicago: Univ. of Chicago Press, 1968. Widow of Enrico Fermi, émigré physicist at the Univ. of Chicago and Nobel laureate.

Literature. *Current Biography*, 1958, pp. 137-139.

Papers. Univ. of Chicago Library, Dept. of Special Collections: *Illustrious Immigrants* Papers, 0.5 ft, include a list of 1900 names of refugee intellectuals, interviews with prominent refugees, correspondence, research notes, and manuscripts.

417. FEUCHTWANGER, LUDWIG, 1885-1947

German-Jewish publisher, editor, author, and communal leader, emigrated to England 1939.

Literature. Max Gruenewald, "Critic of German Jewry—Ludwig Feuchtwanger and His Gemeindezeitung." In *Leo Baeck Institute Year Book* XVII (1972), pp. 75-92.
International Biographical Dictionary, vol. I.

Papers. Leo Baeck Institute Archives: papers, 1915-47, ca. 5.5 ft, include 13 manuscripts concerning emigration from Germany, refugees in England, postwar refugee problems, and *Wiedergutmachung*, most of which were coauthored by Eugen Strauss, a German-Jewish communal leader who also emigrated to England. Finding aid: unpublished inventory (16 pp.).

418. FIELD, HENRY, 1902-

Anthropologist; curator, Field Museum of Natural History, Chicago 1926-41.
    Special adviser to President *Franklin D. Roosevelt on migration problems and minority groups. Director of *"M" [Migration] Project (studies of migration and resettlement) 1943-45, undertaken at the request of the President to explore settlement opportunities for refugees.

Literature. *Current Biography*, 1955, pp. 207-209.
Henry Field, *The Track of Man: Adventures of an Anthropologist.* Garden City, NY: Doubleday, 1953.

Papers. Franklin D. Roosevelt Library: papers, 1920-72, 92 ft. Although the papers contain no primary documentation about, or studies produced by, "M" Project, they include 2 boxes of "Memoranda on the Near East by 'M' Project Staff Members" that consist primarily of reports by the U.S. Federal Communications Commission's Foreign Broadcast Intelligence Service. *NUCMC* MS 65-36.

419. FIELD, WILLIAM LUCK WEBSTER, 1876-1963

Headmaster, Milton Academy (Milton, MA) 1917-42, then headmaster emeritus.
    Active member of Friends of Refugee Teachers, a Boston-based group which attempted to find jobs for refugee teachers during the late 1930s and early 1940s.

Literature. *New York Times*, Mar. 30, 1963, p. 7.

Papers. Milton Academy Library: papers include one folder on Friends of Refugee Teachers, consisting of material regarding Ernst L. Loewenberg, a refugee tutor, and correspondence on efforts made to place six others.

420. FISHER, DOROTHY (CANFIELD), 1879-1958

Novelist and educator. Organized relief work in France during World War I. Active in numerous humanitarian causes. Pro-Zionist.

Supported activities in aid of refugees, especially in behalf of refugee writers. Arranged for summer vacations at the homes of Vermont farmers for 52 German- and Austrian-Jewish refugee children.

Literature. David Baumgardt, "Dorothy Canfield Fisher: Friend of Jews in Life and Work." *Publication of the American Jewish Historical Society* 48 (June 1959): 245-255.

Elizabeth Yates, *Lady from Vermont: Dorothy Canfield Fisher's Life and World.* Brattleboro, VT: S. Greene Press, 1971.

Papers. Univ. of Vermont Library, Wilbur Collection: papers, 1851-1958, ca. 26 ft, include correspondence on the emigration of German Jews, e.g., with David Baumgardt, refugee philosopher who immigrated to the U.S.A. in 1939. *NUCMC* MS 64-791.

421. FLEXNER, ABRAHAM, 1866-1959

Educator. Founder 1930, director 1930-39, *Institute for Advanced Study, Princeton, NJ (succeeded by *Frank Aydelotte). Brother of *Simon Flexner and *Bernard Flexner and uncle of Jennie M. Flexner (librarian and chairman, *American Library Association Committee to Aid Refugee Librarians).

Member of general committee, *Emergency Committee in Aid of Displaced Foreign Scholars.

Literature. Abraham Flexner, *I Remember.* New York: Simon and Schuster, 1940. "Finding Men," chap. 28.

——, *Abraham Flexner: An Autobiography.* New York: Simon and Schuster, 1960. "Finding Men," chap. 28.

Papers. Library of Congress, Manuscript Div.: papers, 1870-1955, 9 ft (ca. 11,000 items), include material relating to the Institute for Advanced Study and to refugee scholars. *NUCMC* MS 66-1404. Finding aid: unpublished inventory.

422. FLEXNER, BERNARD, 1865-1945

Lawyer and Jewish communal leader; active in Zionist and refugee aid activities. Brother of *Abraham Flexner and *Simon Flexner. President 1925-31, and chairman 1931-44, Palestine Economic Corp. (*PEC Israel Economic Corp.). Member of executive committee, *American Jewish Joint Distribution Committee and Jewish Agency for Palestine (*World Zionist Organization—American Section).

Founder and member of executive committee, *Emergency Committee in Aid of Displaced Foreign Scholars. Officer, *Refugee Economic Corp.

Literature. *D.A.B.*, suppl. 3, pp. 279-280.

Papers. Princeton Univ., Manuscript Library: papers, 1881-1944, 16 boxes and 3 vols., consist mostly of correspondence, including an extended exchange with *Felix Frankfurter, 1929-44, and ca. one box relating to Flexner's work for the Emergency Committee and the *League of Nations High Commissioner for Refugees (Jewish and Other) Coming from Germany.

423. FLEXNER, SIMON, 1863-1946

Medical researcher. Founder 1903, and director 1903-35, Rockefeller Institute for Medical Research, New York. Brother of *Abraham Flexner and *Bernard Flexner. Trustee, *The Rockefeller Foundation and *Carnegie Corporation of New York.
Assisted in placement of refugee scholars.

Literature. D.A.B., suppl. 4, pp. 286-289.
Dictionary of Scientific Biography, vol. V, pp. 39-41.

Papers. American Philosophical Society Library: papers, 1891-1946, ca. 200,000 items, consist of correspondence, diaries, drafts of articles, and speeches. The finding aid does not indicate subject matter of correspondence; collection is presumed to contain relevant material on refugees. *NUCMC* MS 68-1470. Finding aid: unpublished list of correspondents (126 pp.).
Rockefeller Archive Center: microfilm (128 reels) of papers at American Philosophical Society Library.

424. FRANKFURTER, FELIX, 1882-1965

Austrian-born American jurist; professor of law, Harvard Univ. Law School 1914-39. Held many government positions prior to his appointment in 1939 by President *Franklin D. Roosevelt as Associate Justice of the U.S. Supreme Court.
Frankfurter acted as a link between President Roosevelt and Jewish leaders on many issues including immigration and rescue.

Literature. Felix Frankfurter with Harlan B. Phillips, *Felix Frankfurter Reminisces.* New York: Reynal, 1960.
Henry L. Stimson and McGeorge Bundy, *On Active Service in Peace and War.* New York: Harper, 1948.

Papers. Library of Congress, Manuscript Div.: papers, 1907-65, 105 ft (ca. 70,000 items). Frankfurter considered this collection to be his "personal papers." Subject file series includes material on German refugees (box 137) and the University in Exile of the *New School for Social Research (boxes 160 and 188). There may be other relevant material in this series and in the General Correspondence series. Available on microfilm at Harvard Univ., Law School Library. *NUCMC* MS 68-2033. Finding aid: Library of Congress, Manuscript Div., *Felix Frankfurter: A Register of His Papers in the Library of Congress.* Washington, DC, 1971.
Central Zionist Archives, Israel: papers, 1885-1965, 2.6 ft, consist of corre-

spondence and printed materials on Zionism, anti-Semitism, and Frankfurter's activities in the Supreme Court, including documentation on Jews in Germany, Nazism, and immigration matters of the Nazi years. Available on microfilm at Library of Congress, Manuscript Div.; American Jewish Archives; and Harvard Univ., Law School Library.

425. FRIEDENWALD, HARRY F., 1864-1950

Physician, author, and Zionist leader, Baltimore, MD. Charter member, *American Jewish Committee 1906; president, Federation of American Zionists 1904-18; delegate to World Jewish Congress, Geneva 1936.

Active on behalf of the rescue and resettlement of German Jews and their emigration to Palestine and the U.S.A. Assisted several Jewish refugees in their immigration and resettlement in the U.S.A.

Literature. Alexandra Lee Levin, *Vision: A Biography of Harry Friedenwald.* Philadelphia: Jewish Publication Society, 1964, pp. 346-391.

Papers. Central Zionist Archives, Israel: papers, 1856-1953, 7.6 ft, include correspondence with leading Jewish figures, refugees, organizations, and other political agencies regarding Jewish and other issues, including Nazi Germany and refugee persecution and resettlement. Available on microfilm (30 reels) at Zionist Archives and Library, American Jewish Archives, and Baltimore Hebrew College/ Jewish Historical Society of Maryland.

Baltimore Hebrew College has 9 cartons of notebooks and papers not believed to be on the above microfilm. It is not known whether there is any material in this collection relating to refugees and immigration.

426. FRY, VARIAN M., 1907-1967

Writer on foreign affairs. Representative of the Emergency Rescue Committee (ERC) and its successor, the International Rescue and Relief Committee (IRRC) (*International Rescue Committee) in France 1940-42, where he assisted refugee intellectuals to escape from Axis-occupied Europe via Spain and Portugal.

Literature. Varian Fry, *Assignment: Rescue.* New York: Four Winds Press, 1968.
——, *Surrender on Demand.* New York: Random House, 1945.

Papers. Columbia Univ., Rare Book and Manuscript Library: papers, ca. 1940-67, 6 ft, include materials concerning his activities with ERC and IRRC, and manuscripts and notes for his books. *NUCMC* MS 71-953.

427. GIBSON, JOHN W., 1910-1976

Labor official in Michigan: official of United Dairy Workers 1934-41; chairman, State Dept. of Labor and Industry 1941-43; president, Michigan CIO Council

1943-45. Special Assistant to the Secretary of Labor and Assistant Secretary of Labor, *U.S. Dept. of Labor 1945-50.
Chairman, *U.S. Displaced Persons Commission (DPC) 1950-52.

Literature. *Current Biography*, 1947, pp. 239-240.

Papers. Harry S. Truman Library: papers, 1935-54, 19 ft, include ca. 4 ft on postwar immigration matters, concerning Gibson's service with the DPC. *NUCMC* MS 65-111.

428. GINZBERG, LOUIS, 1873-1953

Rabbinic scholar and professor of Talmud, Jewish Theological Seminary of America, New York.

Literature. Eli Ginzberg, *Keeper of the Law: Louis Ginzberg.* Philadelphia: Jewish Publication Society, 1966.

Papers. Jewish Theological Seminary of America, Archives: papers, 8.7 ft, include one folder of correspondence with Albert Einstein regarding Jacob Klatzkin, German refugee scholar who immigrated to the U.S.A. in 1941, as well as other materials relating to Ginzberg's efforts to place refugee scholars.

429. GLICK, DAVID, 189?-1964

Lawyer in Pittsburgh, PA.
Went to Germany 1936-38 at the request of *Felix M. Warburg and *Paul Baerwald to assist Jews to emigrate and to save their property. In 1939, Glick and Frederick W. Borchardt, a German-Jewish organization executive and immigrant to the U.S.A., visited every country in South America on behalf of the *American Jewish Joint Distribution Committee (JDC) to survey the needs of German- and Austrian-Jewish refugees who had settled there.

Literature. David Glick, "Some Were Rescued: Memories of a Private Mission." *Harvard Law School Bulletin* 12 (Dec. 1960): 6-9.

Papers. American Jewish Archives: in part in the Irwin S. Rhodes Collection, photostats of documents 1937 and typescript of the published account prepared by Glick in 1960 relating to his experiences in Germany 1936-38, and the reports prepared with Borchardt for the JDC in 1939.
Copies also at Leo Baeck Institute Archives.

430. GOTTSCHALK, MAX, 1889-

Belgian social scientist, author, attorney, and Jewish leader. Immigrated to the U.S.A. in 1940. Correspondent for Belgium and Luxembourg, International Labor Office 1934-40; professor, École Libre des Hautes Études, *New School for Social Research, New York 1940-49; director, Research Institute on Peace and Post-War Problems, *American Jewish Committee 1940-49. Returned to Belgium in 1949.

As president of the Belgian Committee for Refugees from Nazi Germany 1933-40, Gottschalk was instrumental in the rescue of the passengers of the *S.S. St. Louis.* President, HICEM (*HIAS-ICA-Emigration Association) 1938-46, and member of the board since 1929; vice-president, Jewish Colonization Association (ICA) 1929-54; member of the board, Alliance Israélite Universelle 1924-40, and World ORT Union (*American ORT Federation).

Literature. Encyclopaedia Judaica, vol. 7, col. 830.
Universal Jewish Encyclopedia, vol. 5, pp. 73-74.

Papers. YIVO Institute for Jewish Research: papers, 1939-45, one box, also on microfilm (1 reel), consist of correspondence, memoranda, press releases, statistical surveys, printed material, and newspaper clippings relating to Gottschalk's activities and family.

431. GOUDSMIT, SAMUEL ABRAHAM, 1902-

Professor of physics, University of Michigan, Ann Arbor 1932-46; senior scientist, Brookhaven National Laboratory, NY 1948-70, chairman of Physics Department 1952-60. Guggenheim Foundation Fellow, Rome and Paris 1938.

Literature. Current Biography, 1954, pp. 304-306.

Papers. American Institute of Physics, Center for the History of Physics, Niels Bohr Library: papers, 1921-41, 2 cartons and microfilm (6 reels), include correspondence with scientists in Europe and the U.S.A., 1931 and 1933-41, some of which deals with refugee scientists. Finding aid: unpublished inventory.

432. GRAETZ, WILLIAM, 1879-1974

German-Jewish banker and community leader, emigrated to Argentina in 1940, immigrated to the U.S.A. in 1947 (Philadelphia). Member of executive board, Berlin Jewish Community 1931-36.

Cofounder and president, ORT Committee in Germany (*American ORT Federation). Visited Argentina on behalf of ORT in 1937 in connection with efforts to organize ORT training schools in countries of resettlement. Special assistant for *Wiedergutmachungs*-cases, *Legal Aid Society of Philadelphia. Honorary president, *B'nai B'rith Heinrich Graetz Lodge, Philadelphia.

Literature. International Biographical Dictionary, vol. I.

Papers. Leo Baeck Institute Archives: papers, 1915-73, 1 ft. consist of correspondence, minutes, reports, financial records, newspaper clippings, and circulars relating to Graetz' ORT activities in Germany 1926-37, France 1935-40, Argentina 1937-43, and the U.S.A. 1934-70; brochures and clippings about ORT in South Africa 1936-39, Bolivia 1942, Brazil 1943, and Switzerland 1956; also correspondence, financial statements, pamphlets, and clippings concerning the executive board of the Berlin Jewish Community 1929-31. The ORT material relates in part to refugee resettlement. Finding aid: unpublished inventory (15 pp.).

YIVO Institute for Jewish Research: records of American ORT Federation include correspondence with Graetz 1940-42, regarding Argentina and South America.

433. GREENFIELD, ALBERT MONROE, 1887-1967

Financier, business leader, and philanthropist, Philadelphia. Active in local and national Jewish and nonsectarian community affairs.

Literature. *National Cyclopedia of American Biography*, vol. K, pp. 293-297.

Papers. Historical Society of Pennsylvania, Manuscript Dept.: papers, 1923-66, ca. 400 ft. Correspondence, 1933-45, occupies 40 boxes and includes some materials on Jewish refugees and emigration. Materials are arranged by year and alphabetically by subject within each year. Restricted. *NUCMC* MS 71-374.

434. GREENSTEIN, HARRY, 1896-1971

Social worker and lawyer. Executive director, Associated Jewish Charities and Welfare Fund, Baltimore 1928-65.

Author of *Reorganization Study of the *National Coordinating Committee and Its Affiliated Agencies*, New York 1939, and originator of *National Refugee Service 1939. General consultant on welfare programs, U.S. Office of Foreign Relief and Rehabilitation Operations (OFRRO) 1943; Welfare Director, Balkan Mission in Cairo, United Nations Relief and Rehabilitation Administration (UNRRA–successor to OFRRO) 1943-45. Advisor on Jewish Affairs in Germany and Austria to U.S. Army of Occupation 1949, with displaced persons and restitution legislation as major concerns.

Literature. Jewish Historical Society of Maryland, *The Papers of Harry Greenstein: Saga of a Humanitarian.* By Hymen Saye. Baltimore, 1976.
Louis L. Kaplan and Theodor Schuchat, *Justice, Not Charity: A Biography of Harry Greenstein.* New York: Crown, 1967.

Papers. Baltimore Hebrew College/Jewish Historical Society of Maryland: papers, 1928-70, 3 ft, include material relating to Greenstein's activities on behalf of refugees and displaced persons. Finding aid: card index.
American Jewish Archives: microfilm (1 reel) contains a part of the material at Baltimore Hebrew College.

435. GROSSMANN, KURT RICHARD, 1897-1972

German-Jewish political journalist, public official, and author, emigrated Prague 1933, Paris 1938, New York 1939. General secretary, *Deutsche Liga für Menschenrechte* (German League for Human Rights), Berlin 1926-33.

Executive director, *Demokratische Flüchtlingsfürsorge* (Democratic Refugee Relief Committee), Prague and Paris 1933-39; executive assistant, *World Jewish Congress, New York 1943-50; consultant on restitution and indemnification problems, Jewish Agency—American Section (*World Zionist Organization) 1952-66. Author of *The Jewish Refugee* with A. Tartakower), New York: World Jewish Congress, 1944; *The Jewish DP Problem*, New York: World Jewish Congress, 1951; *Hitler's Refugees*, 1961; *Die Ehrenschuld: Kurzgeschichte der Wiedergutmachung*, Frankfurt am Main: Ullstein, 1967; and *Emigration: Geschichte der Hitlerflüchtlinge, 1933-1945*, Frankfurt am Main: Europäische Verlagsanstalt, 1969.

Literature. *Encyclopaedia Judaica*, vol. 7, cols. 936-937. *International Biographical Dictionary*, vol. I.

Papers. Leo Baeck Institute Archives: papers, 1933-69, 41 ft, consist of correspondence, manuscripts, source material, research notes, articles, memos, newspaper clippings, and printed matter, relating mainly to human rights, prosecution of Nazi criminals, refugee and immigration problems, *Wiedergutmachung*, and the German-Israeli agreement of 1954. Correspondents include *Sol Bloom, *Emanuel Celler, and *Stephen S. Wise. *NUCMC* MS 75-713. Finding aid: unpublished inventory.

YIVO Institute for Jewish Research: papers, 1938-45, ca. 1 ft, also on microfilm (2 reels), consist of correspondence, memoranda, reports, bulletins, and press releases. Include materials concerning various organizations and activities in aid of refugees. Finding aid: unpublished inventory (6 pp.).

Stanford Univ., Hoover Institution on War, Revolution, and Peace: papers, 1926-73, ca. 22 ft, consist of manuscripts, correspondence, clippings, and printed matter, concerning Jewish refugees from Nazi Germany, German and Austrian *Wiedergutmachungs*-payments to Nazi victims, German-Israeli relations, the condition of Jews throughout the world, and civil liberties in the U.S.A. and Germany.

Yad Vashem Archives, Israel: Collection on Claims Against Germany, ca. 53 ft, consists of newspaper clippings, gathered for Grossmann's *Digest of Germany and Austria—Jewish Claims and Related Subjects*. Includes West German government publications, and reports and surveys by Jewish and non-Jewish organizations on German-Jewish relations.

436. GRUENEWALD, MAX, 1899-

German rabbi and communal leader, emigrated to Palestine in 1938, immigrated to the U.S.A. in 1939. Rabbi 1925-37, and president 1934-37 Jüdische Gemeinde, Mannheim, Germany; member of executive, Reichsvertretung 1936-38. Rabbi, Congregation B'nai Israel, Millburn, NJ since 1939; member of executive board, cultural department of *World Jewish Congress 1942-45; vice-president, *Jewish Cultural Reconstruction 1951-76.

President, *Theodor Herzl Society, New York 1940-43; president 1952-62, and honorary president since 1962, *American Federation of Jews from Central Europe; member of presidium, *Council of Jews from Germany; chairman 1956, and president since 1974, *Leo Baeck Institute, New York, and international president, Leo Baeck Institutes; cochairman, *Gustav Wurzweiler Foundation.

Literature. *International Biographical Dictionary*, vol. I.

Lessing, *Oral History.*
Who's Who in World Jewry, 1972, p. 362.

Papers. Leo Baeck Institute Archives: papers include materials relating to Gruenewald's various professional, communal, and organizational activities, many of which concern former refugees from Germany.

437. GUMBEL, EMIL JULIUS, 1891-1966

German-Jewish mathematical statistician. Emigrated to France in 1933, settled in New York in 1940. Leading pacifist and polemicist against nationalism, fascism, and Nazism. Faculty member, Heidelberg Univ. 1923-33, Univ. Lyons 1934-40, *New School for Social Research 1940-46, Columbia Univ. 1953-66.
   Extensively engaged in anti-Nazi activities, before and after emigration. During World War II, prepared reports for U.S. Office of Strategic Services (OSS) concerning activities of subversive German political groups in the 1920s-30s.

Literature. *International Biographical Dictionary*, vol. II.

Papers. Leo Baeck Institute Archives: papers, 1928-60, ca. 6 ft, include materials on political activities on behalf of persecuted German scholars of the Nazi period. *NUCMC* MS 72-231.
   Univ. of Chicago Library, Dept. of Special Collections: papers, 1940s, 4 boxes, consist of general personal correspondence and topical files. Materials relate in part to other German émigrés and to his political activities. Finding aid: unpublished inventory (9 pp.).

438. HARRISON, ROSS GRANVILLE, 1870-1959

Professor of biology, Yale Univ. 1907-59, and director, Osborn Zoological Laboratory.
   As a result of study and travel in Germany and marriage to a German woman, he developed special concern for persecuted scientists in Germany and assisted refugee scholars to find positions in the U.S.A. The U.S. National Research Council, of which he was chairman 1938-46, cooperated with the *Emergency Committee in Aid of Displaced Foreign Scholars to this end.

Literature. *Dictionary of Scientific Biography*, vol. VI, pp. 131-135.

Papers. Yale Univ. Library, Dept. of Manuscripts and Archives: papers, 1907-59, ca. 165 boxes, include correspondence with refugee biologists Victor Hamburger and Johannes F. K. Holtfreter regarding their immigration, and other documentation on Harrison's concern with refugee scientists. Finding aid: unpublished inventory.

439. HART, HENRY MELVIN, JR., 1904-1969

Professor of law, Harvard Univ. Law School; arbitrator of labor disputes. In U.S. government service 1940-46, including Special Assistant to the *U.S. Immigration and Naturalization Service in the U.S. Attorney General's Office 1940-41.

Active in research on, and for liberalization of, immigration legislation from 1935 on.

Literature. *New York Times*, Mar. 25, 1969, p. 56.

Papers. Harvard Univ., Law School Library, Manuscript Div.: papers, 1927–69, 21 ft, include material on Hart's activities on immigration, in series I, Correspondence, and VII, Immigration. *NUCMC* MS 74-331. Finding aid: unpublished guide.

440. HAYES, CARLTON JOSEPH HUNTLEY, 1882-1964

Professor of history, Columbia Univ. 1919-50. An authority on the history of modern Europe and nationalism. Cochairman, National Conference of Christians and Jews.

U.S. Ambassador to Spain 1942-45, where he came into contact with the refugee problem.

Literature. Carlton J. H. Hayes, *Wartime Mission in Spain, 1942-1945.* New York: Macmillan, 1945.
John P. Willson, "Carlton J. H. Hayes in Spain, 1942-1945." Unpublished Ph.D. dissertation, Syracuse Univ., 1969.
——, "Carlton J. H. Hayes, Spain, and the Refugee Crisis 1942-45." *American Jewish Historical Quarterly* 52 (Dec. 1972): 99-110.

Papers. Columbia Univ., Rare Book and Manuscript Library: papers, 1920-62, 17 boxes, include material relating to Hayes' diplomatic activities and his contact with organizations aiding refugees. *NUCMC* MS 67-795.

441. HERWALD, T. B., 18??-195?

Active in London in the Territorialist movement and in the *Freeland League.

Literature. *News of the YIVO* 34 (Sept. 1949): 8*.

Papers. YIVO Institute for Jewish Research: papers, 1893-1948, 1 ft. This collection on Territorialism, consisting of correspondence, memoranda, clippings, and personal documents, includes materials relating to the Freeland League and to the proposed establishment of refugee colonies in various countries.

442. HIRSCHMANN, IRA ARTHUR, 1901-

Business executive, New York.

Cofounder 1933, and board chairman, University in Exile, and trustee, *New School for Social Research, New York. Member, *Emergency Committee to Save the Jewish People of Europe. In October 1943, the Committee asked Hirschmann to go to Turkey as its agent, but instead he became special representative of the *U.S. War Refugee Board to the U.S. Embassy at Ankara, Turkey

1944-45, where he was associated with U.S. Ambassador *Laurence A. Steinhardt. Special Inspector General, United Nations Relief and Rehabilitation Administration (UNRRA) 1946.

Literature. Ira Hirschmann, *Caution to the Winds.* New York: McKay, 1962.
——, *The Embers Still Burn.* New York: Simon and Schuster, 1949.
——, *Lifeline to a Promised Land.* New York: Vanguard Press, 1946.

Papers. Papers, with Hirschmann (1075 Park Ave., New York, NY 10028), include materials relating to his refugee aid activities, such as cables and copies of reports to and from the *U.S. Dept. of State.

443. HOLLANDER, SIDNEY, 1881-1972

Business executive, communal leader, and social activist, Baltimore. Active in local and national Jewish and nonsectarian organizations.

President, *Council of Jewish Federations and Welfare Funds 1939-45; vice-president, *American Jewish Congress; executive board member, *American Jewish Committee; board member, *Jewish Family and Children's Service, Baltimore. Advocated legislation in the *U.S. Congress to admit German refugee children into the U.S.A.

Literature. Jewish Historical Society of Maryland, *Sidney Hollander: Beloved Warrior.* By Jack L. Levin. Baltimore, 1976.

Papers. Maryland Historical Society: papers, 1926-72, 37.5 ft (ca. 30,000 items), consist largely of correspondence with numerous social welfare and social action agencies, including the *National Refugee Service, Non-Sectarian Foundation for Refugee Children, *United HIAS Service, *United Service for New Americans, and *United States Committee for the Care of European Children. Finding aid: unpublished inventory and card index.

444. HOOVER, HERBERT, 1874-1964

U.S. President 1929-33.
Restricted immigration as part of his policies for dealing with the Depression of 1929. His Executive Order of September 8, 1930, which instructed consular officers to refuse visas to applicants who could not prove that they would not at any future time become public charges, set the pattern for U.S. immigration policy toward refugees from Germany.

Literature. Lewis L. Strauss, *Men and Decisions.* Garden City, NY: Doubleday, 1962.

Papers. Herbert Hoover Presidential Library: papers include Presidential subject files on immigration, 1929-33; statements regarding immigration, 1929-32; and post-Presidential subject files dealing with refugees, immigration, and Jewish matters, 1933-64. The latter files contain correspondence with *Lewis L. Strauss on the *Baruch-*Hoover Resettlement Plan, a scheme for resettling refugees in Africa, 1939. *NUCMC* MS 70-185, 70-186. Finding aid: unpublished guides.

445. HOPKINS, HARRY LLOYD, 1890-1946

Social worker and U.S. government official 1933-41. Close adviser to President *Franklin D. Roosevelt and special personal envoy 1942-45.

Literature. Henry H. Adams, *Harry Hopkins: A Biography.* New York: Putnam, 1977.
D.A.B., suppl. 4, pp. 391-394.

Papers. Franklin D. Roosevelt Library: papers, 1928-46, 117 ft, and microfilm (24 reels), include correspondence concerning refugee children, the *Intergovernmental Committee on Refugees, and Palestine; reports of the U.S. Board of Appeals on Visa Cases (*U.S. Dept. of State) on individual refugees; and files concerning the refugee problem, postwar immigration, and visa cases. *NUCMC* MS 65-43.

446. HUEBSCH, BENJAMIN W., 1876-1964

Publisher. Editor-in-chief and vice president, Viking Press. Member of national committee and treasurer, *American Civil Liberties Union; member of executive committee, *P.E.N. American Center. Special U.S. representative to UNESCO.

Assisted and maintained contact with refugee authors; supported Emergency Rescue Committee (*International Rescue Committee); arranged for affidavits and assisted with other activities in aid of refugees.

Literature. András Sándor, "Ein amerikanischer Verleger und die Exilautoren." In *Deutsche Exilliteratur seit 1933.* Bd. 1, Kalifornien. John M. Spalek and Joseph Strelka, eds. Bern and München: Francke, 1976. Teil 1, pp. 117-134, especially p. 121.

Papers. Library of Congress, Manuscript Div.: papers, 1893-1964, 17 ft (10,515 items), include correspondence with various refugee authors, 1930s-40s. *NUCMC* MS 66-1421. Finding aids: unpublished inventory; *Deutsche Exilliteratur seit 1933.* Bd. 1, Kalifornien. Teil 2, pp. 184-185.

447. HULL, CORDELL, 1871-1955

Jurist. U.S. Congressman from Tennessee 1907-31 and Senator 1931-33. U.S. Secretary of State 1933-44. Awarded Nobel Peace Prize 1945.

As Secretary of State (*U.S. Dept. of State), he participated in shaping American policies and activities toward refugees from Nazi Germany and occupied Europe.

Literature. Richard Burns, "Cordell Hull: A Study in Diplomacy, 1933-1941." Unpublished Ph.D. dissertation, Univ. of Illinois, 1960.
D.A.B., suppl. 5, pp. 331-335.
Cordell Hull, *The Memoirs of Cordell Hull.* 2 vols. New York: Macmillan, 1948.

Papers. Library of Congress, Manuscript Div.: papers, 1908-56, 106 ft (ca. 70,000 items), also on microfilm (118 reels), consist of correspondence, memoranda, diaries, speeches, statements, scrapbooks, and printed matter, chiefly from the period 1933-44. Include substantial materials on European affairs and Nazi Germany. *NUCMC* MS 76-163. Finding aid: Library of Congress, Manuscript Div., *Cordell Hull: A Register of His Papers in the Library of Congress.* Washington, DC, 1975.

448. HUTCHINS, ROBERT MAYNARD, 1899-1977

Foundation executive and educator. President, Univ. of Chicago 1929-45, chancellor 1945-51. Chairman, Commission on International Economic Relations 1933-36. After 1951, held leading positions at Ford Foundation, Fund for the Republic, and Center for the Study of Democratic Institutions.

Active in efforts to find positions for refugee scholars. Member, *Emergency Committee in Aid of Displaced Foreign Scholars and Emergency Rescue Committee (*International Rescue Committee).

Literature. *Current Biography*, 1954, pp. 356-358.
Laura Fermi, *Illustrious Immigrants: The Intellectual Migration from Europe, 1930-41.* Chicago: Univ. of Chicago Press, 1968, pp. 72, 76.

Papers. Univ. of Chicago Library, Dept. of Special Collections: papers include materials regarding the placement of refugee scholars.

449. ICKES, HAROLD LECLAIRE, 1874-1952

U.S. Secretary of the Interior 1933-46. Advocate of political and social reforms during the Progressive and New Deal periods.

Advocated the resettlement of refugees in Alaska and the Virgin Islands, through the *U.S. Dept. of the Interior and the *U.S. Div. of Territories and Island Possessions. Favored liberalized immigration policies and the admission of political refugees.

Literature. *D.A.B.*, suppl. 5, pp. 341-344.
Harold L. Ickes, *The Secret Diaries of Harold L. Ickes. Vol. III: The Lowering Clouds, 1939-41.* New York: Simon and Schuster, 1954.
Linda J. Lear, "The Aggressive Progressive: The Political Career of Harold L. Ickes, 1874-1933." Unpublished Ph.D. dissertation, George Washington Univ., 1974.

Papers. Library of Congress, Manuscript Div.: papers, 1906-52, 158 ft (ca. 117,000 items). "Secret diaries," 1933-51, are also on microfilm (12 reels). *NUCMC* MS 60-145. Finding aid: card index and unpublished inventory.

450. JELLIFFE, SMITH ELY, 1866-1945

Neuropsychiatrist and pioneer in the field of psychoanalysis. Managing editor, *Journal of Nervous and Mental Disease* 1902-1945, and *Psychoanalytic Review* 1913-45.

Through extensive correspondence and frequent travel abroad, Jelliffe had been acquainted with many European psychoanalysts who subsequently found refuge in the U.S.A. In his last years, he advised and assisted these émigrés, who influenced the development of psychoanalysis in the U.S.A.

Literature. *D.A.B.*, suppl. 3, pp. 384-386.
Quarterly Journal of the Library of Congress 34 (Oct. 1977): 360-363.

Papers. Library of Congress, Manuscript Div.: papers, 1896-1944, ca. 9000 items, include materials relating to the rescue, immigration, and resettlement of refugee physicians, especially neurologists, psychiatrists, and psychoanalysts.

451. JOHNSON, ALVIN SAUNDERS, 1874-1971

Economist and educator. Founder and editor, *The Encyclopedia of the Social Sciences*; editor, *The New Republic* 1917-23. *New School for Social Research, New York: cofounder 1919, director 1923-45, chairman, Graduate Faculty of Political and Social Science 1945; president emeritus 1945-71.

Founded the University in Exile (renamed the Graduate Faculty of Political and Social Science) at the New School in 1933 to resettle displaced German scholars, and to transplant German-style graduate teaching to the U.S.A. In 1940, the École Libre des Hautes Études was organized at the New School to aid displaced French and Belgian scholars.

Head of the Alvin Corp., established in 1939 to resettle refugees in North Carolina. Active in numerous organizations in aid of refugees, including *American Council for Émigrés in the Professions (ACEP), an outgrowth of the University in Exile; *Emergency Committee in Aid of Displaced Foreign Scholars; and *American Guild for German Cultural Freedom.

Literature. Alvin Johnson, *Pioneer's Progress, An Autobiography.* New York: Viking Press, 1952.
Wetzel, "American Rescue," pp. 182-236.

Papers. Yale Univ. Library, Dept. of Manuscripts and Archives: papers, 1902-69, 6 ft, include correspondence and other material relating to the New School, University in Exile, and Johnson's efforts to help refugee scholars and artists. Some of this material was originally part of the records of the University in Exile (at the New School, separately described). Photocopies of documents removed to Yale Univ. have been retained at the New School. The materials identified by Wetzel, *op. cit.*, as the Agnes DeLima Papers at the New School are now part of this collection at Yale Univ. *NUCMC* MS 77-2110. Finding aid: unpublished register.

452. KAHN, BERNHARD, 1876-1955

German-Jewish social worker and communal leader, immigrated to France in 1933, and the U.S.A. in 1939. As *Generalsekretär* of the Hilfsverein der deutschen Juden in Berlin, 1904-20, Kahn helped to direct a large number of Jewish emigrants from Eastern and Central Europe via Germany to the U.S.A. He was succeeded by *Mark Wischnitzer.

In 1920, Kahn became director of the refugee department of the *American Jewish Joint Distribution Committee (JDC) in Berlin (whose European office was transferred to Paris in 1933) and, in 1924, overall European director of JDC, as well as managing director of its subsidiary *American Joint Reconstruction Foundation.

From 1933 to 1939, Kahn directed the office of the JDC in Paris, a major center of Jewish assistance to refugees from Germany and Austria, and was active in several major investment and financial aid agencies serving the colonization and economic upbuilding of Palestine (including the Palestine Economic Corp.–*PEC Israel Economic Corp.), and the Jewish settlement in the Dominican Republic (*Dominican Republic Settlement Association). Honorary chairman, JDC European Council 1939-50. Vice-chairman, JDC 1950-55.

Literature. *International Biographical Dictionary*, vol. I.

Papers. Leo Baeck Institute Archives: papers, 1906-55, 200 items, include some correspondence with *Paul Baerwald, *James N. Rosenberg, *Felix M. Warburg, and others on refugee matters. *NUCMC* MS 75-715. Finding aid: unpublished inventory (7 pp.).

453. KALLEN, HORACE MEYER, 1882-1974

Professor of social philosophy, *New School for Social Research, New York. As member (and dean 1944-46) of the New School's Graduate Faculty of Political and Social Science, Kallen took an active part in national and international efforts to fight fascism and Nazism. His insistence on the link between thought and action led him to work for the extension of democracy at home and abroad, especially in relation to civil liberties and minority rights.

Supported numerous organizations in the U.S.A. and overseas, including democratic refugee organizations in the U.S.A., the anti-Nazi boycott movement, and groups aiding refugee scholars, artists, and professionals. Assisted in founding *Selfhelp of German Émigrés in 1936 and served on its board of directors.

Literature. Milton R. Konvitz, "Horace Meyer Kallen: Philosopher of the Hebraic-American Idea." *American Jewish Year Book 1974-75*, vol. 75, pp. 55-80.

Papers. YIVO Institute for Jewish Research: papers, 1922-52, 24 ft, consist of correspondence, manuscripts, publications, and other materials, including documentation on many organizations in aid of refugees and correspondence with refugee scholars and intellectuals. *NUCMC* MS 60-2600. Finding aids: unpublished inventory (200 pp.); *News of the YIVO* 61 (June 1956): 6*-7*.

American Jewish Archives: papers, 1902-75, 37.5 ft (ca. 36,000 items), consist of correspondence, manuscripts, publications, and other materials, some of which concern Nazi Germany and refugee scholars. (The bulk of this collection concerns the years prior to 1921 and after 1940; the interim years are primarily covered by the collection at YIVO.) *NUCMC* MS 65-1728. Finding aid: unpublished inventory (48 pp.).

454. KANNER, LEO, 1894–

Austrian-born, German-trained child psychiatrist, immigrated to the U.S.A. in 1924. Professor of child psychiatry, Johns Hopkins Univ. School of Medicine.

Member of board of directors, Baltimore Refugee Adjustment Committee 1938–40s, and its successor, *Jewish Family and Children's Service. Actively involved in the immigration and resettlement of refugee physicians 1933–45.

Literature. Louise A. Alpert, "The Economic and Vocational Adjustment of Refugees in Baltimore." Unpublished master's thesis, New York School of Social Work, Columbia University, Sept. 1941, pp. 46–47.

Leo Kanner, "Freedom Is Within." Unpublished autobiography, in the author's possession.

Edith Raddatz, *Leo Kanner, Leben und Werk.* Dissertation, Johannes Gutenberg-Univ. Mainz, 1976.

Ferne Walpert, "Dr. Leo Kanner and the Resettlement of Central European Refugee Medical Personnel in the United States of America." Unpublished master's thesis, Baltimore Hebrew College, May 1976.

Papers. Baltimore Hebrew College/Jewish Historical Society of Maryland: papers, 1934–45, comprise several hundred items of correspondence (946 pp.) on the rescue of Jewish physicians from Central Europe and their resettlement in the U.S.A., primarily in Maryland.

455. KATZ, LABEL ABRAHAM, 1919–1975

Businessman, attorney, and Jewish communal leader, New Orleans. President, *B'nai B'rith International 1959–65.

Board member, *United HIAS Service; member, Jewish Agency for Israel (*World Zionist Organization—American Section); member, national cabinet, *United Jewish Appeal.

Literature. *Current Biography*, 1960, pp. 208–209.

Papers. American Jewish Historical Society: papers, 1931–68, 19 boxes, include B'nai B'rith material concerning German-Jewish refugees and claims against Germany for indemnification of German-Jewish B'nai B'rith property confiscated by the Nazi government in Germany. *NUCMC* MS 72-1379.

456. KAUFMAN, STANLEY L., 1900–

Businessman, Chicago.

Papers. Univ. of Illinois at Urbana–Champaign, Univ. Archives: papers, 1932–50, 2 ft, include correspondence, circulars, and affidavits regarding efforts made by Kaufman and Jewish aid organizations to assist relatives of U.S. residents in Germany and other European countries to emigrate to America, 1936–40; and a letter, 1938, describing the political, social, and economic conditions of Jews in Germany. *NUCMC* MS 77-1179.

457. KEPPEL, FREDERICK PAUL, 1875-1943

Educator; dean, Columbia College, New York 1910-18; president, *Carnegie Corp. of New York 1923-41.

Member, *U.S. Board of Appeals on Visa Cases 1941-43; member, *U.S. President's War Relief Control Board 1942-43.

Literature. *D.A.B.*, suppl. 3, pp. 415-417.

Papers. Columbia Univ., Rare Book and Manuscript Library: papers, 1880-1943, 71 boxes (ca. 38,000 items), comprise correspondence and memoranda dealing largely with Keppel's personal and professional life during his tenure with the Carnegie Corp. Include one folder on the Board of Appeals on Visa Cases, several folders on the War Relief Control Board, and material on the *National Refugee Service. *NUCMC* MS 66-1591.

458. KILGORE, HARLEY MARTIN, 1893-1956

U.S. Senator from West Virginia 1940-56; member, *Senate Judiciary Committee 1941-56 and member of its Immigration Subcommittee. Liberal Senate leader and supporter of *Franklin D. Roosevelt.

Active for legislation to admit displaced persons following World War II.

Literature. Robert F. Maddox, "Senator Harley M. Kilgore and World War II."
Unpublished Ph.D. dissertation, Univ. of Kentucky, 1974.
National Cyclopaedia of American Biography, vol. 42, pp. 94-95.

Papers. West Virginia Univ. Library, West Virginia Collection: papers, 1937-56, 54 boxes and 5 bundles, consist of correspondence, speeches, and printed items. Include several folders on displaced German Jews, the Displaced Persons Act of 1948, and Kilgore's service on the Senate Immigration Subcommittee. *NUCMC* MS 60-352, 66-689.

Franklin D. Roosevelt Library: papers, 1941-56, 59 ft, include materials on displaced persons, immigration, and anti-Semitism. *NUCMC* MS 65-46.

459. KINGDON, FRANK, 1894-1972

Radio commentator, author, and columnist. President, Univ. of Newark (now Rutgers Univ.), Newark, NJ 1935-38.

Cofounder 1940, and chairman, Emergency Rescue Committee (ERC); chairman of its successor, the *International Rescue and Relief Committee (IRRC). Member, *United States Committee for the Care of European Children. Member of executive committee, *Committee for Refugee Education, New York.

Literature. *Current Biography*, 1944, pp. 342-344.
Wetzel, "American Rescue," pp. 106-120.

Papers. Papers in the possession of his family include several folders dealing with the ERC and IRRC, and manuscripts for two unpublished autobiographies. For access, contact Henry L. Blumenthal, 565 Fifth Ave., New York, NY 10017.

460. KOHLER, MAX JAMES, 1871-1934

Attorney, author of legal studies, specialist in immigration and naturalization law, and spokesman for the legal and public rights of immigrants, naturalized citizens, and aliens. Represented various national Jewish organizations with respect to immigration and naturalization legislation. Opposed alien registration laws and the use of the term "Hebrew Race" to classify Jewish immigrants, and was concerned with the conditions of Jews in European countries, including Germany. His *Immigration and Aliens in the United States: Studies of American Immigration Laws and the Legal Status of Aliens in the United States* was published in New York, 1936.

Leading member, *American Jewish Committee. Representative of *B'nai B'rith on the Joint Consultative Council, which Kohler frequently represented before Congressional committees. (The Council was established in June 1933 by B'nai B'rith, the American Jewish Committee, and the *American Jewish Congress for a united American-Jewish response to the German problem. The Council did not live up to the expectations of the founding organizations, which pursued separate ways on various issues, and collapsed in 1936.) Kohler was the founder and chairman of the Council's Committee on German-Jewish Immigration Policy, whose deliberations resulted in the establishment of the German Jewish Children's Aid (*European Jewish Children's Aid) and the Joint Clearing Bureau (*National Coordinating Committee). Active in numerous immigrant aid organizations. Proponent of the establishment of the *League of Nations High Commission for Refugees (Jewish and Other) Coming from Germany in 1933.

Literature. D.A.B., suppl. 1, pp. 472-473.
Irving Lehman, "Max J. Kohler." *American Jewish Year Book* 37 (1935-36): 21-25.

Papers. American Jewish Historical Society: papers, 1888-1934, 11 ft, include correspondence with individuals, organizations, and government agencies; reports, law briefs, and other materials on refugees, immigration, and related issues. *NUCMC* MS 68-143. Finding aid: unpublished guide.

461. KOHN, ESTHER (LOEB), 1875-1965

Social worker, Chicago; planned and managed the campaign which led to the enactment of progressive child labor laws in Illinois.

Papers. Univ. of Illinois, Chicago Circle Library, Dept. of Special Collections: papers, 1896-1965, 24 ft, include budget committee material, 1941-42, and constitution and bylaws, n.d., of Chicago Committee for Jewish Refugees (*Jewish Family and Community Service); a folder on German refugee children, 1939-40; and extensive materials on Jewish welfare, service, and charitable organizations, 1930s-50s, some of which concern the immigration of European Jews to the U.S.A. and to Palestine. *NUCMC* MS 68-1864. Finding aid: unpublished inventory.

462. KOHS, SAMUEL CALMIN, 1890–

Psychologist, social worker, and community leader, Burlingame, CA.

Director, Resettlement Div., *National Coordinating Committee (NCC) and *National Refugee Service (NRS) 1938-40; director, Refugee Service Committee (*Jewish Family Service of Los Angeles) 1940-41; director, Bureau of War Records, *National Jewish Welfare Board 1942-47.

Literature. *Encyclopaedia Judaica*, vol. 10, cols. 1148-1149.

Papers. American Jewish Historical Society: papers, 1916-60, 4 ft, contain unpublished and printed materials, and personal correspondence of a general nature and with Jewish communal institutions. The majority relate to NCC, NRS, and Jewish immigrants, including speeches delivered at conferences on aid to refugees in New York 1939 and 1940, and Chicago 1940. *NUCMC* MS 72-7.

Western Jewish History Center: papers, ca. 1920-57, 3 boxes, consist of correspondence, memorabilia, and printed matter, probably not related to Kohs' activities in aid to immigrants. Finding aid: unpublished inventory.

463. KOLB, LEON, 1890–

Austrian-Jewish physician and educator, immigrated to the U.S.A. (San Francisco) in 1937.

Kolb and his wife welcomed and resettled fellow immigrants from Central Europe. Founder and leader of *San Francisco branch of *Selfhelp of Émigrés from Central Europe 1940-41.

Literature. *International Biographical Dictionary*, vol. I.
Who's Who in World Jewry, 1972, p. 491.

Papers. Research Foundation for Jewish Immigration: scrapbook, 1940-44 and 1949, contains newspaper clippings, recital invitations and programs, guest lists, and other materials relating to events for newcomers which the Kolbs hosted in their home.

464. KRAUS, HERTHA, 1897–1968

Immigrated to the U.S.A. from Germany in 1933. Professor of social economy and social research, Bryn Mawr College 1936-68. Consultant on social welfare matters. Active for the American Friends Service Committee (AFSC) in Germany and the U.S.A. since 1920, including German child-feeding mission 1920-23.

Counselor for refugees 1937-38, and consultant to refugee section, AFSC 1939-43. President, Cooperative Residence Club 1942-48; president, *New Jersey Fellowship Fund for the Aged 1948-52. Member of executive committee, *Emergency Committee in Aid of Displaced Foreign Scholars 1940-45.

Literature. *International Biographical Dictionary*, vol. I.
Wetzel, "American Rescue," pp. 237-287.

Papers. Bryn Mawr College Archives: papers, 1930s-60s, 2 cartons, consist of personal documents, course outlines, reprints, and AFSC materials from the 1960s. The only materials relevant to refugees are seminar notes, a reprint of an article, and one file on a refugee family Kraus had brought from Switzerland to the U.S.A. during World War II.

465. KUBIE, LAWRENCE SCHLESINGER, 1896-1973

Psychiatrist and psychoanalyst. Secretary, *American Psychoanalytic Association, and cochairman of its Emergency Committee on Relief and Immigration 1938-43.

Founder and officer, *National Committee for the Resettlement of Foreign Physicians and member of its general advisory committee.

Literature. New York Times, Oct. 28, 1973, p. 61.
Who's Who in American Jewry, 1938-39, p. 574.

Papers. Papers relating to Kubie's activities on behalf of refugee physicians, 1938-39, 2 folders, are with Bettina Warburg, M.D. (former cochairman, Emergency Committee on Relief and Immigration), 203 E. 72 St., New York, NY 10021. Photocopies are at Research Foundation for Jewish Immigration. Consist of positive and negative replies, Feb.-May, 1939, which Kubie received from physicians in response to his invitation to join the Central Advisory Council of Physicians of the newly founded National Committee for the Resettlement of Foreign Physicians; an unmailed letter to Dr. *Ernst P. Boas, Feb. 4, 1939, in which Kubie expresses his frustration with the efforts being made to coordinate the resettlement of physicians; minutes of meetings 1938, concerning aid to refugee physicians; published report 1938, of the Resettlement Div. of the *National Coordinating Committee; and copies of a bill proposed in the New York State Assembly 1939, about licensing of professionals.

466. LAMPORT, ARTHUR MATTHEW, 1883-1940

Investment banker, economist, philanthropist, and communal leader, New York. Government adviser on economic problems.

One of the key figures involved in negotiations to resettle European refugees in the Dominican Republic and to create the *Dominican Republic Settlement Association (DORSA) in 1939. Established first free loan society for refugees in the DORSA colony at Sosúa. Treasurer, United Palestine Appeal and *United Jewish Appeal.

Literature. Who's Who in American Jewry, 1938-39, p. 583.

Papers. YIVO Institute for Jewish Research: papers, 1939-40, 0.25 ft, consist of materials relating to the settlement of refugees in the Dominican Republic. Include correspondence with the Dominican government, *James N. Rosenberg, and DORSA, minutes of meetings, notes regarding Lamport's visits to the Dominican Republic, and other documents.

467. LANDAUER, CARL, 1891–

German-Jewish economist, immigrated to the U.S.A. in 1933. Professor, Univ. of California, Berkeley.

Active in a variety of efforts to assist with the immigration and resettlement of refugees from Nazism. Charter member, *Selfhelp of German Émigrés 1936. Promoted founding of the *San Francisco branch of Selfhelp since 1937.

Literature. *International Biographical Dictionary*, vol. II. Lessing, *Oral History.*

Papers. In 1978, papers were with Landauer, 1317 Arch St., Berkeley, CA 94708. They will eventually be deposited at Stanford Univ., Hoover Institution on War, Revolution, and Peace. Include correspondence, 8 folders, relating to his efforts to assist with the immigration and resettlement of immigrants from Nazism. Organizations represented in these files include: Selfhelp, New York; Selfhelp, San Francisco; *Jewish Council of 1933, San Francisco; *U.S. Committee of International Student Service; San Francisco Committee for Service to Émigrés (*Jewish Family Service Agency, San Francisco); Academic Assistance Council, London; American Committee for Émigré Scholars, Writers and Artists (*American Council for Émigrés in the Professions); Hilfsverein der Juden in Deutschland. Photocopies are at Leo Baeck Institute Archives and at Research Foundation for Jewish Immigration.

468. LANDAUER, GEORG, 1895–1954

German-Jewish lawyer and Zionist leader, emigrated to Palestine in 1934.

Active primarily on behalf of the immigration and resettlement of German Jews in Palestine/Israel. Executive director, Palästina-Amt, Berlin 1925–33; executive director, Zionistische Vereinigung für Deutschland 1929–33. Director, Central Bureau for the Settlement of German Jews in Palestine (later renamed German Dept.) of the Jewish Agency for Palestine (*World Zionist Organization) 1934–47. Director, Restitution of German-Jewish Property Dept., Jewish Agency 1947–54. His primary activities were the organization of *aliyah*, capital transfer (*Haavara*), agricultural settlement, Youth Aliyah (cofounder with *Henrietta Szold), and German *Wiedergutmachung.* Chairman, Irgun Olei Merkaz Europa (Association of Olim from Central Europe), Israel 1948–54.

Literature. *International Biographical Dictionary*, vol. I.

Papers. Leo Baeck Institute Archives: papers, 1916–53, ca. 3 ft, include correspondence relating to Landauer's activities on behalf of Zionist organizations, the Jewish Agency, Youth Aliyah, and *Wiedergutmachung*, and newspaper clippings and articles dealing with immigration and *Wiedergutmachung. NUCMC* MS 72-233. Finding aid: unpublished inventory (27 pp.).

469. LEHMAN, HERBERT HENRY, 1878–1963

Banker, philanthropist, and political leader. Governor of New York State 1933–42, U.S. Senator from New York 1949–56.

Director General, United Nations Relief and Rehabilitation Administration (UNRRA) 1943-46. Concerned with refugee and immigration matters, and with the role of American Jewish leadership in matters of rescue, migration, and resettlement.

Literature. Allan Nevins, *Herbert H. Lehman and His Era.* New York: Scribner, 1963.

Alan Silverstein, "New Perspectives Concerning the Response of American Jewish Leadership to the Nazi Peril, Oct. 28, 1938-May 1940." Unpublished master's thesis, Columbia Univ., 1974.

Papers. Columbia Univ., School of International Affairs: papers, 1895-1963, ca. 1,250,000 items, include correspondence dealing with immigration, refugees, and organizations aiding refugees. *NUCMC* MS 74-292. Finding aid: Columbia Univ., School of International Affairs, *The Herbert H. Lehman Papers: An Introduction, Checklist, and Guide.* By William B. Liebmann. New York, 1968.

470. LEVENE, PHOEBUS AARON THEODOR, 1869-1940

Biochemist. Member and head of the laboratory of chemistry, Rockefeller Institute for Medical Research, New York; succeeded upon his retirement in 1937 by *Max Bergmann.

Assisted in the placement of refugee physicians.

Literature. *D.A.B.*, suppl. 2, pp. 378-379.

Melville L. Wolfrom, "Phoebus Aaron Theodor Levene, 1869-1940." In *Great Chemists*, Eduard Farber, ed. New York: Interscience, 1961, pp. 1313-1324.

Papers. New York Public Library, Manuscripts and Archives Div.: papers, 0.5 ft, consisting of correspondence with immigrant physicians, 1933-40, are a part of the records of the *Emergency Committee in Aid of Displaced Foreign Scholars (box 195).

471. LIFSCHITZ, SAMUEL, 1883-1961

Austrian-born Jewish social worker who moved to Berlin in 1905. Staff member, Hilfsverein der deutschen Juden 1907-38, and head of its *Auswandererberatungsstelle* (Emigrant Advisory Office). Immigrated to the U.S.A. ca. 1938.

Literature. *News of the YIVO* 80 (Oct. 1961): 2*.

Papers. YIVO Institute for Jewish Research: papers, 1906-50s, 1.25 ft, also on microfilm (3 reels), consist of correspondence, documents, and reports relating to migration and to Lifschitz's Hilfsverein activities and personal life. Include materials on emigration of the 1930s and refugees in the U.S.A. and elsewhere. Finding aid: unpublished inventory (2 pp.).

472. LOCHNER, LOUIS PAUL, 1887-1975

News commentator, foreign correspondent, and author. Chief, Berlin Bureau, Associated Press 1928-41. Awarded Pulitzer Prize for distinguished service as foreign correspondent 1939. During his tour of duty in Berlin, Lochner had numerous contacts with Jews persecuted in Nazi Germany, to many of whom he provided moral, financial, and personal assistance.

Literature. William C. Haygood and Paul H. Haas, eds., "Round Robins from Berlin: Louis P. Lochner's Letters to His Children, 1932-1941." *Wisconsin Magazine of History* 50 (Summer 1967): 291-336.

Louis P. Lochner, *Always the Unexpected: A Book of Reminiscences.* New York: Macmillan, 1956.

Papers. State Historical Society of Wisconsin: papers, 1905-61, 54 boxes. Personal correspondence describes living conditions and political developments in Central Europe, 1925-42. Includes correspondence, 1942-52, with Betty Hirsch, a blind Jewish refugee who had directed a school for the blind and returned to Berlin in 1946 following her emigration to England in 1933. *NUCMC* MS 64-1615. Finding aid: Josephine L. Harper, *Guide to the Manuscripts of the State Historical Society of Wisconsin, Supplement Number Two.* Madison, WI, 1966, pp. 118-119.

473. LONG, BRECKINRIDGE, 1881-1958

U.S. Ambassador to Italy 1933-36. Assistant Secretary of State for Special Problems 1939-44.

Administered the restrictive application of U.S. immigration laws for refugees. Influential advocate of restrictions on immigration and on the admission of Jewish refugees to the U.S.A. during the *Franklin D. Roosevelt administration.

Literature. Fred L. Israel, ed., *The War Diary of Breckinridge Long. Selections from the Years 1939-1944.* Lincoln, NE: Univ. of Nebraska Press, 1966.

James F. Watts, "The Public Life of Breckinridge Long, 1916-44." Unpublished Ph.D. dissertation, Univ. of Missouri, 1965.

Papers. Library of Congress, Manuscript Div.: papers, 1908-46, 60 ft, include documentation regarding the *U.S. Dept. of State's policies on refugees. *NUCMC* MS 59-6. Finding aid: unpublished inventory.

474. LOWENTHAL, MARVIN, 1890-1969

Historian, lecturer, and editor. Author of *The Jews of Germany: A Story of Sixteen Centuries*, Philadelphia: Jewish Publication Society, 1936, and *Henrietta Szold: Life and Letters*, New York: Viking 1942. European editor, *Menorah Journal* (published by *Menorah Association) 1924-29; European representative, *American Jewish Congress 1926-29; member, Zionist Advisory Commission 1946-49.

Literature. Charles A. Madison, "Marvin Lowenthal, 1890-1969," *Jewish Book Annual*, vol. 28 (5731/1970-1971), pp. 94-98.

Papers. American Jewish Historical Society: papers, 1890-1950, 7 ft, include material on the condition of Jews in Germany and relief activities on their behalf, 1933-35; notes, drafts, illustrations, publicity, and reviews relating to his book, *The Jews of Germany*; and material on the Conference on Jewish Relations (*Conference on Jewish Social Studies) 1933-34. *NUCMC* MS 77-37.

475. LUBIN, ISADOR, 1896-1978

Economist, statistician, and diplomat. Commissioner, U.S. Bureau of Labor Statistics 1933-46; Special Assistant to President *Franklin D. Roosevelt on statistical matters 1941-45. U.S. Associate Representative with rank of Minister, Allied Reparations Commission, Moscow 1945; U.S. Representative to Economic and Employment Commission, U.N. Economic and Social Council 1946-49. Special Assistant to Assistant Secretary of State 1949-50. U.S. Representative with rank of Minister, U.N. Economic and Social Council 1950-53.

Active in *American Jewish Committee, *American Jewish Joint Distribution Committee, *United HIAS Service, and other Jewish organizations. In 1944, Lubin advocated increased U.S. efforts to rescue Jewish victims of Nazi persecution.

Literature. *Current Biography*, 1953, pp. 372-375.

Papers. Franklin D. Roosevelt Library: papers, 1928-48, 22 ft, include materials, 1941-48, relating to Jewish refugees, Jews in Germany, and Palestine. *NUCMC* MS 65-48. Finding aid: unpublished shelf list.

476. McDONALD, JAMES GROVER, 1886-1964

Journalist, expert on foreign affairs, international civil servant, and U.S. diplomat. Chairman of the board, Foreign Policy Association 1919-33; member of editorial staff, *The New York Times* 1936-38; member, Anglo-American Committee of Inquiry on Jewish Problems in Palestine and Europe 1946. U.S. Special Representative to Israel 1948-49; first U.S. Ambassador to Israel 1949-51; chairman of Advisory Council, Development Corp. for Israel 1951-61.

*League of Nations High Commissioner for Refugees (Jewish and Other) Coming from Germany 1933-35; chairman, *U.S. President's Advisory Committee on Political Refugees (PACPR) 1938-45; chairman, *Refugee Relief Trustees 1945-46; honorary chairman, *National Coordinating Committee.

His *Letter of Resignation . . . Addressed to the Secretary General of the League of Nations*, published in London on Dec. 27, 1935, written in cooperation with the *American Jewish Committee, was publicized to alert the world to the worsening situation in Germany.

Literature. *Current Biography*, 1949, pp. 373-375.
Haim Genizi, "James G. McDonald: High Commissioner for Refugees, 1933-35," *The Wiener Library Bulletin*, vol. 30, n.s. nos. 43-44 (1977), pp. 40-52.

Barbara McDonald Stewart, "United States Government Policy on Refugees from Nazism, 1933-1940." Unpublished Ph.D. dissertation, Columbia Univ., 1969. (The author, McDonald's daughter, made extensive use of his papers.)

Papers. Columbia Univ., School of International Affairs, Herbert H. Lehman Papers: papers, 1909-64, 18 ft, include correspondence relating to McDonald's service as High Commissioner for Refugees and as chairman of the PACPR. *NUCMC* MS 74-293. Finding aid: unpublished checklist.

Leo Baeck Institute Archives: documentary materials from the period of McDonald's service as High Commissioner 1933-35, 1.75 ft, consist of copies of correspondence and of High Commission minutes and documents dealing with finances, passports, travel regulations, and the special emigration problems faced by professionals.

477. MACK, JULIAN WILLIAM, 1866-1943

Judge and Zionist leader. Chairman, *Survey Associates 1938-43.

Charter member, *American Jewish Committee, on whose behalf he pleaded the cause of German Jews before the U.S. Depts. of *Labor and *State. Active in helping German-Jewish refugees to enter the U.S.A.

Literature. Harry Barnard, *The Forging of an American Jew, The Life and Times of Judge Julian W. Mack.* New York: Herzl Press, 1974.
D.A.B., suppl. 3, pp. 487-490.

Papers. Zionist Archives and Library: papers, ca. 10 ft, include 2 folders on German Jewry and the growing problem of anti-Semitic legislation in Nazi Germany, 1933-36 [box 23, folders 83-84]. A major portion of this correspondence consists of letters by *Stephen S. Wise, who provided Mack with information on the situation. Finding aid: unpublished index.

478. MacMASTER, GILBERT, 1869-1967

Representative of the *American Friends Service Committee (AFSC) in Germany and Switzerland 1920s-40s.

During the 1930s as head of the Friends' Centre, Hamburg, Germany, assisted Nazi persecutees to emigrate to the U.S.A.

Papers. Haverford College Library, Quaker Collection: papers, 1901-68, 3 ft (693 items), comprise correspondence, diaries, clippings, and other materials relating to MacMaster's activities overseas for the AFSC. His diary contains references to his contacts with, and aid to, Jews in Germany. *NUCMC* MS 71-1035.

479. MARRINER, J. THEODORE, 1892-1937

U.S. Foreign Service officer. Chief, Div. of Western European Affairs, *U.S. Dept. of State 1935-37. (*Jay Pierrepont Moffat preceded and followed him in that post.) Assassinated in Beirut while serving as U.S. Consul General.

Papers. Columbia Univ., Rare Book and Manuscript Library: papers, 1918-37, 5 boxes, include Marriner's diaries, 1918-37, which reflect his activities in the State Dept. during the Nazi years. *NUCMC* MS 64-1348.

480. MARX, ALEXANDER, 1878-1953

Professor of history and librarian, Jewish Theological Seminary of America, New York. Immigrated to the U.S.A. in 1903 from Germany. President, American Academy for Jewish Research 1931-33.

Literature. Jewish Theological Seminary of America, *Alexander Marx: Jubilee Volume on the Occasion of His Seventieth Birthday.* New York, 1950.

Papers. Jewish Theological Seminary of America, Archives: papers, 24.5 ft, include letters from European scholars and other correspondence relating to Marx's efforts to place refugee scholars in positions in the U.S.A.

481. MESSERSMITH, GEORGE STRAUSSER, 1883-1960

U.S. Foreign Service officer: Consul General in Berlin 1930-34; Minister to Austria 1934-37; Assistant Secretary of State 1937-40 (successor to Wilbur J. Carr and replaced by *Breckinridge Long); Ambassador to Cuba 1940-41, Mexico 1941-42, and Argentina 1942-46.

Literature. Shlomo Shafir, "George S. Messersmith: An Anti-Nazi Diplomat's View of the German-Jewish Crisis." *Jewish Social Studies* 35 (Jan. 1973): 32-41.

Papers. Univ. of Delaware Library, Special Collections Dept.: papers, 1932-46, ca. 4 ft, include correspondence, dispatches, and notes for his memoirs, reflecting his interest in refugees and immigration. *NUCMC* MS 62-1434. Finding aid: calendar and index.

482. MOFFAT, JAY PIERREPONT, 1896-1943

U.S. Foreign Service officer: Chief, Div. of Western European Affairs 1932-35; Chief, Div. of European Affairs 1937-40; *U.S. Dept. of State; Consul General in Sydney, Australia 1935-37; Minister to Canada 1940-43; Minister to exiled government of Grand Duchy of Luxembourg 1941-43.

Literature. *D.A.B.*, suppl. 3, pp. 528-529.

Nancy Harrison Hooker, ed., *The Moffat Papers: Selections from the Diplomatic Journals of Jay Pierrepont Moffat, 1919-1943.* Cambridge, MA: Harvard Univ. Press, 1956.

Papers. Harvard Univ., Houghton Library: papers, 1917-43, 44 vols. and 5 boxes, consist of personal correspondence, 1922-42, memoranda, 1931-35 and 1942, and diplomatic journals, 1917-43. The latter contain information on the

State Department's reaction to public opinion after *Kristallnacht*, Nov. 9-10, 1938. Finding aid: unpublished index.

483. MOORE, R(OBERT) WALTON, 1859-1941

U.S. Representative from Virginia 1919-31. Assistant Secretary of State 1933-37; Counselor, *U.S. Dept. of State 1937-41. Expert on international law. Chairman of board of trustees, U.S. Export-Import Bank.

Papers. Franklin D. Roosevelt Library: papers, 1922-41, 13 ft, include several boxes of correspondence with *William E. Dodd, U.S. Ambassador to Germany 1933-37, and materials on Jewish refugees in Europe 1938-41. *NUCMC* MS 65-53.

484. MORGENTHAU, HENRY, JR., 1891-1967

Agricultural expert, entrepreneur, and civil servant. Influential adviser of President *Franklin D. Roosevelt. Under Secretary of the Treasury 1933-34, Secretary of the Treasury 1934-45. Author of *Germany Is Our Problem*, New York: Harper, 1945, the "Morgenthau Plan" for Allied postwar policies toward Germany.

In 1943, Morgenthau obtained Secretary of State *Cordell Hull's approval for a plan of the *World Jewish Congress to transfer private U.S. funds to Europe to rescue French and Rumanian Jews. At Morgenthau's suggestion, Roosevelt established the *U.S. War Refugee Board as a presidential executive agency in January 1944. General chairman 1947-50, and honorary chairman 1951-53, *United Jewish Appeal.

Literature. John M. Blum, *From the Morgenthau Diaries.* 3 vols. Boston: Houghton Mifflin, 1959-67.
——, *Roosevelt and Morgenthau: A Revision and Condensation of the Morgenthau Diaries.* Boston: Houghton Mifflin, 1970.

Papers. Franklin D. Roosevelt Library: papers, 1866-1953, 414 ft, include diaries and other materials relating to Jewish matters, immigration, and rescue efforts. *NUCMC* MS 65-54. Finding aid: unpublished index to the diaries.

485. MORRIS, HOMER LAWRENCE, 1886-1951

Professor of economics, Earlham College, Richmond, IN. Director, German Child Feeding Relief 1921, and Special Commissioner for *American Friends Service Committee (AFSC) in the Ruhr area following its occupation in 1923.
Commissioner to Europe for Refugee Problems, AFSC 1939.

Literature. *New York Times*, Nov. 29, 1951, p. 33.

Papers. Earlham College Archives: papers, 1908-51, 12 ft, include 3 in. of documents, including diary, correspondence, and printed matter, dealing with his activities on behalf of refugees in 1939. *NUCMC* MS 64-962.

486. MORSE, ARTHUR DAVID, 1920-1971

Journalist, television producer, and writer.

Author of *While Six Million Died: A Chronicle of American Apathy*, New York: Random House, 1967, a critical study of the U.S. government's response to the Nazi persecution and the genocide of European Jews.

Literature. Rabbi William Berkowitz, ed., *Conversations with . . . .* New York: Bloch, 1975, pp. 83-109.

Papers. New York Public Library, Manuscripts and Archives Div.: papers, 1945-71, 20 ft, include 6 ft of research notes, drafts, page proofs, reviews, etc. related to Morse's *While Six Million Died.* Finding aid: unpublished inventory (1 p.).

487. MOWSCHOWICH, DAVID, 1887-1957

Russian-born Jewish journalist and organization executive. Foreign affairs expert, Board of Deputies of British Jews.

Literature. *News of the YIVO* 71 (July 1959): 3*, 6*.

Papers. YIVO Institute for Jewish Research: papers, 1870-1956, 15 ft, consist of reports, memoranda, summaries, news clippings, and other materials relating to the political and economic conditions of Jews in various countries, and to the Conjoint Foreign Committee of the Board of Deputies and the Anglo-Jewish Association. A large part deals with the rise of Nazism in the 1930s and British-Jewish efforts to aid refugees. *NUCMC* MS 60-2406. Finding aid: *YIVO Bleter* 43 (1966): 283-296 (Yiddish).

488. NEILSON, WILLIAM ALLAN, 1869-1946

President 1917-39, and professor of English, Smith College, Northampton, MA.

Assisted refugee scholars through personal sponsorship of their immigration, appointments to the Smith College faculty, and placement in other colleges and universities. Active with Emergency Rescue Committee and International Rescue and Relief Committee (*International Rescue Committee), Institute of International Education, University in Exile (*New School for Social Research, New York), and *National Refugee Service. With his daughter Caroline, Neilson wrote *We Escaped; Twelve Personal Narratives of the Flight to America*, New York: Macmillan, 1941, which includes autobiographical accounts by seven German-speaking refugees. Neilson's wife chaired the Progressive Schools' Committee for Refugee Children.

Literature. *D.A.B.*, suppl. 4, pp. 624-625.
Margaret Ferrand Thorp, *Neilson of Smith.* New York: Oxford Univ. Press, 1956, pp. 348-349.

Papers. Smith College Archives: papers, ca. 56 ft. Correspondence and subject files include clippings on Jewish scholars and on the *American Committee for the Protection of Foreign Born (one folder each) and materials on World War

II. Additional documentation on Neilson's activities concerning refugees may be identified as a result of the arrangement of these papers in 1978.

489. NIEBUHR, REINHOLD, 1892-1971

Protestant theologian and spokesman for "Christian realism," socialism, and the non-Communist left. Professor of Applied Christianity 1930-55, and of ethics and theology 1955-71, Union Theological Seminary, New York. Opposed the pacifism of U.S. left-liberals prevailing in the 1930s and 1940s, and supported Zionism.

Active in the rescue of persecuted German intellectuals and politicians. Chairman, American Friends of German Freedom, an organization offering material aid to Germans and Austrians opposing Nazism. Supported *American Christian Committee for Refugees and International Relief Association (*International Rescue Committee). After World War II, chairman, Resettlement Campaign for Exiled Professionals, an organization active for the resettlement of refugee professionals and artists in the U.S.A.

Literature. June Bingham, *Courage to Change: An Introduction to the Life and Thought of Reinhold Niebuhr.* New York: Scribner, 1961.

Paul C. Merkley, *Reinhold Niebuhr: A Political Account.* Montreal: McGill-Queen Univ. Press, 1975, especially pp. 155-157.

Papers. Library of Congress, Manuscript Div.: papers, 1913-72, ca. 7000 items, contain materials regarding Germany and refugees, including correspondence with Europeans seeking sponsors for their immigration to the U.S.A., with U.S. clergymen and university teachers who might have served as such sponsors, with colleges and theological seminaries on the placement of refugee scholars, with *U.S. Dept. of State officials, and with American acquaintances who might have provided the necessary funds. *NUCMC* MS 67-622. Finding aid: unpublished inventory.

490. NORMAN, DOROTHY (STECKER), 1905-

Journalist; columnist for *New York Post* in the 1940s. Active in social and political movements.

Literature. *Contemporary Authors*, vols. 25-28, p. 539.

Papers. Columbia Univ., Rare Book and Manuscript Library: papers, 1923-60, 131 boxes (ca. 17,000 items), consist of correspondence and published materials, including items dealing with refugees, refugee organizations, exile governments, and the Free Germany movement. *NUCMC* MS 67-803.

491. PAPANEK, ERNST, 1900-1973

Austrian-born educator and psychologist, immigrated to the U.S.A. in 1940. Professor of education, Queens College, New York 1959-71.

Organizer and general director, Children's Home and School for Refugee Children, Union OSE-Organisation pour la Santé et l'Éducation, France (*American Committee of OSE) 1938-40. Director of Child Projects, *Unitarian Service Committee 1945-57.

Literature. *International Biographical Dictionary*, vol. II.
Ernst Papanek, with Edward Linn, *Out of the Fire.* New York: Morrow, 1975. (About Papanek's experiences with refugee children.)

Papers. New York Public Library, Manuscripts and Archives Div.: papers, 1936-73, 18 ft, include 4 ft of materials regarding Papanek's work with refugee children, including correspondence, interviews, reports, newspaper and magazine articles, writings by Papanek and others, studies of refugee children, and documentation relating to his book *Out of the Fire. NUCMC* MS 76-1534. Finding aid: unpublished inventory (10 pp.).

492. PELL, HERBERT CLAIBORNE ("BIRDIE"), 1884-1961

U.S. Representative from New York 1919-21; U.S. Minister to Portugal 1937-41, and Hungary 1941-42; American representative on U.N. War Crimes Commission 1943-45.
Concerned with refugee problems while serving as Minister to Portugal in Lisbon.

Literature. Michael S. Blayney, "Diplomat and Humanist: The Diplomatic Career of Herbert Claiborne Pell." Unpublished Ph.D. dissertation, Washington State Univ., 1973.
———, "Herbert Pell, War Crimes, and the Jews." *American Jewish Historical Quarterly* 65 (June 1976): 335-352.

Papers. Franklin D. Roosevelt Library: papers, 1912-60, 23 ft, include correspondence concerning refugees, 1940, and material on Germany's treatment of Jews. *NUCMC* MS 65-57.
Washington State Univ. Library, Manuscripts-Archives Div.: papers, 1916-46, ca. 300 items, consist of photocopies of materials in the Roosevelt Library, selected by M. S. Blayney for research on his dissertation. Finding aid: unpublished container list.

493. PERKINS, FRANCES, 1882-1965

U.S. Secretary of Labor 1933-45. Had a positive influence on questions of refugee admission, and favored legislation admitting refugee children. (Until 1940, the *U.S. Dept. of Labor administered the *U.S. Immigration and Naturalization Service.)

Literature. George Martin, *Madam Secretary: Frances Perkins.* Boston: Houghton Mifflin, 1976.
Frances Perkins, *The Roosevelt I Knew.* New York: Viking Press, 1947.

Papers. Columbia Univ., Rare Book and Manuscript Library: papers, 1908-63,

105 boxes (ca. 49,500 items), include office files and correspondence, 1933-45. A part of the correspondence is also on microfilm (22 reels). It has not been determined which parts of the collection concern immigration and refugees. *NUCMC* MS 77-119.

494. PINSON, KOPPEL SHUB, 1904-1961

Russian-born and U.S.-educated professor of history, Queens College, New York. Expert on the history of nationalism, and author of works on German and Jewish history and anti-Semitism. Sympathized with Jewish territorialism (*Freeland League for Jewish Territorial Colonization).

Vice-president 1952-58, president 1958-61, *Conference on Jewish Social Studies (formerly Conference on Jewish Relations) and cofounder and editor of its journal, *Jewish Social Studies* 1938-61. Director of education and culture for Jewish displaced persons in Germany and Austria, United Nations Relief and Rehabilitation Administration (UNRRA) 1945-46. Active in salvaging Jewish books and cultural treasures found in Europe following World War II. Assisted in placing refugee scholars in U.S. colleges and universities.

Literature. *Encyclopaedia Judaica*, vol. 13, col. 551.

Papers. Leo Baeck Institute Archives: papers, 1931-58, ca. 1.5 in. (ca. 100 items), include ca. 30 letters from such refugee correspondents as writer Thomas Mann, economist Emil Lederer, and others concerning questions of emigration, 1933-39.

New York Public Library, Manuscripts and Archives Div.: papers, primarily concerning his teaching at Queens College.

495. PURVIN, JENNIE (FRANKLIN), 1873-1958

Business executive and communal leader, Chicago.

Literature. *Who's Who in World Jewry*, 1955, p. 595.

Papers. American Jewish Archives: papers, 1868-1958, 7 ft, include one folder concerning the immigration from Germany to the U.S.A. of relatives and friends of the Purvin family, 1938-46. *NUCMC* MS 65-1736.

496. RAZOVSKY, CECILIA, 1886-1968

Executive in Jewish and nonsectarian organizations concerned with immigration and refugees. Proponent of advanced social legislation for women and children.

Organizations with which she was connected include: *National Council of Jewish Women—Service to Foreign Born; *European (formerly German) Jewish Children's Aid; *National Coordinating Committee; *National Refugee Service; *United Service for New Americans; *General Committee of Immigrant Aid at Ellis Island; *Selfhelp. Conducted intensive surveys of conditions of Jewish refugees in European ports, in Cuba, Mexico, Canada, Brazil, and Argentina, 1923-1936. In 1939, sent to Cuba by *American Jewish Joint Distribution

Committee in connection with the *S.S. *St. Louis* affair. Resettlement supervisor in postwar European camps for displaced persons.

Literature. *Universal Jewish Encyclopedia*, vol. 9, p. 88.

Papers. American Jewish Historical Society: papers, 1912-68, 6 cartons, include correspondence, reports, documents, and clippings relating to her activities on behalf of refugees from Nazi Germany and other immigrants.

497. REZEK, PHILIPP RAPHAEL, 1894-1963

Vienna-born refugee physician, immigrated to the U.S.A. in 1938. Associated with Jackson Memorial Hospital, Miami, and Univ. of Miami Medical School. Helped to resettle refugees in the U.S.A.

Literature. Dade County Medical Association, *Bulletin* 33 (Oct. 1963): 31.

Papers. Joint University Libraries, Nashville, Special Collections Dept: papers, 1939-41, 54 items, consist of letters to Rezek and members of his family from Jewish refugees asking for his help.

498. RICHARDS, ALFRED NEWTON, 1876-1966

Professor of pharmacology, vice-president for medical affairs, and associate trustee, Univ. of Pennsylvania, Philadelphia. Chairman, Committee on Medical Research, U.S. Office of Scientific Research and Development 1941-46; president, National Academy of Science 1947-50; trustee 1937-41, and informal adviser through the 1930s, *The Rockefeller Foundation.

Explored job opportunities for refugee scientists and enlisted numerous scientists in his placement efforts.

Literature. "Alfred Newton Richards, Scientist and Man." *Annals of Internal Medicine*, vol. 71, no. 5, pt. 2, suppl. 8 (Nov. 1969).

Papers. Univ. of Pennsylvania Archives: papers, 1910-66, ca. 150 ft, include a large number of folders of correspondence relating to Richards' efforts to find positions for immigrant scientists from Germany. One file contains correspondence with and about Otto Meyerhof, immigrant biochemist and Nobel Prize winner, who became a professor at the Univ. of Pennsylvania Medical School. Finding aid: *Survey of Sources* [for the History of Biochemistry and Molecular Biology] *Newsletter*, vol. 1, no. 1 (Nov. 1975): 9-10.

499. ROGERS, EDITH (NOURSE), 1881-1960

U.S. Representative from Lowell, MA 1925-60.

Cosponsor in 1939 with Senator *Robert F. Wagner of New York of the Wagner-Rogers bill for the admission to the U.S.A. of 20,000 German refugee children outside national quotas.

Literature. *Current Biography*, 1942, pp. 698-699.

Papers. Radcliffe College, Schlesinger Library on the History of Women in America: papers, 1881-1961, 19 ft. Except for a photograph of Rogers, Wagner, and Helen Hayes, on the occasion of Hayes' testimony on behalf of the child refugee bill, the papers are reported not to contain material concerning refugees. *NUCMC* MS 74-940. Finding aid: unpublished inventory.

500. ROHRHEIMER, RENA M.

High school teacher, Philadelphia.

Papers. American Jewish Archives: papers, 1936-50, 2 boxes, include correspondence with relatives, friends, and organizations documenting Rohrheimer's efforts, as a private citizen, to rescue a number of refugees from Europe. *NUCMC* MS 67-1023.

501. ROOSEVELT, ELEANOR, 1884-1962

Wife of President *Franklin D. Roosevelt. Diplomat, humanitarian, and author. Defended minority groups against discrimination. Advocated a Jewish state in Palestine and sponsored Youth Aliyah. U.S. representative 1945-52, and delegate 1961, to United Nations General Assembly. Chairwoman, U.N. Commission on Human Rights, until 1953.

Recipient of numerous appeals to help refugees, and of many letters opposing the admission of refugees to the U.S.A. Supported *Good Neighbor Committee on the Émigré and the Community. Honorary president, *United States Committee for the Care of European Children.

Literature. Stella K. Hershan, *A Woman of Quality: Eleanor Roosevelt.* New York: Crown, 1970. Chap. 3, "The Refugees," discusses Mrs. Roosevelt's concern for refugees.

Papers. Franklin D. Roosevelt Library: papers, 1884-1964, 1330 ft, include correspondence with Jewish leaders and a file "Refugee Letters, 1940-1945." *NUCMC* MS 75-557.

502. ROOSEVELT, FRANKLIN DELANO, 1882-1945

U.S. President 1933-45.

Beginning in 1933, the administration of Franklin D. Roosevelt took a variety of not very effective diplomatic and political steps to protest the persecution of Jews in Germany and the plight of political and Jewish refugees, responding to intercessions by Jewish spokesmen and to public opinion trends reflecting American condemnation of Nazi policies. In the early 1940s, a secret study (*"M" [Migration] Project) was undertaken on Roosevelt's initiative to explore settlement policies for homeless refugees around the globe. His endorsement of several plans for Jewish settlement remained without results.

In the U.S.A., Roosevelt eased some of the restrictions imposed upon the issuing of visas to refugees by U.S. consuls in compliance with President

*Herbert Hoover's Executive Order of Sept. 8, 1930. Following the *Kristallnacht* of Nov. 9-10, 1938, restrictions were eased further and refugees were admitted to the U.S.A. to the full extent permitted by the German-Austrian immigration quotas. In 1940, Roosevelt established the *U.S. President's Advisory Committee on Political Refugees, and in 1944, the *U.S. War Refugee Board to facilitate rescue efforts in Europe.

However, Roosevelt's policies toward a liberalization of U.S. immigration laws reflected contradictory (and in part anti-Semitic) trends in U.S. public opinion and in the Roosevelt administration during a period of economic difficulties on a number of major issues touching immigration to the U.S.A., international rescue efforts, British admission policies to Palestine, *U.S. Dept. of State delays in issuing visas, and related matters. Roosevelt has been criticized by historians for his failure to press for more effective policies through which the lives of more Nazi victims might have been saved.

Literature. D.A.B., suppl. 3, pp. 641-667.
Feingold, *Politics of Rescue.*
Saul S. Friedman, *No Haven for the Oppressed: United States Policy Toward Jewish Refugees, 1938-1945.* Detroit: Wayne State Univ. Press, 1973.
Arthur D. Morse, *While Six Million Died: A Chronicle of American Apathy.* New York: Random House, 1967.
Wyman, *Paper Walls.*

Papers. Franklin D. Roosevelt Library: the Roosevelt Papers contain material relating to Jews and Jewish refugees in the Official File (OF), the President's Personal File (PPF), the President's Secretary's File (PSF), and the Map Room (MR).

Much of this material is found among correspondence with leading American Jews, including *Louis D. Brandeis (PPF 2335), *Felix Frankfurter (PPF 140), Rabbi *Stephen S. Wise (PPF 3292), Rabbi *Abba Hillel Silver (PPF 4520), Jesse Straus (PPF 283), *Bernard Baruch (PPF 88), Alexander Sachs (PPF 8792), and *Henry Morgenthau, Jr. (PPF 357).

There is further correspondence with *Myron C. Taylor (OF 3865 and PPF 423) and Raymond Fosdick (PPF 328). 36 files in PPF and one file in OF relate to various Jewish organizations or topics, the most important of which are "Jewish Church Matters" (OF 76-c), "Jewish Matters" (PPF 19), and *National Jewish Welfare Board (PPF 4553).

The PSF contains a file on Palestine, files on correspondence with F. Frankfurter, diplomatic files on Germany, Great Britain, and Poland that include materials on Jews, and a file on refugees.

The MR files contain materials relating to refugees, the establishment of a Jewish state in Palestine, and German atrocities. *NUCMC* MS 75-579 (OF), 75-562 (PPF), 75-581 (PSF), 75-578 (MR). Finding aids: unpublished inventories.

503. ROSENAU, WILLIAM, 1865-1943

German-born Reform rabbi, immigrated to the U.S.A. in 1876. Served Congregation Oheb Shalom, Baltimore 1892-1943. Associate professor of post-Biblical

Hebrew, Johns Hopkins Univ. 1902–32. Active in the Jewish and general communities of Baltimore and in national Jewish affairs.

Literature. *Universal Jewish Encyclopedia*, vol. 9, pp. 204–205.

Papers. American Jewish Archives: papers, 1889–1943, 9 ft, include some correspondence with German-Jewish refugees and with the *Hebrew Sheltering and Immigrant Aid Society (HIAS). *NUCMC* MS 65-1737.

504. ROSENBERG, JAMES NAUMBURG, 1874–1970

Attorney, artist, and philanthropist.

Active with *American Jewish Joint Distribution Committee (JDC) since the 1920s. Founder 1924, and chairman, *American Jewish Joint Agricultural Corp. (Agro-Joint), a JDC subsidiary. Founder and president, *Dominican Republic Settlement Association (DORSA), another JDC subsidiary. Founder 1925, and director, Palestine Economic Corp. (*PEC Israel Economic Corp.), a JDC affiliate.

Literature. Maxwell D. Geismar, ed., *Unfinished Business: James N. Rosenberg Papers.* Mamaroneck, NY: Marasia Press, 1967.
James N. Rosenberg, *Painter's Self-portrait.* New York: Crown, 1958.

Papers. American Jewish Joint Distribution Committee: Rosenberg's papers relating to his JDC, Agro-Joint, and DORSA activities.

505. ROSENMAN, SAMUEL IRVING, 1896–1973

Liberal jurist and attorney. Justice, Supreme Court of the State of New York 1932–43; adviser to Presidents *Franklin D. Roosevelt and *Harry S. Truman. Special Counsel to the President 1943–46; member of executive committee, *American Jewish Committee, in charge of its schools division 1930s. Link between *U.S. Dept. of State and Chaim Weizmann 1943–48, on policies concerning the establishment of a Jewish state in Palestine.

Active on behalf of Jewish Nazi victims during World War II.

Literature. *Current Biography*, 1942, pp. 715–717.
Samuel B. Hand, "Samuel I. Rosenman: His Public Career." Unpublished Ph.D. dissertation, Syracuse Univ., 1961.

Papers. Franklin D. Roosevelt Library: papers, 1928–72, ca. 34 ft, contain files on the *Intergovernmental Committee on Refugees and the *U.S. President's Advisory Committee on Political Refugees, and numerous references to Jews and Jewish refugees in the general correspondence and in reports and memoranda from liberated Europe. *NUCMC* MS 65-64.
Harry S. Truman Library: papers, 1945–66, 4 ft. *NUCMC* MS 65-135.

506. SABATH, ADOLPH JOACHIM, 1866–1952

U.S. Representative from Chicago 1906–52; member, *House Committee on

Immigration and Naturalization; chairman, House Rules Committee 1939-47, 1949-52. Sought the abolition of the House Committee on Un-American Activities, whose activities also affected immigration issues.

Favored a liberalized immigration policy, but supported stringent deportation laws. One of the first members of Congress to support military preparedness against Nazi Germany.

Literature. Burton A. Boxerman, "Adolph Joachim Sabath in Congress." *Journal of the Illinois State Historical Society* 66 (Autumn 1973): 327-340 [concerning 1907-32] and 66 (Winter 1973): 428-443 [concerning 1933-52].
D.A.B., suppl. 5, pp. 597-600.

Papers. American Jewish Archives: papers, 1903-52, 3.3 ft, consist of correspondence, legislative records, and printed material relating to Sabath's congressional career, including documentation on German-Jewish refugees, Nazism, Jewish affairs, and immigration of the 1930s and 1940s. *NUCMC* MS 68-77. Finding aid: unpublished inventory (9 pp.).

The location of Sabath's other papers has not been established.

507. SCHMIDT, SAMUEL MYER, 1883-1967

Editor and Jewish community leader, Cincinnati.

Special representative 1939-40, European director 1945-49, Vaad Hahatzala, *Union of Orthodox Rabbis of the U.S. and Canada (UOR).

Literature. *Who's Who in World Jewry*, 1965, pp. 850-851.

Papers. American Jewish Archives: papers, 1919-45, microfilm (one reel) and 987 items, include documents, correspondence, and reports regarding Schmidt's activities on behalf of UOR to reestablish the religious life of Jews in Europe after World War II. *NUCMC* MS 68-1148.

508. SCHURMAN, JACOB GOULD, 1854-1942

President, Cornell Univ. 1892-1920. U.S. Minister to China 1921-25, Ambassador to Germany 1925-30.

Attempted to secure teaching positions for refugee intellectuals during the Nazi years.

Literature. Sander A. Diamond, *The Nazi Movement in the United States, 1924-1941.* Ithaca: Cornell Univ. Press, 1974, pp. 58-59.
D.A.B., suppl. 3, pp. 696-699.

Papers. Cornell University Libraries, Dept. of Manuscripts and Univ. Archives: papers, 1878-1942, ca. 26 ft. "Clippings from American Newspapers Regarding the Munich Agreement," 1938, include information on Schurman's efforts to assist refugees. His personal papers, 1930-42, 2 boxes, do not contain material concerning refugees of the Nazi era. *NUCMC* MS 66-1042. Finding aid: unpublished guide.

509. SCHWIMMER, ROSIKA, 1877–1948

Hungarian-born feminist, pacifist, world federalist, and writer. Vice-president, *Women's International League for Peace and Freedom. Was denied U.S. citizenship because of her pacifist beliefs.

Actively involved in problems of refugees, including their immigration, naturalization, and citizenship.

Literature. *D.A.B.*, suppl. 4, pp. 724–728.
Universal Jewish Encyclopedia, vol. 9, pp. 439–440.

Papers. New York Public Library, Manuscripts and Archives Div.: papers, 1920s–48, ca. 100 ft. Correspondence files, scrapbooks, and pamphlets contain documentation concerning refugees of the Nazi era. Finding aids: unpublished guides and indexes.

510. SEIDEN, RUDOLF, 1900–1965

Austrian-born Jewish chemist and Austrian Zionist leader, immigrated to the U.S.A. (Kansas City) in 1935.

Proposed that the U.S.A. turn Alaska into a haven for refugee resettlement and corresponded with various government agencies (*U.S. Dept. of the Interior, *U.S. Div. of Territories and Island Possessions) about his proposal, which was rejected.

Literature. *International Biographical Dictionary*, vol. I.

Papers. Leo Baeck Institute Archives: papers, 1919–58, ca. 1 ft, include material relating to Seiden's 1938 plan for resettling refugees in Alaska. Finding aid: *Leo Baeck Institute Library and Archives News*, no. 6 (May 1977): [8].

511. SHAPLEY, HARLOW, 1885–1972

Professor of astronomy, Harvard University, and director, Harvard College Observatory.

Active in numerous organizations aiding refugees during the 1930s and 1940s, including *Emergency Committee in Aid of Displaced Foreign Scholars, Joint Anti-Fascist Refugee Committee, and *American Council for Émigrés in the Professions. In 1939, he organized the National Research Associates to provide funds to maintain senior refugee scholars at Harvard.

Literature. *Current Biography*, 1952, pp. 533–535.
Stephen Duggan and Betty Drury, *The Rescue of Science and Learning*. New York: Macmillan, 1948, pp. 84–85.

Papers. Harvard Univ. Archives: papers, ca. 1902–65, 127 boxes, include 4 boxes concerning Shapley's activities in aid of refugees, such as biographical files on refugee scholars and correspondence with organizations, including *American Christian Committee for Refugees, Boston Committee on Medical Émigrés, University in Exile (*New School for Social Research), and many others. *NUCMC* MS 71-106. Finding aid: unpublished inventory.

512. SILVER, ABBA HILLEL, 1893-1963

Reform rabbi, Cleveland, OH, and American Zionist leader, active on behalf of refugees. President, United Palestine Appeal 1938-43; cochairman, *United Jewish Appeal 1938-44. President, *Zionist Organization of America 1945-46; chairman, American Zionist Emergency Council 1943-44 and 1945-48; chairman, American Section, Jewish Agency for Palestine (*World Zionist Organization) 1946-48; Jewish Agency representative to the United Nations 1947-48.

Author (with Jonah B. Wise) of *The Refugees*, a pamphlet issued in 1939 by the United Jewish Appeal.

Literature. Leon I. Feuer, "Abba Hillel Silver: A Personal Memoir." *American Jewish Archives* 19 (Nov. 1967): 107-126.

Daniel Jeremy Silver et al., eds., *In the Time of Harvest. Essays in Honor of Abba Hillel Silver on the Occasion of His Seventieth Birthday*. New York: Macmillan, 1963.

Papers. The Temple, Cleveland, Abba Hillel Silver Memorial Archives and Library: papers include materials on refugees and German Jewry. Finding aid: catalog of individual names and topics and chronological list.

513. SOLIS-COHEN, SOLOMON DA SILVA, 1857-1948

Physician, author, and Jewish community leader, Philadelphia. Professor of clinical medicine, Jefferson Medical College of Philadelphia 1902-27.

Literature. David de Sola Pool, "Solomon Solis-Cohen." *Publication of the American Jewish Historical Society* 38 (1948): 336-340.

Papers. American Jewish Historical Society: papers, 1927-41, 167 items, include material concerning German-Jewish refugees, especially refugee physicians. *NUCMC* MS 68-176.

514. STEINHARDT, LAURENCE ADOLPH, 1892-1950

Lawyer, economist, and diplomat. U.S. Foreign Service officer: Minister to Sweden 1933-37; Ambassador to Peru 1937-39, USSR 1939-41, Turkey 1942-45, Czechoslovakia 1945-48, and Canada 1948-50. Nephew of Samuel Untermyer (*Non-Sectarian Anti-Nazi League).

Advised strict application of U.S. immigration restrictions to Jewish, Polish, and Russian refugees during his service in Moscow. Active in rescue operations in Turkey in connection with *U.S. War Refugee Board and in association with *Ira Hirschmann during the latter's stay in Turkey, 1944-45.

Literature. *D.A.B.*, suppl. 4, pp. 771-773.

Feingold, *Politics of Rescue*, pp. 285-289.

Ralph R. Stackman, "Laurence A. Steinhardt: New Deal Diplomat, 1933-1945." Unpublished Ph.D. dissertation, Michigan State Univ., 1967.

Papers. Library of Congress, Manuscript Div.: papers, 1929-50, 42 ft (ca. 42,500 items) include material on Steinhardt's activities in Turkey in connection with Hirschmann. *NUCMC* MS 65-932. Finding aid: unpublished inventory.

515. STRAUSS, LEWIS LICHTENSTEIN, 1896-1974

Banker, government official, and associate of President *Herbert Hoover. Assistant Secretary of the Navy during World War II; member 1946-50, chairman 1953-58, U.S. Atomic Energy Commission. President and trustee, *Institute for Advanced Study, Princeton, NJ.

Member of executive board, *American Jewish Committee. Director 1920-51, and president 1930-37, Jewish Agricultural Society (*Baron de Hirsch Fund). Active on behalf of refugees, including service on management council of Coordinating Foundation (founded in 1939 in connection with the attempts of the *Intergovernmental Committee on Refugees to negotiate the orderly emigration of Jews from Germany with German government officials).

Literature. Richard A. Pfau (Dickinson College, Carlisle, PA). Biography in progress.

Lewis L. Strauss, *Men and Decisions.* Garden City, NY: Doubleday, 1962, pp. 103-119. [autobiography]

Papers. Strauss' papers, which are with his son, Lewis H. Strauss, Washington, DC, are being transferred to the following repositories in 1978-79:

American Jewish Historical Society: papers concerning Strauss' Jewish activities including materials on refugees.

Herbert Hoover Presidential Library: papers concerning Strauss' non-Jewish activities.

516. SZOLD, HENRIETTA, 1860-1945

Jewish communal leader, author, and scholar of Baltimore. Founder of *Hadassah and first president 1912-26. Member, Palestine Zionist Executive 1927-31, in charge of health and education. Member, Vaad Leumi (National Council of Palestinian Jewry) 1931-33.

In October 1933, Szold represented the Vaad Leumi at a conference in London on the German-Jewish emergency and traveled to Berlin, Hamburg, Amsterdam, and Paris. The Youth Aliyah movement, in whose founding she played a major role, began early in 1934 to resettle German-Jewish youths in Palestine.

Literature. D.A.B., suppl. 3, pp. 756-758.

Irving Fineman, *Woman of Valor: The Story of Henrietta Szold.* New York: Simon and Schuster, 1961.

Marvin Lowenthal, *Henrietta Szold: Life and Letters.* New York: Viking Press, 1942.

Papers. Central Zionist Archives, Israel: papers, 1887-1945, 9.6 ft. Microfilm of index to papers is at American Jewish Archives.

Baltimore Hebrew College/Jewish Historical Society of Maryland: papers, 1866-1944, of H. Szold and Rabbi Benjamin Szold, her father.

American Jewish Archives: papers, 1866-1945, microfilm (12 reels) of originals at Baltimore Hebrew College, with the Szold family, and elsewhere. *NUCMC* MS 68-104.

Papers relating to H. Szold's Hadassah and Youth Aliyah activities are included in the records of Hadassah at its office.

517. SZOLD, ROBERT, 1889-1977

Attorney; Zionist and Jewish communal leader. Member of executive committee 1926-61, president 1953-57, chairman of board 1943-61, Palestine Economic Corp. (*PEC Israel Economic Corp.); founder-member, American Emergency Committee for Zionist Affairs; member of executive committee, *American Jewish Conference.

Literature. *Encyclopaedia Judaica*, vol. 15, cols. 668-669.
Who's Who in World Jewry, 1965, p. 975.

Papers. Zionist Archives and Library: papers, 15 ft, concern Zionist activities including correspondence with *Louis D. Brandeis; some documents relate to refugees and immigration. Finding aid: unpublished index.

518. TAFT, CHARLES PHELPS II, 1897-

Lawyer and philanthropist of Cincinnati, Ohio. Brother of U.S. Senator *Robert A. Taft.

Member, U.S. President's Committee on War Relief Agencies 1941-42 and its successor, the *U.S. President's War Relief Control Board 1942-46.

Literature. *Current Biography*, 1945, pp. 590-592.
Quarterly Journal of the Library of Congress 32 (July 1975): 188-192.

Papers. Library of Congress, Manuscript Div.: papers, 1824-1972, ca. 160,000 items, include ca. 1.7 ft relating to the War Relief Control Board. Finding aid: unpublished inventory.

519. TAFT, ROBERT ALPHONSO, 1889-1953

U.S. Senator from Ohio 1939-53. Brother of *Charles P. Taft. Opposed U.S. entry into World War II, but supported the war effort following Pearl Harbor. Approved the partition of Palestine and favored United Nations recognition of Israel.

Opposed the *Wagner-*Rogers bill 1939, which provided for the admission to the U.S.A. of 20,000 Jewish refugee children from Central Europe.

Literature. *D.A.B.*, suppl. 5, pp. 673-677.
James T. Patterson, *Mr. Republican: A Biography of Robert A. Taft.* Boston: Houghton Mifflin, 1972.

Papers. Library of Congress, Manuscript Div.: papers, 1914-53, ca. 500,000 items, relate chiefly to Taft's Senate career. Include one folder on the Wagner-Rogers bill. There is a substantial amount of material on refugees and displaced persons in the legislative and subject files; the bulk of this material concerns the postwar period. *NUCMC* MS 70-978. Finding aid: unpublished inventory.

520. TAUSSIG, CHARLES WILLIAM, 1896-1948

Chairman and president, American Molasses Company. One of six members of President *Franklin D. Roosevelt's "brain trust" in the early stages of the New Deal. Expert on Caribbean affairs, serving as the President's personal representative on many matters affecting the area. An economic adviser to the U.S. delegation to U.N. Charter Conference, San Francisco, 1945.

Chairman, National Advisory Committee, *U.S. National Youth Administration (NYA) 1935-43; appointed a committee to advise NYA on refugee youth.

Literature. National Cyclopaedia of American Biography, vol. 36, pp. 78-79.

Papers. Franklin D. Roosevelt Library: papers, 1928-48, 65 ft, include materials on European refugees and their resettlement in the U.S.A. *NUCMC* MS 65-66. Finding aid: unpublished shelf list.

521. TAYLOR, MYRON CHARLES, 1874-1959

Industrialist, lawyer, and diplomat.

Vice-chairman, *Intergovernmental Committee on Refugees (IGCR) 1938-52; chairman, U.S. delegation to *Évian Conference on Refugees 1938; Presidents *Franklin D. Roosevelt's and *Harry S. Truman's personal representative to Pope Pius XII 1939-50.

Following his arrival in Rome in February 1940, Taylor spent several months investigating civilian refugee problems and the possibilities for peace.

Literature. Feingold, *Politics of Rescue.*
National Cyclopaedia of American Biography, vol. 44, pp. 550-551.

Papers. Franklin D. Roosevelt Library: papers, 1933-52, 10 ft, include correspondence about Jewish refugees and files relating to the Évian Conference and the IGCR. *NUCMC* MS 74-319. Finding aid: unpublished inventory.

Harry S. Truman Library: papers, 1938-52, 1 ft, consist of correspondence, reports, and other materials concerning his service as representative to Pope Pius XII and as U.S. Ambassador on Special Missions, including documentation on the European refugee situation 1938-47. The Library of Congress, Manuscript Div., and Cornell Univ. Libraries, Dept. of Manuscripts and Univ. Archives have copies of these papers. *NUCMC* MS 75-603. Finding aid: unpublished inventory.

Library of Congress, Manuscript Div.: papers, 1928-53, 1250 items, consist of correspondence, reports, and other materials concerning his service as representative to Pope Pius XII. *NUCMC* MS 73-910. Finding aid: unpublished inventory.

National Archives and Records Service, Civil Archives Div.: records of the Personal Representative of the President to Pope Pius XII, Myron C. Taylor, 1942-50, 13 ft, are in Record Group 59 (General Records of the *U.S. Dept. of State). The files of the office are arranged by subject and contain copies of telegrams, dispatches, instructions, reports, and semipersonal correspondence. (Some of this material is duplicated in the decimal file of the Dept. of State.) Also a series of telegrams and airgrams received and sent and a confidential correspondence file, which are arranged chronologically, and a miscellaneous subject file and an administrative file, which are arranged by type of document. Finding aids: register of telegrams, card index to instructions, and card indexes to central file materials.

522. TENENBAUM, JOSEPH L., 1887-1961

Physician, author, and Zionist leader. Chairman of executive committee 1929-36, and vice-president 1943-45, *American Jewish Congress; president, American Federation of Polish Jews 1942-47; president, World Federation of Polish Jews 1943-52.

Founder 1933, and chairman 1933-35, Boycott Committee of American Jewish Congress; cochairman (with *B. Charney Vladeck) 1935-41, *Joint Boycott Council of the American Jewish Congress and the *Jewish Labor Committee.

Literature. *Encyclopaedia Judaica*, vol. 15, cols. 1002-1003.

Papers. YIVO Institute for Jewish Research: papers, 1930s-50s, 8 ft, include materials on Tenenbaum's anti-Nazi boycott activities, some of which deal with refugees and rescue work.

New York Public Library, Manuscripts and Archives Div.: records of the Joint Boycott Council, 1933-41, include materials by and about Tenenbaum. *NUCMC* MS 70-1747.

Yad Vashem Archives, Israel: papers, 1927-57, microfilm (2200 frames). Contents and provenance not identified.

523. THOMPSON, DOROTHY, 1893-1961

Author and journalist, wife of author Sinclair Lewis. Directed the Berlin office of the *New York Evening Post* from 1925 to 1934, when she was expelled from Germany. Wrote *"I Saw Hitler!,"* New York: Farrar & Rinehart, 1932, which expressed a then widely current view of Hitler as an insignificant "little man" with no chance to come to power in Germany.

Active in several organizations aiding refugees, especially political and literary émigrés, including *P.E.N. American Center and Emergency Rescue Committee (*International Rescue Committee). Helped numerous refugees to immigrate to the U.S.A. Appeared as a witness in support of the *Wagner-*Rogers bill in 1939. Author of *Refugees: Anarchy or Organization?*, New York: Random House, 1938; coauthor with refugee actor/director Fritz Kortner, *Another Sun*, New York, 1940, a play dealing with the plight of refugees in New York. Entertained numerous distinguished refugees in her home and persuaded many of them to settle near her home in Vermont.

Literature. Marion K. Sanders, *Dorothy Thompson: A Legend in Her Time.* Boston: Houghton Mifflin, 1973.

Papers. Syracuse Univ. Library, Manuscript Div.: papers, 1917-61, 75 ft, include correspondence on Jewish matters and refugees. *NUCMC* MS 69-521. Finding aid: unpublished inventory.

524. TRUMAN, HARRY S., 1884-1972

U.S. Senator from Missouri 1934-45; U.S. Vice-President 1945; U.S. President 1945-53.

Following his assumption of the presidency in 1945, Truman proposed the admission to Palestine by the British Mandate government of 100,000 Jews displaced in Europe as an immediate relief measure, and issued the so-called Truman Directive of December 22, 1945, which made 3900 additional visas under the U.S. quota system available to homeless persons in Germany, Austria, and Italy. The Displaced Persons Act of 1948, initiated by President Truman, provided for the admission of 200,000 (later raised to 400,000) displaced persons to the U.S.A. outside the quota system. Under this legislation, about 63,000 Jewish refugees, including German-Jewish displaced persons, were admitted to the U.S.A. (of a total displaced persons immigration of about 393,000).

Literature. Harry S. Truman, *Memoirs.* Vol. 1, *Year of Decisions,* vol. 2, *Years of Trial and Hope.* Garden City, NY: Doubleday, 1946 and 1955-56.

Papers. Harry S. Truman Library: papers include ca. 1 ft of materials on postwar immigration. *NUCMC* MS 65-145, 77-910.

525. TYKOCINER, JOSEPH TYKOCINSKI, 1877-1969

Professor of electrical engineering, Univ. of Illinois, Urbana. Inventor of sound for motion pictures.

Assisted family and friends to emigrate from Germany and Poland.

Literature. R. A. Kingery et al., *Men and Ideas in Engineering: Twelve Histories from Illinois.* Urbana: Univ. of Illinois Press, 1967, pp. 19-31.

Papers. Univ. of Illinois at Urbana–Champaign, Univ. Archives: papers, 1900-69, 23.4 ft, include correspondence, 1930s–40s, with relatives in Germany and Poland concerning emigration from Europe. *NUCMC* MS 71-1170. Finding aid: unpublished inventory.

526. VAN TIJN-COHN, GERTRUDE F., 1891-

Dutch-born Jewish communal leader, social worker, and journalist, immigrated to the U.S.A. (Portland, OR) after World War II.

Head, emigration dept., Dutch Committee for Refugees from Germany 1930s; secretary of Council, Stichting Joodsche Arbeid (Jewish Labor Foundation), which established and administered the Jewish training farm for refugees Werkdorp Nieuwesluis in Holland 1934-41. Werkdorp cooperated with Reichsvertretung der Juden in Deutschland, *American Jewish Joint Distribution Committee (JDC), Central British Fund for German Jewry, and HICEM (*HIAS-ICA-Emigration Association), Paris.

Interned in Bergen-Belsen during World War II. Worked for JDC in Holland and for United Nations Relief and Rehabilitation Administration (UNRRA), carrying out rescue activities during and after the war.

Literature. *Hebrew Univ. of Jerusalem, Institute of Contemporary Jewry, Oral History Div., written interview with Van Tijn (5 pp.).

Gertrude Van Tijn, "Werkdorp Nieuwesluis." In *Leo Baeck Institute Year Book* XIV (1969), pp. 182-199.

Papers Leo Baeck Institute Archives: papers, 1934-72, 103 items, include materials about vocational training and other aspects of refugee life in Holland, *Shanghai, and Australia. Finding aid: card index.

Some documents from the "archives of Van Tijn" are at Yad Vashem Archives, Israel. Contents and provenance not identified.

527. VEBLEN, OSWALD, 1880-1960

Professor of mathematics and head of School of Mathematical Sciences, *Institute for Advanced Study, Princeton, NJ.

Active in rescue and placement of refugee scholars. Member of general committee, *Emergency Committee in Aid of Displaced Foreign Scholars. Chairman of an informal committee of the American Mathematical Society, created in 1933 to assist the Emergency Committee in finding employment for refugee mathematicians.

Literature. *Dictionary of Scientific Biography*, vol. 13, pp. 599-600.

Charles Weiner, "A New Site for the Seminar: The Refugees and American Physics in the Thirties." In *The Intellectual Migration: Europe and America, 1930-1960*, Donald Fleming and Bernard Bailyn, eds. Cambridge, MA: Harvard Univ. Press, 1969, pp. 190-234, esp. pp. 213-216.

Papers. Library of Congress, Manuscript Div.: papers, 1902-60, 15 ft (ca. 12,500 items), include 5 boxes ("Refugee File") dealing with rescue and placement matters, especially in connection with the Emergency Committee, and correspondence with various refugee scholars. *NUCMC* MS 70-986. Finding aid: unpublished inventory.

528. VILLARD, OSWALD GARRISON, 1872-1949

Liberal reformer, pacifist, and journalist. Owner and editor until 1932 of *The Nation* and cofounder of National Association for the Advancement of Colored People. His books on Germany included *Within Germany*, New York: D. Appleton-Century, 1940, a firsthand account of Nazi Germany.

Treasurer, *American Guild for German Cultural Freedom; chairman, New World Resettlement Fund; supporter of International Relief Association (*International Rescue Committee).

Literature. *D.A.B.*, suppl. 4, pp. 849-852.

Michael Wreszin, *Oswald Garrison Villard: Pacifist at War.* Bloomington: Indiana Univ. Press, 1965.

Papers. Harvard Univ., Houghton Library: papers, 1886-1949, 150 boxes and one vol., include correspondence with Hubertus Prinz zu Loewenstein (a political refugee and founder and general secretary of the American Guild for German Cultural Freedom), with Helmut Hirsch (a refugee scholar), and with various organizations aiding refugees. *NUCMC* MS 70-516. Finding aid: unpublished index by name of correspondent.

529. VLADECK, BARUCH CHARNEY, 1886-1938

Socialist and Jewish communal leader. General manager, *Jewish Daily Forward* 1918-38; chairman, *Jewish Labor Committee 1934-38; national chairman, *American ORT Federation 1932-38.

Cochairman, *Joint Boycott Council of the *American Jewish Congress and Jewish Labor Committee 1935-38.

Literature. *D.A.B.*, suppl. 2, pp. 683-684.

Papers. New York Univ. Libraries, Tamiment Library of American Labor History: papers, 1907-38, 23 boxes, contain correspondence including scattered materials on refugees, immigration, and organizations aiding Jewish refugees. Finding aid: Tamiment Institute Library, *Library Bulletin*, no. 42, Nov. 1964.

American Jewish Archives: microfilm copy (20 reels) of papers at New York Univ.

530. WAGNER, ROBERT FERDINAND, 1877-1953

U.S. Senator from New York 1927-51. New Deal supporter; sponsored labor measures initiating collective bargaining; introduced housing and slum clearance legislation in Wagner-Steagall Act 1937; sponsored Social Security bill 1935. Chairman, American Palestine Committee.

Active supporter of liberalized immigration laws; cosponsor of Wagner-Rogers bill in 1939 for the admission to the U.S.A. of 20,000 German refugee children outside existing national quotas. (Cosponsor in the House of Representatives was *Edith Nourse Rogers.)

Literature. *D.A.B.*, suppl. 5, pp. 717-719.
Feingold, *Politics of Rescue*, passim.
J. Joseph Huthmacher, *Senator Robert F. Wagner and the Rise of Urban Liberalism.* New York: Atheneum, 1968.
Wyman, *Paper Walls*, passim.

Papers. Georgetown Univ. Library, Special Collections Div.: papers, 1927-49, 734 ft, include "Aliens file," 48 ft of correspondence and other material regarding aliens, refugees from Nazi Germany, U.S. immigration policy, and the Wagner-Rogers bill. *NUCMC* MS 61-1283.

531. WALDMAN, MORRIS DAVID, 1879-1963

Jewish organization executive. Executive secretary 1928-42, executive vice-president 1942-45, *American Jewish Committee (AJC).

A central figure in the intensive political, educational, public relations, and communal efforts of the AJC concerning Nazi Germany, international migration, immigration to the U.S.A., and rescue efforts.

Literature. Naomi W. Cohen, *Not Free to Desist: The American Jewish Committee, 1906-1966.* Philadelphia: Jewish Publication Society, 1972.
Morris D. Waldman, *Nor by Power.* New York: International Universities Press, 1953. [autobiography]

Papers. American Jewish Archives: papers, 1912-63, 2.9 ft (ca. 2800 items), consisting of correspondence, minutes, and other materials on the organizations in which Waldman was active, include correspondence on refugees (with *James N. Rosenberg) and on Nazism (with AJC leaders Cyrus Adler and Sol M. Stroock). Finding aid: unpublished inventory (9 pp.).

American Jewish Committee, Archives and Records Center: papers relating to Waldman's activities as executive officer of AJC include significant documentation concerning refugees and related matters.

532. WARBURG, FELIX MORITZ, 1871-1937

Jewish philanthropist and communal leader. Chairman 1914-32, and honorary chairman 1932-37, *American Jewish Joint Distribution Committee (JDC); member of executive committee, *American Jewish Committee 1929-37; president, *Refugee Economic Corp. 1934-37; president, *New York Foundation 1930-37. Initiator of *Emergency Committee in Aid of Displaced Foreign Scholars 1933.

Cochairman, Council for German Jewry, an Anglo-American group established in 1936, which coordinated the collection of considerable funds for the vocational retraining and resettlement of German-Jewish youth.

Literature. D.A.B., suppl. 2, pp. 694-695.
David Farrer, *The Warburgs: The Story of a Family.* New York: Stein & Day, 1975.
Jerome M. Kutnick, "Felix M. Warburg and the American Jewish Community, 1929-1937." Unpublished Ph.D. dissertation, Brandeis Univ., 1978.

Papers. American Jewish Archives: papers, 1910-37, 103 ft. A major archival resource on the immigration of refugees during the 1930s, including materials on the numerous organizations and activities with which Warburg was connected. *NUCMC* MS 65-1743. Finding aid: *Manuscript Catalog of the American Jewish Archives.* Boston: G. K. Hall, 1971. Vol. 4, app. III, Catalog of the Felix M. Warburg Collection.

Harvard Univ., Graduate School of Business Administration, Baker Library, Manuscripts and Archives Dept.: papers, 1912-36, 2 boxes (ca. 1300 items). It is not known whether this collection contains relevant material. *NUCMC* MS 68-1278. Finding aid: unpublished inventory.

533. WARREN, CHARLES, 1868-1954

Legal historian, constitutional lawyer, and Pulitzer Prize winner in history.

Member, *U.S. President's War Relief Control Board 1943-46.

Literature. *New York Times*, Aug. 17, 1954, p. 21.

Papers. Library of Congress, Manuscript Div.: papers, 1874-1954, 6 ft (ca. 6000 items), include ca. 1 ft of material on the War Relief Control Board. *NUCMC* MS 67-635. Finding aid: unpublished inventory.

534. WARREN, GEORGE LEWIS, 1890-

U.S. government official whose special area of expertise was migration and refugees. With *International Migration Service 1928-38; U.S. government expert, *League of Nations Temporary Commission on Assistance to Indigent Aliens, Geneva 1933, 1936, 1938; adviser to U.S. Representative [*Myron C. Taylor] to *Évian Conference on Refugees 1938; technical adviser, U.S. delegation to *Bermuda Conference on Refugees 1943; consultant, U.S. Foreign Economic Administration 1943; executive secretary, *U.S. President's Advisory Committee on Political Refugees 1938-44; Advisor on Refugees and Displaced Persons, *U.S. Dept. of State 1944-68; U.S. representative, General Council and Executive Committee, International Refugee Organization, Geneva 1948-52; U.S. representative, Intergovernmental Committee for European Migration 1953-66.

Literature. *Who's Who in America*, vol. 31 (1960-61), p. 3034.

Papers. Harry S. Truman Library: papers, 1930-72, 10 in., include material on the international problem of refugees, 1930-64, reports on U.S. participation in aid efforts for refugees, and other documentation relating to Warren's involvement in migration affairs.

535. WEIL, BRUNO, 1883-1961

German-Jewish lawyer, author, politician, and community leader, emigrated to Argentina and, in the 1950s, to the U.S.A. (New York). Vice-president, Central-Verein deutscher Staatsbürger jüdischen Glaubens 1926-35, the main Jewish defense and civil rights organization in Germany, founded in 1893. Active in Kartell-Convent der Verbindungen deutscher Studenten jüdischen Glaubens and its U.S. successor, the *American Jewish K C Fraternity.

In 1935 he traveled to North and South America to study the possible immigration of Jewish refugees. Founder and president, *Axis Victims League, an organization calling for reparations for damages inflicted on Jews in Germany by the Nazi regime. Cofounder, *American Association of Former European Jurists.

Literature. *International Biographical Dictionary*, vol. I.

Papers. Leo Baeck Institute Archives: papers, 1892-1964, ca. 12 ft, include materials on the Axis Victims League and on Weil's speeches and lectures on emigration and *Wiedergutmachung* problems. *NUCMC* MS 72-240. Finding aid: unpublished preliminary inventory.

536. WELLES, SUMNER, 1892-1961

U.S. Assistant Secretary of State 1933-37, Under Secretary of State 1937-43. Influential in setting and implementing *U.S. Dept. of State policy concerning refugees.

Literature. Current Biography, 1940, pp. 850-851.
Feingold, *Politics of Rescue.*
Frank W. Graff, "The Strategy of Involvement: A Diplomatic Biography of Sumner Welles 1933-1943." Unpublished Ph.D. dissertation, Univ. of Michigan, 1971.

Papers. Papers, with Welles' son, Benjamin Welles, Washington, DC, are not available to researchers. Eventually, these papers will be deposited in the Franklin D. Roosevelt Library.

537. WIENER, NORBERT, 1894-1964

Professor of mathematical logic, Massachusetts Institute of Technology 1924-60. Originator of cybernetics.
Guggenheim fellow in Europe (Göttingen and Copenhagen) 1926.

Literature. Dictionary of Scientific Biography, vol. 14, pp. 344-347.
Norbert Wiener, *I Am a Mathematician.* Garden City, NY: Doubleday, 1956. (Includes references to Germany and German scholars, among them refugees.)

Papers. Massachusetts Institute of Technology Libraries, Institute Archives: papers, 1899-1964, 21 ft, comprise personal and professional correspondence and manuscripts. Include 100 to 125 letters concerning Wiener's efforts to aid refugee scholars. Finding aid: unpublished chronological listing.

538. WILSON, HUGH ROBERT, 1885-1946

U.S. Foreign Service officer: Minister to Switzerland 1927-37, Assistant Secretary of State 1937, Ambassador to Germany 1937-38 (successor to *William E. Dodd), recalled following the pogroms of Nov. 9-10, 1938 (*Kristallnacht*).

Literature. D.A.B., suppl. 4, pp. 897-899.
Hugh R. Wilson II, ed., *A Career Diplomat, The Third Chapter: The Third Reich.* New York: Vantage Press, 1960.

Papers. Herbert Hoover Presidential Library: papers, 1923-46, 2 ft, include 42 pp. of correspondence dealing with Jews, refugees, and immigration, 1936, 1938, and 1939. *NUCMC* MS 69-749. Finding aid: unpublished inventory.

539. WINANT, JOHN GILBERT, 1889-1947

State Senator and Governor of New Hampshire and international civil servant of the New Deal period. Chairman, U.S. Social Security Board 1935-37; director,

International Labor Office, Geneva 1939–41. U.S. Ambassador to Great Britain 1941–46.

Literature. Bernard Bellush, *He Walked Alone: A Biography of John Gilbert Winant.* The Hague: Mouton, 1968.

D.A.B., suppl. 4, pp. 899–901.

Papers. Franklin D. Roosevelt Library: papers, 1916–47, 110 ft, include materials relating to refugee matters and to the admission of refugee children to the U.S.A. Restricted. *NUCMC* MS 65-81.

540. WISCHNITZER, MARK, 1882-1955

Russian-born Jewish immigrant historian, sociologist, and organization executive. Emigrated to Berlin 1921, France 1938, Dominican Republic 1940, and the U.S.A. (New York) 1941. Author of various publications on Jewish migration, including *To Dwell in Safety: The Story of Jewish Migration Since 1800*, Philadelphia: Jewish Publication Society, 1948, and *Visas to Freedom: The History of HIAS*, Cleveland: World, 1956.

Generalsekretär, Hilfsverein der deutschen Juden, Berlin 1921-38, as successor to *Bernhard Kahn. From 1933 to 1937, the Hilfsverein, under Wischnitzer's management, assisted Jewish emigrants from Germany to countries other than Palestine. Coedited the Hilfsverein's emigration journal, *Korrespondenzblatt über Auswanderungs- und Siedlungswesen*. In 1936, Wischnitzer was sent by the Hilfsverein and other leading Jewish organizations to Southeastern Europe and Africa to investigate possibilities for the immigration of Jews from Germany.

Research associate, European office (Paris) of the *American Jewish Joint Distribution Committee (JDC) 1938-40. Social work and research in Jewish history in Santo Domingo 1940-41, in connection with *Dominican Republic Settlement Association (DORSA), a JDC subsidiary, and in the U.S.A. with the *Council of Jewish Federations and Welfare Funds (CJFWF), New York.

Literature. *International Biographical Dictionary*, vol. I.

Papers. Papers are with his widow, Mrs. Rachel Wischnitzer, New York, NY. Their future disposition has not been determined. Include materials regarding DORSA, refugees, and migration matters.

541. WISE, STEPHEN SAMUEL, 1874-1949

President, *American Jewish Congress 1936-49, Zionist and political leader, personal adviser to President *Franklin D. Roosevelt. Wise was in contact with many individuals and organizations concerned with the persecution and emigration of Jews from Nazi Germany and Axis-occupied Europe.

Member, *U.S. President's Advisory Committee on Political Refugees (PACPR); member of management council, Coordinating Foundation (*Intergovernmental Committee on Refugees). Assisted numerous German-Jewish immigrants in the U.S.A.

Literature. *D.A.B.*, suppl. 4, pp. 903-906.
Carl Hermann Voss, ed., *Stephen S. Wise: Servant of the People; Selected Letters.* Philadelphia: Jewish Publication Society, 1969.
Stephen S. Wise, *Challenging Years: The Autobiography of Stephen S. Wise.* New York: Putnam, 1949.

Papers. American Jewish Historical Society: papers, 1841–1968, 88 ft, include materials on refugees, organizations aiding refugees, immigration schemes and policies, and individual cases, primarily in sections XII (Refugees—boxes 96–98), X (World Affairs), and XI (American Jewish Congress/*World Jewish Congress). Microfilm copies (100 reels) of most of the papers (161 of a total of 187 boxes) are at American Jewish Archives and at Stephen Wise Free Synagogue, New York. *NUCMC* MS 77-50. Finding aid: unpublished guide and card index.

American Jewish Archives: papers, 1893–1969, 2.5 ft (ca. 2000 items), consist of material concerning Wise's participation in Zionist activities and organizations. Finding aid: unpublished inventory (10 pp.).

542. WOODSMALL, RUTH FRANCES, 1883-1963

Author and feminist. General secretary, World's Council of the YWCA (*Young Women's Christian Association), Geneva, Switzerland 1935-48. Chief of Women's Affairs, U.S. High Commission for Germany 1949-52.

Literature. *Current Biography*, 1949, pp. 645-647.

Papers. Smith College Library, Sophia Smith Collection: papers, 1906-63, 72 ft, include materials on refugees, 1935-48, the period of Woodsmall's administrative position with the YWCA in Geneva. *NUCMC* MS 69-507. Finding aid: unpublished inventory.

Four

ORAL HISTORY COLLECTIONS

543. AMERICAN JEWISH COMMITTEE, WILLIAM E. WIENER ORAL HISTORY LIBRARY
165 E. 56 St., New York, NY 10022

Its oral history program records the experiences of American Jews from different backgrounds in the twentieth century. General collections include memoirs by the following Central European Jewish refugees: Otto L. Bettmann, graphic historian; Theodore Bikel, performing artist; Paul F. Lazarsfeld, sociologist; and Theodor Reik, psychoanalyst.

General collections also include memoirs discussing, in part, refugees and immigration, by *Emanuel Celler, U.S. Congressman, on his legislative activities in the area of immigration; Morris Ernst, lawyer, on his experiences with the pre-World War II refugee problem; Adele Ginzberg, Jewish community activist, widow of *Louis Ginzberg, on her efforts on behalf of the *National Refugee Service; Israel Goldstein, rabbi and communal leader, on attempts to help Jews escape the Holocaust and on the allocation of German reparations; Alexander Kipnis, opera singer, on the condition of Jewish life in Nazi Germany and efforts to help German Jews escape; and *Samuel I. Rosenman, government official, on *Franklin D. Roosevelt's attitude toward Jews and Hitler, and on the American Jewish attitude toward events in Germany.

"Remembering Jacob Blaustein: An Oral History Collection" includes memoirs by Nahum Goldmann, William Haber, Saul Kagan, Rolf Pauls, Dean Rusk, and Mark Uveeler, who were associated in various capacities with J. Blaustein, chairman of the executive board 1942-48 and president 1948-53, of the *American Jewish Committee, in the activities of the *Conference on Jewish Material Claims Against Germany.

"A Study in American Pluralism Through Oral Histories of Holocaust Survivors" comprises 250 interviews with survivors and family members. (A "survivor" was anybody who had lived in Nazi-occupied Europe between 1939 and 1945 and who had immigrated to the U.S.A. by the mid-1950s.) This collection includes ca. 25 memoirs of German-Jewish refugees and their families.

Literature. American Jewish Committee, *Midpoint in a Decade, A Progress Report of the William E. Wiener Oral History Library, 1974-75.* New York, 1975.

——, *News from William E. Wiener Oral History Library.* 1977-date.

"U.S. Immigrants Tape-Record Grim Memories of Nazi Holocaust." *The New York Times*, May 11, 1976, p. 25.

Tapes and Transcripts. William E. Wiener Oral History Library: transcripts for interviews. Most memoirs are open to research; some require permission or are closed for a stated period of time. Finding aid: *Catalog of Memoirs of the William E. Wiener Oral History Library.* New York, 1978. (An annotated listing of 600 oral history transcripts.)

544. AMERICAN MUSEUM OF IMMIGRATION
Statue of Liberty National Monument, Liberty Island, New York, NY 10004

The collection of taped interviews with immigrants to the U.S.A. includes nine interviews with immigrants from Germany and Austria of the Nazi period. None of the interviews are transcribed.

545. BOARD OF JEWISH EDUCATION OF GREATER NEW YORK, BROOKDALE EDUCATIONAL RESOURCE CENTER
426 W. 58 St., New York, NY 10019

Collection includes one video-taped oral history with a refugee from Nazi Germany who immigrated to the U.S.A. 1937.

Literature. *Jewish Week* (New York), Jan. 30-Feb. 5, 1977, p. 3.

546. BRANDEIS UNIVERSITY NATIONAL WOMEN'S COMMITTEE, LIVING HISTORY PROJECT
Waltham, MA 02154

The collection of ca. 300 taped interviews with refugees and Holocaust survivors, conducted between 1972 and 1975 across the U.S.A., includes ca. 35 interviews with German and Austrian refugees.

Literature. Leo Shapiro, "Views of Hitler's victims being compiled on tape." *Boston Evening Globe*, Sept. 26, 1972.

Tapes and Transcripts. Brandeis Univ. Library: tapes and transcripts are on deposit. For access, contact the Executive Committee of the Women's Committee.

547. CENTER FOR HOLOCAUST STUDIES
1609 Avenue J, Brooklyn, NY 11230

Collections include 1000 hours of taped interviews with Holocaust survivors and related documentation concerning the Holocaust experience. There are ca. 50 interviews with German-speaking refugees from Nazism. Very few interviews are transcribed.

Literature. Center for Holocaust Studies, *Newsletter.* 1976–date.

548. COLUMBIA UNIVERSITY, ORAL HISTORY RESEARCH OFFICE
Butler Library, New York, NY 10027

The Columbia University Oral History Collection, the foremost of its kind, includes memoirs, discussing, in part, refugees and immigration, by *Samuel Dickstein, U.S. Congressman, on the *U.S. Emergency Refugee Shelter at Fort Ontario; *Benjamin W. Huebsch, publisher, on his friendship with refugee authors Franz Werfel and Stefan Zweig; *Alvin Johnson, educator, on the University in Exile of the *New School for Social Research; *Herbert H. Lehman, politician, on the United Nations Relief and Rehabilitation Administration; Herbert L. May, lawyer and diplomat, on the High Commission for Refugees of the *League of Nations; *Herbert C. Pell, U.S. diplomat, on his service in Portugal and Jewish refugees; George Rublee, lawyer and director 1938–39 of the *Intergovernmental Committee on Refugees, on German refugee relief; and John C. White, diplomat, on Jewish life in Nazi Germany.

There is also a memoir of refugee psychoanalyst Theodor Reik, and a collection of memoirs concerning the *Carnegie Corporation of New York.

Literature. *Annual Reports of the Columbia University Oral History Research Office.* 1948–date.

Tapes and Transcripts. Columbia Univ., Rare Book and Manuscript Library: transcripts for unrestricted interviews. *NUCMC* MS 70-484, 75-467.

The New York Times Oral History Program has issued the unrestricted transcripts in microform. Published by Microfilming Corporation of America, 21 Harristown Rd., Glen Rock, NJ 07452.

Finding aids: Elizabeth B. Mason and Louis M. Starr, eds., *The Oral History Collection of Columbia University/1978–1983.* New York, 1978. *Columbia University Oral History Collection: An Index to the Memoirs in Part I of the Microform Edition.* Glen Rock, NJ, 1978. *The New York Times Oral History Program: Oral History Guide No. 1.* Glen Rock, NJ, 1976. *The New York Times Oral History Program: Oral History Guide No. 2.* Glen Rock, NJ, 1978.

549. HEBREW UNIVERSITY OF JERUSALEM, INSTITUTE OF CONTEMPORARY JEWRY, ORAL HISTORY DIVISION
Sprinzak Bldg., Givat Ram Campus, Jerusalem, Israel

The Contemporary Jewry Oral History Collection of the Hebrew University covers the entire spectrum of contemporary Jewish history. Some of the memoirs consist of written statements, whereas others are based on interviews. Interviews relevant to refugees, immigration, and German-Jewish history are found among, but not limited to, these projects (number of interviews in each project is shown in parentheses):

Part I: Jewish Communities
The Stand of German Jewry in the Face of Nazi Persecution, 1933-35 (16).
Jewish Nationalism and Israel in the Reform Movement in the United States:
  includes interviews with Julian Morgenstern (*Hebrew Union College) and
  with refugee rabbis Max Nussbaum and Jacob Petuchowski.
American Jewry: includes interview with *Robert Szold.
Jewish Life in Latin America: includes interview with Mr. [Alfred (?)]
  Neumeyer, a German refugee who settled in Argentina.
The Jewish Community in China: consists of interviews conducted by David H.
  Kranzler with refugees who had fled to *Shanghai, China, prior to settling
  in the U.S.A.
The Jewish Community of Brazil: includes interview with Rabbi Dr. Henrique
  Lemle, a German refugee.

Part II: World War II, The Holocaust, Resistance and Rescue
The Joint (*American Jewish Joint Distribution Committee) (26): includes
  interviews with *James N. Rosenberg and *Gertrude Van Tijn.
The Rescue of Jews via Spain and Portugal During World War II (49): includes
  interview with *Elizabeth Dexter.
The Jewish Underground Movement in Wartime France (17).
Jews in the Underground in Belgium 1940-44 (50).
Hiding Children in Belgium During World War II (4).
The Rescue of Children and Youth from Germany, Czechoslovakia, and Austria
  to (or Through) the Countries of Western Europe 1933-40 (35).

Part III: The History of the Yishuv (Jews in Palestine and the State of Israel)
Restitution from Germany (The History of the *Conference on Jewish Material
  Claims Against Germany) (8).

Tapes and Transcripts. Hebrew Univ., Oral History Div.: transcripts for unre-
stricted interviews.
  The New York Times Oral History Program has issued the unrestricted tran-
scripts in microform. Published by Microfilming Corporation of America, 21
Harristown Rd., Glen Rock, NJ 07452.
  Finding aids: Hebrew Univ. of Jerusalem, Institute of Contemporary Jewry,
Oral History Division, Catalogue No. 3, Jerusalem, 1970; and *Oral History
Division, Catalogue No. 4*, Jerusalem, 1975. *The New York Times Oral History
Program: Oral History Guide No. 1.* Glen Rock, NJ, 1976. *The New York Times
Oral History Program: Oral History Guide No. 2.* Glen Rock, NJ, 1978.

**550. RESEARCH FOUNDATION FOR JEWISH IMMIGRATION,
  ORAL HISTORY COLLECTION**
  570 Seventh Ave., New York, NY 10018

The Oral History Collection of the *Research Foundation for Jewish Immigration consists of taped interviews with about 250 Jewish immigrants from Central
Europe of the Nazi period, primarily community leaders in the U.S.A. residing
in Boston, Chicago, Cincinnati, Cleveland, Los Angeles, New York, northern
New Jersey, Philadelphia, Pittsburgh, and San Francisco. Various age and income
levels and occupations are represented in the collection.

The purpose of the interviews is to document the social, economic, and intellectual processes involved in the immigration, resettlement, and acculturation of immigrants from Central Europe of the Nazi period, and the development of the various organizations and institutions established by the immigrant community. Interviews, which have been conducted since 1972, are continuing.

Tapes and Transcripts. Under the transcription program of the Research Foundation, 35 interviews have been transcribed (1978). Completion of transcription is expected in 1979–80. A guide to the interviews and several card indexes are at the Foundation's office. Summary descriptions of the interviews are being published by the Foundation in 1979 as Volume III of *Jewish Immigrants of the Nazi Period in the U.S.A.: Guide to the Oral History Collection of the Research Foundation for Jewish Immigration*, Joan C. Lessing, comp. Interviews bearing on entries in this volume, *Archival Resources*, are identified under the literature section of the entry as "Lessing, *Oral History.*" Access to the collection is by permission of the Foundation.

551. STATE HISTORICAL SOCIETY OF WISCONSIN, WISCONSIN JEWISH ARCHIVES
Madison, WI 53706

Collections include a transcribed interview, ca. 1956, with Rabbi Manfred Swarsensky, formerly of Berlin, who immigrated to the U.S.A. 1939 and occupied a pulpit in Madison, WI. There is no tape recording for this interview. Finding aid: Lindsay B. Nauen, ed., *Guide to the Wisconsin Jewish Archives at The State Historical Society of Wisconsin.* Madison, 1974, p. 20.

552. UNION COLLEGE
c/o Professor Stephen M. Berk, Dept. of History, Schenectady, NY 12308

"Oral History of American Jews Born in Europe Prior to 1914," a project in Schenectady, NY, documents the lives of Jews in Europe before World War I and between the wars. The collection of several dozen taped interviews includes four with individuals who left Nazi Germany and four with persons who fled Austria.

Tapes and Transcripts. Union College, Schaffer Library: transcripts for some interviews, and tapes, are on deposit in a closed collection. *NUCMC* MS 77-1954.

LIST OF REPOSITORIES AND ARCHIVAL HOLDINGS

- American Council for Émigrés in the Professions, Medical Division
  345 E. 46 St., New York, NY 10017
  - 62 Emergency Committee in Aid of Displaced Foreign Medical Scientists
  - 99 National Committee for the Resettlement of Foreign Physicians

- American Federation of Jews from Central Europe
  570 Seventh Ave., New York, NY 10018
  - 59 Council of Jews from Germany
  - 183 Jewish Council of 1933, San Francisco
  - 84 Jewish Philanthropic Fund of 1933
  - 136 United Restitution Organization

- American Institute of Physics, Center for the History of Physics, Niels Bohr Library
  335 E. 45 St., New York, NY 10017
  - 54 Committee for the Study of Recent Immigration from Europe
  - 431 Goudsmit, Samuel Abraham

- American Jewish Archives of the Hebrew Union College-Jewish Institute of Religion
  3101 Clifton Ave., Cincinnati, OH 45220
  - 394 Brandeis, Louis Dembitz
  - 397 Brown, David Abraham
  - 50 Central Conference of American Rabbis
  - 286 Congregation Habonim, New York
  - 406 Cronbach, Abraham
  - 410 Dickstein, Samuel
  - 424 Frankfurter, Felix
  - 425 Friedenwald, Harry F.
  - 429 Glick, David
  - 434 Greenstein, Harry
  - 73 Hebrew Union College-Jewish Institute of Religion
  - 356 HIAS and Council Migration Service of Philadelphia
  - 188 Jewish Family and Children's Service of Colorado

339   Jewish Family Service, Cincinnati
86   Jewish War Veterans of the United States of America
453   Kallen, Horace Meyer
90   Labor Zionist Alliance
379   Manitowoc Coordinating Committee
97   Menorah Association
73   Morgenstern, Julian
340   National Council of Jewish Women, Cincinnati Section
109   Non-Sectarian Anti-Nazi League to Champion Human Rights
495   Purvin, Jennie (Franklin)
500   Rohrheimer, Rena M.
503   Rosenau, William
506   Sabath, Adolph Joachim
507   Schmidt, Samuel Myer
154   U.S. Office of Education
529   Vladeck, Baruch Charney
531   Waldman, Morris David
532   Warburg, Felix Moritz
541   Wise, Stephen Samuel
164   World Union for Progressive Judaism

- American Jewish Committee, Archives and Records Center
  165 E. 56 St., New York, NY 10022
  531   Waldman, Morris David

- American Jewish Historical Society
  2 Thornton Rd., Waltham, MA 02154
  23   American Jewish Conference
  24   American Jewish Congress
  39   Baron de Hirsch Fund
  58   Council of Jewish Federations and Welfare Funds
  60   Delaware Valley College of Science and Agriculture
  409   Diamond, David
  228   Hebrew Immigrant Aid Society, Boston
  229   Immigrants Mutual Aid Society, Boston
  312   Jewish Child Care Association of New York
  188   Jewish Family and Children's Service of Colorado
  86   Jewish War Veterans of the United States of America
  455   Katz, Label Abraham
  460   Kohler, Max James
  462   Kohs, Samuel Calmin
  474   Lowenthal, Marvin
  104   National Jewish Welfare Board
  105   National Refugee Service
  115   Phi Epsilon Pi Fraternity
  496   Razovsky, Cecilia
  513   Solis-Cohen, Solomon da Silva
  515   Strauss, Lewis Lichtenstein
  128   Synagogue Council of America
  137   United Service for New Americans
  151   U.S. Emergency Refugee Shelter at Fort Ontario, Oswego, NY
  541   Wise, Stephen Samuel

• American Jewish Joint Distribution Committee
60 E. 42 St., New York, NY 10017
117   Refugee Economic Corp.
504   Rosenberg, James Naumburg

• American Jewish Periodicals Center
3101 Clifton Ave., Cincinnati, OH 45220
229   Immigrants Mutual Aid Society, Boston

• American Philosophical Society Library
105 S. Fifth St., Philadelphia, PA 19106
386   Bergmann, Max
392   Boas, Franz
414   Dunn, Leslie Clarence
423   Flexner, Simon

• Archives and Historical Collections of the Episcopal Church
P.O. Box 2247, Austin, TX 78767
65   Episcopal Committee for European Refugees

• Archives and Museum of the Jewish Labor Movement
Beit Lessin, 34 Weizmann St., Tel Aviv, Israel
90   Labor Zionist Alliance

• Balch Institute for Ethnic Studies
18 S. Seventh St., Philadelphia, PA 19106
18   American Friends Service Committee
392   Boas, Franz

• Baltimore Hebrew College/Jewish Historical Society of Maryland
5800 Park Heights Ave., Baltimore, MD 21215
425   Friedenwald, Harry F.
434   Greenstein, Harry
454   Kanner, Leo
516   Szold, Henrietta

• Boston Public Library
Boston, MA 02117
74   Immigration Restriction League

• Brandeis University Library
Waltham, MA 02154
6   American Civil Liberties Union
394   Brandeis, Louis Dembitz
546   Brandeis University National Women's Committee, Living History Project

• Brick Presbyterian Church
62 E. 92 St., New York, NY 10028
303   Friendship House for Refugees, New York

• Brown University Library, University Archives
Providence, RI 02912
408   Dexter, Robert Cloutman, and Dexter, Elizabeth Williams (Anthony)

- Bryn Mawr College Archives
  Bryn Mawr, PA 19010
  464   Kraus, Hertha

- Bund Archives of the Jewish Labor Movement
  25 E. 78 St., New York, NY 10021
  82   Jewish Labor Committee

- Center for Migration Studies of New York
  209 Flagg Pl., Staten Island, NY 10304
  138   U.S. Catholic Conference, Division of Migration and Refugee Services

- Central Archives for the History of the Jewish People
  P.O.B. 1149, Jerusalem, Israel
  55   Conference on Jewish Material Claims Against Germany
  85   Jewish Restitution Successor Organization
   9   World Union OSE

- Central Zionist Archives
  1 Ibn Gabirol St., Jerusalem, Israel
  394   Brandeis, Louis Dembitz
  424   Frankfurter, Felix
  425   Friedenwald, Harry F.
  516   Szold, Henrietta
  165   World Zionist Organization—American Section

- Chicago Historical Society, Manuscript Division
  Clark St. and North Ave., Chicago, IL 60614
  211   National Council of Jewish Women, Chicago Section
  215   United Charities of Chicago

- City College Library, Dept. of Archives and Special Collections
  New York, NY 10031
  398   Brunswick, Mark

- Columbia University Library
  New York, NY 10027
  392   Boas, Franz

- Columbia University, Rare Book and Manuscript Library
  New York, NY 10027
  399   Butler, Nicholas Murray
   49   Carnegie Endowment for International Peace
  548   Columbia University, Oral History Research Office
  426   Fry, Varian M.
  440   Hayes, Carlton Joseph Huntley
  457   Keppel, Frederick Paul
  479   Marriner, J. Theodore
  109   Non-Sectarian Anti-Nazi League to Champion Human Rights
  490   Norman, Dorothy (Stecker)
  493   Perkins, Frances
  151   U.S. Emergency Refugee Shelter at Fort Ontario, Oswego, NY

- Columbia University, School of International Affairs, Herbert H. Lehman Papers
  420 W. 118 St., New York, NY 10027

383   Baerwald, Paul
469   Lehman, Herbert Henry
476   McDonald, James Grover
109   Non-Sectarian Anti-Nazi League to Champion Human Rights

- Congregation Beth Ahabah Archives
  1111 W. Franklin St., Richmond, VA 23220
  373   New American Jewish Club, Richmond

- Cornell University Libraries, Dept. of Manuscripts and University Archives
  Ithaca, NY 14853
  385   Becker, Carl Lotus
    57   Cornell University, German Dept.
    63   Emergency Committee in Aid of Displaced Foreign Scholars
  508   Schurman, Jacob Gould
  521   Taylor, Myron Charles

- Cornell University, School of Industrial and Labor Relations Library
  Ithaca, NY 14853
  143   U.S. Committee on Fair Employment Practice

- Delaware Division of Historical and Cultural Affairs
  Hall of Records, Dover, DE 19901
  194   State of Delaware, Service for Foreign Born

- Deutsche Bibliothek
  Frankfurt am Main, Federal Republic of Germany
    19   American Guild for German Cultural Freedom
    80   International Rescue Committee

- Earlham College Archives
  Richmond, IN 47374
  485   Morris, Homer Lawrence

- Franklin D. Roosevelt Library
  Hyde Park, NY 12538
  387   Berle, Adolf Augustus, Jr.
  415   Ezekiel, Mordecai
  418   Field, Henry
  445   Hopkins, Harry Lloyd
  458   Kilgore, Harley Martin
  475   Lubin, Isador
    95   "M" [Migration] Project
  483   Moore, R(obert) Walton
  484   Morgenthau, Henry, Jr.
  492   Pell, Herbert Claiborne
  501   Roosevelt, Eleanor
  502   Roosevelt, Franklin Delano
  505   Rosenman, Samuel Irving
  520   Taussig, Charles William
  521   Taylor, Myron Charles
  539   Winant, John Gilbert
  159   U.S. War Refugee Board

- Genealogical Society of Utah
  50 E. North Temple St., Salt Lake City, UT 84150
  114 Passenger lists: Hamburg departures

- Georgetown University Library, Special Collections Division
  Washington, DC 20057
  530 Wagner, Robert Ferdinand

- Harry S. Truman Library
  Independence, MO 64050
  427 Gibson, John W.
   95 "M" [Migration] Project
  505 Rosenman, Samuel Irving
  521 Taylor, Myron Charles
  524 Truman, Harry S.
  534 Warren, George Lewis

- Harvard University Archives
  Cambridge, MA 02138
   77 Harvard Committee to Aid German Student Refugees
  511 Shapley, Harlow

- Harvard University, Divinity School, Andover-Harvard Theological Library
  Cambridge, MA 02138
  131 Unitarian–Universalist Service Committee

- Harvard University, Graduate School of Business Administration, Baker Library,
  Manuscripts and Archives Dept.
  Boston, MA 02163
  106 Aldrich, Winthrop W.
  532 Warburg, Felix Moritz

- Harvard University, Houghton Library
  Cambridge, MA 02138
   74 Immigration Restriction League
   93 "Life in Germany" Contest
  482 Moffat, Jay Pierrepont
  528 Villard, Oswald Garrison

- Harvard University, Law School Library, Manuscript Division
  Cambridge, MA 02138
  439 Hart, Henry Melvin, Jr.

- Haverford College Library, Quaker Collection
  Haverford, PA 19041
  478 MacMaster, Gilbert

- Hebrew Union College–Jewish Institute of Religion, Klau Library
  3101 Clifton Ave., Cincinnati, OH 45220
  337 Congregation New Hope (Tikvoh Chadoshoh), Cincinnati

- Herbert Hoover Presidential Library
  West Branch, IA 52358
  444 Hoover, Herbert

515   Strauss, Lewis Lichtenstein
538   Wilson, Hugh Robert

• HIAS
200 Park Ave. S., New York, NY 10003
321   National Council of Jewish Women, New York Section

• Historical Society of Pennsylvania, Manuscript Dept.
1300 Locust St., Philadelphia, PA 19107

433   Greenfield, Albert Monroe

• Institute for Mediterranean Affairs
1078 Madison Ave., New York, NY 10028
64   Emergency Committee to Save the Jewish People of Europe

• International Synagogue Museum at JFK International Airport
Jamaica, NY 11430
315   Jewish Veterans Association, New York

• Jabotinsky Institute
38 King George St., P.O.B. 23110, Tel Aviv, Israel
64   Emergency Committee to Save the Jewish People of Europe

• Jewish Historical Society of Oregon
6651 S.W. Capitol Highway, Portland, OR 97219
350   Oregon Émigré Committee

• Jewish Theological Seminary of America, Archives
3080 Broadway, New York, NY 10027
428   Ginzberg, Louis
480   Marx, Alexander

• Johns Hopkins University Archives
Baltimore, MD 21218
393   Walter Hines Page School of International Relations

• Johns Hopkins University Library, Dept. of Special Collections
Baltimore, MD 21218
393   Bowman, Isaiah

• Joint University Libraries, Special Collections Dept.
Nashville, TN 37203
497   Rezek, Philipp Raphael

• Leo Baeck Institute Archives
129 E. 73 St., New York, NY 10021
14   American Danzig Association
17   American Federation of Jews from Central Europe
395   Breslauer, Walter
417   Feuchtwanger, Ludwig
429   Glick, David
432   Graetz, William
435   Grossmann, Kurt Richard
436   Gruenewald, Max

437   Gumbel, Emil Julius
315   Jewish Veterans Association, New York
452   Kahn, Bernhard
166   *Konzentrationslager Frankreich* collection
467   Landauer, Carl
468   Landauer, Georg
476   McDonald, James Grover
494   Pinson, Koppel Shub
510   Seiden, Rudolf
526   Van Tijn-Cohn, Gertrude F.
535   Weil, Bruno

• Leo Baeck Institute Library
  129 E. 73 St., New York, NY 10021
  281   Congregation Beth Hillel of Washington Heights, New York
  286   Congregation Habonim, New York
   87   *The Jewish Way*

• Library of Congress
  Washington, DC 20540
   95   "M" [Migration] Project

• Library of Congress, Manuscript Division
  Washington, DC 20540
   35   American Psychological Association
  400   Celler, Emanuel
  407   Davies, Joseph Edward
  412   Dodd, William Edward
  421   Flexner, Abraham
  424   Frankfurter, Felix
  446   Huebsch, Benjamin W.
  447   Hull, Cordell
  449   Ickes, Harold Leclaire
  450   Jelliffe, Smith Ely
  473   Long, Breckinridge
  101   National Council of Jewish Women
  489   Niebuhr, Reinhold
  514   Steinhardt, Laurence Adolph
  518   Taft, Charles Phelps II
  519   Taft, Robert Alphonso
  521   Taylor, Myron Charles
  527   Veblen, Oswald
  533   Warren, Charles

• Louisiana State University Library, Dept. of Archives and Manuscripts
  Baton Rouge, LA 70803
  413   Douglas, Judith Hyams

• Maryland Historical Society
  201 W. Monument St., Baltimore, MD 21201
  443   Hollander, Sidney

• Massachusetts Institute of Technology Libraries, Institute Archives
  Cambridge, MA 02139
  537   Wiener, Norbert

- Milton Academy Library
  Milton, MA 02186
  419   Field, William Luck Webster

- Minnesota Historical Society, Division of Archives and Manuscripts
  690 Cedar St., St. Paul, MN 55101
  396   Brin, Fanny (Fligelman)
  243   Jewish Family and Children's Service of Minneapolis
  244   National Council of Jewish Women, Minneapolis Section

- Missouri Historical Society
  Jefferson Memorial Bldg., St. Louis, MO 63112
  404   Cook, Fannie (Frank)

- National Archives and Records Service, Audiovisual Archives Division
  Washington, DC 20408
  148   U.S. Department of the Interior
  154   U.S. Office of Education

- National Archives and Records Service, Civil Archives Division
  Washington, DC 20408
  141   U.S. Bureau of Foreign and Domestic Commerce
  142   U.S. Children's Bureau
  143   U.S. Committee on Fair Employment Practice
  144   U.S. Congress: House of Representatives and Senate
  145   U.S. Department of Justice
  146   U.S. Department of Labor
  147   U.S. Department of State
  148   U.S. Department of the Interior
  149   U.S. Displaced Persons Commission
  150   U.S. Division of Territories and Island Possessions
  151   U.S. Emergency Refugee Shelter at Fort Ontario, Oswego, NY
  152   U.S. Immigration and Naturalization Service
  153   U.S. National Youth Administration
  154   U.S. Office of Education
  157   U.S. Public Health Service
  159   U.S. War Refugee Board
  160   U.S. War Relocation Authority
  161   U.S. Work Projects Administration
  521   Personal Representative of the President to Pope Pius XII, Myron Charles
        Taylor

- National Archives and Records Service, Federal Records Center
  Bayonne, NJ 07002
  149   U.S. Displaced Persons Commission

- National Archives and Records Service, Military Archives Division
  Washington, DC 20408
  158   U.S. War Department

- National Archives and Records Service, Washington National Records Center
  Washington, DC 20409
  31   American National Red Cross
  142   U.S. Children's Bureau

    150   U.S. Division of Territories and Island Possessions
    156   U.S. President's War Relief Control Board

- National Carl Schurz Association
  339 Walnut St., Philadelphia, PA 19106
      110   The Oberlaender Trust

- New School for Social Research Library
  65 Fifth Ave., New York, NY 10003
      392   Boas, Franz

- New York Academy of Medicine Library
  2 E. 103 St., New York, NY 10029
      333   Virchow–Pirquet Society, New York

- New York Public Library, General Research and Humanities Division
  Fifth Ave. and 42 St., New York, NY 10018
        6   American Civil Liberties Union
      95   "M" [Migration] Project
     143   U.S. Committee on Fair Employment Practice

- New York Public Library, Jewish Division
  Fifth Ave. and 42 St., New York, NY 10018
     286   Congregation Habonim, New York
     315   Jewish Veterans Association, New York
      87   *The Jewish Way*
     267   *Jüdisches Familienblatt*, New York
     296   *Jüdisches Gemeindeblatt*, New York

- New York Public Library, Manuscripts and Archives Division
  521 W. 43 St., New York, NY 10036
       7   American Committee for the Guidance of Professional Personnel
     390   Bloom, Sol
      63   Emergency Committee in Aid of Displaced Foreign Scholars
      89   Joint Boycott Council of the American Jewish Congress and Jewish Labor Committee
     470   Levene, Phoebus Aaron Theodor
     486   Morse, Arthur David
     112   Palestine Economic Corp.
     491   Papanek, Ernst
     494   Pinson, Koppel Shub
     509   Schwimmer, Rosika

- New York University Libraries, Tamiment Library of American Labor History
  New York, NY 10003
     529   Vladeck, Baruch Charney

- North Carolina Department of Cultural Resources, Division of Archives and History
  Raleigh, NC 27611
      41   Black Mountain College

- Ohio Historical Society
  Interstate 71 and 17th Ave., Columbus, OH 43211

347 Jewish Family Service, Columbus
348 National Council of Jewish Women, Columbus Section

● Philadelphia Jewish Archives Center
625 Walnut St., Philadelphia, PA 19106
351 Association for Jewish Children of Philadelphia
356 HIAS and Council Migration Service of Philadelphia
357 Jewish Family Service of Philadelphia

● Presbyterian Historical Society
425 Lombard St., Philadelphia, PA 19147
5 Church World Service
102 National Council of the Churches of Christ in the U.S.A.
135 United Presbyterian Church in the U.S.A.

● Princeton University, Manuscript Library
Princeton, NJ 08540
6 American Civil Liberties Union
384 Baruch, Bernard Mannes
422 Flexner, Bernard

● Queens College Library
Flushing, NY 11367
143 U.S. Committee on Fair Employment Practice

● Radcliffe College, Schlesinger Library on the History of Women in America
Cambridge, MA 02138
499 Rogers, Edith (Nourse)

● Research Foundation for Jewish Immigration
570 Seventh Ave., New York, NY 10018
34 American Psychoanalytic Association, Emergency Committee on Relief and Immigration
277 Conference of Jewish Immigrant Congregations, New York
77 Intercollegiate Committee to Aid Student Refugees
463 Kolb, Leon
465 Kubie, Lawrence Schlesinger
467 Landauer, Carl
245 New World Club of Minneapolis
550 Research Foundation for Jewish Immigration, Oral History Collection

● Rhode Island College Library, Special Collections Dept.
Providence, RI 02908
364 International Institute of Providence

● Rockefeller Archive Center
Hillcrest, Pocantico Hills, N. Tarrytown, NY 10591
423 Flexner, Simon
120 The Rockefeller Foundation

● Rockefeller University Archives
1230 York Ave., New York, NY 10021
403 Cohn, Alfred Einstein

- Rocky Mountain Jewish Historical Society
  Center for Judaic Studies, University of Denver, Denver, CO 80208
  189   National Council of Jewish Women, Denver Section

- Roper Public Opinion Research Center
  Williams College, Williamstown, MA 01267
  116   Public Opinion Polls

- Smith College Archives
  Northampton, MA 01060
  488   Neilson, William Allan

- Smith College Library, Sophia Smith Collection
  Northampton, MA 01060
  542   Woodsmall, Ruth Frances
  167   Young Women's Christian Association

- Spertus College of Judaica, Asher Library
  618 S. Michigan Ave., Chicago, IL 60605
  206   Congregation Ezra Habonim, Chicago
  213   Temple B'nai Yehuda, Chicago

- Stanford University, Hoover Institution on War, Revolution, and Peace
  Stanford, CA 94305
  435   Grossmann, Kurt Richard
  136   United Restitution Organization

- State Historical Society of Wisconsin
  816 State St., Madison, WI 53706
  6   American Civil Liberties Union
  389   Blaine, Anita (McCormick)
  472   Lochner, Louis Paul
  378   Madison Citizens' Committee for Displaced Persons
  377   Wisconsin Jewish Military Service Records

- State University of New York at Albany, Dept. of Germanic Languages and Literatures
  Albany, NY 12222
  80   International Rescue Committee

- Stephen Wise Free Synagogue
  30 W. 68 St., New York, NY 10023
  541   Wise, Stephen Samuel

- Swarthmore College, Friends Historical Library
  Swarthmore, PA 19081
  382   Aydelotte, Frank

- Swarthmore College Peace Collection
  Swarthmore, PA 19081
  162   Women's International League for Peace and Freedom

- Syracuse University Library, Manuscript Division
  Syracuse, NY 13210
  - 405   Corsi, Edward
  - 523   Thompson, Dorothy

- The Temple, Abba Hillel Silver Memorial Archives and Library
  University Circle at Silver Park, Cleveland, OH 44106
  - 512   Silver, Abba Hillel

- Temple University, Urban Archives Center
  Philadelphia, PA 19122
  - 358   Legal Aid Society of Philadelphia
  - 359   Nationalities Service Center, Philadelphia

- Union College, Schaffer Library
  Schenectady, NY 12308
  - 552   Union College, Oral History Collection

- United Nations Library
  Palais des Nations, Geneva, Switzerland
  - 91   League of Nations High Commission for Refugees

- University of Akron, Archives of the History of American Psychology
  Akron, OH 44325
  - 35   American Psychological Association

- University of California at Berkeley, Bancroft Library
  Berkeley, CA 94720
  - 169   State of California, Division of Immigration and Housing

- University of Chicago Library, Dept. of Special Collections
  Chicago, IL 60637
  - 416   Fermi, Laura (Capon)
  - 437   Gumbel, Emil Julius
  - 448   Hutchins, Robert Maynard

- University of Delaware Library, Special Collections Dept.
  Newark, DE 19711
  - 481   Messersmith, George Strausser

- University of Illinois, Chicago Circle Library, Dept. of Special Collections
  Chicago, IL 60680
  - 76   Institute of Design (New Bauhaus)
  - 461   Kohn, Esther (Loeb)
  - 214   Travelers Aid Society of Metropolitan Chicago–Immigrants' Service League

- University of Illinois at Urbana–Champaign, University Archives
  Urbana, IL 61801
  - 30   American Library Association
  - 456   Kaufman, Stanley L.
  - 525   Tykociner, Joseph Tykocinski

- University of Iowa Libraries, Manuscripts Dept.
  Iowa City, IA 52242
  - 382   Aydelotte, Frank

- University of Louisville, Law Library
  Louisville, KY 40208
  394   Brandeis, Louis Dembitz

- University of Michigan Library, Labadie Collection
  Ann Arbor, MI 48104
  8   American Committee for the Protection of Foreign Born

- University of Minnesota, Immigration History Research Center
  826 Berry St., St. Paul, MN 55114
  10   American Council for Émigrés in the Professions
  12   American Council for Nationalities Service
  220   Baltimore Young Women's Christian Association
  53   Citizens' Committee on Displaced Persons
  230   International Institute of Boston
  247   International Institute of Metropolitan St. Louis
  242   International Institute of Minnesota
  309   International Institute of New York City
  79   International Institutes
  99   National Committee for the Resettlement of Foreign Physicians

- University of Minnesota Libraries, Social Welfare History Archives Center
  Minneapolis, MN 55455
  20   American Immigration and Citizenship Conference
  103   National Federation of Settlements and Neighborhood Centers
  127   Survey Associates
  129   Travelers Aid–International Social Service of America
  332   United Neighborhood Houses of New York

- University of Oklahoma Library, Western History Collections
  Norman, OK 73069
  45   *Books Abroad*

- University of Pennsylvania Archives
  North Arcade, Franklin Field, Philadelphia, PA 19174
  498   Richards, Alfred Newton

- University of Pittsburgh Libraries, Archives of Industrial Society
  Pittsburgh, PA 15260
  360   American Service Institute of Allegheny County
  361   Friendship Club of Pittsburgh
  363   National Council of Jewish Women, Pittsburgh Section

- University of Vermont Library, Wilbur Collection
  Burlington, VT 05401
  420   Fisher, Dorothy (Canfield)

- University of Washington Libraries, Archives and Manuscripts Division
  Seattle, WA 98195
  375   Jewish Family and Child Service, Seattle
  376   National Council of Jewish Women, Seattle Section

- University of Wisconsin, Green Bay Area Research Center
  Green Bay, WI 54302
  379 Manitowoc Coordinating Committee

- Washington State University Library, Manuscripts–Archives Division
  Pullman, WA 99163
  492 Pell, Herbert Claiborne

- Wayne State University, Archives of Labor History and Urban Affairs
  Detroit, MI 48202
  238 Michigan Commission on Displaced Persons and Refugees

- West Virginia University Library, West Virginia Collection
  Morgantown, WV 26505
  458 Kilgore, Harley Martin

- Western Jewish History Center of the Judah L. Magnes Memorial Museum
  2911 Russell Ave., Berkeley, CA 94705
  183 Jewish Council of 1933, San Francisco
  462 Kohs, Samuel Calmin

- Western Reserve Historical Society (Cleveland Jewish Archives)
  10825 East Blvd., Cleveland, OH 44106
  342 ˌJewish Family Service Association, Cleveland
  343 League for Human Rights, Cleveland
  345 National Council of Jewish Women, Cleveland Section
  346 Nationalities Service Center, Cleveland

- Yad Vashem Archives
  Har Hazikaron, Jerusalem, Israel
  51 Central Location Index
  435 Grossmann, Kurt Richard
  522 Tenenbaum, Joseph L.
  526 Van Tijn-Cohn, Gertrude F.
  163 World Jewish Congress

- Yale University Library, Dept. of Manuscripts and Archives
  New Haven, CT 06520
  21 American Immigration Conference Board
  64 Emergency Committee to Save the Jewish People of Europe
  438 Harrison, Ross Granville
  451 Johnson, Alvin Saunders

- Yeshiva University Archives
  New York, NY 10033
  320 National Council of Jewish Women, Brooklyn Section
  321 National Council of Jewish Women, New York Section
  130 Vaad Hahatzala

- YIVO Institute for Jewish Research
  1048 Fifth Ave., New York, NY 10028
  9 American Committee of OSE
  26 American Jewish Joint Distribution Committee
  28 American Joint Reconstruction Foundation

 32   American ORT Federation
 39   Baron de Hirsch Fund/Jewish Agricultural Society
388   Birman, Meyer
401   Chamberlain, Joseph Perkins
402   Cohen, Israel
 54   Committee for the Study of Recent Immigration from Europe
411   Dijour, Ilja M.
 66   European Jewish Children's Aid
430   Gottschalk, Max
435   Grossmann, Kurt Richard
 72   Hebrew Sheltering and Immigrant Aid Society of America (HIAS)
441   Herwald, T. B.
 70   HIAS–ICA–Emigration Association (HICEM)
240   Jewish Family and Children's Service, Detroit
 87   *The Jewish Way*
453   Kallen, Horace Meyer
 90   Labor Zionist Alliance
466   Lamport, Arthur Matthew
471   Lifschitz, Samuel
487   Mowschowich, David
100   National Coordinating Committee for Aid to Refugees and Emigrants
      Coming from Germany
320   National Council of Jewish Women, Brooklyn Section
321   National Council of Jewish Women, New York Section
105   National Refugee Service
110   The Oberlaender Trust
124   Shanghai Refugee Community
 68   Steinberg, Isaac Nahman
522   Tenenbaum, Joseph L.
133   United HIAS Service
137   United Service for New Americans
155   U.S. President's Advisory Committee on Political Refugees

• YWCA of the City of New York, Archives and Resource Center
  610 Lexington Ave., New York, NY 10022
309   International Institute of New York City

• Zionist Archives and Library
  515 Park Ave., New York, NY 10022
 23   American Jewish Conference
394   Brandeis, Louis Dembitz
425   Friedenwald, Harry F.
477   Mack, Julian William
517   Szold, Robert
159   U.S. War Refugee Board
165   World Zionist Organization–American Section
168   Zionist Organization of America

Numbers in this Index refer to entry, not page numbers. Numbers in boldface indicate main entries.